FATHERHOOD
IN
THE UNITED STATES
OF
AMERICA

— An Historical, Prophetic & Practical Guide

For Biblical Male Leadership in Family Development

Numbers 10: 1 - 10

By:
Michael D. Juzwick

DENVER, COLORADO

Dedication

For the Advancement
&
Propagation of the Holy Gospel
of our Lord & Saviour Jesus Christ

-- Book of Acts chapter 1 verse 8;
Gospel of Matthew chapter 28 verses 17 - 20;
Gospel of Mark chapter 16 verses 14 - 20

" God, who at sundry times and in diverse manners
spake in time past unto the fathers by the prophets,
Has in these last days spoken unto us by His Son, Whom He has
appointed heir of all things, by Whom also He made the worlds;
Who being the brightness of His glory, and the express image of
His person, and upholding all things by the Word of His power,
when He had by Himself - " purged " [Greek = katharismon - to
make clean, pure, unsoiled. clean from guilt, guiltless, innocent. To
cleanse from filth. to cleanse from sin, make expiation] sat down
on the right hand of the majesty on high; "

-- Book of Hebrews chapter 1 verses 1 - 3

Acknowledgements

We acknowledge the Lord Jesus Christ & His Father God Almighty to have granted the gifts and capacities to write this book for the betterment of men who are fathers. After all, we are made in His likeness, and image, with the blessed capacities to bring forth sons and daughters for His glory in this earthly realm. We are thankful to our Creator for the blessing of trust He places in our hands to fulfill His purposes in our lives, and, those of our children. May we learn to do those things He commands in His excellent Words of righteousness - the Holy Bible.

Also, it is acknowledged that many kind individuals took part in the task to produce this treatment. My brother, Joseph W. Juzwick, served to scan the original text from the ASCII format from the handwritten manuscript transcript typed by my Christian sister Janet of Tech Type in Southern California. We utilized the Logitech scanner software back then. I was not educated in the use of a personal computer during my grade school and college education years. My brother brought me up to speed in the use of computer age technologies. Over the years of producing this book & eBook we sought to follow the trends of men in how they were attending to their families so we could better understand how to address their successes, or, failures in the great task of male parenting God's way. Joseph also set up the process to produce this title with the original Aldus PageMaker 4.0 software, which had to be upgraded up to 7.0, which became the property of Adobe which was finished in their InDesign Creative Suite 5.5 programs. My YouTube video producer - Charlie

Jirov, now living in Sofia, Bulgaria, helped me in many ways to deal with computer related improvements to produce & publish. My son, Justin W. Juzwick, helped move data to newer computer systems & set up the hardware. My good Christian brother and friend Matthew Bell and Grey McCoy, assisted with the final details required for printing & publishing this book.

About the Cover

The Great Seal of the United States of America reflects the founding and history of our American Republic. The eagle was chosen to be our National symbol because of its characteristics. Biblical accounts like in Isaiah chapter 40 verse 31 teaches us that -

"..they that wait upon the Lord shall renew their strength; they shall mount up with wings as eagles; they shall run, and not be weary; and the shall walk, and not faint. "

But, this is not the main reference we can look at in learning God Almighty's purpose for this land. The main prophetic Word of God can be seen in the book of the Revelation of Jesus Christ our Lord and Saviour. Revelation chapter 12 verses 13 - 17, reveals the prophetic history we have seen the United States of America fulfill in its founding and development. We will quote only verse 14, for brevity here -

" And to the woman were given two wings of a great eagle, that she might fly into the wilderness, into her place, where she is nourished for a time, and times, and a half a time, from the face of the serpent."

The trumpet below the eagle is the symbol of the command God Almighty gave to His ancient people Israel in the book of Numbers chapter 10 verses 1 - 9, in which He told them to make 2 silver trumpets to use as announcements to call the assembly of God's people and for the manner in which they could call upon the Creator to assist them in defeating their oppressors in war - verse 9. The silver trumpets were also to call out to assemble - " And if they blow with one trumpet, then the princes, which are the heads of the thousands of Israel, shall gather themselves unto thee. "

The male leaders were to assemble for battle when one trumpet is blown. "..and you shall be remembered before the Lord your God, and you shall be saved from your enemies . " Amen!!!

Other Lifetime Written Works
by: Michael D. Juzwick

The Original Intent of the First Amendment - According to the Founding Fathers - By: Michael E. Citriniti & Michael D. Juzwick

The Effects of Pornography on the United States of America

The Differences Between A Christian Republic & A Humanist Democracy

Satanic Feminism Verses The American Home

Forbidden Masonic Objects Planted in the Founding of the United States of America - previous title - God's Word on the Grove & Ashtoreth

The Symposium on God's Deliverance

The Symposium on Parenthood & Husbandry

My Pre - Marital Commitment to Moral Purity

Western Pennsylvania Teen Challenge Presentation

Healing for the Wounded Spirit

Further information on obtaining these book & eBook titles may be obtained by contacting the publisher @ Ph. 206. 497. 8553, or, via email - lighteternalpublications@gmail.com

You may connect with Michael D. Juzwick via the URL website - lighteternalpublications.wordpress.com/

Also, his facebook group site - My " America Bless God! " Last Call to Repentance - National movement.

Contents

Part 5
Appendix A

Preface

The preliminary objective in preparing the minds of those who would undertake to examine the profound subject of fatherhood is to explain our purpose. The United States of America has been a nation conceived in liberty, as our founders envisioned. The Apostle Paul, in Galatians 5:1, made mention of the ".. liberty that Jesus Christ has made us free..". Though this nation has undergone an evolution of development into what we are now experiencing. Early American colonists had a specific purpose in the founding of the nation as a Christian republic. This purpose has been removed by powerful political forces bent on creating America into an all inclusive democracy that expels the rule of God, and His eternal Word, from our National mindset. This profane objective has been achieved by numerous methods. The triangulation of accomodation of all ethnic, racial, religious creeds into what we have referred to as, " the melting pot " approach to nation - building, has brought into our National experience certain curses we are all now experiencing. The admixture of all points of view, and belief systems of this fallen world, has created specific problems now facing us as a nation of people.

If wisdom speaks to these calamitous difficulties we all face as American citizens, He says to us as a nation -

"..Remember therefore from whence thou art fallen, and repent, and do the first works: .." - the book of Revelation 2: 5.

Liberty, as any other freedom granted by our Maker, can be profaned, and squandered. America has been under an evil spiritual attack from its inception. Christ shall judge the nations. - see Matthew 25:31-32. The big secret now being hidden is that He will do it through the repentance, and obedience, of His faithful fathers and mothers. We have been a perversely patient people. What would have not even been tolerated say, fifty years ago, is now considered normal Public discourse. And woe be to any who challenges that notion! This corruption and profaning of the American people, has transpired over quite a number of years. Much of the problem is centered in the overthrow, and attack, now being leveled at parental leadership and authority. Our evolution as a nation has created an ungodly, and disparaging disposition of men, who are responsible for the fathering of this nation's children. In September 1953, the month and year of the author's birth, a new and intoxicating profane idea came into vogue among men. It was called the Playboy philosophy. It began deluding the male population of America into seeing the prostitution of women as being normal and healthy. Marilyn Monroe [Norma Jean] was the tragic example of the consequences of "..causing your daughters to become whores.." spoken of in God's warning to Old Testament Israel [see - Leviticus 19:29]. This was not the initial blow to turn America's eyes to worship whoredoms. Historical evidence reveals that the foolish corruption of men's view of women began many years prior. This book will examine these matters in detail as we proceed. But, we must state that America's judicial Courts of law have perfidiously corrupted our nation's system of law. What was once considered evil and profane, is now viewed as good. What was considered holy and virtuous, is now considered evil. God's Word pronounces doom, and woe, upon all nations that think to behave in such a manner - see - Romans chapter 1 verses 17 - 28.

Though the content of this book may offend certain interest groups that have been assimilated into our American culture at large, we will speak to those that are revealed in God's Word to be an abomination in His sight. Our ultimate goal in doing this is to cause those who have been deceived, to find their way out of their entanglement with that which God hates. This will hopefully produce the spiritual blessing of repentance and restoration.

The second goal in the matter of addressing this subject of fatherhood, will be to reveal the numerous guidelines the Holy Bible gives on being an effective husband and father. Practical application of spiritual truth must follow repentance. Otherwise, people will only languish in the great sea of apathy and ignorance. God has issued His eternal call to all men to repent in the book of Acts17:30-31. Repentance is not a bad thing to avoid. It is the Lord God's work in the lives of men. He has sent His Holy Spirit from Heaven to give us the power necessary to do His good will. That will is found contained in the sixty-six books of the Holy Bible.

Our efforts in this treatment of the subject of - Fatherhood in the United States of America - is to grant us a greater capacity to carry out the great purposes ordained by our Lord God from the beginning of time. And, was re - established by our Lord & Savior Jesus Christ in His Great Commission - see - the Gospel of Matthew chapter 28 verses 17 - 20; Gospel of Mark chapter 16 verses 14 - 20; the Gospel of Luke chapter 24 verses 36 - 53; Acts chapter 1 verse 8. His truth is marching on. Amen.

Disclaimer

Since we will endeavor to reveal to our readers, specific errors promoted by certain religious entities now existing in America. We wish to make a disclaimer up front as to our honest, and conscience-based convictions. The subject of fatherhood can conjure up a number of opinions, hostilities, and judgments that can cloud, and confuse the important examination of this particular subject. Our personal life experience can color our disposition in intense and profound ways, that can obscure, and hinder the creation of a healthy and Biblical perspective. In recent years, there have been many news Media reports of molestation of children in America by Roman Catholic priests called " father " . Millions of dollars have been paid out to hush up these abuses by religious authorities, which is also a horrible shame. These evil acts have sullied the name of Jesus Christ, and those called Christians.

With that stated, we must confront an heretical error now propagated by the world entity known as the Roman Catholic religion. The Lord Jesus Christ commanded His people to avoid a specific error in Matthew 23:9. We are instructed of the Lord to not call any man *".. father.."* . He specifically laid this ordinance down in order to counter the spiritual usurpation of His lordship, and fatherhood honor. For He said, ***"..for one is your Father, which is in Heaven."*** This part of God's eternal Word of righteousness makes the Roman Catholic practice of calling their priests- " father " a damnable heresy. It opens up those who practice this evil, to other demonic delusions, and curses. We call on the people of this religious belief system to repent of this disobedience against the Lord Jesus Christ. We wish to confront these errors in the love of Christ. And counteract any effort to paint our intentions as being anything other than benevolent. God's grace and love is now reaching out to all men and women. Even those who might be embracing error, and heretical beliefs, contrary to His written Word. Other major entities, now firmly established into our American culture, are addressed in order to call those participating in them, out. As commanded in Revelation 18: 4 . We are to hate that which God hates. We are to love the deluded sinner into Christ's kingdom by every means at our disposal. Doing this serves God's highest purposes.

Additionally, we state that our expose of the religion of the Masonic Orders is to educate them about the danger they are in for promoting and establishing sins of idolatry in the United States of America by renaming their images & icons relational to their founder King Nimrod and his mother Semiramis. We teach the actual history that goes back to the account of Genesis chapter 10 verses 8 - 20, where Nimrod was the infamous builder of many cities and ancient Babylon after the flood of the patriarch Noah as recorded in Genesis chapters 6 - 9. And, his mother started the propagation of idolatry & image worship forbidden by the Creator. We intend to help men and women in these two major religious systems to understand why they need to repent and come out of the delusions so God may have mercy upon their souls. We warn others about the curses associated with these religious belief systems of antiquities.

Mankind is still *" shaking off the dust of Babylon from their feet "*. Our ministry and work for our Lord & Master Jesus Christ and His Holy Father, is to help assist our brothers and sisters to come out of every false religion, cult, and belief system that is contrary to the Creator God's will. Our true purpose in confrontation of error is to follow Christ in Matthew 13:12-17. Calling your brother to obedience is an act of love. I trust our readers will fully understand this.

PART 1

The Prophetic & Historical American Experience

Light Eternal Publications, USA
- Biblical Light for America's Christian Families -
Mountlake Terrace, Washington 98043-2913

CHAPTER 1

Fatherhood &
The Founding of Our Nation

WHAT IT WAS -

13) And when the dragon [Satan] saw that he was cast unto the earth, he persecuted the woman which brought forth the man child.

14) And to the woman were given two wings of a great eagle, that she might fly into the wilderness into her place, where she is nourished for a time, and times, and half a time, from the face of the serpent. [Satan's onslaught].

— Revelation 12:13 &14

THE FACE OF THE SERPENT

After the resurrection and ascension of the Lord Jesus Christ, Holy Scripture informs us that various things took place in the realm of spiritual beings and powers. Colossians 2:15 tells us that Jesus Christ spoiled both principalities and powers. This means that God the Father, through the incarnation of His Son, regained authority in the earth over which Satan had been given control. Now, through the sacrificial death, shedding of blood by the Son of God, and His resurrection, man could again come under the authority of God the Father by faith in the redemptive work of Jesus Christ. The manifestation

3

of God's love for man would prove to be the worst thing that could happen within Satan's kingdom of darkness.

Needless to say, the enemy of God and man had to become infuriated. He definitely enjoyed inspiring wicked men to crucify Jesus Christ, but the resurrection had not been considered (see 1st Corinthians 2:8). Satan and his powers could not stop the resurrection and ascension of the Lord Jesus Christ, yet as the Bible, and historians record, he went to work immediately to stop the spreading of the Gospel of Jesus Christ. To halt and hinder the preaching of all God had done by word of mouth, was job-one for God's enemies.

The persecution of God's believing Church began by the religious Jewish leaders in Israel. They conspired to use the Roman authorities to rid the land of any followers of Jesus Christ, and especially any who were leading others to faith in the resurrected Lord. Those who believed Jesus to be the Messiah were accused of blasphemy and idolatry. Believers were either thrown into prison or put to death for their faith in Jesus Christ (see Acts 5:17-20; Acts 7:57-60; Acts 8:1-4). Both Satan and earthly authorities despise any competition.

After Satan worked through the Jewish religious authorities to put a stop to God's works in the new believers, he moved into the leadership of the Roman Empire to destroy the works of God in that early Church. Satan gained control of the Emperors and Ceasars of Rome and began a time of vicious attacks against God's people through their corrupted lives. Caligula and Nero were notorious for their attacks on the Christian believers. The Roman Ceasars degenerated to begin to view themselves as gods. Emperor worship began to be challenged by allegiance to Jesus Christ by believers. This began to produce attacks on this fledgling new faith, though Christianity was spreading rapidly due to the powerful outpouring of God's Holy Spirit. Foxe's Book of Martyrs gives to us a history of martyrdom in the early days of the Age of Grace. It is said that the Roman Ceasars would feed Christians to lions and wild beasts in the Roman Colosseum for entertainment. That Nero would even put young children who had expressed faith in Christ, in to be attacked by wild beasts. Nero also is said to have dipped believers into tar. And then hung them in his courtyard, and lit them as torches. This all forced God's people underground. And into the catacombs of Rome.

After an evil time of persecution from Satan, through these emperors, a man named Constantine (280? - 337 A.D.), *supposedly* became a convert to Christianity. Through his policies he worked to convert the entire Roman Empire to Catholicism, and in the process married a perverted form of Christianity, and all the pagan religious systems of the Roman world. In essence, yet unofficially, he became the first pope. The name " pope " was invented later on. This effort by Constantine had the effect of changing the name of the corrupt and degenerating Roman Empire to the " *Holy* Roman Empire ". The false spawn of Satan put on a new religious face.

After future successions to power in this " State - Church "system, it transpired into a full-blown religious institution eventually named " the Holy Roman Catholic Church". Through this system of a succession of various popes, millions of believers had been tortured and burned at the stake for " heresies ". The inquisitions throughout Europe, made this religious system rich with the confiscated wealth of those who were accused of heresy, and put to death. Many innocent people died cruel deaths and the earth plunged into the Dark Ages. Satan and his powers reigned terror upon any and all who opposed " the Holy Roman Mother Church." He will even put on the face, and name *Christian,* if necessary to deceive mankind.

God began to raise up bold and courageous men such as John Huss, Swingley, Wycliffe, Tyndale and others. Martin Luther, with his ninety five thesis, challenged the heretical errors of Roman Catholic theology. Popes ruled without accountability until then.

The invention of the printing press, and the translation of the Holy Scriptures into English, began to break mankind out of the

Dark Ages. The Renaissance and the "Age of Enlightenment" followed. There were many people who held fast to the genuine faith of the Lord Jesus Christ through the centuries, yet Satan had sown much fear among God's people. Attacking God's work in His People.

Much hatred of, and skepticism of, " the Church " (Roman Catholic Institution) was produced by the many atrocities it committed during the Dark Ages. Many intelligent men, who would form the intelligence of the " Age of Enlightenment ", were very bitter against all that referred to God, or the Bible, and the representation of " Christianity " by the Roman Catholic heretical institution. This caused true Christians much trouble and misunderstanding among people as they continued Christ's Great Commission.

The animosity against anything " *Christian* ", prepared the ground of the minds of these apostate men inside America, for the propagation of the revival of the ancient system of the religion of Secular Humanism, espoused by the Greek and Roman world, prior to the birth of the Church of Jesus Christ our Lord.

This anti-God, anti-Creator, anti-Christ philosophy of Secular Humanism, now in power over America, was first generated by the minds of Aristotle, Socrates, and Plato. The idolatrous philosophy purports to make sinful men and their reasoning, supreme over God's Word and rule in the earth, which is anti-Christ. It exists in full force in American public schools today because of parental ignorance and indifference. Two sins now overthrowing our American Republic. One witch named Madalyn Murray-OHair was Satan's agent to turn America apostate in its Public schools in 1962.

After the Dark Ages and the Renaissance, the Age of Enlightenment became ruled by men who were skeptics, and had a great desire to see the Catholic Institution opposed with all its evils of persecution, domination and control over people. This seemed good even to the members of the Protestant Churches. So it was even respected, to some degree, by the various religious communities of the Western European nations. Papal rule was despised by most people due to its atrocities over the centuries.

Voltaire and Rousseau, two men who were even educated in the subversive sub-system of Roman Catholicism, the Jesuit Colleges [began by Ignatius Loyola (from hence, American Jesuit Loyola Universities) in 1534] worked in their time to produce an educational system devoid of respect for God and morality. These men were not stupid. They were extremely intelligent. And, with their intelligence revived the amoral humanistic philosophy to prepare educators to teach (the systems of empirical scientism) we know today espoused in our American national systems of education. This was the beginning of satanic Secular Humanism, that has succeeded in expelling the Christian world view in America's Public School systems as unlawful, because of their own perverse Humanist view of the so-called " Separation of Church and State " dogma. Our nation has degenerated morally since this evil philosophy took hold as Public policy. Romans 1: 17-32, specifically verse 28, warns mankind of the heinous results of removing God from the acquisition of knowledge. Psalm 9:17 warns of being *"..turned into hell.."* for it.

It should be stated at this point that God, through the Apostle Paul, warned us of this in his letter to the Colossians 2:6-10. That we, as God's people, should beware, and make our children aware, of men who would "spoil" them by false or corrupt philosophy. False and corrupt ideas intended to cause the rejection of Christ and His place of lordship and rule over and through mankind.

It should be stated at this point that the word " philosophy " actually means - "lover of wisdom ". And there are various sources of wisdom God's Word refers to, both good and evil.

1st Corinthians 3:18-20:

18) Let no man deceive himself if any man among you seems to be wise in this world, let him become a fool, that he may be wise.

19)   For the wisdom of this world is foolishness with God.
        For it is written, he takes the wise in their own craftiness.

20)   And again, the Lord knows the thoughts of the wise,
        That they are vain.

Also,
James 3:15, 17:

15)   This wisdom descends not from above, but is earthly,
        sensual, demonic.

17)   But the wisdom that is from above is first pure, then
        peaceable, gentle, and easy to be entreated, full of
        mercy and good fruits, without partiality, and with-
        out hypocrisy.

We also know and realize that Satan is referred to in Ezekiel 28:12-17
as being " full of wisdom ", but the wisdom which he possesses is corrupted (Ezekiel 28:17) and is utilized by him to turn the creation away
from God. Herein we see that Satan has wisdom and he gives wisdom
to certain men, but that the wisdom he gives is not only deceitful and
corrupt, but that it is designed by God's enemy to turn people from
faith in God. This is the basic root of Secular humanism as espoused
by men such as Charles Darwin and John Dewey. To give humanity a
"religion" that they could "believe" in, but that is devoid of a Creator to
whom man was responsible to for his actions upon the earth. Though
the US Supreme Court has allowed the adoption of this false idea of
religion being defined as Secular Humanism, this was not the intention of the Founding Fathers. When they framed the U.S. Constitution
and First Amendment to be exclusively "Christian" in its restriction to
not allow any specific Christian Church denomination to become the
official National religion [see source bottom of page[1]]. Now, we see

---

1   The Myth of Separation - Pages 26-40, David Barton, Wall Builder Press 1993.

all Christian religious freedom censored in public schools, and false religions are taught and promoted like Witchcraft. For this cause "The Theory of Evolution" espoused by Charles Darwin and John Dewey is a false system of wisdom, but it is designed to take the place of God, who is Creator, and sustainer of all life. It is, therefore, satanic and demonic in its origin. The Holy Spirit forewarned us of this activity of Satan, and his demon forces at the end of time, in I Timothy chapter 4 : 1 - 2 -

1) Now the Spirit speaks expressly, that in the latter times some shall depart from the faith, giving heed to seducing spirits, and doctrines (teachings) of demons;

2) Speaking lies in hypocrisy: having their conscience seared with a hot iron; [emphasis added]

The author, at this juncture, must say that just as God the Father, and His Son our Lord Jesus Christ, has a plan for the future. Satan and his angels have contrived a plan, whereby they can move the world to a system through which he can force all humanity to worship him and proclaim him as being God (see Revelation 13). Satan has, from the beginning of the Church age, energized to secure for himself a segment of humanity to work at establishing a one-world system over which he is the head. The Lord Jesus Christ is still building His Church during this time, and will continue to extend His grace to even those who are now working to build this Anti-Christ system. But there is an appointed time in which all will have heard God's message of salvation, and then the end will begin to take place (see Matthew 24:14).

We conclude this segment *" the face of the serpent "* with the religious, socio-political conditions which prompted Christianity's movement to the " New World ", i.e. the Americas. We also must state at this time that the establishment of colonies in the Americas was not just for religious freedom, but mostly for the exploitation of the " riches " the Americas offered to the English, French, and Spanish kings and rulers. Babylonish " powers " were preparing to establish a brand new conquest in the Americas. The " dragon " of Revelation 12:11 had persecuted the woman through earthly human authorities in the old world i.e., the European nations. This persecution proceeded from religious and secular governmental establishments. The spiritual connection of the activity of Satan in earthly authorities is explained in Ephesians 6:12. Freedom from this persecution by Satan was the desire of the Christian men and women who held true and faithful to the commandments of the Lord Jesus Christ. Most American school textbooks have been *"secularized"* to avoid teaching of the evil atrocities committed by Satan's men, through Roman Catholicism, in the old world. The truth is that over 68 million were maimed, tortured, and murdered in those periods of history. It is said that in one town of Ana-Baptists (rebaptizers), that during certain inquisitions these evil Satan-inspired men cut the heads off all the men of the town, and stuck them on poles, and lined the entrance of the town with them. In certain pockets of the old world there was a definite desire for God's mercy and grace to deliver men, women, and their families from this vicious onslaught of Satan's powers. The *" face of the serpent "* had been clearly seen by those who appreciated and loved the Lord Jesus Christ. We close with a quote from Max Sevelle's - History of Colonial America - The significance of a century of colonization -

> The true age of colonization opens at the end of the century and was due chiefly to certain important developments. During the century (15th) that brought considerable numbers of people to consider leaving their motherlands forever. The two most important of these factors were the development of an economic situation, particularly in England, that created a large body of people detached from the land who looked longingly to America toward the free land that might be had there, and the situation created by the protestant's revolt, which split western Christendom into warring sects,

one or another of which was constantly under persecution during two entire centuries - a situation that prompted many to seek escape to religious freedom in the new world. [2]

EXPLORERS PREVIOUS TO COLUMBUS

October 12th of every year our national educational system makes our children acknowledge, that in 1492 a Roman Catholic Spaniard, under commission of the King of Spain, and Catholic Pope, discovered America. This erroneous idea gives the Roman Catholic Church a foot-hold of political power in the United States federal government, and " special " privileges in our National media, something our national Constitution prohibits! Naming the seat of our Federal government - District of " Columbia ", verifies this has occurred. The First Amendment to the U.S. Constitution, "the Law of the Land" clearly states -

" Congress (the assembly of elected representatives) shall make no law respecting an establishment of religion, (i.e., no certain Christian religion gets special favor, or power, from the federal government to make them the official State - Church of America) nor prohibit- ing the free exercise thereof. " [Emphasis added]

Yet, more and more, we see total coverage, by our National Media, of every move the pope of the Catholic religion makes. Political moves, during the Reagan administration, acknowledged the Vatican as a center of world government to be acknowledged, by installing a U.S. ambassador at the Vatican. In the purest sense of the United States Constitutional law, this act violates our First Amendment. The framers of the Constitution knew, that if one sect of Christianity was

---

2   A History of Colonial America, Max Sevelle pp., 35 - 36

respected officially by the Federal government, all others must be also to be fair. Christopher Columbus did not discover the United States. He did explore the regions of the West Indies [Caribbean] and Florida coastline and reported certain findings to the king of Spain. But, to say he discovered America himself, is erroneous. And leads to a favoring, to some degree, of Catholicism as *the* Christian religion.

We know, though we do not acknowledge, because of our political persuasions, that many various tribes of " *Indians* " inhabited the North Americas before any explorers arrived to the coasts of America. The first recorded explorers from the European continent, were Leif and his brother Thorwald Ericsson. In the year 1003 A.D., these Norsmen explored and discovered the North American Coast long before Columbus. These Vikings, Leif and Thorwald Erickson, discovered and named it Vineland. Leif Erickson's brother, Thorwald, stayed on the Continent and became the first American homesteader.

After various other explorations by various other men, the three most powerful political forces in Europe vied for control of the exploitation of the American Continent. There were wars for the monopoly of the riches that the new world had to offer. Wars on the high seas took place between the kings of England, France, and Spain. Each strived for " their piece of the American Pie ". (See Bibliography #2). Protestant English, and Catholic French and Spanish forces, fought for spiritual dominance over new land conquests.

Various treaties were signed, in diplomatic efforts, to establish control over pirate activities on the high seas against these three kings of Europe, and the British Isles. Through these wars English, French, and Spanish colonies were being established.

A man by the name of Martin Waldseemuller, a German Cosmographer [map maker], in 1507 in contract with Amerigo Vespucci, produced a Latinized form the Spanish name - *Amerrique* (which was the name of a mountain range in Nicaragua [Central America today]. This was used by early explorers as the name of the continent. We today call it - *"America"*. Today, we know that

France received control of the land area called Canada. The Protestant English established control of what today is called the United States of America. The Catholic Spanish conquered and gained control of Mexico, and the Southern hemisphere portion of the continent.

Therefore, with all due respect, Christopher Columbus did not discover America. Neither should we be deceived in thinking he alone located this area of the New World. Neither should he, nor the Roman Catholic religion, be credited with having done so. Neither should our U.S. Capitol be called the District of Columbia. Nor should the United States be personified and feminized as the woman - i.e., Columbia. [refer to Webster's New World Dictionary, Page 281 - 1970 edition].

THE PILGRIM FATHERS & PLYMOUTH PLANTATION

In reference to our previous segment on the face of the serpent, we learned that there were severely persecuted sects of Christianity, Christian people who yearned for the freedom to worship God and practice their faith as they believed God would have them to. These displaced individuals were Pilgrims in the truest sense of the term. God heard their cry for freedom to serve and worship him as Holy Scripture directed. Their great faith and perseverance was about to be rewarded by their Lord Jesus Christ, and would prove to be the source of all the wondrous blessings and benefits the United States of America now enjoys. For it is when fathers and mothers honor their Creator, and worship Him, that God pours forth His blessings upon His creation.

14) And to the woman were given two wings of a great eagle, that she might fly into the wilderness, into her place, where she is nourished for a time, and times, and half a time, **from the face of the serpent**. [bold emphasis added]

— Revelation 12:14

13

The fatherhood, and founding of the United States of America, began at this juncture of western civilization. Some have called this reality - the Chain of Christianity. The Western propagation of the Gospel of the Lord Jesus Christ. Many apostate Church leaders deny, and reject these historical facts in America's development as a nation, and world power. See - 2nd Peter 2: 1-21.

Prophetically speaking, as Revelation 12:14 states, and the history books tell us, *"the wilderness"* was that place God had prepared to give His people a time of refuge from the wicked attacks Satan had perpetrated upon them " through religious authorities " for centuries. If you notice the prophecy says - *"...where she is nourished..."* The Holy Scripture was held in control by Roman Catholic - State sponsored religious men, who held all people in bondage to *their* interpretation of Holy Scripture. The rulers allowed the common people to know and understand only what *they* deemed necessary. Even one of the reformers said to one of the popes that " ..his goal in life was to cause the youngest plowboy to know more of the Holy Scripture than the pope". This control by European Roman Catholic "religious" men over the minds of humanity was about to end in this establishment of Plymouth Plantation. The profound Christian founding of America can be learned and understood by studying founding father - William Bradford's History of this subject. Satan has worked to hide these facts.

Religious freedom and liberty, which was the cry of the hearts of the Pilgrim fathers was soon to be their portion, yet not without great difficulty. Many of those early American parents died the first winter at Plymouth. Native American " Indian " leaders Samaset, Squanto and Massasoyt did help the Plymouth colonists survive. Evil white men, bent on self-centered greed, created hostilities with the native American tribes as time progressed. Plymouth Plantation was just that. A planting of a seed which would germinate, sprout, and eventually grow into the mighty nation we know today as the United States of America. But all the difficulties of starting a nation were in the hands of the men listed below. The women who helped them were very special women of God. The children born of this generation would help their parents build the dream they came to create. We place a quote from the American Historian Leonard Bacon.

Who and what were they? Whatever ecclesiastical or political prejudice against them may linger in some quarters, no intelligent reader of history can think of them as frantic enthusiasts, as dupes of knavish leaders, or as in any way dangerous members of society. Some of them were men trained at the English Universities, and skilled in the learning and the controversies of their time. Some were not without experience of life in the great world, and the connection with Public affairs; Others were plain people of the old English Yeomanry, who lived on their hereditary acres - the type and original of our New English farmers. All had gained the intelligence that comes from the diligent study of the Bible, and all were honest and earnest believers in the Christ of the New Testament. Such were the men and the women who were thus driven out of their native England, yet hunted and intercepted in their flight, as if they were criminals escaping from justice. Why did they suffer the spoiling of their goods, arrest, imprisonment, exile?... They had caught from the Bible the idea of a Church independent alike of the pope and the queen, independent of parliament as well as of prelates, and dependent only upon Christ. It was their mission to work out and organize that idea... [3]

This quote should give us a good look and understanding of the Christian roots of our nation. Wherein lied the great strength of those who gave to us, by their great suffering, a nation of freedom and

---

3   The Christian History of the Constitution of the United States of America- Verna M. Hall, 1975
     - " Genesis of the New England Churches "1874.

liberty. Not to do what we please, but rather, to do what would honor the God, Creator, and Saviour of man. American parents have failed in maintaining this love, honor, and, fear of the Lord.

We close this segment with a Pilgrim fathers and mothers as they began to establish this nation, after their arduous voyage across the stormy Atlantic Ocean.

" The Virginia Company had no rights in New England, and therefore their patent could confer none, and there was no other recognized authority there. Under these circum- stances it was found there was danger of disorder arising. Some of the company, Probably the hired labourers, were putting forth the idea that there was an end of all authority, every man might go his own way and do as he liked. The leaders saw the peril of this, and resolved to guard against it. If there was no other government over them, either of king or company, they would make a government for themselves. " They therefore called the adult males into the cabin of the Mayflower, and there entered into that memorable compact which became the basis of the Constitution for the infant colony.[4] It also represents our beginning. Which is -

' In ye name of God, amen. We, whose names are under- written, the loyal subjects of our dread sovereign lord, King James, by ye grace of God, of Great Britain, France, and Ireland King, defender of ye faith, and, having undertaken, for ye glory of God and advancement of ye Christian faith, and honor of our king and country, a voyage to plant ye first colonie in ye Northern parts of Virginia, do by these presents solemnly and mutually in ye presence of God, and of one another, covenant and combine ourselves together into a civil body politic, for our better ordering and preserving and furtherance of ye ends aforesaid; and by virtue hereof, to enact, constitute and frame such

4   Explorations in America Before Columbus, Hjalmarr Holland, 1958.

just and equal laws, ordinances, acts, constitutions and offices from time to time, as shall be thought most mete and convenient for ye general good of ye colonie, unto which we promise all due submission and obedience. In witness whereof we have here under subscribed our names at Cape-Codd, ye 11th of November, in ye year of ye reign of our soveraigne Lord, King James of England, France and Ireland ye eighteenth, and of Scotland ye fiftie-fourth,

Ano. Dom. 1620.'

The Mayflower's Pilgrim Fathers --

John Carver	John Turner
William Bradford	Francis Eaton
Edward Winslow	James Chilton
William Brewster	John Crickston
Isaac Allerton	John Billington
Miles Standish	Moses Fletcher
John Alden	John Goodman
Samuel Fuller	Degory Priest
Christopher Martin	Thomas Williams
William Mullins	Gilbert Winslow
William White	Edmuno Marteson
Richard Warren	Pete Brown
John Howland	Richard Britterbridge
Stephen Hopkins	George Soule
Edward Tilley	Richard Clarke
John Tilley	Richard Gardiner
Francis Cook	John Allerton
Thomas Rodgers	Thomas English
Thomas Tinker	Edward Dotey
John Rigdale	Edward Lister
Edward Fuller	

A Nation Dedicated to the Proclamation and Propagation of the Gospel of Jesus Christ

The Mayflower compact proves, without a shadow of doubt, the truth that the founding of this nation, the United States of America, was for the proclamation and propagation of the good news the Lord Jesus Christ brought to us from God the Father. This is the calling of the nation. To fail to see this basic fact of our nation's history is to grope in darkness concerning our purpose and identity. The men who signed the Mayflower Compact followed through with the establishment of our nation. The reality of this is found on all our national currency. It is everywhere present in our nation's capitol, Washington D.C. "One Nation Under God". No other nation, other than Israel, has ever claimed that subjection to the Lord. And, before we fell out of touch with who He is, we had the greatest blessing any nation could ever have. The blessing that God was with us and for us. The author, in study of early American history, found that most every book published in the beginning of our nation had this dedication - " For the proclamation and propagation of the Gospel of the Lord Jesus Christ ". This one reality is what has created a nation so blessed with God's hand.

It has been our relationship with God and His wisdom that has brought about the great inventions this nation has produced to the envy of all nations. The Soviet Union has spied out our inventions and copied our technology because, when they entered outer space, one of their atheistic cosmonauts radioed back, "..we are looking for God out here, but we do not see him anywhere..". But, in America, the freedom and liberty of God's Word, the Holy Bible, gave to us the ability to be superior to our great national adversary. Proverb 8:12 states -

12)   " I wisdom dwell with prudence, and find out knowledge of witty inventions. "

18

Yes, the greatness of the United States of America is only found in her relationship with her purpose. That of being dedicated for the proclamation and propagation of the Gospel of our great Lord and Savior Jesus Christ. We only deceive ourselves to think it is in anything else!

THE AMERICAN COVENANT

The Pilgrim fathers, as stated in the Mayflower compact," covenanted " together with God and each other to advance the Christian faith. This seed of faith germinated into a nation for that purpose. The trouble America faces today is because she has lost knowledge of her purpose in the earth.

It is very important to examine the covenant to which you commit yourself. Today the legal term is " contract ". The Biblical word "covenant " has been abandoned, and with its abandon the strength it provides to those who enter into it.

In the Old Testament of the Bible, a covenant entered into by two people was very sacred and binding. So much so that usually those who fell out of their part of the agreement died. To cite some examples we see that God covenanted with Adam. Adam was to care for and protect the Garden of Eden. Part of the agreement was - "..not to eat of the tree of knowledge of good and evil." We know what happened. He did. And he died. God covenanted with Noah and his sons. Every person who entered into that covenant with God lived. All others died in a watery grave. God made a very special covenant with Abraham, father of the nation of Israel (Genesis 17:1-14). Many blessings came to Abraham and his children. And when the nation of Israel fell out of fellowship with God and broke the covenant, the nation died. This happened slowly over many years and disobedience generationally.

This is all to say that the American covenant has been not only forgotten, but the covenant has been broken by the fathers in our nation who are now in control. Therefore, we are seeing the nation slowly die. The way we view ourselves and our nation dictates our activities and pursuits. Fatherhood in the United States must be addressed if we would hope to see the children we are bringing into this world have a God - honoring purpose in life. Our national strength lies only within the strength of the moral fibers we hold as dear for the protection of our young. God's strength and blessing is found in the power of an individual or nation who keeps covenant with Him. The weakness and degeneration of our nation, comes from its citizen's failure to do His will and keep covenant.

For God says -

"Know therefore that the Lord your God, he is God, the faithful God, which keeps covenant and mercy with them that love him and keep his commandments to a thousand generations." — Deuteronomy 7: 9-11

It has not been God's unfaithfulness that has almost ruined this nation! It is the outright disobedience of the American people. Parents, both fathers and mothers have caused America to become a profaned and corrupted land before the Lord God. The men of this nation, who are now fathers, can change this if they repent.

THE SEEDS OF DESTRUCTION

Each time a man becomes a father, it is because he has entered into a relationship with a woman. Through his marriage relationship, (hopefully being love centered) a child is conceived. But, a basic understanding of man's ways upon the earth, proves to us many children have not been conceived in love. Many children are conceived after the fact. And many men are willfully ignorant, and irresponsible concerning God's commands to nurture their children in God's ways. And this means that love, other than God's sacrificial kind of love, is very seldom the motivation in which children are conceived. This is an aspect of sin in American men.

If a man does not view himself as being a servant of God upon the earth, it will be most unlikely that any child he is responsible for bringing into the world, will see himself as being one of God's servants. This is a very simple summation, but oh the destructions that proceed from men who refuse to be God's servants. And therefore, by default, become God's enemy - Satan's servants. Or, should we say corrupted and degenerate slaves providing no godly leadership for their children.

We do not want, at this time, to go into too much detail in this area now, since it will be covered in detail in chapter eight. But to touch upon it, there has been a very clever deception which has been propagated by Satan's spirit-beings of immorality and lust. That deception has been the source of many of the destructions our nation is suffering from at this time. The evil seeds of profanity.

The Pilgrim fathers and mothers, in their devotion and obedience to God, and His Word, had a saying that has merit in speaking of on this subject of " seeds ". Their efforts and desires before God was that they would endeavor to raise up " a godly seed ". William Penn, founding father of Pennsylvania, willed that the freedom and liberty, gained from England, would become - " The Seed of the Nation." Sons and daughters of liberty and religious freedom under God's lordship and direction. Not antiChrist independence!

The generation of life begins within the womb of a woman. If a man views himself as God's servant, his duties of husbandry and fatherhood are numerous and very important in relation to being successful at raising a godly seed. If it is possible to raise a godly seed. It stands to reason, that one also can, by refusal to carry out God's requirements for being a godly husband and father, raise an "ungodly seed". Helloooo America's men and fathers! Are you listening?

It all comes down to this. Who will our children be raised to manifest the likeness of when they grow up. The basic war, that is being waged today, and has been waged throughout man's history is this basic fact. Who will be manifested, and glorified in the earth. God the Father, and His Son Jesus Christ, through the workings of the Holy Spirit of God in us? Or Satan, through the workings of all his evil angels and demons? It is this author's belief that this basic question must be answered by the fathers and mothers of our nation. And their decision to obey and serve the Lord God, or not.

Basic demonology and deliverance tells us that Satan and his angels desire to manifest their likeness and personalities through human beings (Ref. Gen. 2:7 & 3:14). Basic Christianity and Biblical theology proper tells us that God the Father, and His Son Jesus Christ, desire to manifest their likeness in men and women's lives. The name " Christian " was a mockery by the heathen Roman world and meant " Christ - like " or " Little Christs " (Ref. Genesis 1:26 & John 17:16-22). Glorifying God means to demonstrate Him in your words and actions.

It is important to know and understand that both God, and His enemy Satan, must have a body through which to manifest their nature in. Jesus said, in John 10:10, that one aspect of Satan and his angel's activity is to " destroy ". There are many ways and methods he employs to bring about these destructions, which we will discuss later in this book. But suffice it to say now that he seeks out those fathers and mothers who do not acknowledge God, nor serve Him, to gain control over their " seed " children's lives. This fact was so in the founding of our United States of America. And also, today, these basic problems exist. Even God's people are suffering certain destructions. And He gives us the reason in Hosea 4: 6 -7.

We conclude this segment and chapter now by saying this. That it is, as each father and mother join themselves together, under God's lordship, united in His Spirit, and Word found in the Holy Bible, that their " seed " children; will be beneficial for the future of our nation. To bring His saving knowledge, healing, and deliverance into people's lives. Constant attacks upon the state of marriage, by the damaging effects of divorce, and the other national sins chapter two and eight will address. Will we be used, as fathers and mothers, to bring about further destructions in our nation's future generations? Or, begin to allow our Maker to work through our lives to bless those under our authority and care? This present generation is commanded by God Himself to follow His eternal Word concerning parenthood,. And, be obedient. Let us learn where we have fallen. And, repent in humility.

12/7/1991

CHAPTER 2

Fatherhood &
The Development
Of Our Nation

WHAT IT IS -

" Mystery, Babylon the Great, the Mother of Harlots and
Abominations of the Earth. "

— Revelation 17:5 (b)

9)   When you come into the land which the Lord your
God gives to you, you shall not learn to do after the
abominations (wicked and evil practices) of those
nations.

10)   There shall not be found among you anyone that
makes his son, or his daughter to pass through the
fire, (put your child or offspring to death in immoral
Baal worship) or that uses divination, (fortune telling) or an observer of times, (astrology / horoscope)
or an enchanter, (musicians who entice to inordinate
lust and immorality) or a witch (a man, or woman,
who employs demons and/or manipulates people to
act against God's will),

11)   Or a charmer, (hypnotist) or a consulter with famil-
iar spirits, (a medium in a seance communications
with demons, or a psychic) or a wizard, (magician)
or a necromancer (one who purports to talk with the
dead, yet really conjures up demon spirits).

For all that do these things are an abomination unto
the Lord: and because of these abominations, the
Lord your God does drive them out from before you.

13)   You shall be perfect with the Lord your God.

14)   For these nations, which you shall possess, listen to
astrologers and horoscopes, and to diviners: But as
for you, the Lord your God has not permitted you to
do so.

— Deuteronomy 18: 9 -14

In this first segment of chapter two, we will attempt to discern whether, or not, our nation could very well be. Or, be part of,
the *"..Mystery, Babylon the Great, the Mother of Harlots, and
Abominations of the Earth"*.....described in detail in the seventeenth
and eighteenth chapters of the book of the Revelation of Jesus Christ.
We first will define each of the words and names from Webster's
Dictionary.

"Mystery" means: 2. Anything, or event, that remains so secret, or
obscure, as to excite curiosity 8. Theology: any religious truth known
to man only through Divine revelation, and to be accepted by faith.

"Babylon " was, and is: an ancient city on the lower Euphrates
River, the Capital of Babylonia, famous for wealth, luxury, and wickedness - .. any city or place of great wealth, luxury, and vice.

" The Great.." Orig. Greek - η μεγαλη - extremely big,
magnificent.

" Mother " means: a woman, as she is related to her child, or children. 4. that which gives birth to something, is the origin, or source of something.

" Harlot " means: (an euphemism for whore) same as prostitute, a woman as she is related to harlotry collectively - [a woman who is used for any other purpose, than the purpose for which God created her for [author].

" Abomination " means: 1- an abominating; great hatred, and disgust, loathing, 2. anything hateful, and disgusting.

" Earth " means: 3. all the people on the earth, 6. (poet.) A.) the substance of the human body, C.) the concerns, interests of human life.

God's Word is the source of all truth in the earth. Whether it is positive truth, or negative truth, it is the source of our knowledge of the mind of God. That which God is pleased to see done on the earth is in the Holy Bible. That which displeases God is also there. John 1:14 informs us that Jesus Christ is that Word in physical manifestation. It is also revealed to us that God's purpose in the earth is that we all be like He is, as His children (Ephesians 5:1-2). Today, in the United States of America, we are seeing a great amount of tolerance to what God calls abominations. That which is loathesome, and hated by the Creator, is accepted as " part of the world system ". With little, or no condemnation, and abhorrence by His children. Those of God's children, who along with Him, detest these wicked practices are even called radical fanatics, and overzealous by the more "open-minded". Yet, perversely tolerant segment of "Christianity" in America. Yet the same Bible they say they believe, commands "all" men everywhere to repent (see Acts 17:30 & 31). *"..Mystery, Babylon the great, the mother of harlots, and abominations of the earth"*, is an apt description of what we have seen the United States of America develop into. We will cite specific developments within our nation, and their corresponding counterparts in the descriptions of Mystery Babylon in the book of Revelation chapters 17 & 18. If we were to just cite the description of ancient Babylon, we would have sufficient evidence to accuse our nation of such character. Wealth, luxury, and wickedness were the characteristics. They are also aspects of the United States of America. Now, there is nothing wrong with wealth. If it is utilized to do God's will (see Deuteronomy 8:18). But wealth utilized to corrupt people, or, to oppress the poor, is wickedness.

To understand some of the aspects of this **Mystery, Babylon the Great**, we must first understand. And know something of *ancient* Babylon. For, this new Babylon, is patterned after the old. Ancient Babylon historians say, was a very wealthy, and religious empire. As a matter of fact, it was one of the major civilizations established after the great flood, and deluge of Noah, recorded in the book of Genesis chapters 6-10. Genesis chapter 11 records an incident which displeased the Lord God. That, a man named Nimrod, organized the people of the earth, to build a tower to Heaven. It was named: The Tower of "Babel". From which comes "Babyl-on". It is said that Nimrod had developed a system of religion today known as Astrology. At the top of this tower he inscribed the *Signs of the Zodiac*- and led people to worship the stars. The Babylonish connection of this area today, in the United States of America, is that just about all the newspapers, in each and every city, has either horoscopes, or astrographs daily. Which is a Biblically forbidden occult practice. Also, Jean Dixon had a national phone number customers can call to receive council regarding their astrological forecast. It is also not uncommon to be asked what *" sign of the zodiac "* you were born under. The Masonic influences of Nimrod are also present in America's automobile industries. Ford corporate leaders have named their best selling model by the Zodiac name - *' Taurus '*. Lincoln-Mercury had a model named- *'Scorpio'*. Many of America's teen magazines open up our daughters to this forbidden practice of divination, by putting Astrological charts for teens in their every edition. This was abhorred by God at Nimrod's Tower of Babel. And, He decided to confuse the languages of these rebels, who began these Babylonish mystery religions of the antiquities. These same people, of the post-deluvian civilization created, under Satan's direction, ancient Babylon. In that empire was immense wealth, occult, and military power. So much so, that in Jeremiah 42:11, God encouraged His people not to be afraid of it. Also, when Israel began to practice Baal worship, and sacrifice their offspring, God used wicked Babylon to destroy Old Testament Israel as a nation. And take them all captive as slaves for the occult King Nebuchadnezzar (See Jeremiah 52, and Daniel 1).

All occultic religions had their beginning in ancient Babylon. Nimrod, and his idolatrous mother Semiramis, were Satan's mediums to bring in these evil curses upon this earth. And Babylon's influences have continued under Satan's direction to this day. To worship anything but the true God, and Creator, is just right by him.

As we begin to see the connection between ancient Babylon, and the United States, we will first review the first commandment God gave to Moses His servant, to give to His people. The abomination of idolatry is the first connection between Babylon, and the United States. Exodus 20:1-6 -

1). And God spake all these words, saying, 2) I am the Lord your God, which have brought you out of the land of Egypt, out of the house of bondage. 3) You shall have no other gods before me. 4) You shall not make to yourself any graven image, or any likeness of anything that is in heaven above (stars and astrology), or that is in the earth beneath, or that is in the water under the earth; 5) You shall not bow yourself down to them nor serve them: For the Lord your God am a jealous God, visiting the iniquity of the fathers upon the children to the third and fourth generations of them that hate me. 6) And showing mercy to thousands of them that love me, and keep my commandments.

God warned us not to make any graven image in our nation of anything in heaven, or in the earth, or sea. This must include statues of presidents who are men. Men who are made out of earth. It is also to be noticed, that there has been in the development of the United States, many gymnastics with semantics. What in ancient times would be called an idol, or devotion (see Acts 17:22-31) is now called - *a statue.* This has been done by the enemy to take away the stigma the word **idol** has been given by the Lord God. Idolatry is rampant in our nation today. Having been to Washington D.C., the author has witnessed the occult images, statues, and pictures. Which would cause those visiting America to see our people, as a people that worships men, rather than God. AntiChrist Humanism is all that can be deduced by any who visits our center of national government. The worship of the founding fathers is an idolatry, and affront to God. This does not mean we should not honor them for their Christian faith. But he said to".. make no image, or likeness of anything..."[review Exodus 20:3-4]. And we have! This is an abomination to the Creator. It is also interesting that we as parents have a gift we give to our children. It used to be given just to little girls. Now little boys also receive these gifts. They are called *"dolls"* Little do most Christian parents know, or understand, this name is derived from the word " *idol* ". You just drop the " *i* " and add a " *l* ".

Another aspect of idolatry in the United States of America, is the Hollywood, and New York, movie and film industries. It is all based upon the " worship " of certain " stars " . Most Christians to-day know more about their favorite movie stars, than they do about Jesus Christ, who is *" The Bright and Morning Star "*(Revelation 22:16). What is so abominable about these film industries, is that they usually display some kind of immorality to the viewers. Some illicit " lust " scene is utilized to captivate their audiences. Very seldom are wholesome marriage, and family values, and morals presented, if at all. What is sad is that little children are having their young minds corrupted through the eye-gate before they even are old enough to understand what morality is about. For this reason, they are an abomination. What is so insidious about these systems of pervasive national indoctrination, is that the advertising companies who sponsor these programs and movies receive their wealth from us the consumers of their products. How wicked this is. Investigation and boycotting of these companies should be a weapon through which we, the fathers and mothers of this nation, take authority over this area of wickedness in our land. The entire advertising industry of America's networks, is based upon the doctrine of Balaam found in the book of Numbers chapters 22 through 25. And Numbers 31:1-16. This will be discussed in chapter 16 at length.

Next, in this segment, we will touch lightly upon the phrase *"..Mother of Harlots.. "*. We will not say much, because it is to be dealt with entirely before the end of the book. Whoredoms, and harlotry was a major description of ancient Babylon. And Satan's activity with women, has not changed since then. In the United States of America whoredom and harlotry is also rampant. Pornography in general, and pornography in our national media, is the cause. The profane works of Hollywood have endeavored to help the United States of America be called "Babylon the Great". For, Revelation 18:3 states -*"..For all nations have drunk of the wine of the wrath of her fornication.. "* Literal Greek τασ πορνειασ αυτᾶσ(of her porneias) i.e., pornography (pictures of fornication). There has been continual use of America's daughters to produce immoral, and illicit pictures, for the entire world to see. This has produced *"..the wine of the wrath.. "* Or, the despising of women, and their God-ordained position of bringing children into the earth. The Baal worship (offering of your seed to Molech) i.e., abortion of infants, has been fomented by this Babylonish form of wickedness in America. The United States government promotes child sacrifice technology worldwide. (See Revelation 18:24) *"..All that were slain upon the earth.. "*. CBS - Los Angeles, Channel 2 News, recently had a segment which declared Southern California, specifically the San Fernando Valley, as the Pornographic

Capitol of the entire earth. Next, we see in Revelation 18:11-19 that *"..the merchants.."* Or, in today's vernacular, men and women of commerce, were made rich by all her goods. The United States trade, and commerce systems, are without a doubt the "greatest" the world has ever seen. The flow of goods, in and out, of the United States is immense. Ships and aircraft are in continual operation to distribute goods around the world. By way of explanation, the word "chariots" in Rev. 18:13, has been reduced to the word "cars" in today's vernacular. The two last aspects of the abominations of "Mystery, Babylon the Great", is what is found in Rev. 18:22 & 23. The rock music industry has, in its more degenerated segments, been used by Satan, and his demonic powers (See Rev. 18:2). It is interesting that one rock star has been given the name Billy "Idol". Also, a female rock star who is named "Madonna", which is a Latin name for: ***women in rule, or dominion over men sexually***. This religious perversion also came out of ancient Babylon as *"..Queen of Heaven Worship.."*. It is also used by the Roman Catholic institution to deify Mary as the "Queen of Heaven". (Refer to Jeremiah 7:18, 44:15-25). One of her hit songs was *"Material Girl"*. In which she glorifies the receiving of carnal possessions as the answer to every girls dreams. Madonna, by the way, also exposed her naked body to two of the leading prominent producers of pornography worldwide, Playboy and Penthouse. God abhors the use of ***musical enchantments*** to seduce people to commit adultery, and fornication. And so should we! Yet, these abominations have indoctrinated our nation. And filled our young children with lascivious attitudes, and evil concupiscence. It has produced millions of unwanted teenage pregnancies. And, the resultant slaughter of in-nocent unborn babies by abortion. Not to mention the destruction of the self-worth and esteem of our children. We can, and must, force our Federal, and State governments to destroy these abominations. Before God has to destroy us (See Leviticus 20:1-5).

Lastly, we see an aspect of ancient Babylon, and its connection in the United States of America in Revelation 18:23(d). "...for by your *sorcery..* (Greek-φαρμακεια- transliterated - pharmakeia) were all the nations deceived." The word "sorcery", in the Greek, is the word from which we get "pharmacy". It means: the utilizing of mind altering potions, to make people believe something is so. When it, in reality, is not. This is, without a doubt, a major abomination which exists in great force in these United States of America. It is interesting that Revelation 17:3, and Revelation 12:14, both speak of *"..a wilderness.. "* The name pilgrim fathers, and pioneers called this land area prior to its development into the United States of America.

THE MYSTERIOUS MASONIC ORDERS

Very few American citizens know much about Masonry. The reason is that it is a highly secretive organization. Which literally blankets the entire United States. There is a Masonic Temple in just about every city, township, in every State. The members of this secretive organization meet regularly. And conduct "religious" exercises. Much like those who attend Church regularly. Yet, they do not espouse to worship the Lord Jesus Christ, or, His Father God.

The Mysterious Masonic Orders had their beginnings also in ancient Babylon. The Masons of Babylon prided themselves with their creations of architecture. At this point we must turn to the book *The Two Babylons* - by: late author Alexander Hislop pg. 43 -

"It is admitted that the secret system of Freemasonry was originally founded on the mysteries of the Egyptians. It is, the union of a Masonic body with these mysteries, had they not had particular reference to architecture, and had the god who was worshipped in them not been celebrated for his success in perfecting the arts of fortification and building? Now, if such were the case, considering the relation in which, as we have already seen, Egypt stood to Babylon, who would naturally be looked up to there as the great patron of the Masonic art? The strong presumption is, that Nimrod must have been the man. He was the first to gain fame in this way (at Babel) as the child of the

Babylonian goddess-mother (Semiramis), he was worshipped, as we have seen, in character of Ala Mohozim, " the god of fortifications ". Osiris, in like manner, the child of the Egyptian Madonna, was equally celebrated as " the strong chief of the building ".[5]

This system of "..the worship of the works of men's hands", is just another aspect of Satan's myriad of tactics used to deceive mankind. And distract him from worshipping the true God. Creator of life on earth. Yet the Mysterious Masonic Orders will continue to " build " Mystery Babylon. That is, until God's judgments of the book of Revelation begin (please study Rev. 9: 20 & 21).

We say at this time that the reason we write these things is that God does not want His children associated with any of these " ..abominations of the earth.. ". As fathers, we are to warn our children, to beware of them. Also, something is seriously wrong when we, as Americans, must pay thousands of dollars. And go in-to life long debt to purchase a house, while we are encouraged by groups like Planned Parenthood, to destroy our children by abortion, because it costs too much to raise them!

We close this segment now with selected quotes from
Demolishing the Hosts of Hell - by: Win Worley.

"...In every symbol, ceremony, and emblem of Freemasonry we are confronted with nothing but the sun-god [Lucifer]. That ancient Baal worship, in every religion from the Druids, to Hinduism.

By embracing such rituals, and vows, rooted in ancient witchcraft, and demonic worship. Men, and women, are placing themselves under occult power. The secret signs, passwords, handgrips, etc. Which are so highly prized, in reality brings lives under secret bondages. And churches are paralyzed where these secret loyalties exist. And the Holy

---

5   *The Two Babylons* - Alexander Hislop, Pg. 43, Loizeaux Bros., Inc. 1959.

Spirit cannot flow freely. Jesus said,*".. He had done all things openly, and had done nothing in secret,.."* A startling contrast to secret [Masonic]orders. Which enforce secrecy on their members. We are commanded*".. to renounce the hidden things of darkness.."* (Romans 13:12).

" The point within a circle.." is another thinly disguised " lift " from paganism. Borrowed from Baal mythology. It is a true representation of the lascivious Moabite idol Baal-peor...[see Numbers 25:1-18]. The point within a circle is, in reality, an ancient phallic symbol, and alludes to [ancient] sun worship [Satan] according to Masonic authority Mackey.

He states further that, Phallic (obelisk) worship, was a peculiar modification of ancient sun-worship. The Phallus was a sculptured representation of the male organ of generation. And, the worship of it originated in Egypt. Where it was venerated as a [cultish fertility] religious rite. This was the Baal-peor of the Moabite [review Numbers chapter 25]. And, the Tammuz, or Adonis (review Ezekiel chapter eight) of the account of Holy Scripture.

This occult pornographic phallus symbol, has been placed in St. Peter's Square, at the Vatican (by Roman Emperor Caligula). And, in the center of Washington, D.C. (District of Columbia) with a circle of American-Flags making it -*" A Point within a Circle"*. [See appendix on - The Grove & Ashtoreth]. These facts reveal the Roman Catholic - antiquitous Babylon connection.

Masons *changed names* in the Egyptian mysteries from Osiris to Hiram Abiff, but retained a similar legend for the initiations. They burned their manuscripts in 1720, interspersed the names of Hiram and Solomon to secure acceptance by Jew and Gentile. And appropriated the Bible, and Apostle John, to give it a " Christian " veneer. i., e., transformed into - Freemasonry. Both in whole, and in part, is literally, and truly the secret worship of Baal. Or, the sun god." An ex-witch quotes from a Masonic book. Which is to be read by 33rd, 32nd, 31st, and 30th degree Masons. Whose lives prove they are not Christians : " ..That which we must say to the crowd [inquiring non-members] is we worship a god. But it is a god that one adores without superstition. To you, Sovereign Grand Inspectors General. We say this. That you may repeat it to the brethren of the 32nd, 31st, and 30th degree. The Masonic religion should be, by all of us initiates of high degree, maintained in the purity of the Luciferian doctrine. If Lucifer were not god, would Adonay- Jesus, the God of the Christians. Whose deeds prove His cruelty and hatred of men, barbarism, and repulsion for science - would Adonay and his priests calumniate him? Yet Lucifer is god: Thus, the doctrine of Satanism is a heresy. And the true, and pure philosophical religion is: The belief in Lucifer. The equal of Adonay- Jesus Christ. But Lucifer, god of light. And god of good. Is struggling for humanity against Adonay, the god of darkness and evil."

From: *Locked Keys of Freemasonry*. -

When the Mason learns that the key to the warrior on the block is the proper application of the dynamo of living power, he has learned the mystery of his craft. The seething energies of Lucifer are in his hands, and before he may step onward and upward, he must prove his ability to properly apply energy. He must follow in the footsteps of his forefather Kubal-Cain, who with the mighty strength of the war god [Lucifer] hammered his sword into a plowshare." (The ' *warrior on the block* ' rite is one of human sacrifice).[6]

---

6   *Demolishing the Hosts of Hell* - By: Win Worley Pgs. 77-79 Hedgewich Baptist Church, Box 626, Lansing, ILL 60438 1978.

AMERICA'S PROPHETS OF BAAL

In chapter eight we will go into detail as to what actually Baal worship is. And, we have already touched upon it. But, to effectively produce a discernment in the minds of men concerning fatherhood, relating to this matter; we must expose the reality of a very evil, and wicked philosophy, which has developed to immense proportions within the boundaries of our nation. We must again state that Satan's purpose is to take God's place. God's place in the lives of men, and women. In any, and all ways possible. To produce an alternative way of life, contrary to the Creator God's way of life, and ordained plan, is job one. These attacks come from religious and secular sources.

The relationship men and women have between each other is a major area of activity by Satan. And his demonic spirits. Especially the area of physical carnal relationship. To put it simply. The most precious and personal gift, God has provided man with, has been one of the most intense areas of Satan's attacks. And, evil works.

The name God gives to men, He charges to explain His will through, is the name " prophet ". The Old Testament term was also " Seer ". A visionary for God. The purest definition of this name is:

1)   A person who speaks for God, or a god, or, as though under divine guidance. One who has been divinely [or satanically] inspired to interpret God's will. A spokesman for a specific cause.

In 1st Peter 4:11 God instructed us to be sure that -

11)   If any man speak, let him speak as the oracles of God..

In other words. Let him speak as God's *" mouthpiece "* in the earth.

The way God sets up the ordination of His authority on the earth; is that He speaks to men, and women, through " preachers ". Or, in the purest sense, *" prophets "*. We will cover this in detail in chapter thirteen on the use of the tongue. But now we explain that Satan, and his demon powers, also need mouths to speak through. And, also, through which he can propagate his anti - God life styles. Specifically relating to " sexual " activity. [This word is actually a Roman profanity in Latin linguistics - *sexus* equated with- *fornication* of the Greek profanity derivative]. Satan's prophets in America, are the same kind of religious men we find in 1st Kings 18: 21-22

21)   And Elijah came unto all the people, and said, how long halt you between two opinions (life-styles)? If the Lord be God, follow Him: But if Baal, then follow him: and the people answered him not a word. 22) Then said Elijah to the people, I, even I only, remain a prophet of the Lord; but Baal's prophets are four hundred and fifty men.

Today, in the United States of America, there are prophets of Baal as in Old Testament Israel's time. The problem we face, as God's people, is that they are not called, or known, as such. This can produce a very dangerous delusion. A condition of acceptability among God's people. An attitude of- *" well that's the world, and we cannot change the world."* When God said, *" ..Be the salt of the earth..."* (Mt. 5:13). And, *".. to those who know to do good, and do it not, to them it is sin."* (James 4:17). These prophets of Baal in America, are developing a condition in the United States, that will accept their profane " Playboy " philosophy. And continue to make our nation's daughters into harlots. And, our sons into whoremongers. We all, as God's men, must organize ourselves into a body politic nation - wide. In every city. And appeal to, and demand our federal, State, and local laws concerning obscenity be strictly enforced! Hugh Hefner, in the year1953, " started " or, should we say *"fathered"*, his immoral playboy philosophy. He did it by satanic, and demonic inspiration, to mock God's standards of morality, purity, and virtue. It used to be a hidden thing. Something "Dad" kept in his office desk drawer. But now, it is aired worldwide, by cable and satellite television into every home. The video market is exploding to supply pornographic videos to the fathers, and mothers in our nation. Even young children are having their young minds polluted, and molested by these prophets of Baal, via the Internet. Bob Guccione, of Penthouse Magazine, and Larry Flint, of Hustler; are the other two major prophets of Baal. Who should, at this time, be in prison for the destructive influence they all have perpetrated upon our lives in America. It is interesting that all the major television networks, ABC, NBC & CBS, and FOX, give air time to promote these pornographers. Yet never permit one of God's true prophets to speak of God's design for marriage, and procreation. And we are supposed to have freedom of speech in every form of media in our nation. They are hypocrites.

Evidence is mounting that all child molestations. And most rapes, and violence against women, are fueled, as an effect of pornography. For this cause, we all, as God's people, must unite nationwide. To eradicate this source of wickedness in our beloved nation. The author guarantees, that we would see a dramatic drop in the epidemic of sexual assaults upon our families, if this is done. If it is not we shall see greater wickedness.

The author believes it necessary to organize parents in each city of our nation. Parents, who are committed to destroy this destructive force corrupting our nation. As was said in the book- ***Satanic Feminism v. The American Home***, those who espouse that *"morality cannot be legislated "*, speak by demon spirits out of Hell. Because, the truth is, that some kind of morality. Or immorality, will prevail in our nation, if good men, and women do nothing! (read Romans 13:3-4). Pornography. Or, as those who wish to soften its offense with euphemisms like- "adult entertainment". Is to be punished by moral laws. Inspired by godly men, and women, in public office. Today, our government is taking in corrupt tax revenue from this industry. A profanity that is destroying our moral lives. We must stop it. We can, and we will, by God's mighty Word. For His glory!

Sowing Wild Oats

So goes the phrase that the fathers of immorality use to describe their son's profane sexual activity before marriage. It is even received with pats on the back. And words like- "..he's a chip off the old block..". A phrase probably derived from the Masonic Orders. But what does God say in Galatians 6:7 & 8.

7)   Be not deceived; God is not mocked: for whatsoever a man sows, that shall he also reap.

8).   For he, that sows to his flesh, shall of the flesh, reap corruption; But, he that sows to the Spirit, shall of the Spirit, reap life everlasting.

Fathers. If you teach.,or, approve of your son, or, daughter to sow to their flesh. You will cause them to reap a life of corruption. No man mocks the Creator and gets away with it. Much of the suffering, and wickedness in our land, is because of men who are deceived by Satan. And themselves, to believe they can get away with violating God's order involving procreation. God created us to have rule over our bodies. Not to allow our flesh, and its desires, to rule us. The *"sowing of wild oats"* has produced terrible conditions for young women, and children, in our nation. The irresponsible evil attitude perpetrated, by Hugh Hefner's Playboy philosophy, has caused horrendous conditions in the lives of many in our nation. If those men think they are going to get away with these atrocities, they have God to answer to. For their whoremongering, fornicating, and adulterous activities. There is a just God who will render to every man according to his activities (read Revelation 22:7-15.) But, the fathers in our nation who encourage, and allow their children to do these things, will reap the consequences. Which is: corruption and death. Let us not forget that God has prepared a place for those who follow Satan's ways and suggestions called- *"....the lake of fire."* (See Rev. 20:15). We do well to fear God. And, His warnings, to those who practice wickedness in the earth. (Read Revelation 21:8).

A LITTLE LEAVEN

"A little leaven leavens the whole lump."

— Galatians 5:9

The Apostle Paul, and Jesus Christ our Lord, gave us this spiritual principle to understand. They both utilized it to explain that profane, and erroneous teaching, and doctrine, would corrupt the people they were trying to protect from Satan's systems of false teaching. The author Tim LaHaye summed much of this up in his excellent book - *" The Battle for the Mind "*. But, as we stated before, the intention of Satan's system of education is to take the place of God's way in the earth. This leaven of - satanically inspired doctrine, is to be opposed by God's people. (Read 1st Timothy 4:1-16). Leaven must be placed into the lump of dough to have any effect. We are to hinder, and guard our children from the enemy of their souls. We must hinder Satan, and his demons, from having any opportunity to do his destructive work in their minds, and hearts.

OUR STOLEN HERITAGE - APOSTATE EDUCATORS
IN OUR SYSTEM OF NATIONAL EDUCATION

The founding fathers, as shown in chapter one, labored diligently to provide us a nation in which we could enjoy all of God's richest blessings. They beseeched God to bless us in the song- *" God Bless*

America - land that I love"! They were truly blessed fathers and mothers. That gave us a heritage of God's blessing. The " kind " of planting that took place at Plymouth Plantation, gave this nation's people, their blessings, and wealth. But, as the true proverb goes-

" ..It is the little foxes that spoil the vine."
— Song Solomon 2:15

Only the foxes [educators] have- *"..transformed themselves into ravening wolves in sheep's clothing.."*(study 2nd Corinthians 11:13-15). Satan is the first apostate. And father of all apostasy. He, before the fall, " knew " all the deep truths of God. He was the *"anointed cherub"* (Ezekiel 28:12-19). Today, he energizes the people of the earth to apostatize from God. Who is the Truth (John 14:6). This has been his work in our national system of education. The purest definition of apostasy is- when an individual who knows the truth. And has been intimately associated with the truth. Deliberately turns from the truth. To maliciously teach, and propagate falsehood. This is definitely the activity of Satan, and his educators. There are many abominable teachings in our school systems nationwide. But the basic undermining began as Charles Darwin's philosophy of evolution, and origin of species, was received to secularize State funded education. God warned us through the apostle Paul of these teachings of demons in 1st Timothy 4:1-

1)   " Now the Spirit speaks expressly, that in the latter times some shall depart from the faith, [faith that God is Creator of earth, and all life upon it] giving heed to seducing spirits, and doctrines of demons;..."

Evolution is a satanic, and demonic doctrine, which purports that life on earth just came about over millions of years. It has produced many forms of reprobation in the minds of our intelligentsia. Who

41

educate our children. This has divorced our young from the faith that God, is the Creator, and sustainer of our life. God has warned us not to separate our knowledge, from our respect of Him, in the book of Proverbs 1:7-

7)   The fear of the Lord is the beginning of knowledge: but fools despise wisdom and instruction.

It is no wonder our children are growing up to despise our authority. It is because we rebel. And, refuse to submit to God's authority, the Holy Bible. It is no wonder we see our children flirting with Satan worship. When, in reality, our refusal to submit to God's authority, is an aspect of satanism. We cannot claim we were not warned of these things. For, in Romans 1: 21-28, we find God's prognosis of our national education system. Specifically in Romans 1: 28-

And even as they did not like to retain God in their knowledge, [but rather turned to demonic evolutionary lies] God gave them over to a reprobate mind, to do those things which are not convenient; [emphasis added]

There has been a militant antiChrist effort to remove all references to God out of our children's school textbooks by these apostates. Yet, *"..we the parents.."*, who pay our taxes to develop these books; are not even consulted as to whether, or not, we mind if this is done to the minds of our offspring. We must get back to the principle of our Government that said, *"..no taxation without representation"*. In reality, those feverishly working to get all references to God out of our nation's textbooks, should be fired for working to undermine the very principles that made our nation great. For they are working for Satan. And doing his work as described in John 10:10. *Stealing* from our young. Stealing the Christian American heritage many have died shedding their blood to provide us with. This has recently been called deconstructing the American Republic. We close this segment with God's warning found in 2nd Peter 2: 1 & 2 -

1)   But there were false prophets also among the people, even as there shall be false teachers among you, who sneakily shall bring in damnable heresies, even denying the Lord that bought them, and bring upon themselves swift destruction. 2) And many shall follow their pernicious [evil] ways; by reason of whom the way of truth shall be evil spoken of.

Our job before God is to work in every way we possibly can to protect our youngsters from these heresies. And the false teachings these people who serve Satan are propagating. We should do all we can to stop our hard earned tax monies from being utilized to corrupt our children's minds. It is not the Government's job to do this. It is the job of fathers and mothers! The way we allow our children's minds to be formed today, will in essence, produce for us the kind of Government we will have in the future of our nation. We need to realize just exactly what the Lord Jesus Christ meant in Matthew 16:19 when he said-

19)   And I will give to you [those in authority over your children] the keys of the kingdom of heaven: And whatsoever you shall bind on earth shall be bound in heaven. [emphasis added]

Some say this power was given only to Peter the Apostle. Some say it was given only to the original apostles. Some say it was given to the Church. But what is the Church? But all those fathers and mothers who love, and serve Jesus Christ as their Savior and Lord? Our authority, and power in the earth, is far more powerful than Satan and his angels want us to understand!

To gain more insight into the causes of apostasy in the educational elite in the United States public school systems, please read the recommended reading book titles at the end of this chapter. Also, it was a major work of Satan to allow Madalyn Murray - OHair to manipulate the US Supreme court to ban both daily prayer and Holy Bible reading in our Public schools Nationwide on June 17th,1963. It is high time to reverse her curse.

THE BINDING OF ANTI-CHRIST AND THE U.S. CONSTITUTION

The forefathers who framed the United States Constitution, and our form of government, knew that if any man was given control, and authority in our government for too long; that man would have the potential to begin to oppress, and destroy the nation. Therefore, they set up our electoral process of executive, and legislative branches of government. To be limited to two years legislative. And four years executive respectively. With the possibility of impeachment if a leader went bad too quickly before the voters could get him out of office. The framers knew the reality of Proverbs 29:2. *" When the righteous are in authority, the people rejoice: But when the wicked bear rule, the people mourn."* The third branch of our system of government is the judicial branch. From the term Judaic - Law. Or, the law God gave to Moses. Judges in our Supreme Court are supposed to interpret the laws of God. And the conduct of the nation's citizens. Then rule by decree righteously, and lawfully. That is why our nation is developing a precarious nature at this time. There are forces (demonic) and people working to throw out all law that derives its origin from Holy Scripture. American judges are fearful to make righteous judgments. Because, they fear reprisals from the atheistic God-haters. Who always lobby in Washington, D.C. And who would accuse them of being " Bible Thumpers ". The author believes it is a definite mistake to allow judgeships for lifelong tenures. The atrocities of pornography. And - abortion on demand - is a wickedness. That if the judges in our Court systems knew the Biblical position about- *"..offering a nation's seed to Molech.."* being an abomination to God, the Supreme Judge of the earth, they would decree a judgment of national repentance immediately! They would fear God. the Judge of judges more, than American wicked rebellious God-haters. With every passing day though, there are forces at work to undermine, and abolish the righteous laws in our nation's law libraries. Specifically on moral issues. Historical revisionists, who hate America, seek to corrupt our children with evil views of this nation's founders. We must heed at this time God's admonition in Psalm 11:3 -3) *"..If the foundations be destroyed, what can the righteous do."* This verse should be read right along side of Mt. 5:13. If we fail to do something now we may see the- *"....But be cast out and be trodden under foot of men."* part of Mt. 5:13.

The electoral process of the United States, and the purest interpretation of our Constitution, binds any anti-Christ individual (Read Rev. 13) from coming to power in our nation. Also, the influence, and political power our nation has around the world "at this time", also would hinder such a man from gaining that much authority in the earth. Adolf Hitler was an example of this, by the way the military forces of the United States destroyed his efforts to control all of Europe. This is not to say, that if certain elements have their way, a continued destruction of righteous principles of our government would allow for such an individual to take power over the free world quickly.

Readers can learn how the U.S. Constitution has been corrupted over the 394 years [from the Pilgrims landing in 1620] of our American history by reading- *The Original Intent of the First Amendment - According to the Founding Fathers* - By: Michael Citriniti & Michael D. Juzwick, from: Light Eternal Publications, 1996. Information on America's Christian history can be obtained from them.

APOSTLESHIP IN THE UNITED STATES

Probably the greatest reason God has withheld His judgment against the wicked activities in our nation, is that our nation has been a fountainhead of missionary endeavor worldwide. The Mayflower Compact was signed by the Pilgrim American founding fathers specifically- *"..to Advance the Christian faith.."*[review chapter 1, page 12]. The Church that Jesus Christ is building, will be built. And, though Satan is doing all he can to stop it, he will not. Because, Matthew 16:18 & 19 declares -

18)   ...And upon this rock I will build my Church; and the gates of Hell shall not prevail against it. 19) And I will give unto you the keys of the kingdom of Heaven: And whatsoever you shall bind on earth shall be bound in heaven: And whatsoever you shall loose (allow) on earth shall be loosed [allowed] in Heaven.

We, at this time, wish to define the Bible term: apostle. The Greek word, which is transliterated *" apostle "* is a word which means: someone who is sent on a mission for a specific purpose. That means if a mother sent her son, or daughter to the store to pick something up. He, or she, would be in the purest sense of the word be an apostle for that purpose. For all the word apostle means is "sent one." The Great Commission of Mark16-14-20, is to be carried out by all God's children. Not just " apostles " For, we are all sent by our Lord Jesus Christ. And, we have His power, and authority, as we do. Especially as the fathers and mothers of our children. If we could see more apostleship in our homes, and neighborhoods in the cities across our land, we would see many great things take place to heal America our land. And, that would glorify the Lord Jesus Christ. (Read Mark 12:28-34).

Recommended Reading:

1. *NEA; Trojan Horse in American Education* - Samuel L. Blumenfield, Paradigm ID., 1984.
2. *Book Burning* - Cal Thomas, Crossway Books, 1983.
3. *Textbooks on Trial* - James C. Hefley Distributed by: Educational Research, P.O.. Box 7518 Longview, TX 75602.
4. *Child Abuse in the Classroom* - Phyllis Schlafly, Pere-Marguette Press 1984.
5. The War Against Boys - Christina Hoff Sommers, 2000.

CHAPTER 3

Fatherhood & The Future of The United States of America

WHAT IT COULD BE -

The precarious nature which our nation has at this time is because there has been a waning of godly spiritual leadership. As the saying and proverb goes- *"Everything rises and falls through leadership"*. God intends for the fathers in a nation to reflect Him, and do His will in the earth. God desires to manifest His nature through our lives. This is one reason there is so much wickedness in our land. The ignorance and disobedience of the men in our nation has produced it. But God always looks for men who will do His perfect will, and glorify Him. The desire of the author is that what has been written in this book will encourage and inspire many fathers to develop their spiritual leadership capacities before God. And assist their sons and daughters to do the same. For this is America's salvation and deliverance from the evil one. (ref. 1st John 5:18).

FATHERHOOD AND LEADERSHIP 1

"If My People..." 2nd Chronicles 7:12-14 12 -

12)   And the Lord appeared to Solomon by night, and said to him, I have heard your prayer, and have chosen this place to myself for a house of sacrifice.

13)   If I shut up heaven that there be no rain, or if I command the locusts to devour the land, or if I send pestilence among my people; 14) If my people, which are called by my name, shall humble themselves, and pray, and seek my face, and turn from their wicked ways; then will I hear from Heaven, and will forgive their sin, and will heal their land.

The two-letter word *"if"* is a very important word in Biblical revelation. It sets forth the conditions through which the Lord God of hosts operates in the earth, and moves His mighty hand. God's majesty and glory is revealed and demonstrated to us as we meet His righteous and holy conditions. All the terrible destructions we see happening around us daily are the result of our national sins that are against a holy God who executes His righteous judgment in the earth. God has issued His command to repent, and do His will (ref. Acts 17:30-31). He has not made a suggestion. We are all under command. At this point we outline God's conditions which He places upon us. And that which He promises to do in response to obedience to His will.

First - We as God's people must *"...humble ourselves."* (read Micah 6: 8).
Second - *"Pray"* (read I Timothy 2:1-6 & Ephesians 6:18)
Third - *"Seek the face of God"* (read Matthew 5: 8 & Jeremiah 29: 11 -13).
Fourth - *"And turn from our wicked ways"* (read Leviticus 19:20; 20: 1 - 8; Matthew 18: 32 - 35; James 4: 17).

If, and only if, we meet these conditions will God do the three things that we in the United States of America desperately need from Him. God promises He will:

First - *"..Hear our cry to Him in Heaven.."* (read Isaiah 59:1 & 2). Second - *".. Forgive our sins."* (Read Ezra. 8:21-23). Third - *"..He will heal our land."* (read Psalms 107:19-22).

Probably the greatest sin we as God's people have committed is the sin of not being "the light of our nation".(See Matthew 5:14-16). We all as His servants should be declaring with our mouths His righteousness in every area of our nation. Whether in the work space, or in the halls of our national, and State governments. It is sin for us to allow, and permit God's righteous laws to be destroyed in our nation by the wicked (ref. Psalm 11:3). We are to be God's voice in the earth. Declaring His holy will to all men everywhere (see Acts 17:30-31). God is not going to take the answer - "I did not know your Word said that." in the day of His judgment. We are to know God's will, and do it. He created us for that purpose. God created man, especially fathers, to enforce His will on this earth. The Lord Jesus affirms this in His pattern for prayer in Matthew 6: 9 -13-*"..your will be done in earth, as it is in Heaven.."*. This is not a prayer request! It is what God expects from us.

FATHERHOOD AND LEADERSHIP 2

" ..to show Himself strong.." 2nd Chronicles 16:9 (a)-

9)(a) For the eyes of the Lord run to and fro throughout the whole earth, to show Himself strong in behalf of them whose heart is perfect toward him.

God tells us He is looking throughout the earth for men and women to be the kind of leaders He can manifest His will through. The condition He requires is that their hearts be perfect before Him. The man who prepares himself, and his children to do God's will is the man whose heart is perfect because God's will is perfect. Another very important part of God's Word, through which we see His divine will, and purpose for men is found in Ezekiel 22:30 - 30-

> "And I sought for a man among them, that should make up the hedge, and stand in the gap before me for the land', that I should not destroy it: But I found none."

What a terrible situation God is in when men refuse to do His will. A good cross reference for this verse is in Numbers 16:44-49. We will cover this area of " hedges " in detail in chapter fourteen. But for now we see this is an extremely important ministry for us to learn about, and begin to practice. God wants, and needs such men who care enough. And love enough. To protect those who are destined for destruction. If they do not receive one to lead. And *"..stand in the gap between them and God"*, they shall perish. Fathers that honor God will stand in the gap. The fathers in our nation today must occupy this very important place of caring, loving, and protecting their children. Intercessors are being called by God today to not only pray, but also to take action in our land before God must. We shall see great things begin to manifest in our nation, if we will work to carry out this very purpose of the Lord God's in the earth. May we all, as fathers, and mothers, commit ourselves to God to carry out this blessed purpose. We will be very glad if we do. We will be very sad if we fail to.

THE DESTRUCTION OF BABYLON

The Prophetic Holy Scripture warns us to know, and understand, that the end times political and religious Babylon shall, without a doubt, be destroyed by God's judgments. Ancient Babylon was both political and religious. *"..Mystery, Babylon the great, the Mother of harlots and abominations of the earth.."* is also political, and religious (see-Revelation 17:1-18). It is also made up of physical architectural buildings. Created and built by the Mysterious Masonic

Orders. The destructions will come in phases of judgments according to the Revelation of our Lord Jesus Christ. The beginnings of which will be to encourage God's people to remove themselves from the Satanic and demonic inspired (See Rev. 18:2) system opposed to God, and His plan for the earth. Revelation 18:4 says, -

> 4) And I heard another voice from heaven, saying, come out of her, My people, that you be not partakers of her sins, and that you receive not of her plagues.

The next point the author wishes to make is that the earth we live on is still experiencing the effects of the last major judgment God had to execute because of the wickedness of men. The flood of Noah's day produced radical changes upon this earth. The flood waters literally washed much of the trace minerals of the dry ground off into the ocean floors producing vast deserts where no food could grow causing famines. The climatic changes were drastic also. There was no snow, or arctic regions, prior to the flood. There was no rain. The earth was set up by God with a green-house type of canopy around the atmosphere producing lush vegetation. The climate was perfect around the entire earth's surface. There was no reason to build protective buildings to live inside. And pay mortgage payments on. And maintain for the majority of your life on earth! We say this because man has moved more and more away from God's plan for this earth as instituted in the Garden of Eden. God's plan will be reinstituted by Jesus Christ during the millinial reign referred to in Revelation 20:1-7. Prior to that reinstitution of God's way on this planet, God's mighty judgments shall take place to prepare the earth to be changed into the condition God wants it to be. Utter destruction, and *"..all the works of men's hands shall be destroyed.."* (see 2nd Peter 3:7-13). The details of what those works are can be found by the study of the book of Revelation chapters 17 & 18. We, in this segment, wish to reveal the aspects of Mystery Babylon's destruction. Revelation 18:8-

8)   Therefore shall her plagues come in one day, death, and mourning, and famine; and she shall be utterly burned with fire: For [because] strong is the Lord God who judges her. Revelation 18:17 (a)

17(a)   For in one hour so great riches is come to nothing. Revelation 18:21 (b)

21(b)   Thus with violence shall that great city Babylon be thrown down, and shall be found no more at all.

THE FLOOD OUT OF THE SERPENT'S MOUTH

Revelation 12:15-17 -

15)   And the serpent [Satan] - [ref. Rev. 12:9] cast out of his mouth water as a flood after the woman, that he might cause her to be carried away of the flood..

As we explained in our first chapter the first stage of Satan's attack against God's people in the true Church was vehement persecution by Satan through evil men. Religious evil men using political men. This is represented in the political- *" ..beast.. "* that has *a religious "..whore.."* riding on its back for those who understand the prophecy. The verse we just gave reference to is the second phase of evil activity against true the Church. The Christian pilgrim fathers and mothers came to this *"..wilderness.."* [America] (Rev. 12:14) *".. prepared for her, to be protected, and nourished from the face of the serpent for a specified time.."* Our U.S. Constitution's First Amendment was designed by its framers to stop all persecution of any Christian Church. Religious freedom was their mandate. Not freedom for pornographers. As wicked lawyers have twisted its meaning in order to create infidelity between men and women. And thereby produce havoc in marriages, and child rearing tasks. Attorneys gain vast sums of money by illegally defending, and promoting pornography. Indirectly weakening families, in divorce courts during family court litigation. They financially gain from both the promoting of profanity, and the destroying of marriages. But, as we all know, freedom misused is freedom abused. The same First Amendment that closed the door to Satan's persecution of God's people through political government; now has been twisted, and distorted by corrupt attorneys in order to open the door for the second phase of Satan's attack. Specifically the *"perversion"* of God's people by profane books, video tapes, cable TV, and even regular network television programming. The same Constitution that was intended to provide liberty and protection for the persecuted Christians of the old European world, now has been perverted to permit the overthrow of God's people morally. By supposing to grant license to the wicked and immoral of the nation. Corrupt judges, and attorneys, have twisted the concept of liberty for righteous and Biblical ".. speech and expression..", as intended by the Christian founding fathers; and fathered the use of the First Amendment to give unlimited freedom to pornographers and Hollywood industries. This is a very cleaver deception being propagated by Satan, and those attorneys who serve him against God's people. Namely, that pornography is allowed by the First Amendment. And, the evil it creates must be tolerated by us as God's people. This is contrary to Romans 13:1-7 which tells us that the law-making bodies in our State and National congresses are to insure all evil is legislated against, and, punished by them. That is their major function according to the Holy Bible. Yet, the federal laws prohibiting such obscenity, profanity, pornography, and prostitution are not being enforced throughout our land by the Federal Communications Commission [FCC]. Which is to be a watch dog and punisher against evil communications in our Media networks. This has without a doubt allowed (see Mt. 16:19; 18: 18-20) Satan to open his mouth, and spew out this- *"..flood of wickedness..",* into our lives as God's people. Profane books, magazines, and movies are

54

supposed to be censored by the mandates set forth in Federal statutes. Most Christians in America have been desensitized to profane and obscene expression. And know very little about how it destroys them, and their families. The previously recommended reading on the First Amendment to the U. S. Constitution, has a review of terms relating to what actually profanity is at its end. To assist in the development of discernment by those who read it. Fathers, who remain ignorant on this subject, cannot be effective protectors of their households. Film industries know how to seduce us. They are like demon spirits. As long as you want to entertain them they will accommodate. They receive your wealth from the products they advertise to you, as they destroy your household's virtues and morals with their profane pro-gramming. We are to use money for God's will! It is interesting that the word *" ..wilderness.. "* is used by God to describe the place for God's people's nourishment and rest. And also the place-*" Mystery, Babylon the Great"*, exists (see Revelation 17:3). The flood which has been permitted to be unleashed by Satan, has occurred by God's people's sinful indifference. These sins are beginning to be recog-nized, and dealt with by God, and His people. This is revealed in Revelation 12:16 -

16)   And the earth [people who serve God] helped the woman, and the earth opened her mouth, and swal-lowed up the flood which the dragon (see Rev. 12: 7) cast out of his mouth.

In chapter thirteen we will deal in detail on the use of *the mouth and tongue*. But, we must say at this point, that as God uses our mouths to speak through to accomplish things. So, also Satan has been using the tongues and mouths of his followers to cause situa-tions to exist in our land. False statements like- *" You cannot legis-late morality "*, is a very powerful lie, that binds execution of moral laws. The championing of this false idea that there is a separation of political government from executing moral law is absurd. Romans 13: 1-7 reveals to us that God expects us to see police officers as *".. His ministers of justice specifically ordained to punish evil.."* Our tax monies are supposed to go for this very purpose as God's Word says. Any law imposes *" moral "* rules. And principles established are for the well-being of all people. As the Lord God rules heaven by His Word, so He created man to rule the earth by His spoken, written and enforced Word. Those who are punished for criminal activity by governmental law enforcement officials and judges are only God's hand of warning of His horrible wrath in Hell. Warning that if they fail to repent of their sinful behavior, that also effects citizens of the community, there is a future punishment to avoid. True Christian citizens in our nation are God's salt and light into even our places of law and government. We must be active in these matters, so that God's moral laws are kept in force for our own protection. And even those who are unbelievers. True, and pure law comes only from God's Word, the Holy Bible. Those who hate God, and His standards in His Word would naturally want them overthrown. Galatians 3:24 shows us that the law is designed to teach us when we are doing evil. And are sinners. So we can turn to the Lord Jesus Christ to gain His strength to overcome sin that will put us in Hell. To try to get rid of moral laws, is to increase the idea that there is no need for the salvation of Jesus Christ. Law is good to restrain evil. And try to show men their need to repent. If there is no law to reveal sinfulness, what purpose would people need to be saved from their nature to do evil? That is what is so wonderful about this prophetic promise in Revelation 12:16. Those who are bold, and courageous enough to but *".. open their mouths.."* will see God's hand of deliverance and healing move to overthrow these powerful deceptions (ref. Proverb 28: 1(b)). The book of Proverbs also tells us God's blessing, and delight will be ours if we will but - *".. open up our mouths.."* Proverbs 24: 24 & 25 -

24) He that says to the wicked, you are righteous; him shall the people curse, nations shall abhor him:

25) But to them that rebuke him shall be delight, and a good blessing shall come upon them.

This is God's promise to us, if we will begin to speak out. And use our words to overthrow the flood of wickedness and perversion Satan has poured out of his mouth, because of our fear and silence today! The author reminds the reader of another passage of God's majestic Word concerning prophetic occurrences relating to " floods ". In conclusion to this segment on- ***The flood out of the serpent's mouth*** we see God's prophecy. Isaiah 59:16-19 -

16) And He saw that there was no man and wondered that there was no intercessor: Therefore His arm brought salvation to Him: and His righteousness it sustained Him.

17) For He put on righteousness as a breastplate, and a helmet of salvation upon His head: And He put on the garments of vengeance for clothing and was clad with zeal as a cloak.

18) According to their deeds, accordingly He will repay, fury to His adversaries, recompense to His enemies; to the islands He will repay recompense.

19) So shall they fear the name of Lord ***from the west***, and His glory from the rising of the sun, When the enemy [Satan] shall come in like a flood, the Spirit of the Lord shall lift up a standard against him. [emphasis added]

God's enemy has come into this nation. Which is in *" ..the west"*. And we, as God's people, must prepare ourselves. And our children, to allow *".. the Spirit of the Lord to energize through us that He might raise up a standard against him in our land."* Amen!

WHEAT AND TARES

Most people know something about wheat since it is a staple of American life. Nutritional experts tell us that whole wheat bread is better for the human body than the more refined and adulterated products. But the parable that is found in Matthew 13:24-30 is spoken by Jesus Christ in a figurative way to explain a spiritual truth. We know that if we fail to eat physical food, and nourish our bodies properly, our physical bodies will begin to manifest weakness and illness. The food giants today are placing various chemicals and additives which have been proven to cause cancer into our foods. We all have common sense enough to not place any toxic substance into our physical bodies because doing so can cause us to die. Yet, today in America, there are *"spiritual and moral"* toxins, which have flooded into our lives in an insidious, and subtle way via today's media. They are poisoning, not only our lives, but also our dear children's lives. As fathers and mothers we must act to protect our families from these realities. You might say what does this have to do with wheat and tares? It has much to do with it. Normally we think only of physical food when we think of nutrition. But the Holy Scriptures speak of spiritual food for the spirit and soul of man. In the temptation of Jesus Christ, at the point of starvation, Satan came to Jesus to entice Him to obey Satan's words rather than His Father in heaven. Matthew 4:1 - 4 -

1)   Then was Jesus led up of the Spirit into the wilderness to be tempted of the Devil.
2)   And when he had fasted forty days and forty nights, he afterward ahungered.

58

3)   And when the tempter came to him, he said, if you be the Son of God, command that these stones be made bread.

4)   But he answered and said, man shall not live by bread alone, but by every word that proceeds out of the mouth of God.

There is something for fathers and mothers to " chew " on. We are told by God that we are to take into our lives God's words and live by their nourishment. Jesus Christ is referred to in John 1:1 as- *"..the Word of God.."*. Also, in John 6:31-63, Jesus informed us that He is *" ..the bread of life.."*. That, by eating this bread, we receive life from God. Even eternal life. This is a very deep aspect of understanding who Jesus Christ is to us. When we take God's Word into our lives by faith, we become capable of sharing that bread of life with others. Our children desperately need us as fathers to give this life-giving bread to them. If we fail to, they can become infested with various spiritual poisons which Satan can use to destroy them. And others, with whom they come into contact. This is the aspect of the work of being a good husband. Which will be discussed later in this book. Tares are something the average father, or husband, know little about. Except maybe that it is a weed that grows near wheat. But we shall define this word *"..tares.. "* And some words associated with it. And attempt to draw spiritual conclusions from doing so. There are four words we will at this time define. Afterward, we will draw spiritual truths from this study. Jesus used parables about natural matters to bring light. The definitions are from Webster's dictionary.

Tare: 1. Any of several vetches, esp. the common vetch. 2. The seed of any of these plants. 3. Bible - a noxious weed thought to be darnel: ref. Mt. 13: 25-40.

Darnel: (stupefied, black caraway, Latin - niger, black: so called from its supposed stupefying qualities). A weedy rye grass often occuring in grain fields: When its seeds are infested with a certain fungus they become poisonous.

Vetch: Any number of leafy, climbing or trailing plants of the legume family, grown chiefly for fodder, and as a green manure.

Manure: Orig., to farm (land) to cultivate, literally to work with the hands:

It is very interesting to see that " manure " originally meant to cultivate land. For this is precisely what God commanded man to do in the Garden of Eden (ref. Genesis 2:15). And, from studying darnel, we learn that if "certain fungus" gets into the seeds of this rye grass, it becomes poisonous. As fathers, and mothers we are to cultivate the land God has given to us to take care of . If we permit the " fungus " of satanic, and demonic activity to enter our children's lives, they too will grow up to be poisonous to themselves, their offspring, and others. The author believes that all those in our nation, who are being used by Satan to poison our lives in our school systems, or National Media networks, have been neglected and uncultivated by their parents. This tragedy flows from generation to generation (see Ex. 20:5 & 6) if not handled by fathers who desire to stop the "fungus" of spiritual wickedness from entering into their children's lives. This will be covered further in chapters 11 & 12. We sum up this segment with a short pun. Which should give light to our eyes.

Tares become tares when nobody cares!

And as Jesus said, if tares do not respond to our care, "..let them both grow till the harvest." (ref. Mt. 13:24-30).

THE SALT OF THE EARTH

Physical salt has various uses to man to produce specific results. We shall review Webster's definitions of these uses.

Salt: White crystalline substance with a characteristic taste, found in natural beds, in sea water, etc., and used for seasoning and preserving food, etc. 5. As a restorative. 6. To give artificial value to; specifically. to alter...in order to deceive prospective buyers.

From these definitions we see that there are positive and negative uses for salt. It is in the administration of the salt that it finds its positive or negative effects in the physical realm. We will give some examples of this first. Then we will apply it to spiritual realities. The precise amount of salt on a specific culinary creation can make it a delight to the palate. Too little can make it bland, and fail to bring out the flavors. Too much, can ruin it altogether. Those with high blood pressure, and cardio-vascular problems are warned by their doctors to refrain from sodium in order to hinder the thickening and clotting of blood in their systems. Salt is known to cause corrosion in metals, and weaken its strength. It is also interesting that the food processing giants utilize both salt, and sugar, to increase a consumer's desire and craving for their specific food products. Why do you think they say, *"you can't only eat just one!"* It is important as fathers and mothers to realize the food giants can have adverse effects on your families health. With the amount of sugar that is being placed in our children's food by these ' big profit ' only minded companies, it is no wonder the youngsters run around with the *"psychological "* problem *" hyperactivity "*, and *" attention deficit disorders "*. After dumping all the sugar they dump into their little bodies. Also, that as adults grow older, they start developing the sugar metabolism problems of hypoglycemia and sugar diabetes. The symptoms of which are irritability, crankiness, outbursts of anger, fatigue, memory failure and even black-outs in extreme cases.

Now we will look at the spiritual effects of spiritual salt. God desires us as parents to understand how to make spiritual food taste good to our children, and our neighbors (please refer to Psalm 119:103; 19:7-10). The author is reminded of a comment a California pastor made concerning people's desire for God's Word. He felt by the lack of spiritual growth in some Church members, that they were spitting out the Word they were hearing in the services as they left the building! Maybe a case of spiritual anorexia nervosa toward God's Word. The Lord Jesus Christ told us of the dire necessity of salt in our lives as true believers in Matthew 5:13 -

13)   You are the salt of the earth: But if the salt has lost his savor, where with shall it be salted? It is henceforth good for nothing, but to be cast out, and to be trodden under foot of men.

In this passage of God's Word we see three aspects to our relationship with spiritual salt. We say at this time that spiritual salt is a mixture of God's Word and the Holy Spirit which pours out of our lives by the words of our mouths and our actions (see Colossians 4:6). As only a master chef can create a culinary masterpiece, so only parents under the direction of the Holy Spirit can prepare a palatable spiritual meal for the family. The first of the three aspects of Christ's words are descriptive of us His followers. We are the salt of the earth. Our functioning in the earth is for this purpose. The second aspect of God's words to us is His appeal to us. How is the earth to be salted if we as His people lose our ability to be what God wills us to be as His children? It is an appeal of urgency that He asks us. " How shall the earth be salted? " The pressure is on us to be salty fathers and mothers. The last aspect of Christ's words are words of warning and judgment. The judgment of Christ is that if we fail to be salt of this earth we are "..good for nothing." What a terrible judgment. The author is hoping that through this book - Fatherhood in the United States of America, all who read it will learn how not to be good for nothing. The warning Christ gives us at the end of this verse is to be heeded by us. Christ tells us that if we fail to be salt in the earth, we will be developing by our indifference to God, and the people in our spheres of influence, a potential for being repulsive to them. The Lord Christ has warned *"..to be cast out and trodden underfoot of men. "*, will be the condition we will produce. In order for the people who need to hear us, as we speak for God in the earth, we all must do acts of kindness and love. Or, they will become repulsed, and intolerant of us as those who claim to know God (ref. 1 John 2:3-6). Let your speech be seasoned with salt - see book of Colossians chapter 4 verse 6.

In concluding this chapter we say that Satan also uses salt to deceive. Much like if someone knew something was spoiled, and tried to get you to eat it by spicing it up. He tries to use God's Word erroneously to deceive. All false religions, and cults have a certain amount of truth. Otherwise people would not accept them (ref. Mt. 4: 5 - 7). This passage shows us that our enemy knows God's Word. And does work to use it to deceive us today. We must know it better to survive his deceptions. As fathers in our nation we must receive the information, and understanding, as to the causes of our national problems. This is necessary to produce effective leadership in the homes of the United States of America. God's Word gives to us the causes, and solutions to every problem. If we listen to its instructions. After we learn of the causes, and repent toward God, and if we begin to obey His Word, we can effect change and restoration. This is God's promise in Isaiah the prophet's book 55: 4 -7. We must first heed God's eternal warning we find in Psalm 9:17 -

17)   The wicked shall be turned into hell, and all the nations that forget God.

You just cannot squeeze any "..Separation of Church and State.." into that verse of Holy Scripture!

Recommended reading:

The Original Intent of The First Amendment - According to the Founding Fathers, By: Michael E. Citriniti & Michael D. Juzwick; published by: Light Eternal Publications, Seattle, WA © 1996. Phone - 206. 497. 8553 to leave voice mail to order.

PART 2

The Biblical Theology
of Fatherhood

Light Eternal Publications, USA

- Biblical Light for America's Christian Families -

Mountlake Terrace, Washington 98043-2913

CHAPTER 4

The Fatherhood of God

IN THE BEGINNING —

Before anything that is, ever was, God existed. He never had a beginning. He shall never have an end. This is difficult for us, as human beings, to grasp because the opposite is true of us. We have a beginning at conception in the womb. And, in our earthly sphere, we have an end at physical death.

In this chapter we will explore some basic aspects of God as a Father. Fatherhood began with God. It is through His immense power, and unlimited wisdom, and knowledge, that all that exists came into being. One of His names is - our Maker.

At this point we will review some semantics. The name *father* means: one who starts something, one who causes something, or someone, to come into being, to be the *originator* of something. To begin something. To be responsible for the existence of anything. The Hebrew word *"father "* is found in Strong's Exhausitve Concordance Page # 335. It is the first word defined in the Hebrew lexicon. The actual word utilized in the Hebrew language is [אָב - transliterated - ahu]. Gesenius' Hebrew Chaldee Lexicon pages 1-2 defines the term as:

(2)   founder, or first ancestor of a nation. (3) Of the author, or maker, of anything, specially of the Creator. (4) Father is applied to a bringer up, nourisher, as bestowing his benefits like a parent. (5) It is used of

a master, or teacher. And hence priests and prophets, as being teachers endued with divine authority,.. The Biblical patriarch Joseph was *"..father.."* to Pharoah [Genesis 45:8]. Literally, chief counsel, or, teacher held in close confidence, and reverence.

The Greek language utilizes the word [πατηρ- transliterated - pater] Hence, the term paternal. As the designation *" father "*. Literally, father, parent. The common American designations of male parents have been dad, daddy, pappy, pap, pops. Which expresses a close, and loving relationship of an endearing nature. Yet, these terms of endearment have been corrupted by male sin, and now somewhat carry a certain level of disrespect and dishonor. Today, in our world, we know of individual men who are considered *fathers* of something in relation to our environment. To cite some examples we have the father of modern science. The father of modern medicine. The father of the automobile, Henry Ford. The fathers of aviation - the Wright Brothers. The father of psychology- William James. The father of the telephone - Alexander Graham Bell. The father of electricity - Benjamin Franklin and Thomas Edison. And on, and on. The term father in these examples is to give credit to the man who has been responsible for something coming into existence. It is respecting someone's contribution to mankind, to name him the father of something. Yet, there are those in our national intellectual and educational systems who refuse to respect God, as Creator of our world. And the life upon it. And, as we shall see in chapter six, by failing to give honor, to whom honor is due, another has become their father.

The Book of Genesis, in the Holy Bible, is called " Genesis " because it is the book which records the beginning of all that God cre- ated in the heavens, and in the earth. The word **generation** is derived in its etymology from this word which means: the beginning. And the duration of the life of man, and woman by procreation. Contemporary scientists use the word "genetics" to describe the realm of DNA studies of life. Micro -biology now boasts successes in mastering areas of God's created universe due to inventions of microscopic instruments. Genetic scientists are now seeking to alter the earthly creations of God by tampering with the genetic codes of plants, animals, and human life. Some advances are fearful, such as the science of cloning. Some of these activities are rebellious in nature.

But God is the one who started all the works of the entire universe. Both spiritual and physical. Whether seen, or, unseen. His majestic works are to be held in wonder and awe. His works are cause to give worship, praise, and glory to Him. For He is great, and greatly to be praised. (read out loud Psalm 145).

"..THE FATHER OF SPIRITS..."

We can learn from Holy Scripture that God has fathered two types of spirit beings. 1st Cor. 15:40 says -

40)   There are also celestial [spiritual] bodies, and bodies terrestrial [physical]: But the glory of the celestial is one, and the glory of the terrestrial is another.

Holy Scripture reveals to us that there are first spiritual angelic beings. Celestial beings. As the book of Hebrews 12:22 reveals:

22)   But you are come to Mount Zion and to the City of the living God, the heavenly Jerusalem, and to an innumerable company of angels.

Of these angels, we know from the study of God's Word, that there are various kinds of angels who have different purposes.

LUCIFER-SATAN

Isaiah 14:12-20 shows us that Lucifer was one of God's leading created angelic beings. Ezekiel 28:12-19 shows us that Lucifer was created with an anointing of being capable of creating musical worship and praise. And covering God's throne with it. He was prime-minister of leading in the worship of the Creator. A very powerful position. Lucifer had authority over a third of angelic beings (see Revelation 12:4-9). These spirit beings are now referred to in Holy Scripture as " chief princes "(Ezekiel 38:2), " Principalities and powers. " (Ephesians 3:10), "...rulers, and spiritual wickednesses..." (demon spirits - which are the buck-privates of Satan's warring army (Ephesians 6:10-12). These are earth bound spiritual creatures. The war the Devil started in heaven to overthrow God's throne, has continued upon earth because of Adam's disobedience in the Garden of Eden (See Genesis 2:15- 17; 3:1-7). And, mankind's disobedience since that time. Our personal obedience to God overthrows Satan, and, his cooperating evil spirits.

MICHAEL THE ARCH-ANGEL

Michael [means: Who is like Yahweh - Eloh - heem?] is the Arch- angel charged by God, and anointed to be God's Chief warrior angel. He is always seen in Holy Scriptural revelation as one who leads in warfare against those who are God's enemies. This is seen in Daniel 10:13, 21; 12:1. The Arch-angel Michael goes to war for God to attack the forces of Satan which rule in the heavens, and the earth. He will be used by God in the end to put an end to all of Satan's activity in God's creation (Rev. 12:7-8; 20:10). Ephesians 1:19-22 declares that Jesus Christ is Lord over every angelic power. They are ministering spirits under His direct authority. We may call on their assistance by the leading of the Holy Spirit as Hebrews 1:14 states.

GABRIEL THE ARCH-ANGEL

Gabriel [means: God's might, valiant, warrior] is God's anointed messenger of divine revelation (see Daniel 8:16; 9:21). He also brings to the earth messages of God's love and care (Luke 1:19; 1:26). He is God's announcer of good things, and glad tidings.

SERAPHIM

There is another realm of angelic beings which surround God's throne with exquisite worship called Seraphim (see Isaiah 6:2-3 & 6-7). They are created to worship and honor the holiness of God the Father, Jesus Christ His Son, and Holy Spirit. The book of Revelation 4: 6-9 speaks of other creatures which serve in various capacities for God in Heaven. Some of which it is not for us to know of at this time.

CREATURES OF THE EARTHLY REALM

But God the Father also created a unique creature after he creat-ed the physical universe (Genesis 2:7)

7) And the Lord God formed man of the dust of the ground, and breathed into his nostrils the breath of " lives " (Lit. Hebrew- חַי - transliterated - ghah'y, adj. lit.- thriving, living forever) and man became a living " soul " (lit. Hebrew - נֶפֶשׁ - translit- neh'-phesh, com. lit. that by which the body lives. The actual person. Heart, mind, will and emotions).

Genesis 1:26-28; 2:15 tells us the purpose of God for man made in His image. God created man that he might have sons and daughters in the earth. Sons and daughters who should be subject unto Him as their Father (Hebrews 12:9) -

9)   Furthermore we have had fathers of our flesh which corrected us, and we gave them reverence: shall we not much rather be in subjection unto the Father of spirits, and live?

The nature of man is that he is like God because he is a spirit being, who has a soul, and dwells inside an earthly body created by God's wisdom, and knowledge out of the earth's substances (Ref. 1st Thess. 5:13). Man, being a spirit being, gives to him the capacity to know and commune with God. It also allows him to relate in various ways with other earthly people, and angelic beings [see Daniel 10:8-21]. Adam, and all men, were to rule earth for their Father God.

"OUR FATHER..."

Not every man, or, woman, on earth reverences God as their Father. They are as a result "...children of disobedience..."(Eph.2:2). Only those, who by submitting to the lordship of Jesus Christ, and His Word, can rightfully claim God as their Father (see chapter 7). Those who are born again, by the Holy Spirit of God, and His Word, become the sons and daughters of God the Father. (Ref. John 1:12 & 13; 3:1-8). No man gains entrance into the favorable Father's presence without God's Son, the Lord Jesus Christ. No man, or woman, can claim to be God's son, or daughter. Or, claim God to be his, or her Father except by Jesus Christ (John 14: 6).

But the majestic glory and benefits to those who can truthfully receive the Lord Jesus as their personal Saviour are great. Eternity will be filled with wonderful events due to His love on Calvary. We who honestly pray, "...Our Father..." have blessings that are without number. " ..whereby we cry " Abba, Father. " - read Romans chapter 8. Let us be grateful, and thankful, that the Lord Jesus Christ gave the ultimate sacrifice of Himself to make that possible!

"..Wherefore God also has highly exalted Him, and given Him a name which is above every name:

That at the name of Jesus every knee should bow, of things in heaven, of things in earth, and things under the earth;

And, that every tongue should confess that Jesus Christ is Lord, to the glory of God the Father."
                                        -- Book of Philippians chapter 2 verses 1 - 11.

When the disciple of the Lord asked Him how to pray, He gave them all His primary guidelines in Matthew 6: 5 - 18. He continued the directions in chapter 7, verses 7 - 11. Jesus Christ, God's Son, gave us insight into how to approach God the Father. Then, He accomplished the task it took to restore and heal the broken relationship with God the Father every man suffered because of sin. This has given us confidence and full assurance to boldly approach God's throne of grace to ask His help. We can now come before Him free of the guilt and shame of our previous sinfulness.

CHAPTER 5

The Fatherhood of Man

THE FIRST EARTHLY FATHER

As recorded in Genesis chapters one and two, God the Father decided to create a being who could rule over all that He had created in the physical earth. This being had total dominion over the entire earth. He was in charge of all the earth. God gave to him the dominion and authority to rule over all of God's works in the earth.

Adam, whose name meant: " *spiritual being made with dust* ", ruled the earth as God's servant in the physical realm. God saw that Adam was lonely as he cared for the Garden of Eden, so he decided to create another aspect of the physical earth which would provide companionship for man. Adam was to view this new creation of God as part of God's creation to be protected and cared for. Genesis 2:18 records:

18) And the Lord God said, it is not good that the man should be alone; I will make *a help meet* for him.

This new creation of God was to help Adam bring glory to God. Her ministry in the earth would not only be to provide company for Adam, but also be the instrument for assisting Adam to be capable of taking on the full nature of his Father, and Creator God, the "... *image and likeness...* " of also being a father. Oh the wonderous glory God created in the earthly sphere of His creation! Adam, and his wife's union would begin, or father, millions of sons and daughters of infinite physical variety. And numerous personality descriptions. The genes of Adam and Eve, held the D.N.A. blueprint for a myriad of physical beings by the fiat of their marriage and procreation . Yes, Adam, as God's authority over all the earth, would, by God's created design, father the entire race of mankind with all its variations. He would become the first earthly father of the earth. What a divine responsibility! What a tremendous glory Adam had to take on this aspect of the nature of God his heavenly Father!

THE ADAMIC COVENANT

Adam Means: " Spiritual being made with dust." A spiritual being with a physical body. Created to rule over the physical earth.

26)   And God said, let us make man in our image, after our likeness: And let them have dominion over the fish of the sea, and over the fowl of the air, and over the cattle, and over all the earth, and over every creeping thing that creeps upon the earth. 27) So God created man in his own image, in the image of God created he him; male and female created he them. 28) And God blessed them, and God said to them, be fruitful and multiply, and replenish the earth, and subdue it and have dominion over the fish of the sea, and over the fowl of the air, and over every living thing that moves upon the earth.

God's command, which has never been rescinded, was to take authority and dominion over the earth, and everything in it. Adam and Eve, male and female, husbands and wives, were commanded to: "...be fruitful and multiply..". Something the Planned Parenthood, and abortion groups are against. It must be stated now, that once God decrees something. Or commands something to be done, that is the final Word on the subject. He should not have to repeat Himself again. When God speaks He does not speak flippantly. Nor does He say something in a light manner. The words which proceed from God's mouth are perfect and pure (see Proverbs 30:5&6). God speaks words of faith (See Hebrews 11:3). God speaks words of life (see John 6:63). God created us in His image, and likeness. We are to live like Him. We are to speak right words. This was an aspect of Adam's dominion mandate as we shall see as we proceed further. At this point we will review Adam's creation and purpose in the earth in detail. It must be understood that God's purposes for man, and woman, has never changed since He first decreed them in the beginning. A failure to obey God's commands has produced the kind of world we live in today. We speak of all the miseries and wickedness occuring today.

Genesis 2:7-9:

7)   And the Lord God formed man of the dust of the ground. And breathed into his nostrils the breath of life [Lit. Hebrew = " lives "] and man became a living soul. 8) And the Lord God planted a garden eastward in Eden; and there he put the man whom he had formed.

9)   And out of the ground made the Lord God to grow every tree that is pleasant to the sight, and good for food; the tree of life also in the midst of the garden, and the tree of knowledge of good and evil.

Genesis 2:15-18:

15)   And the Lord God took the man, and put him into the Garden of Eden to dress (Literal - Hebrew = gahvad "..take care over it..") and "..to keep (Lit. Heb. shamar: provide protection for) it.

16) And the Lord God commanded the man saying, of
     every tree of the garden you may freely eat:
17) But of the tree of the knowledge of good and evil,
     you shall not eat of it: For in the day that you eat of
     it you shall surely die. [You shall be cut off from me
     the source of eternal life - emphasis added].
18) and the Lord God said, it is not good that the man
     should be alone, I will make him a help meet for him.

In these passages of God's Holy Word we find His purpose and
will for men. God's will and purpose is eternal. God does not make
mistakes. Or create something for one purpose, and change that
original purpose. In this basic fact we find the Adamic Covenant. The
average reader would read Genesis 2:1-25 as a story of past events
which occured in past history. This would be an error if you are a
Biblicist. Since a Biblicist believes that God's eternal Word is living
and active, as 2nd Timothy 3:16-17, and Hebrews 4: 12 declares to
us. Unless he had the faith to believe these events actually took place,
he would doubt that they in fact did transpire. But a wise man, who
is full of faith, would not only read this passage of God's Word for
information, but would also look into it to find out how to return to do
that which was pleasing to the Lord God. What God's will was before
the Adamic Covenant was broken by Eve and Adam. The Adamic
Covenant was a simple, yet profound covenant. God created the earth,
and a wonderful garden in Eden. He created a being like Himself to
rule over this earth. As Genesis 2:15 states, he was to watch over the
garden, and care for its needs. He was also created by God to protect
it from all enemies opposed to the spiritual state in which God created
it to exist in. These commands, and orders from God, are not just a
story we read in the Holy Bible. They are eternal orders of faith given
from the mouth of God (reference Deut. 8:3). The blessings of God
come to man in direct proportion to man's adherence to God's explicit
commands. Adam was created to rule over, care for and protect the

garden God created. He was also commanded not to eat of one tree in the Garden. " The tree of the knowledge of good and evil ". This one stipulation of obedience was the only prohibition Adam, and his wife Eve, received from God. As we explained in chapter one, in the segment of the American Covenant, the breaking of Old Testament covenants produced *death*. The solemn agreement God had with man, did require death, if it was broken. Genesis 2:17(c):

17(c)   ..For in the day that you eat thereof you shall surely die.

ICHABOD - THE GLORY DEPARTED

We borrow this name, Ichabod, and expression from 1st Samuel 4:10-22. Eli, the high priest of Israel at this time in history, had two sons Hophni, and Phinehas. During the wars of the nation of Israel with the Philistines, Israel was being severely beaten by their enemies. So much so that the Philistines captured the "Ark of the Covenant of Israel" (please read Exodus, 25:10-22). The state of Israel, and its spiritual leadership at the time was apostate. Eli's sons were smittent by the Lord God for fornicating with the women that came into the temple. They also disregarded the sanctity of God's things [ref. I Samuel 2: 22 -35]. When the wife of Phinehas, who was about to deliver a child, heard the Ark of the Covenant was taken by the Philistines, she named Phinehas' son, " Ichabod ". Which was to express the religious state of the nation of Israel at that point. Ichabod means: " God's glory had departed ". The Ark of the Covenant was to be a symbol of the presence of God among the people of the nation of Israel (See Exodus 25:22). It literally meant to Israel, that God was no longer with them. Because of the sins of the fathers of Israel, and the priesthood of the Levites, God was against them now. And permitting their enemies to destroy them.

This occurrence in the Old Testament, is an excellent analogy of that which took place at the point of Eve, and Adam's disobedience, in the beginning of earth's history (refer Genesis 3:1-13). Before their disobedience, Adam, and Eve, flowed with God's will and purpose in the earth. God's Spirit (i.e., His presence) was with them, and in them. The Garden of Eden was in the perfect condition in which God created it to be. Adam was prime minister of all God created in the physical earth. All was flowing in harmony with God's plan. The peace of God flowed throughout the earth like a river. The word peace means: " cessation of againstness ". There was nothing, which had taken place in the garden, that was against its Creator.

Then, at the suggestion of God's arch-enemy Satan, death took place in the Garden of God. Adam, and Eve his helpmeet, did that which God forbade. They did the very act God warned would produce death. Adam loosed, or allowed, new spiritual principles to take over the earth. God, who by His Holy Spirit ruled the earth through Adam, now was rejected from ruling the earth. At the very point of disobedience to God's command, Adam chose who he wanted to rule over the earth. Prior to the point of disobedience, God's principles were utilized by Adam, and Eve, to control the earth. For Adam, and Eve to obey the suggestion of Lucifer through the serpent's mouth, put Satan in command of the Garden of Eden. This is substantiated in Luke 4:5-7, and 2nd Corinthians 4:3 & 4. Also, Romans 6:4-18. It is a very mysterious thing to understand that Adam lost his God-given rule when he disobeyed God's command. The kind of authority, and rulership God created the earth to be ruled by, was lost when Adam sinned in the Garden. The glory of God flowed throughout the earth, and Garden of Eden. God's glory rested upon Adam, God's creature made of earth, to rule the earth in God's likeness.

The curse began at the point of Adam's refusal to keep, and protect the Garden, as God commanded him to. The curse began when Satan's words through the Serpent (see Genesis 3:1-4) took control of Eve, and then Adam, rather than God's commands. The glory of

78

God departed from Adam and Eve, because they obeyed the words of Satan. Instead of God's benevolent, and kind words. The curse began when Satan took over the earth, at the point of Adam's adherence to his lies, rather than God's truth. Jesus Christ the Lord came to earth to overthrow this usurpation of God's earthly authority. This curse has continued from generation to generation. Only because of each man's refusal to obey God's commands. And refusal to allow God's Holy Spirit to rule his life. For we see that is true in the Apostle Paul's letter to the Romans 3:23:

> 23)   For all have sinned, and come short of the glory of God.

God's glory is manifested in the earth when Satan, or his evil spirits are cast out (see Mark 16:17 1 Luke 11:9-23). And the Holy Spirit of God is allowed to rule in all the aspects of men and women's lives (Refer to Mat.thew 18:18-20). It must be emphasized that it is in each man's, or woman's power and authority, to allow God to rule their life. Or Satan, and his demonic spirits. To stop God from ruling in their lives. Or stop Satan, and his demons from ruling their lives. Or their children's lives. It is in the area of earthly parental authority that either God, through the workings of His Holy Spirit rule. Or that Satan, and his evil spirits bear rule. There is no middle ground. 1st Kings 18:15-40, and Luke 11: 1-28, prove to us all that God allows for no neutral place for any man, or woman to exist.

Adam[spiritual being made with dust] was prime minister of all God created in the physical earth. All was flowing in harmony with God's plan. The word peace means: cessation of againstness. There was nothing which had taken place in the garden that was against its Creator.

Then, at the suggestion of God's arch-enemy Satan, death took place in the Garden of God. Adam and Eve did that which God forbade. They did the very act God warned would produce death.

Adam loosed, and allowed, new spiritual principles to take over the earth. God, who by His Holy Spirit, ruled the earth through Adam previously, was now was rejected from ruling the earth through His appointed authority. At the very point of obedience to God's command. Or disobedience, Adam chose whom he wanted to rule over the earth. Prior to the point of disobedience, God's principles were utilized by Adam and Eve to control the earth. For Adam, and Eve to obey the suggestion of Lucifer, through the serpent's mouth, put Satan in command of the Garden of Eden. This is substantiated in Luke 4:5-7, and 2nd Corinthians 4:3 & 40. Also Romans 6:4-18.

It is a very mysterious thing to understand, that Adam lost his God-given rule, when he disobeyed God's command. The kind of authority, and rulership, God created the earth to be ruled by, was lost when Adam sinned in the garden. The glory of God flowed throughout the earth and Garden of Eden. God's glory rested upon Adam. God's creature made of earth, to rule the earth in God's likeness. The curse began at the point of Adam's refusal to keep, and protect the garden as God commanded him to. The curse began when Satan's words through the Serpent (see Genesis 3:1-4) took control of Eve, and Adam, rather than God's commands. The glory of God departed from Adam, and Eve his wife, because they obeyed the words of Satan, instead of God's benevolent, and kind words. The curse began when Satan took over the earth at the point of Adam's adherence to his lies, rather than God's truth. This curse has continued from generation, to generation. Only because of each man's refusal to obey God's commands. And allow God's Holy Spirit to rule his life. We see that is true in Romans 3:23.

There is no neutral place for any man, or woman to exist in. Each man, woman, male-child, or female-child, must decide to obey the Lord God, and His eternal Word. Or choose to follow the Devil's lies and deceptions. Each person's eternal destiny is decided on this crucial point. As fathers, who honor the Lord God's work, through His Son, our Lord Jesus Christ, we must address this curse in each, and every generation we are responsible for causing to be fathered. The fatherhood of man will produce children that serve and honor God. Or, be responsible for allowing Satan to continue his wicked rule over generations yet to come into existence.

CHAPTER 6

The Fatherhood Of Satan

At the outset of this chapter we must state that God never intended for Lucifer to be a father. God anointed and ordained him to perform specific duties for his Creator God. In his fallen state, everything he has done, or is doing, or will do, is against God's will for him. We see this in various revelations of God's Word. We must reiterate that the designation: *father* means: The originator of something, one who starts something. This can be in the positive, or, negative sense.

THE FATHER OF REBELLION

Isaiah 14:12-14 states:

12) How you are fallen from Heaven, O Lucifer, son of the morning! How you are cut down to the ground, which did weaken the nations! 13) For you have said in your heart, I will ascend into heaven, I will exalt my throne above the stars of God: I will sit also upon the mount of the congregation, [in the place of authority, or control] in the sides of the north; 14) I will ascend above the heights of the clouds; I will be like the Most High.

Lucifer's fathering of rebellion, God says, started in his heart [Isaiah 14:13(a)]. He did not have to utter a word from his mouth. God read his evil, and corrupted heart. It is important to understand that there are two spheres referred to in this passage of God's revelation:

82

" *Heaven* " and, the " *ground* ". These are the places that Satan is waging his warfare against God. Satan started the rebellion against God, by refusing to occupy his place of leading in the worship and praise of God, and wishing to see himself worshipped. The five.. " *I wills..* " of Satan's declaration, were a direct affront, and rebellion to God's will, and purpose for him. We learn from Revelation 12:7-9 that Lucifer has led, and organized all the angels originally assigned to his authority, to cooperate with him in his rebellion against God's purpose in heaven, and on the earth.

It should also be stated, that every kind of rebellion is inspired by Satan, and his demons. He is the father of all rebellion. Another aspect of rebellion, which we should explain, is found in I Samuel 15:23. God tells us through Samuel the prophet that " rebellion " is " like " the sin of witchcraft. And that stubbornness is " like " idolatry. Satan used the force of witchcraft in the Garden of Eden. He also used enchantment. Witchcraft is implemented, when one person uses anything to manipulate the will of another person, to do their will, rather than God's will. It is working to take the place of God's Holy Spirit by anyone. Stubbornness is like idolatry, because it says " I " make all decisions, not God. It is usurping God's place of rule in an effort to rule instead of Him. This is the very essence of what the Apostle John referred to in I John 4:1-3, when he described -"..the spirit of antiChrist.." It is rebelling against God, and His Word. And placing yourself, as final authority, to any area in your life. This is the very essence of Satan's activity in the lives of men, women, and their children. Evil men are in tune with Satan [see Prov.17:11].

THE FATHER OF LIES

4)   And the serpent [Satan's mouthpiece] said to the woman, you shall not surely die. — book of Genesis 3:4

God had already warned Adam, and Eve, that to eat of the tree of knowledge of good and evil, would bring death to them. God's kind of life would depart from them. What Satan used to deceive Eve was a lie. The first lie. That first lie brought death to the man, and woman, and all subsequent children since them. Satan's plan was to entice Eve to believe his lie, that they would not die. So that he could take, or receive control over the earth, instead of Adam. It is interesting that Satan said, in Genesis 3:5(b) *"...then your eyes shall be opened, and you shall be as (like) gods..."* Satan is very interested in people's eyes. It is through the eyes of an individual, that he, or his evil spirits gain entrance into the life of that man or woman. Jesus Christ the Lord, made reference to this fact in Matthew 6:22 & 23:

22)   The light of the body is the eye; if therefore your eye be clear, your whole body shall be full of light. 23) But if your eye be evil, your whole body shall be full of darkness. If therefore the light that is in you be darkness, how great is that darkness!

Jesus Christ claimed Himself to be the light of the world. And that His disciples, are also, the light of the world. Satan, and his angels work to appear as "..angels of light.." (See 2nd Corinthians 11:13-15). The light that Satan uses is corrupted. And, used by him to deceive people into following his rebellion.

Without the Holy Spirit, and God's Word, any man, or woman can follow a deceptive light of Satan. It takes keen discernment to see clearly, what is God's truth. Or, Satan's lies. Satan used God's truth in Matthew 4: 5-6 to try to deceive Jesus Christ into obeying him in the temptation. Satan still mixes a little truth, with his lies, to allure simple minds to follow his ways. All false faith, and false religions, have been started by Satan, and his demons, to deceive mankind. And take the place of true faith in the true God. To follow any way, which seems religious, rather than God's only way, is the center of Satan's activity in the life of the people on the earth.

Satan is not only the father of lies, he always lies. All the time. His entire kingdom of darkness is organized around lies. He lies to men, women, and children by telling them they can sin, and not be hurt by it (see Galatians 6:7). He is always lying to men, and women to put off their salvation to a more convenient time. So that they will wait until it is too late, and they have died, and go to hell to suffer for their sins forever (See Hebrews 9:27).

Jesus Christ warned us of this lying activity, and its effect on those who reject His Word, in John 8:42-44.

42) Jesus said to them, if God were your Father, you would love Me: For I proceed forth, and came from God, neither came I of Myself, but He sent Me. 43) Why do you not understand my speech? Even because you cannot hear My Word.

44) You are of your father the Devil, and the lusts of your father you will do. He was a murderer from the beginning [see Gen. 4:8],and abode not in the truth, because there is no truth in him. When he speaks a lie, he speaks of his own: For [because] he is a liar, and the father of it [all lies].

Those who hate the Words of God, and, of Jesus Christ, are of their father the Devil. Satan is their god, and father. Those who love God's Word, and the Words of Jesus Christ the Lord, have the true God as their Father. Satan, as Jesus said, originated and started all lies. He uses his lies to thwart the purposes of God in the earth. He is using many lies to rule over our nation even today. The demonic doctrine of *evolution* is one great lie he has sold to our national education system by fiat of the NEA (National Education Association) using our tax monies to propagate it. " Abortion on demand " is another big lie, which says pre-born children are not people.

" Morality cannot be legislated by our government " is another profane lie from Satan's mouth (See Romans 13:1-7).

Most of Satan's lies are such that they sound true. It is a lie that sounds like it may be valid, that is most dangerous. At the time that Satan organizes his one-world government, he will be spewing forth lies everywhere (See 2 Thessalonians 2:3-12, and Revelation 13:1-18). He will most likely have more access to, and control over the many sources of the Media of the world by then.

Yes, Satan has lied continually since he started in the Garden of Eden with Eve. He has uttered his lies ever since that time. And, he will continue to lie until, as Revelation 20:3(b) states, God's mighty angel casts him chained into the bottomless pit.

<u>"..and shuts him up! "</u>

Only then will God's creation be free from having to listen to his lies. For us as God's children, the knowledge of God's truth gives us the ability to overcome the Devil's lies (See John 8:31-32). Inasmuch as you are willing to saturate you heart and mind with the total content of God's book the Holy Bible, will you be capable of escaping his evil lying ways. As a father, your obedience to God's Word is critical to the deliverance, and salvation of your children.

THE FATHER OF IMMORALITY & INIQUITY

To begin this segment we explain that Lucifer led a third of the angels of God into rebellion against God (Ref. Rev. 12:4-9). Satan, and his angelic beings, and princes are now corrupted from the state they once were prior to Lucifer's fall. 2nd Peter 2: 4, and, Jude verse 6, both shows us this reality. 2nd Peter 2:4:

4)   For [because] if God spared not the angels that sinned, but cast them down to Hell, and delivered them into chains of darkness, to be reserved unto judgment;

Jude verse 6:

6)   And, the angels which kept not their first estate, but, left their own habitation, he has reserved in everlasting chains under darkness unto judgment of the great day.

Lucifer, and all these angels, had previously held a position, and an estate, which was an honorable place to occupy before God their Creator. Now, as fallen beings, their place is dishonorable. Their place is corrupted. The power, wisdom and authority God gave them is now twisted and perverted against their original purpose in their futile war against their Creator, and us.

Prior to assisting our readers to gain a greater understanding of discernment regarding whereof we speak in this segment. We should define the two terms referred to in its title. First, the word *immorality* is defined by Webster's Dictionary in this way: not in conformity with established principles of right and wrong behavior; contrary to the moral code of the community; wicked; sometimes, specif., not in conformity with the accepted standards of sexual behavior; unchaste, lewd — Biblically, it means to be amoral and/ or, profane.

Since the United States of America has been constantly attacked with numerous forms of profanity, and sexual rebellion, this word must come into the equation of our discussion of the fatherhood of Satan in America. This should also be considered since *the fatherhood of man* has been defiled sexually. It has created much evil, and destruction among men, women, and their children. Fatherlessness in America has created many curses, and criminal behavior - see Malachi

4: 4 - 6. The evil hourds of the Prince of Darkness have been very active in this nation that claims to be " Under God ". This important area will be covered in more detail in chapter 8.

Secondly, we define the Bible word - iniquity. The Hebrew word [עָוֹן - transliterated - gah-vohn'] is the term the Lord God utilizes to describe the conditions that exist within the lives of all who have turned in rebellion against His rightful place as Sovereign over His created universe. Gesenius, in his Hebrew - Chaldee Lexicon, page 614, defines iniquity as: perversity, depravity; hence — 1. a depravedacation, a crime, a sin. It is often guilt contracted by sinning, as " *the guilt of the fathers..* ". 2. Sometimes it is the penalty for sin, Isaiah 5:18; calamity, misery. These explanations and definitions reveal to us the evil intentions of Satan, father of immorality and iniquity. He is master of these profane and corrupt realities of human existence in the earth. His demonic legions serve his interests well in these wicked intentions and machinations against mankind.

We could explain it like this. An angelic being, in the pre-fallen state, was ordained by God to minister virtue and purity. Now, in his fallen state, he ministers uncleanness and debauchery [see Matthew 12: 43 - 45]. A spirit, which use to represent righteousness, will propagate unrighteousness. A spirit, representative of truth, will now be ".. a lying spirit "[see 1st Kings 22: 21-23]. An angel, that was to exalt morality and virtue, is now a spirit of whoredom and immorality [see Hosea 5: 4]. A spirit of trust, turned into "..a spirit of jealousy." [Numbers 5:30]. An angel of praise, became a demonic power of depression [ref. Isaiah 61:3]. A spiritual power of obedience, now works and energizes as "..a spirit of disobedience." [Ref. Ephesians 2:2]. An angelic authority, that exalted humility, now promotes pride and arrogancy [see Job 41: 34]. A spiritual principality that promoted the blessing of giving, now works to promote stealing and thievery. An angel that exalted honor and respect, now compels others to be disrespectful and dishonorable.

As fathers in our nation, we are to be filled with God's Holy Spirit, who gives to us the ability to discern these evil spirits, that attempting to rule our lives, or our children's lives [Ref. 1st Corinthians 12:10 (c)]. If we discern by God's Word, and His Holy Spirit, we are commanded by God "..to cast them out "[study Mark 1: 21-28]. Cast them out with our words, in the power of the Holy Spirit, and God's Word. We are to take authority over them. By speaking in the name of Jesus Christ the Lord (See Mark 16:17 (a) & (b)). We will cover this area further in chapters 11 through 14.

We close this chapter now, by stating that Satan has loosed the spirits of immorality, iniquity, and whoredoms against the parents of United States. Virtue, and virginity are mocked, and despised by these enemies of God and man. They know the horrible devastation that will come upon all who disobey and ignore the veracity of God's holy Word of righteousness. As the fathers of the United States, God charges us to bind these powers, and cast them out of our families, cities and states. These evil beings are, at this point in our nation's history, ruling in our national network media. The light of the body is the eye. Some of the Hollywood films are actually creating visual images that reflect the demonic realm. We are responsible to God to clean our land of these spirits of immorality and vice. God shall hold us accountable if we refuse to obey His eternal Word. We are to protect our children's eyes, and ears, from those people who allow Satan, and his demons, to speak through their mouths, and immoral life styles. The immoral rock star Madonna, is not the kind of woman, our daughters should be looking to as an example of what women should be like. The demonic power using her, and other men, and women in television rock videos are to be censored by us as parents. By demanding that Federal Communications Commission [FCC], do their job (paid for by taxpaying parents) of policing vulgarity, and sexual vice, on all our national media sources. Whether television, radio, or print mediums (See Romans 13: 1-7).

Finally, we review God's judgment of the father of rebellion, lies, immorality, and iniquity in Ezekiel 28: 12 - 19 -

12)   Son of man, take up a lamentation upon the King of Tyrus, and say to him, thus says the Lord God; you seal up the sum, full of wisdom, and perfect in beauty.

13)   You have been in Eden the Garden of God: Every precious stone was your covering, the sardius, topaz, and the diamond, the beryl, the onyx, and the jasper, the sapphire, the emerald, and the carbuncle, and gold:
The workmanship of your taborets and of your pipes was prepared in you in the day that you were created.
[The musical instruments of worship and praise (taborets and pipes) were designed by God].

14)   You are the anointed cherub that covers; and I have set you so: You were upon the holy mountain of God, you have walked up and down in the midst of the stones of fire.

15)   You were perfect in your ways from the day that you were created, until iniquity was found in you.

16)   By the multitude of your merchandise they have filled the midst of you with violence, and you have sinned: Therefore, I will cast you - as profane - out of the mountain of God: And I will destroy you, O covering cherub, from the midst of the stones of fire.

17)   Your heart was lifted up because of your beauty, you have corrupted your wisdom by reason of your brightness: I will cast you to the ground, I will lay you before kings, that they may behold you.

18)   You have defiled your sanctuaries by the multitude of your iniquities, [Satan corrupted all his angels with

numerous kinds of iniquity] by the iniquity of your traffic; therefore, will I bring forth a fire from the midst of you, it shall devour you. And I will bring you to ashes upon the earth in the sight of all them that behold you.

19) All they that know you among the people shall be astonished at you: you shall be a terror, and never shall you be anymore.

Satan's judgment is decided by God his Creator. He is a criminal awaiting the carrying out of his execution. In his corrupted mind, he still believes he will win the war against God Almighty. He is deceived by his pride, and self-will. As Revelation chapter 12 verse 12 tells us, he will, at a point in history, probably soon, begin to see, and understand his time is short. This will be the most evil, and terrible period, this earth has ever experienced, or ever will. No man, woman, or, child would survive this attack of Satanic power on earth, unless God, by His almighty power, puts an end to it [Review Matthew 24:3-22]. We must, as fathers, determine to cast every form of iniquity out of our families, and households. We have specific authority as parents to remove any power from Satan's kingdom out of those who are under our place of dominion assigned by God the Father.

The fatherhood of Satan ends in Revelation 20:10 -

10) And the Devil that deceived them was cast into the lake of fire and brimstone, where the beast and the false prophet are. And shall be tormented day and night forever and ever.

There will be a shout of praise that will rise eternally before the Lord God Almighty, the day this takes place! Oh happy day!!!

91

CHAPTER 7

The Person and Work
of the Lord Jesus Christ

What Christ Came to Do

May we begin this preeminent chapter, by stating that God by His mercy, and grace, decided to make it possible for any man to be reinstated to the position in which the first father, Adam, held prior to the great transgression in the garden of God. Man, by a direct disobedience to the heavenly Father's eternal will, allowed new spiritual principles to take over the earth. Adam was God's appointed authority over this planet. He enjoyed the power of God's Holy Spirit, which aided him to walk in continuous harmony, and fellowship with the eternal God-head. God had warned Adam, and Eve, not to eat of the tree of the knowledge of good and evil. And, that the consequence of doing so would be death (Ref. Genesis 2:16 & 17). We know that Adam and Eve did not die physically at the moment of disobedience, nor did their soul (psyche) die. Yet God said "...the day you eat of it, you shall surely die...". This death God warned of was the death, or separation from the life, which God provided. The Holy Spirit, the eternal Spirit of God, gave man the ability to be an eternal being. Adam was an immortal being prior to his decision to follow Lucifer's rebellion. God created (fathered) Adam to be indwelt by Himself by His Holy Spirit. This is stated in Genesis 2:7 -

7) And the Lord God formed man of the dust of the ground, and breathed into his nostrils the breath of lifes; [Lit. Hebrew - חַי transliterated - 'ghah'y, adj.] and man became *a living soul* [נֶפֶשׁ transliterated - neh' - phesh, com.].

Man was created as a separate individual, yet dependent upon God as his source of life. The Hebrew word translated - nehphesh expresses that the name Adam means: a spiritual being made with the dust. The numerous mental, emotional, volitional, and physical aspects of man's creation were bound up in the wondrous wisdom and power God released by the breath of His mouth into man's physical frame. Even the physical part of God's creation contained numerous life systems medical science has discovered to their amazement. To clarify now we explain it like this. The triune God-head said "*Let us make man* (of the dust of the earth) *in our image, after our likeness.*" (Ref. Genesis 1:26). Man was created, therefore, to be a physical-spiritual being like God Himself. After he formed the physical part of man out of the substances of the physical earth, he breathed into that formation His own life, and in the process of God's creation, man became a separate living soul; a new being with all the characteristics of God his Creator. This meant Adam had emotional feelings and a mind, and will of his own. This was all united with God's mind, will, and emotion prior to the fall. Adam's authority was inspired, and or-dained by God. Adam relinquished that power and authority over to Satan, and his evil angels, by disobeying and rebelling against God's revealed will for the earth. Satan, and his angels became the rulers of the earth which was contrary to God's purpose and still is! From that point of the transgressing of God's purpose, both Adam and Eve lost their life-sustaining relationship with God their Creator. Also, Adam and Eve became the father, and mother of children procreated after their likeness of spiritual deadness. Every child born since has come into the world needing to have their relationship with God restored.

And, if that relationship fails to be restored, that soul shall suffer eternal death, i.e., separation from the life giving Creator-God. Adam, the first father of earth, placed all his offspring under this condition. You and I were born into the world lacking a relationship with God. And, in a sinful state. Some kind of occurrence had to transpire in order to make a way out of this destitute condition that every soul, born of woman, finds himself, or, herself (Ref. 1st John 3: 8 (b) -

> 8(b)   For this purpose the Son of God was manifested, that He might destroy the works [Lit. Greek - ε"ργα - transliterated erga - meaning the operations, energizings, course of action, traffic, business] of the Devil.

The name 'Jesus' means: God is salvation. The name 'Christ' means: anointed promised Messiah. Jesus Christ is God's appointed authority for the salvation, and deliverance, of each, and every man or, woman, son, or, daughter alive now, or, to be born. The Lord God continually promised throughout the Old Testament, that He would be faithful to send the Deliverer and Saviour for man's need. All who looked forward by faith to that day, had their eternal destiny established. Those, who by unbelief, and sin, refused to seek God's forgiveness and grace died without God, to await His eternal judgment at the end of time. God made His promise good. He did exactly as He said He would. Yet, the extent of His love will forever be held in wonder and amazement by all those who receive it.

We know, and understand from the standpoint of Biblical revelation, that there are three persons who make up the God-head. The Holy Father, the Son, and Holy Spirit. They are all one (Ref. 1st John 5:7). Each person is God, though each person, is an individual. Their will, mind, and emotions are the same. Yet one person within that structure was chosen to bring God and man back into fellowship. That person was God's Son (Ref. John 3:16 & 17)-

16) For God so loved the world, [mankind] that He gave His only begotten Son, that whoever believes in Him should not perish, but have everlasting life. 17) For God sent not His Son into the world to condemn the world [men and women]; but that the world [men and women] through Him might be saved.

The Lord Jesus Christ was ordained by God the Father to become the eternal mediator between the holiness of God, and the sinfulness of men, and women. This is explained in Hebrews 9:15 -

15) And for this cause He [Christ] is the mediator of the New Testament, that by means of death, for the redemption [payment] of the transgressions that were under the first Testament, they which are called might receive the promise of eternal inheritance.

Satan deceived Eve to disobey God's direct command in Genesis 2: 17. Adam followed Eve's direct disobedience, rather than taking authority over the situation, Eve had been deceived into by God's enemy. This very act transferred power and authority of the entire earth over to the fallen Lucifer. Satan gained legal rights over the creation God placed under Adam's control (see 2 Cor. 4: 4). This was, and still is, totally out of God's will. The Lord Jesus Christ came to this earth for specific purpose. To gain back for God the Father man's authority over the earth. He came down from the place of glory He had with His Father to be born of a virgin. In order to become an earthly man. Since God created the earth to be ruled over by an earthly man, this was necessary. The incarnation of Jesus Christ, the eternal Son of God, accomplished this. This act potentially had the power to destroy Satan's authority in the physical beings of the earth. Yet, to be totally complete, the death, and shedding of blood by the Lamb of sacrifice, had to take place.

Adam and Eve, through their sin against God, placed themselves, and all the peoples of the earth, into a spiritual situation that would be totally impossible to bring themselves out of. Satan would reign, with despotism, over God's beautiful creations of the earth. Death would reign. Murder would reign. Perversion would reign. Disease would reign. Rebellion would reign. Hatred would reign. Greed would reign. Pride would reign. Deceit would reign. Destruction would reign. God's way was peace. Satan's would be war! Everything contrary to the spiritual state in which God created the earth would take place. This is the purpose for which God the Father sent His Son to this earth. Let's read it again, 1st John 3:8(b) -

> 8(b)   For this purpose the Son of God was manifested, that
>   [in order that] He might destroy the works [opera-
>   tions- deeds- energizings - activities] of the Devil.

The Lord Jesus Christ is still doing this same thing today. He is still at work destroying Satan's works! But, as we continue in our learning about the subject of fatherhood, we will come to understand that He continues to destroy the works of the enemy, not by Himself alone. But through us, who dwell upon the earth! We shall learn that Jesus Christ came not just to gain back authority in the earth for Himself alone. But, also, that He has transferred this authority over to all of us, who by faith believe in Him, and His name (Ref. John 1:12 & Ephesians 1:18-23). When each father, mother, son, or daughter become totally obedient to God's Word. The works of Satan are destroyed through our lives! When you, and I, honor and love the Lord God. And, are totally obedient to His Son, the Lord Jesus Christ, we enter into the special work of God Almighty. The great work of destroying the operations of Satan, and all his evil angels! Jesus Christ did not come to this earth to play games with Satan. He came to do warfare against our great enemy. He came to set the spiritual prisoners of war free (Ref. Isaiah 61:1-3, and Luke 40:1-21). He came to cancel out all the indictments of God's holy Word, that were against us. And held us all captive in Satan's prison world-system (Ref. Colossians 2:13-15). As the negro slave was subject to the cruelty of his slave-master, so we also were held in bondage to the wickedness, and cruelty of Satan, and his demons. It is very necessary that you understand that Christ is at this time engaged in armed warfare with Satan, and his angels. We all must develop ourselves to join in the Spirit of Christ as literal soldiers of His warring army. As men, and fathers, we need to take on this military disposition, that the Lord Jesus Christ has ordained for this time in eternity. We will cover this more in chapter 12. On Fatherhood & Shahmar [the Hebrew word for warfare administration]. As long as we breath air on this earth, we are to be always ready to go to war spiritually with the enemy's forces, arrayed against our families. This is what Christ came to do.

First, He came to reveal to us what God the Father was truly like (Ref. Gospel of John 14: 6-15). Secondly, He came to destroy all the activity of Satan, and his demons, in the life of man (1st John 3:8(b)). He does this today by proxy. He does it through the lives of obedient, Word of God and Holy Spirit-filled fathers, and, mothers.

THE MAGNIFICENT POWER OF THE BLOOD OF JESUS CHRIST

Someone had to satisfy God's justice against sin. That person had to be without any fault. That person had to pay for each, and every sin, ever committed from Adam and Eve's sin, until the last person to be born. That person had to be willing to do this great sacrifice for God and man. That person had to taste death for every man. That person's blood had to be without spot. It had to be pure, and holy blood, to have the power to wash, and cleanse, the filthiest sin against God's righteous law. It had to pay for the forgiveness God would provide, because every sin must be paid for if God is to remain righteous, and just. It had to be God Himself to fulfill these awesome requirements! No angel of Heaven could do it. No person on earth could.

1st Peter 1: 18 - 20 reveals precious facts on this matter -

18) Forasmuch as you know that you were not redeemed [purchased back] with corruptible things, as [like] silver and gold, from your vain [empty] conversation [way of viewing life] received [handed down] by tradition from your fathers; 19) But [rather] with the precious blood of Christ, as of a lamb without blemish and without spot: 20) Who truly was foreordained before the foundation of the world, but was manifest in these last times for you. [emphasis added]

The Lord God first manifested the kind of sacrifice that would be necessary to satisfy His justice against sin first in the slaughtering of animals in the Garden of Eden (Ref. Genesis 3:21). God had to slay innocent animals to cover the nakedness of the guilty, fallen pair. It is very likely the animals God used were lambs. Adam and Eve saw first-hand the bloody consequences of sin, and rebellion against God's perfect way. Those who promote nudity as normal, and that using animal skins, and fur for clothing as evil, really hate God. Who was the first to set down these ordinances in the beginning as His will during the process of ridding the earth of sin [see 1st Timothy 4: 1-5]. God has established these things due to sin's effects.

The second example of the need for a blood sacrifice was seen in Genesis 4:4. Abel, who was Adam and Eve's second-born son, was anointed, and blessed by God, because he honored the Lord with a blood sacrifice. In Hebrews 11: 40 we see that Abel's excellent sacrifice has given him a voice in the earth to this day. Satan, and Abel's brother Cain, hated God's respect for Abel's sacrifice. So Satan energized spirits of jealousy, and hatred, in Cain to inspire him to murder Abel, his younger brother (see John 8: 44). All the men of faith in Old Testament times would honor the Lord God with the blood of animal sacrifice. The economy of those times made it a sacrifice to give a lamb, sheep, bullock, or goat as an offering to the Lord. A man's wealth was equated with the number of cattle he owned.

The next major example of offering a blood sacrifice to God is found in Genesis 22:1-14. We will discuss this major offering of sacrifice in the first segment of chapter ten on Abraham, the father of faith.

The next example of the offering of a blood sacrifice is seen in God's judgment of the land of Egypt, for not listening to the voice of God's leader Moses. Plague after plague was visited upon the land of Egypt because their Pharaoh refused to release God's people, the Israelites, from slavery and bondage. So, God commanded Moses, His servant, to institute the sacrifice of the Passover to protect the first-born male in each household of Israel. It is a great blessing to see the manner God chose to manifest His deliverance from bondage and slavery, the people of Israel. For God still uses these same principles today in our households and families. We see God's great deliverance of the Israelite captives first in Moses' prophetic pronouncement. Exodus 11:4-8 -

4)   And Moses said, thus says the Lord, about midnight I will go out into the midst of Egypt:

5)   And all the first-born in the land of Egypt shall die, from the first-born of Pharaoh that sits upon his throne, even to the first-born of the maidservant that is behind the mill; and all the first born of the beast.

6)   And there shall be a great cry throughout all the land of Egypt, such as there was none like it, nor shall be like it anymore.

7)   But against any of the children of Israel shall not a dog move his tongue, against man or beast. That you may know how that the Lord does put a difference between the Egyptians and Israel.

8) And all these your servants shall come down to me, and bow down themselves to me, saying get you out, and all the people that follow you: and after that I will go out. And he went out from Pharaoh in a great anger.

This situation in the land of Egypt, is similar to the reality of satanic, and demonic bondage existing in our nation even today. The Pharaoh of Egypt is representative of Satan. The servants of Pharaoh are likened to Satan's principalities, and demon spirits. Moses represents the likeness of Jesus Christ our Lord. The fathers, and families of Israel, correlate with the fathers of the United States of America, and their families. We continue now by reviewing the Lord God's instructions to Moses regarding the passover lamb, and its administration by the fathers of Israel. (Exodus 12:3-5, 7, 12-13; 21-23) -

3) You speak to all the congregation of Israel, saying, in the tenth day of this month, they shall take to them every man a lamb, according to the house of their fathers, a lamb for a house:

4) And if the household be too little for the lamb, let him and his neighbor next to his house, take it according to the number of the souls, every man according to his eating, shall make your count for the lamb.

5) Your lamb shall be without blemish, a male of the first year: You shall take it out from the sheep, or from the goats.

7) And they shall take the blood, and strike it on the two side posts, and on the upper door post of the houses, wherein they shall eat it.

12) for (because) I will pass through the land of Egypt this night, and will smite all the first-born in the land

of Egypt, both male and female, and against all the gods of Egypt I will execute judgment: I am the Lord.

13) And the blood shall be to you for a token upon the houses where you are. And when I see the blood, I will pass over you, and the plague shall not be upon you to destroy you, when I smite the land of Egypt.

21) Then Moses called for all the elders of Israel, and said to them, draw out, and take you a lamb according to your families, and kill the passover.

22) And you shall take a bunch of hyssop, and dip it in the blood that is in the basin, and strike the lintel (cross beam) and the two side posts with the blood that is in the basin, and none of you shall go out at the door of his house until the morning.

23) For the Lord will pass through to smite the Egyptians: and when he sees the blood upon the lintel, and on the two side posts, the Lord will pass over the door, and will not allow the destroyer to come into your houses to smite you.

It is interesting that to strike the top cross-beam, and the two side posts of each family's door, would produce the lines of " a cross " from each point. A pre-incarnate symbolizing of salvation and deliverance through the blood of the cross of the Lord Jesus Christ for each family. Today, as fathers, we must apply the blood of God's Lamb to ourselves, and lead our children to receive it, for their own salvation, and deliverance from " the destroyer " who is Satan himself [see John 10:10]. The nation of Israel observed the passover instituted by God, throughout their generations, by the sacrifice of a lamb without blemish. This ordinance was conducted by the office of the high priest of the priestly tribe of Levi. Once a year, the entire nation of Israel, would portray what God would do with His own Son to pay for the sins of all men everywhere. In studying the yearly blood sacrifice of Israel, we can see God's holiness, and justice pictured. Once a year, the high priest of Israel's family, would go through specific steps to procure God's forgiveness of the sins of the family - nation of Abraham's grandson Jacob-Israel. The high priest would first make atonement for his own sins. And then, he would represent the people of Israel before God. God demanded specific procedures to be obeyed by those responsible for the administration of National atonement. Leviticus 16 records those procedures. The high priest would enter into the place called " the holy of holies ", where the Ark of God's Covenant with Israel was placed. The robe of the high priest had bells sown on it at the bottom hem, and a rope tied to it. In the event he entered into the Holy of Holies improperly. He would continually walk around the Ark of the Covenant so that the assisting priests could hear the bells on his priestly robe. Because, if the bells stopped ringing, the other priests would know God had smitten him. As Leviticus 16:2 warned.

In the Ark of the Covenant were two cherubic angels, who's wing-tips touched. This symbolized God's righteous judgment against the sinfulness of the people of Israel. The two cherubs were placed to be looking down upon the tablets of testimony. Or, the tablets containing the ten commandments the nation received from God, through the hands of His servant Moses (Ref. Deuteronomy 5:1-29). The administration of Israel's high priest, was to enter into the holy of holies, intercede for the nation, and sprinkle the blood of the sacrifice seven times over the mercy seat. Which contained the ten commandments. This all symbolized that God would not see the failure of Israel to obey His laws through the blood sprinkled over the law.

This ordinance God instituted in the nation of Israel, was designed by Him to prepare their understanding for the blood sacrifice of His own Son, the Lord Jesus Christ, the Lamb of God (Ref. Genesis 11:8 & John 1:19). To show how the work of the Levitical priesthood contrasted with the actual work of the Lord Jesus Christ, we must understand two words, and their meanings. The Hebrew word atonement [כָּפַר - transliterated - kah-phar' means: to make a covering, to smear over, obliterate, expiate. The blood of the yearly sacrificial lamb of Israel's High Priest only " covered " the sins of the people. In contrast the Greek word for remission [ἄφεσις - translit. aphesis] means: forgiveness, liberty, pardon, deliverance from sin. Pardon means: cancellation of, or, release from a debt, or penalty. Romans 3:15 shows us that the magnificent power of the blood of Jesus Christ does not just cover over our sins. It totally cancels them out! The actions of Israel's High Priest were honored by the Lord God in light of His knowledge of future events by His Son. Israel's sins were rolled over each year up until Christ's death on His cross. When we exercise proper faith in His blood, we can know all our sins are totally cleansed, and forgiven by God. When the Lord Jesus Christ ascended into the holy of holies in Heaven, and offered the precious blood He poured out on the cross, the Father said, " Whoever will repent of their sins, and exercise faith in your blood, I will totally forgive ". God the Father was totally pleased with the blood of Jesus Christ. God set His total approval upon Christ's blood to have the magnificent authority, and power, to cleanse, and cancel out all sins of those who appropriate it to their own lives by faith. The blood of Jesus is a spiritual cleanser and purifier. It disinfects our lives from the pollutants of Satan, and his demon powers. They hate the mention of the blood of the Lord Jesus Christ. Revelation 12:11 reveals that we gain power to overcome Satan through Christ's blood. In the spiritual sense we need it for daily cleansing much like we use a bar of soap to clean our physical bodies [ref. 1st John 1: 7].

7) But if we walk in the light, as He is in the light, we have fellowship one with another, and the blood of Jesus Christ His Son cleanses us from all sin.

We close this segment by stating that all deliverance and healing occurs when the blood of Jesus Christ is honored. Hebrews chapters 9 through 10, shows us that the blood of Jesus is central to the new covenant He has established with His blood. Hebrews 12:22-24 shows us that the blood of Jesus Christ will be eternally honored in Heaven. His blood will be "continually sprinkled" in the city of the living God. Satan, and all his demons, hate, and loathe the blood of Christ. Deliverance comes easier when it is fully honored.

Medical science has now proven that the man who fathers a child carries the blood line. A doctor can determine the father of a specific child, by examining the blood. Leviticus 17:11, shows that God said *"..the life of all flesh is in the blood.. "*. Adam, the first father, brought death and disease upon all humanity. Through the blood-line of Adam, flows the disease, and cancer of sin. Even in our fallen condition man's blood has miraculous powers. In studying human blood we find it to be a liquid tissue. The red blood cells, which are created by God, within our bone marrow, contain iron, which attracts molecules of oxygen. These molecules of oxygen are magnetically drawn to the surface of each red blood cell, and carried throughout the entire human body system. Supplying the life-sustaining oxygen to each cell. The blood also contains various hormones, vitamins, proteins, and enzymes. The blood is a servant, which supplies all the needs of our body through a system of arteries, veins, and capillaries. In the five and a half quarts of blood in the adult human, about one-tenth of one percent, contains a host of warriors known as white blood cells. They have been created by God inside our lymphatic system. This system runs somewhat parallel to our blood vessel systems. The white blood cells attack all kinds of various germs, and viruses, or other enemies to the health of the body. Phagocytes and lymphocytes are the major soldiers which attack destructive bacteria which enter through a cut, or abrasion. They engulf foreign trespassers in a fraction of a second. The deadly disease A.I.D.S. breaks down the immune system, and allows the viral enemies of health to have victory. Other elements of the blood go to work building a network of fibers to produce the repair, or, healing of an injury. This is the reason God said that - "..the life of all flesh is in the blood." If the blood system is interrupted, or stops in our bodies, death comes to that member that is deprived of the life-giving qualities of our blood. This is also true of each member of the human race that is deprived of, or refuses the blood of our Lord Jesus Christ. His blood must flow to each of us. If we wish to live forever. Only this blood can give eternal life. Joel 3:20 & 21 reveals that this is so. Jesus Christ, who is " The Lion of the tribe of Judah ", has become God's agent for cleansing our blood, and restoring life to us. Evil spirits are attracted to dying, and sinful blood. They fear and tremble at the speaking about the blood of Jesus Christ. From 1908-1912 great revivals broke out in places where God's people honored, and spoke out about the blood of Jesus Christ. Some ministers would even sprinkle the blood by faith over audiences and salvations, deliverances, and healings took place. Wherever the blood of Christ is honored, magnificent and miraculous events take place. John Lakey, who was a missionary, was in Africa at the time of a break out of Bubonic Plague among the people there. Victims would begin frothing at the mouth, their eyes would turn up, and then they would be totally dead in a few days. John Lakey learned that the blood of Jesus was more powerful than Bubonic Plague. He would go into the houses stricken with the plague, and lay hands on the people [see Mark 16:18], rebuke the fever, rebuke the plague, and they would come out of it, and be healed. Doctors came to Lakey and asked him, " How is it that when we enter these households we also get sick, yet you go in, and pray, and they are healed? What do you do?" Lakey answered, " I am honoring the blood of Jesus Christ my Lord." They said, "What is this? How do you do it?" He said, "Bring me a microscope slide full of froth." So they went down to one of the people dying, and took froth from their mouth with the Bubonic Plague in it. He said, " Put that froth under the microscope." They put it under the microscope and there were the Bubonic Plague germs. Demonic power crawling around in it. Then Lakey took the slide, and he said, "I'm going to wave my hand over it and plead the blood of Jesus Christ over it. Instantly, within seconds, they placed the slide back under the microscope, and every Bubonic Plague germ had died! Praise God! There is great power in Christ's blood!

The blood of Jesus Christ has magnificent authority and power to destroy disease, and bring life, and healing. God will heal, when we plead, and speak the blood of Jesus Christ the Lord. Amen. The Lord Jesus Christ, the Lamb of God, became the blood sacrifice. He became the person to provide peace between sinfulness, and holiness. The blood of Jesus Christ provided everything necessary for man and woman, son and daughter, to return to the Father (Ref. Hebrews 10:19). By the sacrifice of His own life He has opened to man the blessings of God forever. The Lord Jesus Christ shall stand as the eternal Mediator between God and man. He has made it possible for every person born of woman to be " Born Again " into God's eternal family (Ref. John 3:1-7). Take the time to praise Him for it!

THE RESTORER OF AUTHORITY AND DIGNITY TO MAN

Prior to the crucifixion, and shedding of blood by the Son of God, Satan made an attempt to give Jesus Christ an easy way out of accomplishing the work His Father gave to Him. This is seen in Luke 4:5-8 -

5) And the Devil taking him up into a high mountain showed him all the kingdoms [places of the inhabited earth] of the world in a moment of time.

6) And the Devil said to him, all this power [literal Greek την εξουσιαν ταυτην - transliterated - tan exousian tautan] and the glory [lit. Greek - την δοξ-αν αυτον - tan doxan auton] of them: for that is delivered to me; and to whomsoever I will, I give it.

7) If you will therefore worship me, all shall be yours.

106

8) And Jesus answered and said to him, you get behind Me, Satan: for it is written, you shall worship
the Lord your God, and Him only shall you serve. [
Emphasis added]

We find very important information in this section of God's Word.
We find a war for control and authority. We find out that Satan desires
to be worshiped in the place of God. We find that the glory and authority [Greek - doxan & exousian] was delivered, or given to Satan.
Let us study this for a minute. Who gave this authority, and glory into
Satan's hands? Some believe God did. Did He? As we continue in
our study of the subject of fatherhood, we will see that God did not
give authority over this earth to Satan. Genesis 1:26 clearly reveals
the perfect plan of God was to give this authority, and dominion,
into the hands of Adam. He gave it to man, the spiritual being He
had formed out of the dust of the earth. God created an earthly man,
created to be like Himself, to rule over His earthly creations in the
physical earth. So what happened to cause Adam to lose this authority
and dignity? We will see in chapters 11 & 12, that God commanded
Adam, the first earthly father, to care for, and protect God's garden
in the earth. To provide for its need, and "guard it from any forces
opposed to the spiritual state in which God created it." God entrusted
into man's hands the authority to observe Genesis 2:15-17. Adam was
king, and prime minister, over all God's works in the earth. When
the fallen, despotic Lucifer came down, and entered the garden in
the body of the serpent (Genesis 3:1-6) he did so with the intent of
stealing away from Adam this God-given authority and power. He
said in Isaiah 14:13 & 14 that ".. he would take God's place." " ..He
would be worshipped like the Most High." What does this mean in
relation to Adam? Satan was the rebellious, and wicked spirit from
Heaven. The only way for Satan to gain the authority over God's earth
was to somehow get man to do something disobedient to God the
Father. There was only one law God asked Adam and Eve to observe.

Genesis 2:15-17 was God's covenant, or agreement with His servant on the earth. Obedience would retain God as the Lord in Adam's life. Disobedience, by listening to, and following Satan's voice, would make Satan the ruler over this earth. This sounds quite simple, but this is the truth. God did not give Satan control over this earth. Adam, as he followed his deceived wife, gave it over to the enemy. God's purpose now is to restore the earth to its original glory and beauty. In the next segment we will see that God, through the lordship of His Son Jesus Christ, will return this earth back to the state God originally created it. He will do this through men, who He has restored to the authority and dignity He created man to display. The [exousian & doxan] Satan stole from Adam, Jesus Christ is restoring to each, and every man, and woman, that submits to the lordship of Jesus Christ. This is God's ultimate purpose in the earth. Satan is still warring to hold this [exousian & doxan] authority and dignity. But each time a man, or woman, acknowledges the shed blood of Jesus Christ for their sins. His death on the cross. His burial. His resurrection from the dead by God, and His ascension into Heaven to be seated at God's right hand, Satan loses the authority over that soul! When that soul learns more about what God is like, and develops into the likeness of Jesus Christ (2nd Peter 1:2-8; 3:18), Satan also loses the glory of that individual. That soul gains, as John 1:12 states, the authority to become sons of God. Sons who are like God's first begotten the Lord Jesus Christ!

This is God's purpose in the person, and work of His Son Jesus Christ. He is the restorer of God's authority, and glory, or dignity to man. Satan came to make man his slave. Jesus Christ came to set us all free. And release us to the honor and glory of serving the living God! Hebrews 9:14 -

14) How much more shall the blood of Christ, who through the eternal Spirit offered himself without spot to God, purge [cleanse by fire] your conscience

from dead works [literal Greek = energizings] to serve the living God.

Recommended reading- MAN'S CROWN OF GLORY- Jerry Savelle, Harrison House Publishers - Tulsa, OK 1982.

BAPTIZER WITH THE HOLY SPIRIT & FIRE

16) John [the Baptist] answered, saying to them all, I indeed baptize you with water, but one mightier than I comes, the latchet of whose shoes I am not worthy to unloose: He shall baptize you with the Holy Spirit, and with fire:

17) Whose fan is in His hand, and He will thoroughly purge His floor, and will gather the wheat into His garner [grainery]; but the chaff He will burn with fire unquenchable. — The Gospel of Luke 3:16 -17

In Isaiah 66:1, God says, that ".. heaven is His throne, and the earth is His footstool:.." God spoke through His servant John the Baptist prophetically. By announcing that Jesus Christ was ordained to baptize God's children with His Holy Spirit, and with fire. John also said that, through the work of Jesus Christ, He would totally, and "..thoroughly purge [cleanse] his floor,..". What does that mean? We shall study it a little to give us a fuller understanding of Jesus Christ, and His future work with us upon this earth. Ezekiel 28:18 tells is that Satan has used "..a multitude of iniquities to defile' his sanctuaries.." This is speaking of those men and women, sons and daughters who by lack of faith in Jesus Christ have become "defiled" by Satan's various forms of iniquity. When we, as an act of faith, come to the Father by faith in Jesus Christ. God, through the work, and ministry of His Holy Spirit, and His Word, begin to cleanse us of all the defilement of Satan, and his demon powers. This work manifests in us very much the same way as a burning fire. What has a greater ability to cleanse and purify other than intense fire? It destroys all impurities, and germs in the physical realm. In the spiritual realm, it burns out wicked spirits of Satan, that have entered our spirits, souls, or bodies prior to our faith in the Lord Jesus Christ. At the point that we begin to repent of sins, and begin to walk in God's righteousness, we progressively become conformed to the likeness of Jesus the Christ [see Romans 8:29]. God utilized trials & afflictions to do this.

In Acts 2:2-3, the Holy Spirit manifested in an appearance similar to fire. God, in the person of the Holy Spirit, always operates with the Word of God [i.,e., the Holy Bible]. We see this connection in Jeremiah 5:14 & 23:29. Jeremiah 5:14 states to Jeremiah-

14)   Wherefore this says the Lord God of hosts, because you speak this Word, behold, I will make My Words in your mouth fire, and this people wood, and it shall devour them.

Jeremiah 23:29 - shows us how we must perceive God's Word -

29)   Is not My Word like a fire? Says the Lord; and a hammer that breaks the rock in pieces?

There is an analogy to draw from on this subject of " fire ", by observing the reason our nation has experienced huge fires in the recent years. Especially in our western States, hundreds of thousands of acres have been destroyed by raging fires out of control. Any fireman will tell you the main reason for these immense fires that consume the countryside. It is the absence of water, and abundance of dry, dead trees, plants, and brush. This applies to our lives in that if we fail to keep ourselves full of the water of the Spirit of God, and His Word, we will become dried out. And, good for nothing, but to be burned [refer to Christ's warning in John 15: 6].

God has promised, through His servant John the Baptist, that He is in the process of thoroughly purging [cleansing-burning] His floor [His footstool - Isaiah 66:1]. This is happening now in the lives of those who allow God's Spirit, and holy Word, to purge out every area of uncleanness, or, wickedness. It will happen thoroughly as the judgments of the book of the Revelation of Jesus Christ begin to unfold in the future. Refer to Revelation 18: 8 - 9.

To conduct a word study in the Holy Bible on the word fire, would give more light on this subject of the "..fire.." of God's Spirit, and Word. We encourage such a study.

We say, in conclusion to this chapter on the Person and Work of the Lord Jesus Christ, that He will continue to purge this floor [this earth] with unquenchable fire. This fire will prepare all those, who by faith, allow God to cleanse their lives with His Holy Spirit, and holy Word. We are to release this fire into the minds, and hearts, of those in our families, who have been defiled by the enemy. This is accomplished by laying on our hands, and speaking it into their lives as needed. We must recognize that God has warned that, *"..there shall be in no way enter into it* [God's city - New Jerusalem] *anything that defiles..."* God's fire shall burn up all that defiles.

We close with a few selected verses concerning those who refuse to acknowledge God, and obey our Lord Jesus Christ. The end of evil must come as God has determined to end all opposition to His will. He has given that power to His Son.

2nd Thessalonians 1: 6 - 9 -

6)   Seeing it is a righteous thing with God to recompense tribulation to them that trouble you;

7)   And to you who are troubled rest with us, when the Lord Jesus shall be revealed from Heaven with His mighty angels,

8)	In flaming fire taking vengence on them that know not God, *and that obey not the gospel of our Lord Jesus Christ:*

9)	Who shall be punished with everlasting destruction from the presence of the Lord, and from the glory of his power;

2nd Peter 3:10 -

10)	But the day of the Lord will come as a thief in the night, in the which the heaven shall pass away with a great noise, and the elements shall melt with fervent heat, the earth also, and the works that are therein shall be burned up.

Hebrews 12: 28 & 29 -

28)	Wherefore we receiving a kingdom which cannot be moved, let us have grace, whereby we may serve God acceptably with reverence and godly fear:

29)	for [because] our God is a consuming fire. [emphasis added]

CHAPTER 8

Fatherhood & Procreation

GOD'S DESIGN FOR REPRODUCTION

When God the Father, His Son Jesus Christ, and the Holy Spirit created the spiritual and physical universe they had a beautiful design in their mind before anything actually came into being. The majestic knowledge and wisdom of the triune God-head was about to be demonstrated. The immense and eternal power of God was about to be released through the creative power of God's Words and actions. The glory and majesty of God's ability to create things with divine perfection must be in our minds prior to any study of the procreative ability within us as those who have been created in His image and likeness.

Yes, God the Father had a master design in mind in His creation of the first earthly father, Adam, and his wife, Eve, (the mother of all living see - Genesis 3:20). That master design in which God created us has been the object of God's enemy, Satan's, most vicious attack. The perversion of God's created order has been a specific area of satanic and demonic activity in the earth. We shall attempt in this chapter to clarify God's perfect will concerning His design for procreation. And, the enemy's deceptive strategies against that will. Doubt it not that this is a war zone!

May we state at the outset that it is in the absence of the praise and thankfulness to God for His wonderful creative ability that Satan's operations are evident. The profane theory of antiChrist Evolution demonstrates this heresy, that now rules over American

Public schools. It is through the worship and praise of God the Father - Who is our Creator, that the Devil's works are destroyed (see 1st John 3:8). Romans 1:20-28 indicts those who refuse to keep the Lord God - Creator in their education.

20) For the invisible things of Him from the creation of the world are clearly seen, being understood by the things that are made, even His eternal power and God-head; so that they are without excuse:

21) Because that, when they knew God, they glorified Him not as God, neither were thankful, but became vain in their imaginations, and their foolish heart was darkened.— Romans 1:20 & 21

God demands, and deserves our deep admiration, and worship for all His wonderful works. It is in the absence of this attitude of gratefulness in our lives, that the corrupted Lucifer is given place to raise havoc with God's creation (see Ephesians 4: 27). It is in the presence of this thankful attitude in us, that God's glory, and ability is released in, and through us, as His children (see Psalms 22:3).

God the Father created every living thing *"..to bring forth abundantly.."* (study Genesis 1:20-28). *"..to be fruitful and multiply..."* was, and still is, God's most basic command to man. The Global World social planners, and Planned Parenthood organizations, hate this command because it is in the obedience to this basic will of God, that their evil will, and purpose is thwarted. We will expose this evil antichild - antiparent philosophy in detail in the next segment on what actually is ancient, and contemporary " Baal Worship "?

God's design for reproduction is simply majestic in nature. The ability, and privilege of a man, and a woman, to join themselves together in holy marital covenant with God is blessed. And commitment to each other, is one of the most precious gifts He gives to us.

It is in the honor, and respect of God, that this great gift is most appreciated. It is in the dishonor, and disrespect of God, it's Creator, that it is abused, and perverted, in any of the many ways it can be. Fathers, and mothers, are entrusted by God, to insure the sanctity and beauty of marital union; is protected and nurtured in their marriage. And in their children's marriages. All American divorce, and abuse of this basic area of the fathering, and beginning of life, is to be blamed on the neglect of protection and nurturing of marriage in the United States of America! And, those judges, and attorneys, who prey upon this calamity must give Him an account! We have been commanded by God as men to - *"..have respect for the covenant.."* (Psalms chapter 74:20).

20)   Have respect unto the covenant: for the dark places
        of the earth are full of the habitations of cruelty.

Probably the greatest factor, besides the dishonor of God, as the one who has ordained marriage. Is the failure to guard the covenant of God in marriage. We speak at this time of godly husbandry. Protection, and nurture of this creation of God, is in the hands of men and women. God's design includes the aspect of men as a fathers who are *".. made in God's image and likeness..."* Being the protector, and nurturing factor of His creation. Man is responsible to God to care for, and protect, this ordinance of God.

By way of illustration we use an example of a man who was asked by a friend to take care of his plants while on vacation. During his friend's vacation, the man simply forgot to watch over the needs of protection, and care of his friends property. Insects began to eat the leaves of the plants. A fungus developed in the roots, destroying the plants ability to nourish itself. One of the plants was left directly in the sun, and was scorched, and withered up. This man is going to be quite embarrassed, when his friend returns to find how his plants have been abused, and neglected, by the one he thought enough of to trust with their care.

So shall it be with each, and every father, and mother, in God's future day of judgment. His judgment will be based upon the obedience of each of us who take on the responsibility of bringing children into this world. His covenant is not so concerned with how successful you have been to sell cars, or build buildings, or businesses. But, rather, in how you protected and nurtured your marriage and children. Chapters 11 & 12 will detail our duties.

In studying God's design of reproduction, we observe that God throughout Holy Scripture, refers to people, families, and nations, as, or like trees, vineyards, plants, flowers, or gardens. God does this in His wisdom, to show man His design. All God's creatures, whether of the sky, land, or sea, are designed to reproduce themselves. Men and women also have this basic design.

God's design of the procreative anatomy in men, and women, is simply wonderful, and marvelous. The Psalmist declares this in Psalms 139:13-14-

13)   For you have possessed my reins: (i.,e., life systems) you have covered me [protected me] in my mother's womb.

14)   I will praise you; for I am fearfully and wonderfully made: marvelous are your works; and that my soul knows very well.

In opposition to the pro-abortionist's mentality in the United States of America, God views the beginning, starting, or should we say fathering, and mothering of life, when "..the seed of man.." (see Genesis 12:7) and "..the seed of woman.." (see Genesis 3:15 (b), are joined together during the procreative act of marriage. The dissemination of a man's seed, into the procreative womb of woman, begins the process whereby God develops, and creates each and every human being. This is God's design and His work. To destroy this work is to destroy the creative majesty of God's hands. It is an abomination before the eyes of God Almighty (ref. Exodus 1:15-22; 2:1-4; Judges 6:1-29; 11 Kings 9:1-37 (esp. vs. 7); Isaiah 47:9 & 10; Jeremiah 2:34; Proverbs 6:1-17, and Ezekiel 23:36-39). The abortion atrocities, which take place daily throughout our land, must be met with God's judgment in our nation's future, if He is to remain just. As He has been toward all past civilizations who destroyed their offspring. There is, in the United States, a war being waged against the fathering of life. Fear is one of the main forces producing it. Greed is another major force causing this condition. Inordinate lust promoted by Playboy, and other pornography, also. These spiritual forces must be bound, and cast out (ref. Mt. 18:18-20), if we would see our country's attitude change to be in line with God's design.

Before we conclude this segment of God's design for reproduction we must explain that the most neglected aspect of fatherhood and procreation has been the absence of the seeds of God's Word (see Luke 8:4-15) on the subject. We review Webster's definition of " seminary " to establish our thoughts on this subject. Seminary means: seed plot - nursery of seed. 1. A place where something develops- grows, or is bred. 2. A school, esp. A private school... 3. A college where priests, ministers, or rabbis are trained.

The author cannot help but exhort that this is a perfect description of what a family, and home in America should be. If it is true that the leaders in our various places of worship are our examples, we too should be sowing the various seeds of God's Word into the fertile minds of our young ones! This is a very important aspect of total parenting. Our children should be able to learn the words, and ways of God, from the lives, and mouths of fathers, and mothers. This too is an aspect of God's design. We can view this in 1st Corinthians 3:6-9.

6)   I have planted, Apollos watered; But God gave the increase.

7) So then neither is he that plants anything, neither he that waters; but God that gives the increase.

8) Now he that plants and he that waters are one: And every man shall receive his own reward according to his own labor.

9) For we are laborers together with God: You are God's husbandry, you are God's building.

For fathers and mothers to *"...labor together with God..."*, in the protection and nurturing of the lives of their children is truly the design of our Creator. He is pleased, and we are healthy, and joyful when we keep His commands (see Psalms 103: 17-22). The patterns we establish, by our Biblically guided behaviors in our children's minds, grant to them strength to carry out these things when they marry, and have children. We leave them at a great disadvantage if we fail to teach these most important areas.

We now explain an aspect of fatherhood and motherhood, that is usually left to Sunday schools, or others in our children's lives. There is no greater blessing, as the blessing, of exercising the leadership of seeing that your son, or daughter is *" Born Again.."*. This relates to the subject matter we are discussing in this segment. What the seed of God's Word produces. I Peter 1:23-25 reveals -

23) Being born again, not of corruptible seed, but of incorruptible, by the Word of God, which lives and abides forever.

24) For all flesh is like grass. And all the glory of man as the flower of grass. The grass withers, and the flower thereof falls away:

25) But the Word of the Lord endures forever.

Fathers and mothers, God's Word, and His Holy Spirit, have the power to give to you and your children everlasting life. It is in your willingness, or unwillingness to administer these things, that you, and your children are blessed, or suffer in this life, and the life to come. Jesus Christ our Lord, has affirmed God's purpose, and design in reproduction, in the Gospel of John 15 :1-17. To bear fruit, and protect, and nurture that fruit, is God's will for this earth. Let us all be about our Father's business.

We close this segment by reviewing a passage in Psalm 80 : 7-16. The words of the psalmist ask God to restore his nation. Let us apply this request to our land.

7) Turn us [restore us] again, O God of hosts, and cause your face to shine; and we shall be saved.

8) You have brought a vine out of Egypt: You have cast out the heathen, and planted it.

9) You prepared room before it, and did cause it to take deep root, and it filled the land.

10) The hills were covered with the shadow of it, and the boughs thereof were like the goodly cedars.

11) She sent out her boughs to the sea, and her branches to the river.

12) Why have you [ref. Ezekiel 22:30] then broken down her hedges, so that all they which pass by the way pluck her?

13) The boar out of the forest does waste it, and the wild beast of the field does devour it. [ref. John 10: 10]

14) Return, we beseech you, 0 God of hosts: Look down from heaven, and behold, and visit this vine.

15) And the vineyard which your right hand has planted, and the branch that you made strong for yourself.

16) It is burned with fire, it is cut down: They perish at the rebuke of your countenance.[Emphasis & references added]

Baal Worship

As we begin this segment on the meanings behind the worship of Baal, we must begin by recognizing the spiritual forces behind all religious systems of worship. Whether they be true, or false forms of worship, they always are inspired by spiritual powers unseen to the physical eyes of man. This basic fact has been true from the original fall of man in the Garden of Eden. Isaiah 14, and Ezekiel 28, clearly reveal to us, that Satan's basic activity in the earth, is to do all in his power to thwart the worship of the true God. And utilize all the spiritual beings of evil under his authority to lead men, women, and children to worship him as God. The malignancy of the Devil's hatred for God the Father is so acute, that he is even content to lead men to worship anything other than God. This corruption of his original purpose. Which God gave to him, is totally opposite today in his activities. Rather than leading the creation to worship God, he does all in his power to have the creation do anything but that.

Our first segment in this chapter, God's Design for Reproduction, was to establish a few basic principles, God has laid down from the beginning of His creation. God's will, and desire in these areas have never changed. Neither shall they ever (see Hebrews 13:8). God's will concerning procreation is forever settled in heaven. We say this at the beginning of studying what Baal worship is, to encourage both spiritual, and moral discernment. America is morally insane because of certain sins not yet repented of. Watch the " changing of names ".

In chapter two of this book we examined what *" Mystery, Babylon "* was. We worked at comparing the aspects of Ancient Babylon of the antiquities, with the aspects of evil inside our nation. But, at this time, we must review a little about the Patriarch Noah. Since we will review much about him in chapter nine, we say only that God was so grieved with mankind, and their communing rebellion with Satan and his angels, he destroyed all mankind except for Noah, and his three sons. All other men on the face of the earth drowned in the flood. Noah, and his sons, were again charged by God to keep His covenant commands, and repopulate the earth. But, Satan immediately went to work to corrupt the seed of man, as before. This began after years of the repopulation of man on the earth. As we know, Satan found a leader in Nimrod. He organized the making of bricks. And building the tower of Babel (ref. Genesis 10:6-10). As we studied, Nimrod organized the occult system of star worship, today known in the United States, as the Signs of the Zodiac (see Genesis 11:1-9). It has been recorded, that after God judged Nimrod, and his tower at "Babel", Nimrod, and his mother, whose name was "Semiramis", moved south. And began to build ancient Babylon, with all its wicked religious, and immoral systems. The Zodiac was continued there, and developed into the corrupt art of Astrology and Horoscope. It has been recorded in Alexander Hislop's " Two Babylons ", that this mother of Nimrod, sexually seduced her son after his father died, and married him. It was recorded that Noah's sons heard of this perversion in Babylon. And sent men to kill Nimrod. And cut him up, and sent parts of his body to various areas of civilization, with the warning that if any other man did this abomination before God. The same would happen to them. This got the attention of all people. But Semiramis, in her anger against the children of Shem, and, the true God, decided to develop a " Mother-Son " form of religion to preserve the name of her son Nimrod. We say, at this time, that Satan, and his demons, were behind this perverting of God's laws of morality. We follow the contagions into new world powers.

From the 9th Century B.C., Semiramis, propagated this false religious system throughout the world. In the land of Canaan it was named - Ashtarte. In Egypt it was renamed - Isis & Osiris, in Assyria the name was changed to - Rhea (the great goddess mother). In Ephesus she was renamed - Diana. In Greece - Venus, or Dionysus. In Rome - Madonna. There has also been in the Roman Catholic religion, a deification of Mary, as mother of God. Which has repeated this perverted " Mother-Son " system of occult worship. The names of

Semiramis' son Nimrod, were also changed as they were propagated throughout the world under Satan's direction. Nimrod became " Baal " in Assyria, and Canaan. The Sun god " Ra " in Egypt. Aprodites' child in Greece. " Bacchus ", the Eternal boy, or god of partying, in Rome. Semiramis is known in Webster's Dictionary as having been a woman of wisdom (ref. Ezekiel 28:12). Which gave to her the capacity to engineer this abominable system of false religious worship. She, also, was said to be a woman of great beauty. Hugh Hefner's Playboy Magazine would be interested in her, if she were still alive. Yet, he does have the Roman *" Madonna "* of our day. She was also known for *her* sexual excesses. Immorality began to be propagated by her. These examples of profane counterfeits, to the Lord God's design for procreation, show us Satan's efforts to supplant the Lord's place of rule in the lives of men, and women [refer again to Isa.14:14]. We have covered this information so that we might go further now to bring us up to date on Baal worship. Baal worship was scattered throughout the land of promise when God, through the leadership of Joshua, brought them into Canaan. The altars to Baal were to be destroyed, by the Old Testament Israelites, as they took over the land. Immorality was so rampant, even the animals, and children, were diseased with venereal infections. And had to be killed, and burned, under God's orders to Joshua (Deuteronomy 12:29-32; 13:12-18).

Besides these altars to Baal, which the idolaters placed on hills called -*" The High Places "* (see Numbers 33:52), there was what was called *" Groves "* (ref. Judges 6:25-30). The Zondervan Bible

Encyclopedia - p.p. 209 & 210, describes these as obelisks. They were then made out of wood. They were called, by the idolaters, sacred pillars, or poles. Usually, they had to be " cut down " and burned. These same obelisks are today built out stone, or cement. They are said to be found throughout the middle east. The two major world obelisks that we have seen, are to be found in St. Peter's Square, in Rome, at the Vatican. And, in the Federal center of Government for the United States of America, Washington, D.C. The meaning, spiritually speaking, behind the grove, or obelisk, is that it literally calls spiritual powers wickedness, specifically of immorality, prostitution, and child sacrifice, into a nation's powers of government. These evil powers bind the righteous order of governing. And loose, or allow the practice of evil, and wickedness to prevail. It is interesting studying the background of the George Washington Monument. At the time of the beginning of its' construction, certain people came in to destroy it. Because of this, those behind it's construction stopped building it until the 18th century. Others have attempted to blow it up, and have been accused by the American Media of being religious fanatics, or anti-American elements. The first president, George Washington, was a Mason who gave French Mason, Major Pierre L'Enfant, the contract to design the seat of our Federal government. Later on, Masons in our government, selected this most satanic symbol known to man, as Washington's Monument. The author, growing up, never could understand what kind of monument it was. Now he knows! Research reveals, that the obelisk was designed to be representative of the male organ in the ancient fertility cults, or a sexual association. A phallic idol, or pornographic symbol. It also releases the spirit of witchcraft . Being forbidden by God in the Holy Bible as idolatry of the worst and profane sort (see Deut. 4: 15 & 16).

The female representation of ancient Baal worship, was the Ashteroth, Ashtoreth, or statue of Astarte. This idol-statue represented female worship, and fertility. A goddess of [lust and immorality] fortune, and war. It is interesting in reports about The Statue of " **Liberty** ", in New York Harbor, that they admit that Church men vehemently protested its placement in our nation as a symbol of " Liberty ". They admitted that the actual builder of this occult statue, or, idol said that -".. he built it to have " *the face of his mother* ", and the "*..body of his mistress..*". In studying the ashtoreths of ancient times, they made them with " rays of light ". Coming forth from its head. Which represented ancient Nimrod (sun god) worship. The builders of this supposed " gift " from France were members of the

Mysterious Masonic Orders seeking to establish an evil foot-hold, or beach-head, in our nation. Changing the names in order to repropagate their idols, and statues. Most Americans are ignorant of these facts, yet we suffer under the curses of this disobedience. [see appendix A - God's Word on the Grove & Ashtoreth].

At these altars of Baal worship, and at the groves [asherahs], men would bring their daughters, and wives, and practice immoral orgies with them in worship of Baal. The money gathered by the prophets of Baal, was from the prostituting of the daughters, and wives (see Leviticus 19:29). Apparently there was also the " circulation " of pornographic pictures around these corrupted civilizations (ref. Numbers 33:52). Archeologists have found profane images in their digs. Making idols to corrupt men is Satan's work.

The last most abominable practice, which the worshipers Baal and Ashtoreth did, was centered around what was called the chief god (or principality) under Baal, " Molech "[see 2nd Kings 23:10]. After the immoral prostitution, and sex orgies, the participating women naturally became pregnant. So, what they did was that one of their idols to Molech was made out of iron. The hands and arms of this hideous idol were heated red hot by a fire under the hand-bowl structure, and the offspring, or, as pro-abortionists call it, " fetal matter ", or " product of conception " was laid into the hands of Molech. And burned alive to Baal's chief god Molech (Ref. Leviticus 20:1-5). These were the primitive methods of infanticide we today see in every city across America, in abortion clinics, and " Planned Parenthood Centers ". Our rejection of God has opened us up to these evils.

Our daughters, in the United States of America, are also being prostituted by the fathers and mothers to the pornographers. Not at all unlike ancient Baal worship. We state prophetically, that just as God had to judge and destroy His people Israel, for flirting with Baal worship. And then, falling totally into all its aspects, so He must also judge and destroy this nation if we refuse to repent of this abomination, and wickedness. As a nation, we are deceiving ourselves to think

" We, Great America " will not be judged, and destroyed by God. Historical study reveals that this system of Baal worship has been propagated by Satan, and his principalities throughout the earth. And, that God's anger and destruction came upon each, and every empire, or nation, that did it. It is probably the murdering of innocent children that God finally decides to visit with his wrath. In the purest sense of what idolatry, and Baal worship is, the United States of America, has offered their children to Molech in the various excuses given to destroy children inside the womb. Many say children are too expensive, yet they go out and buy expensive cars and possessions. Rather than being " bothered " with the work of raising children. God describes these abominable attitudes in Ezekiel 23: 36 - 49. Sacrificing helpless children to their self-worshiping idols.

We close this segment now with an admonishment from God. As His children we are required to stop this wickedness from going on in our land. We all must organize into body-politics in every city in our nation. And, stop the wickedness, and atrocities going on there. The fathers of America, and the mothers, should repent in every city. They must bow before God, and request His forgiveness. For allowing this great wickedness to develop in our nation. And, then arise, and work in an orderly fashion, to destroy it all in the name of Jesus Christ our Lord. Raising good children to be God honoring and obedient takes love in action against these plagues.

MORALITY VS IMMORALITY

In the year 1980, the Baptist preacher Jerry Falwell, mustered up the boldness, and courage, to organize a group. A civil body politic of morally minded citizens. To confront those, who had been at work for years, destroying and overthrowing all Federal, State, and local laws written against obscenity and profanity. Yes, America has had good laws against all forms of immorality throughout the United States of America. The " Moral Majority, Inc. " was founded, in order to raise up a standard against the floods of wicked pornography corrupting the lives of Americans. Attorneys, for adult entertainment interests, had been mounting an assault to overthrow our nation's moral precepts and righteous principles. Satan's men and women immediately went to work to mock and ridicule this new movement for righteousness in the land. A rock radio station, with the call letters - K.M.E.T. Los Angeles, California, began a mockery against this effort to awaken the nation to morality. They broadcast the saying - " We are the Immoral Majority ". Larry Flint, of Hustler Magazine had the audacity to publish pictures of Jerry Falwell, and his beloved mother, in his magazine of pornography. Stating lies that he had sex with mother. When God's servant, Jerry Falwell, attempted redress these corrupt abuses of Larry Flint in the government, his appeals fell on deaf ears. How abominable! How wicked! But that, my dear readers, is the major force in our nation now destroying the moral fiber of our lives. And, our children's lives. Federal, State, and local judges should be impeached for ruling protections for these corrupters of America. It is past time, that all God's men, and women arise. And, force all law enforcement authorities, throughout our nation, to overthrow all those individuals in our nation, that are promoting spirits of immorality. These are satanic principalities working to break down this nation morally. Fathers are required to fight against these matters in every area that affects our lives. It is required by the Lord God, that men obey Him in protecting their children. Christ has commanded us to cast out these demon forces in the earth. We bind them by good laws against their evil traffic, and by putting constant pressure on all law enforcement agencies to punish evil doers - see - Romans 13.

Today, satanic and demonic powers of immorality are very active throughout our cities. This is so because men and women are overtly worshiping Satan in these sordid, and aberrant behaviors. Our public school systems permit the mockery of the wicked against our daughters who try to protect their virginity, and virtue. The young men watch their dad's pornographic movies, and read their books, and then go into our schools all fired up with spirits of lust and immorality to " conquer " the girls at school. This mockery of morality is now being laughed at by the parents of these young people.

Yes, morality vs. immorality is a reality within our National cities. What is really sad, is that the people who are morally-minded, are afraid to speak out against the wicked for fear of reprisals. That is why we all must organize to work faithfully to restore a respect for virtue, and morality, in each of our cities. The power, and authority of God Almighty, and His holy angels will be with us if we do. Satan's power will definitely increase in our land if we fail to. It is in our hands to insure morality is respected by our city, State, and Federal leaders. And, as we said before, we are not to accept the demonic phrase " morality cannot be legislated ", by those who are allowing themselves to speak for our enemy Satan. We are to follow God's Words found in all Bible verses which speak of earthly authorities. (Ref. Romans 13:1-4; I Timothy 2:1-8; Ephesians 6:11-12). If we discern by God's Holy Spirit, that demonic powers are working our governmental rulers, we are to pray, and fast, to "..cast them out.." As the Lord Jesus Christ has given us direction (see Mark16: 17).

The forces against morality, and for immorality, are very strong in our nation, because those who are moral, have tolerated profanity, and permitted it to be so. It is like the days of the judges of Israel in the United States of America. Not only is the enemy increasing his foothold in our land, those God has given authority over Satan, are afraid of him. We are to fear one power only. God the Almighty who will judge all immorality at His judgment seat (ref. Rev. 20:11). We, who are His leaders in America, are to judge it in our land (see Luke 10:17-20). As fathers, we are to guard our children from these powers of immorality in all ways possible. Many moral mothers could send a flurry of letters, email etc., to all our State, and Federal legislators requesting, *and if they refuse to act*, demanding harsh penalties for the broadcasting, or propagating, of immoral profanity anywhere in our cities. This does take extra effort from us, but we must ask ourselves if truly " an ounce of prevention, is worth a pound of cure ". Our children will suffer, only because we, as their parents, refuse to act against immorality in our nation.

SEXUS VS. THE MARRIAGE COVENANT

The Roman Latin language originated the word *" sex "*. It originally meant: to cut, or divide. And, that, is exactly what Satan has utilized the meaning of the word " sex " to do! The Greek equivalent to the word is: *fornication*. From which we derive the word pornography. The scientific, medical, and psychological minds, have, through their processes of investigation, categorized everything they possibly could. The word sex, is a foreign term to God's Biblical revelation. It is a word that not only cuts into God's creation of marriage, but also, divides men and women, into competing parties. Rather than God's order of cooperation, and togetherness. Our minds have been indoctrinated with this worldly philosophy in America, which generated out of the pagan Roman system. Which, God destroyed for its profanity and wickedness. This evil concept of the American humanistic system, is devoid of God, or His order. It has been propagated by the atheistic, and immoral God-haters now ruling in our national systems of education, and National multimedia. The word *sex* is a pagan term. Which, has been utilized by Satan, and his powers, to overthrow any idea that God is the source of the relationship between man and woman. It has separated, and divided, the principle of responsibility, God ordained in the Garden of Eden, from the actual physical pleasure involved, in what God ordained as the marriage covenant. To propagate the idea that hedonistic pleasure and self-gratification, is the main focus an individual should have as their philosophy in life, is to distort the entire purpose of God in the lives of men and women. Yet, this has been the focus of our nation's men with the 1953 advent of Hugh Hefner's Playboy philosophy. As in every area of life, we usually have two extremes to discern in our decisions about the various life matters which concern us. The Puritan view of married love, which has been besmirched by America's pornographers, was probably the most liberating view the world had heard since the Dark Ages. The Roman Catholic heresy, that espoused that celibacy, and life long virginity, were superior to the married state, was propagated in the early stages of Christianity. So, much so, that Origen, considered by historians as a church father, had himself castrated before his ordination. The opposite position was taken by Martin Luther, who defied the Roman Catholic heresy, by marrying a nun. All kinds of weird, and might we say demonic, ideologies ruled over this very important area of man's existence since mankind's fall. The playboy philosophy, we see so prevalent in our country, was brought into existence by Hugh Hefner by stating that Puritan views held by many of America's founders, repressed man's " sexual " drives. When, the truth is, that the Puritan view of married love, exalted the romantic nature Holy Scripture gives to it as we see in Proverbs 5:15-19. And, the Book of Solomon's Song. Previously, evil religious men propagated an evil disposition toward marriage. And, God's marriage relationship created for men and women out of His loving care. Then, others came along to correct the abuse. Only in an opposite extreme. To say that the married relationship between a man and woman is evil is erroneous. To try to say that the married relationship of a man and woman is for pleasure only, is erroneous. To say that the married relationship of a husband and wife is for bearing children only, is also erroneous. To declare that the married relationship of a husband and wife, within the bonds of God's marriage covenant, is for the good purpose of wedded bliss. And, to bring forth children to glorify our Maker, is God's design, and order. To violate this basic design of God, is to violate the order in which God created marriage. It is not either, or. But, both, and. It is His blessing He created holy.

The marriage covenant was drawn up by the triune God - head, and then implemented in the Garden of Eden. That covenant provided the basic structure relationally, which is best for man, woman, and their offspring. The loyalty, and commitment of love, between a husband and wife, was created to reflect God's desired relationship with us (see Ephesians 5:21-33). The procreation, and development of our children (really God's offspring), is to be cultivated in this environment God prescribed in the beginning. Jesus is Lord and Maker!

It is very abominable the horrendous conditions which have transpired as the result of the fathers in our nation refusing to oppose all antiChrist ideologies contrary to God's marriage covenant. We are required to honor that which is to be obeyed in the earth. Psalm two reveals God's wrath and activity against those who violate His eternal principles of life. This Psalm is about Jesus Christ.

1)   Why do the heathen rage, and the people imagine a vain thing

2)   The kings [political social planners] of the earth set themselves, and the rulers take counsel together, against the Lord, and against His anointed, saying,

3)   Let us break their bands asunder, and cast away their cords from us.

4)   He that sits in the heavens shall laugh: The Lord shall have them in derision.

5)   Then shall He speak to them in his wrath, and vex them in His sore displeasure. [emphasis added]

The violation of God's marriage covenant, which is the *"..bands and cords.."* spoken of by the Psalmist, is met by God's vexation, and judgment. A visit to any one of the Family Law, and divorce courts in our land will confirm this fact. The adulterous, and whoremonger -ing attitudes propagated by America's pornographers (America's prophets of Baal) are the cause of these evil realities in our nation. God's disposition is clearly seen in Hebrews 13: 4-

4) Marriage is honorable in all, and the bed undefiled:
   But whoremongers and adulterers God will judge.

We close this segment by saying that " *sex* " violates God's marriage covenant ordained in the beginning. It divides, and separates, the pleasures God ordained to be experienced in the marriage covenant of male and female, from the awesome responsibility of bringing forth children, and caring for them. Christians must not speak it into their marriage - read Proverbs chapter 18 verse 21.

We conclude this segment with a quote of poetry by the famous John Milton. Who placed into writing, the beauties of God's marriage covenant. This expression is the true Puritan position.

" Hail wedded love, mysterious law, true source of human offspring, sole propriety in paradise of all things common else. By thee adulterous lust was driven from men among the beastial herds to range, by thee founded in reason, loyal, just and pure, relations dear. And all the charities of father, son, and brother first were known. Far be it, that I should write thee sin or blame. Or, think thee unbefitting holiest place, perpetual fountain of domestic sweets. Whose bed is undefiled and chaste pronounced." [7]

THE WICKEDNESS OF PORNOGRAPHY

The conjugated words pornieas, and grapha, are the two Greek words [πορνιεασ - γραπηα]. Which mean respectively: *pornieas* - fornication. And *grapha* - writing, icons - images, or pictures. The word " *pornography* " was derived, and was coined, from these two words. Which mean literally: writings, or pictures of fornication. And

---

[7] The Complete Poetical Works of John Milton, Ed. by Douglas Bush, Houghton Mifflin 1965, Paradise Lost, Book 4 P.P. 750-761-135.

so they are! As in all other areas of Satan's activity, whenever God gives a name to show the ugliness of a specific sin, Satan's first move is to change its name, in order to make it acceptable again. To deceive men, and women, by use of new terminology is an ever present aspect of the works of Satan, and those men who are his followers. Usually the new term the enemy of our souls comes up with sounds acceptable. And even righteous! The stigma God has placed upon abortion was met with the new phrase *" pregnancy termination "*. Sounds kind of good and acceptable does it not! How about alcoholism, for God's sin term *" drunkard "*. How about dissolution of marriage, for God's sin word *" divorce ".* Or, homicide, for the stigma of *" murder ".* The City of Pittsburgh's police department has adopted the false, and might we say illegal designation of the term " actor " instead of the proper term *" suspect ",* when they speak to the Media about a criminal behavior in the city.

This gymnastics with semantics has also been exercised on the word pornography (pictures of fornication). Those who are being controlled by Satan's principalities of immorality in our nation have changed the word pornography to *" Adult Entertainment ".* Before this segment is finished, we will endeavor to convince all of the wickedness of this *so called* " Adult Entertainment ". And, that if it is not overthrown in our land, God's righteous judgment will be our experience. The previous segments in this chapter should have by now built into the reader's mind a more acute discernment between God's righteous judgments, and ordinances concerning fatherhood and procreation, and Satan's myriad of *" alternative life styles ".* But, before we bring out the abominations produced by pornography, we explain the power structures Satan has to propagate his anti-Creator ideologies. The main spiritual principality, which rules over this area of the promotion of pornography is *" the spirit of whoredoms "*[refer Hosea 4: 6-12, et, al]. Under this satanic power are " demon spirits of profane lust ", " spirits of adultery ", " spirits of fornication ", and the most militant demonic power, " the perverse spirit ". There is an entire structure of evil spirits that come into a nation after the previous powers have had success. The breaking of the hedge of the marriage covenant by divorce, opens up the participants, and their children, to spirits of hatred, resentment, and bitterness. It also works to destroy honor and respect between husbands and wives.

Since the drive, and desire to procreate, given to man by God as a gift, is one of the most powerful areas of human existence, Satan's activity is immense in this area. Probably the next area, besides religious and political areas, is the area of *procreation* in Satan's warfare strategy. If we are to be victorious *"..over all the power of the enemy:..."* (Luke 10:19) we must understand his strategies.

Just as Satan was given authority over the earth in Adam and Eve's disobedience, so today, he also gains control in our lives. Or, over our children's lives, by disobedience to God's perfect will. We have been shown by God, through Biblical revelation, the basic reason for all the wickedness in our land today. It is found in Leviticus 19:29 -

> 29) Do not prostitute your daughter, to cause her to be a whore; Lest the land fall to whoredom, and *the land become full of wickedness*. [emphasis added]

This is the single greatest reason pornography is so wicked. It releases *"..the spirits of whoredoms"*, into the daughters of a nation. All the evil spirits described earlier in this segment, are free to enter into our lives, and our children's lives, because of this National sin. Demon powers cannot enter a man, or woman's life, unless they are permitted by the destruction of the spiritual hedges, which God has established in His eternal Word, to protect us from their entrance. Pornography opens the doors for demons, to enter their prey, through the eye-gate. Audio and verbal expressions allow them to enter through the ear-gate. These wicked spirits literally enter through the eyes and ears. This principle is seen in the positive sense in Psalm 119: 130. Both God's Word and Holy Spirit enter us by reason of *these two gateways* being submitted to Him. Romans 10: 6 -17 confirms this. 2 Peter 2: 6 -22 describes this in the negative sense.

14 (a)   Having eyes full of adultery, that cannot cease from sin;

As shown earlier in this book, Jesus Christ the Lord, revealed this reality of the eye -gate principle in Matthew 6: 22 - 23. By way of reinforcement of this basic human life principle and concept, we quote a parallel passage to Mt. 6:22-23, which is Luke 11: 34 -36 -

34)   The light of the body is the eye: Therefore, when your eye is *single* [Greek - ʿαπλουσ - pure], your whole body also is full of light; but when your eye is evil [Greek = πονηροσ - transliterated - ponaros], your body also is full of darkness.

35)   Take heed, therefore, that the light which is in you be not darkness.

36)   if your whole body therefore, be full of light, ***having no part dark***, the whole shall be full of light, as when the bright shining of a candle does give you light. [emphasis added]

These spiritual light, and spiritual darkness Bible passages, are God's descriptions of spiritual discernment. Most men and women, who have allowed demons of inordinate lust, and whoredoms, into their lives through their eye and ear-gate, are generally totally unaware that demon spirits have entered into their souls and bodies. Unless someone with the " discernment of spirits " and knowledge of the power of God's Word, and Holy Spirit, cast out those demons, they will remain indwelt with profane spirits (review Mark 16:17) -

17)   And these signs shall follow them that believe; in My
       name shall they cast out demons...

Once these demonic powers enter into a human life, they energize, compel, and drive their host to acts of perversion against God's
procreative marriage covenant. They stir up, compel, and drive
their victim to licentious, and lascivious behavior. Even those who
have found faith in Christ, and still battle with their thoughts, and
actions, need to fast, and pray, to discern if their " *house* " needs
to be cleansed of wrongful occupants which entered their life prior
to salvation (study carefully 1st Thessalonians 5:23 & 2nd Timothy
2:19 -22). Something a proper study of demonology and deliverance reveals is that once a wicked demonic spirit enters a person, it
must be " *..cast out.. *". The Greek word for this phrase " cast out "
εκβαλουσιν - transliterated - ekbalousen means: to violently throw,
or, force out! Or, walk the plank if you were a US Navy sailor on the
battleship USS Constitution.

We have studied this area because those who either accidentally,
or, purposefully, expose themselves to pornography, are very likely
to have had the moral hedges of protection from God knocked down.
And, demon powers may very well have entered into them. See the
order form for - The Symposium on God's Deliverance.

Immorality and whoredoms become epidemic when a nation
permits pornography to be propagated. It destroys God's view of life
in the minds and hearts of men and women. Then replaces it with dishonor and disrespect. It is a form of idolatry in which the procreative
nature of man and woman is worshiped, rather than God who created
it. It produces child molestation, sodomy [homosexuality], lesbian-
ism, and beastiality in the lives of those whose fathers, or mothers,
have broken down the hedges of their offspring. Daily the evidence
is mounting that all rape, and child molestations, are the result of a
man, or woman, feeding their minds and hearts with pornographic
literature, films, and/or DVDs. Though our current antiChrist judicial

authorities are siding favorably with these profanities by interpreting the First Amendment as legal protection for these abominations, parents can do something about this immoral scourge. We all, as fathers and mothers, need to heed God's warning in Proverbs 26: 2. That -

2)   ..so the curse causeless shall not come.

It is this author's position based upon many years of research that all the divorce, unfaithfulness, child abuse and molestations, domestic violence, satanic feminism, slaying of the innocent unborn children by abortion, homosexual sodomy, is in fact *the land becoming full of wickedness.* That God has already warned us of it in Leviticus 19:29. It is not by coincidence that God warns of His impending wrath, and judgment against any who offers his seed to Molech in Leviticus chapter twenty, and, the first five verses. It should motivate us who know this truth to do all we can to overthrow all pornographers in our nation. Since they are the cause of all this wickedness in our land. It must be stated also that the various women's " romance novels " are pornographic also. We should organize, and boycott, all stores that stock these immoral books in each of our cities across our nation, the United States of America. If we do, we will see what fatherhood in the United States of America should be. If we refuse to, our nation shall continue to be destroyed. We conclude this final segment on the wickedness of pornography by stating that the name *" adult "* entertainment is a misnomer. Because, as Matthew 19: 4-6 reveals, the activities of any man, or woman, effects the lives of their children, and others. This is also confirmed in Proverbs 6: 23-33; 1 Corinthians 6:15-20; and, Romans 14: 7. Romans 12: 21 tells us -

21)   Be not overcome with evil, but overcome [conquer] evil with good.

This meaning that, we who are the righteous children of God by faith in Jesus Christ our Lord, must eradicate all forms of pornography. Whether in immoral romance novels, Playboy, Penthouse, etc., magazines, or movie DVD forms. God expects obedience.

This author believes that, if each, and every believer in Biblical morality, and righteousness, in their specific area of residence, would demand from their law enforcement officials. And store managers, that this evil be removed, it most certainly would be. Also, as Proverbs 24:24 & 25 states,

God's good blessing would come upon them.

If we really desire to be good fathers and mothers, this must be a priority in our lives. To obey God by protecting the children under our authority. And, by removing all that which would defile our lives. Anything that destroys morality and virtue in our nation's cities.

Probably the two greatest forms of wickedness we have learned that pornography produces, is the profane physical molesting of young daughters by trusted adult men who have adopted Hugh Hefner's September 1953 profane Playboy philosophy. Fathers, uncles, or other men who abuse their authority over their daughter's lives. The profane militant feminist curse has been spawned because of the wounds and bitterness demon possessed men have perpetrated upon innocent and helpless young girls in America. And, around the world. Militant Islamic hatred for America is fomented due to our perversely tolerant attitudes toward pornography. It is forbidden in nations ruled by the Koran. Christians are hated for their tolerance of this wickedness - see Proverbs chapter 24 verse 24.

The second greatest evil, is the sexual assaults and molestation of altar boys by Roman Catholic priests, and others[please see book title reference on the next page*]. Those who fill their hearts, and minds, with pornography, begin to find themselves driven, and compelled to molest their children physically. Demonic spirits of inordinate lust, and perversion energize, and drive, those men or women, who have torn down the moral hedges of their lives. The sons or daughters who are victims of these atrocities, and abominations become destroyed emotionally by such profane acts by those adults who abuse their authority. Daughters and sons then grow up with evil memories of these kinds of physical assaults of sexual abuse find a seething hatred of men. And, since God created man to reflect His likeness, those daughters grow up to wrongfully think God is like their abusive fathers and priests who violate their lives. Many girls grow up with deep hurts they can never seem to get over because of a violated trust. Many in mental hospitals are there because of traumatic abusive experiences of sexual assaults early in their childhood. Fathers and mothers, grandfathers and grandmothers, are required by our Lord God - *Whose name is Holy* - to put a quick stop to the very source of the corrupting of our country's morals. His eyes are on us.

Let's work with our Lord God to put these insanities to an end. Putting pressure on Government officials, and removing them from holding Public office for inaction, must be the major tactic we use to correct these evils. This is our proving ground as to whether we truly love both God, and, our children.

Finally, for those who would contradict this Biblical admonition, we encourage a careful study of the Words of our Lord Jesus Christ found in the Gospel of Matthew chapter 5: 13. We find there that we are God's salt of the earth. And, that if we do not function as such, we will be viewed as -

> "...good for nothing, but to be cast out,
> and trodden under foot of men."

Recommended Reading

-The Original Intent of the First Amendment - According to the Founding Fathers - By: Michael E. Citriniti & Michael D. Juzwick

- Available by contacting the publisher @ Phone 206. 497. 8553 [Leave voice mail contact information].

* <u>Lead Us Not Into Temptation</u> *(Roman Catholic Priests and the Sexual Abuse of Children)* - By: Jason Berry, University of Illinois Press © 2000. Available from Amazon.com & Barnes & Noble. com.

PART 3

The Biblical History
of The Patriarchs

Light Eternal Publications, USA

- Biblical Light for America's Christian Families -

Mountlake Terrace, Washington 98043-2913

CHAPTER 9

The Fatherhood of Noah

5)   And God said that the wickedness of man was great in the earth, and that every imagination of the thoughts of his heart was only evil continually.

6)   And it repented the Lord that he had made man on the earth, and it grieved him at his heart.

7)   And the Lord said, I will destroy man whom I have created from the face of the earth: Both man, and beast, and the creeping thing, and all the fowls of the air; for it repents me that I have made them.

8)   But Noah found grace in the eyes of the Lord.

9)   These are the generations of Noah: Noah was a just man and perfect in his generations, and Noah walked with God. 10) And Noah Begat [fathered] three sons, Shem, Ham, and Japheth.

11)   The earth also was corrupt before God, and the earth was filled with violence.

12)   And God looked upon the earth, and behold, it was corrupt: for all flesh had corrupted his way upon the earth.

13)   And God said to Noah, the end of all flesh is come before me; for the earth is filled with violence through them; and, behold, I will destroy them with the earth.

14)   Make you an ark of gopher wood;...— Holy Bible book of Genesis 6:5-14

There was a man named Lamech, who fathered a son, and gave to his son the name " Noah ". Lamech, in Genesis 5:29, looked to his son as a boy who would grow up to bring *comfort* to his parents. For that is the meaning of the name - *Noah*. Lamech was a father, who along with all men in the earth, had a negative disposition towards the curse God instituted because of the sin of Adam and Eve. Rather than humbling themselves, and accepting God's conditions for a sinful mankind, they all rebelled, and turned themselves over to Satan, and his angels. Every man on the face of the earth turned to only wickedness continually. God was so grieved at his heart with the behavior of mankind, he was sorry he even created man. And decided to destroy every human being from off the face of the earth. *"..All in whose nostrils was the breath of life.."* would die (ref. Genesis 7:17-23) Total annihilation of every living creature was God's decision. Only those, who would enter Noah's ark, would survive. It is very unlikely that Lamech, Noah's father, knew the purpose God would have for his son. It is interesting, that it was only God, who spoke out against the evil of Noah's day. The guilt of man's sin against God in the Garden of Eden was still hounding mankind. The state it drove mankind to, was not a state of humility and repentance, but rather, of exceedingly great wickedness. To the point, that God had to destroy them all with the gigantic flood of waters worldwide. Only eight human beings, out of many multitudes [approx. 6 billion] lived through the flood of Noah's day. All others died in the watery grave. Yes, God does get fed up with sin, and man's refusal to live the kind of life God created him to live. A life that brings glory and honor to his Creator God.

The man named Noah was the only man God could find on the earth who would respond to His grace. Only Noah walked with God. Only Noah did all that the Lord God commanded him to do. For this reason, you and I exist today. For if Noah had not found grace in God's eyes, no human being would have lived through God's judgment against sin. We can all thank God, and His servant Noah, that we are alive today.

Noah was a special man. One who gave God the hope, that maybe, he would be trustworthy enough to allow God to start over in His plan for man. To fill the earth with people, and teach them to obey God's purpose. As was God's original intent. Maybe Noah, and his sons, could do what God desired. For this reason, God made an agreement with Noah, and his family.

THE NOAHIC COVENANT

Genesis 8:15;17-

15)   And God spoke unto Noah, saying,...

17)   Bring forth with you every living thing that is with you, of all flesh, both of fowl, and of cattle, and of every creeping thing that creeps upon the earth: that they may breed abundantly in the earth, and be fruitful, and multiply upon the earth.

Genesis 9:1,7- 8; 11 - 15(a) -

1) And God blessed Noah and his sons, and said unto them, be fruitful, and multiply, and *replenish* [Hebrew - מָלְא - translit. - *mallah* - fill up] the earth. 7) And you, be fruitful, and multiply; bring forth abundanty in the earth, and multiply therein.

8)   And God spake unto Noah, and to his sons with him, saying,

9)   And I, behold, I establish my covenant with you, and with your seed after you;

11)   And I will establish my covenant with you; Neither shall all flesh be cut off anymore by the waters of a flood; neither shall there any more be a flood to destroy all the earth,

12) And God said, this is the token of the covenant which I make between me and you and every living creature that is with you, for perpetual generations:

13) I do set my bow in the cloud, and it shall be for a token of a covenant between me and the earth.

14) And it shall come to pass, when I bring a cloud over the earth, that the [rain] bow shall be seen in the cloud:

15) And I will remember My covenant... [emphasis added]

It must have deeply grieved the heart of God to have to destroy everything He created. But God's pure justice forced Him to take such a drastic step in the course of man's evil activity in the earth. God did not like to be so destructive. He had created everything on the earth with divine perfection. It was only because of man's wickedness that His hand of judgment was forced. After the terrible flood, God covenanted with Noah, and his three sons, to never again destroy the entire earth with a flood of waters. 2nd Peter 3:1-18, reveals that God will, in the future, destroy the earth with fire. This will be preliminary to the setting up of the millenial kingdom of Lord Jesus Christ on this earth. This earth shall be ruled by Christ, and His Church for a thousand years (see Revelation 19 & 20:4).

It should be stated that - *God's rainbow* - is His creation. God designed its multifaceted colors and design. It is strange that certain antiChrist world forces, and one world organizers, are utilizing the rainbow as a symbol of a profane world peace. There are evil spiritual powers of political deception, moving throughout the earth doing the work of Satan to organize the whole world in a rebellion against God. Using the rainbow God created, as a symbol of peace, yet refusing to repent of the atrocities and abominations spoken of previously in this book. This is like the use of the *" Peace sign "* during the rebellious sixties. The sign that has an upside-down broken cross, with a circle around it, is a secret symbol of witchcraft. Satanists, during their masses, use a cross, *the symbol of Christianity*, and break the horizonal part down, then draw a circle around it. This declares in their initiation, that they choose to reject Jesus Christ for eternity, while they blaspheme His work on the cross! Most parents have no clue about certain occult images now being promoted in the world specifically targeted toward teenagers, and younger children. We must understand that the purest definition of the Holy Bible Word *peace* - [Hebrew - שָׁלוֹם - translit. *shah-lohm*] means: the cessation of being against God's established covenant. God's earthly covenant is found in obedience to His eternal ordinances of marriage and procreation. And, God renewed His eternal plan with the patriarchs Noah, and his three sons. The Satanic Planned Parenthood organizations of the United States, which are funded by our tax dollars, are diametrically opposed to God's procreative mandate for man on this earth. God, no where says, to start a holocaust against people born, or, unborn when " you " think there are too many. America's current lack of faith for God's provision for raising children. And the self - willed covetous hedonism fomenting obsessive pursuit of material possessions has created America's anti-child mentality. God's design is *"..bring forth abundantly in the earth.., .. and respect the covenant of the nurturing of offspring.* God's covenant with Noah and his sons, Shem, Ham, and Japheth was a repeat of God's original commands and purpose for Adam in Genesis 2:15. *" ..To care for, and protect.."* God's property in the earth. Abortion is an inspiration of Satan to destroy God's creation (See John 10:10). Before moving on, to Noah's sons, are a few new conditions in God's covenant with mankind after the flood. In Genesis 8:22, we see that *"..cold and heat,...summer and winter..."* were new atmospheric conditions after the destructions of the deluge. The water canopy, which existed above the earth in the atmosphere [see Genesis 1: 6-8 & 7:11-12] was destroyed. This produced radical climatic changes. Severe cold and heat. It should also be stated that all plant, animal, and human life was washed down into the crevices of the ground, which over thousands of years, produced fossil oil, and fuels, that we utilize to energize our industries. The internal combustion engine of automobiles, aircraft, ships, farm machinery, etc. all demand crude oil. Fossil fuels, are called fossil fuels, because they are derived from old decayed plant and animal substances from the time of Noah's day. It could very well be that as these fossil fuels dwindle, an economic collapse world-wide may be the situation, which produces in the world, the need for the Antichrist of Revelation 13. Verses 16-18 reveal, that it will be because of economic turmoil, that the last main political world leader will force all mankind to receive his economic mark system - 666.

Another new condition in the earth after the flood was, that man now was permitted to eat animal flesh. (Genesis 9:2-3) This was most likely because most trace minerals, which caused the pre-flood fruits of trees to be nutritious enough to sustain health, now had been washed into the ocean floors, and deep water basins of the planet. Also, the fact that it most likely took some time for trees to grow to the point of bearing fruit again to supply the need for food.

The last area we review is the area which many in our popular culture, and criminal justice systems, are seeming to find difficulty with these days. That of capital punishment. It is clear in God's Word to Noah in Genesis 9:5 & 6, that whoever takes the life of another human being, outside of the accidental killing of another human being. That man, or woman, is to be put to death for it. Who ever among mankind, who knows that someone has taken another's life, they are under obligation before God to see that that person is put to death. It is a perversion in our society that says the murderer is to be protected. When the " rights " of a criminal, are more carefully considered, than their victim's, it is a perversion of justice. There is something seriously defective in anyone who feels sorry for someone who viciously murders anyone. We finish this segment by saying that there shall be another repeat of the condition of mankind prior to the flood of Noah. We are told by Jesus Christ this will be so. Matthew 24:37-39 -

37)   But as the days of Noah were, so shall also the coming of the son of man be.
38)   For as in the days that were before the flood they were eating and drinking, marrying and giving in marriage, until the day that Noah entered into the ark,
39)   And knew not until the flood came, and took them all away; so shall also the coming of the Son of man be.

THE PATRIARCH SHEM

18)   And the sons of Noah, that went forth of the ark, were Shem, and Ham, and Japheth: and Ham is the father of Canaan.
19)   These are the three sons of Noah: and of them was the whole earth overspread. — Genesis 9:18-19 18

As we begin to study the lives of Noah's sons, we will see how accurate the Word of God's revelation is. We will see what a disservice, and travesty it has been, for the United States Public school system to deliberately remove this historical account, that God has provided in the Holy Bible. We will see that God's Word is the best, and most accurate, record of mankind's activity on the earth since the flood. We will also see, that it is in the plan of Satan to remove from the minds of each successive generation of man, the facts of God's activity in relation to man. Satan has, in fact, accomplished this plan in our American National system of Public education. To deny the Biblical account of history, is to steal from the minds of men the most important scholastic facts in the earth. Academic freedom is totally prohibited, and censored, by refusing to allow our sons, and daughters, to review the Genesis record in our tax supported Public schools. As fathers we are to ensure our children are not denied all the facts pertaining to life on the earth. To deny the information that God does visit with harsh judgment when men do wickedly, is a great atrocity, and an abomination. It is like a father who would send his child out into a busy street to be hit by a car, by taking advantage of his ignorance of the dangers of life. It is for reasons such as this that the Charles Darwin Theory of Evolution is deluding. It steals from the minds of the generations coming up in our nation. The corruptions we can see our children going to, are the result of an absence of the reverence, and fear of God. Yet, those who in our educational systems who espouse the Theory of Evolution are today endeavoring to change the textbooks our children learn from, to present this abominable lie, and heresy of evolution, in an even greater convincing falsehood. Their excuse for not being bolder in the past is that they did not want to offend those who believe the Genesis account. This great division between Biblical history, and Secular Humanist's history, began in the 1800's by men such as Charles Darwin, and his proponent Thomas Huxley. What these heretics did, was produce an alternative account of the origins of life, which would supplant the Genesis account in our nation's school systems. To accommodate the ungodly and unbelieving, who would be offended in having to have the truth of God's Word, the Bible, " forced down their throats." Yet, they now are forcing this bold-faced lie of evolution down the throats of all American young people. And, even encourage children of Bible honoring parents, to doubt, and ridicule their parent's faith in God's truth. We now take a quote from - The Human Body series, the volume on - The Cell. The quote includes a quote from Thomas Huxley, who had the audacity to call himself among those who were Christians.

The publication of Darwin's on the origin of species by means of natural selection in 1859 outraged orthodox scientists and church men, but Darwin left its defense to his close friend Thomas Huxley who declared at a famous Oxford debate in 1860 "Genesis is a lie, the whole framework of the book of life [the Holy Bible] falls to pieces, and the revelation of God to man, as we Christians know it, is a delusion and a Sham!" [8] [emphasis added]

This *"friend"* of Charles Darwin, was a perfect description of what the Lord Jesus Christ called *"..ravening wolves in sheep's clothing."* (see Mt. 7:15). He called himself a " Christian " yet denied the Holy Scripture, and called it a lie. This Thomas Huxley, who today rules the minds of our young children, by the fiat of our Public school systems was, by Biblical understanding, possessed and controlled by powerful satanic spirits. God gives us an apt description of this kind of man in 1st Timothy chapter 4: 1 & 2:

1)   Now the Spirit speaks expressly, that in the latter times some shall depart from the faith, giving heed to seducing spirits and doctrines of demons;
2)   Speaking lies in hypocrisy; [i.,e., saying they are believers, while declaring God's Word to be a lie] having their conscience seared with a hot iron; [emphasis added]

It is for these specific reasons that all fathers and mothers in our nation, must learn the Biblical records well, and continually speak of it in the ears of our children [study Deut. 6: 5-9]. Otherwise, the generations to come will become more, and more wicked because of the absence of accountability to their Creator God. This lie of the Theory of Evolution has, and will continue to produce in the minds of our public school children, the evil curse of *reprobation* (the

---

8   *The Human Body, The Cell* - Charles Robert Darwin - *The Origin of Species*, page 121; New York, NY 1985.

inability to discern right from wrong). It is only logical that if you teach a child that he evolved from a lower form of life, and not that God created him in the beginning; children raised in this manner will grow up to scoff at morality, and reject any concept of godliness. The numerous corruptions that have surfaced in the United States Federal Congress and Senate impeachment hearings of past President Bill Clinton, reveal a reprobate condition of enough government officials to verify that evolutionary lies will create havoc with preserving good and righteous government. The founders of America established the Federal law of impeachment to rid our government of profane and evil men. Election laws also were meant to police and punish evil - read Romans 13.

Genesis tells us God created us in His image and likeness. That premise presupposes that we are to reflect His character qualities such as holiness, righteousness, justice, mercy, kindness, etc. If we, according to those who espouse the falsehood of evolution, have come from lower animal forms, we can therefore act and behave like animals and beasts. With no reason to fear God's righteous judgment as revealed in Revelation 20:11-15.

We have dealt with these evolutionary lies because the Biblical Genesis account is the only accurate and complete revelation of why we today find fossils buried in sedimentary rock. The fact that all animal,plant, and human life forms were buried during the deluge explains, perfectly why fossils of animals are found there. And the immense pressures, exerted by the waters of the flood, which reached the height of over one hundred feet above the highest mountain on earth [see Genesis chapter 7 verse 20], would have the ability to instantly fossilize anything.

It has been a very cruel act to deny the historical account found in the Holy Bible. The Genesis account, is in fact, the best source of the history of mankind's life on earth. Let us all endeavor to keep it that way. We will all suffer, if we ignore, and deny these facts.

Now, we will look into the life of Noah's first - born son, Shem. We will elaborate on certain descendants of his family. None of the studies of Noah's sons are complete. We only cover a few in order to gain a basic knowledge of their fatherhood. As we today can understand. How it has some bearing on us today. And, it does!

THE SONS OF SHEM

21) Unto Shem also, the father of all the children of Eber, the brother of Japheth the elder, even to him were children born.

22) The children of Shem; Elam, and Asshur, and Arphaxad, and Lud, and Aram. 23) And the children of Aram; Uz, and Hul, and Gether, and Mash.

24) And Arphaxad begat Salah; and Salah begat Eber.

25) And unto Eber were born two sons: The name of one was Peleg; for in his days was the earth divided; and his brother's name was Joktan.

26) And Joktan begat Almodad, and Sheleph, and Hazar Maveth, and Jerah,

27) And Hadoram, and Uzal, and Diklah,

28) And Obal, and Abimael, and Sheba,

29) And Ophir, and Havilah, and Jobab: all these were the sons of Joktan.

30) And their dwelling was from Mesha, as you come to unto Sephar, a mount of the East.

31) These are the sons of Shem, after their families, after their tongues, in their lands, after their nations.

32) These are the families of the sons of Noah, after their generations, in their nations: and by these were the nations divided in the earth after the flood. — Genesis 10: 21-32

We can observe that Shem was responsible for fathering the Semetic peoples of mankind after the flood. After leaving the Ark, Shem headed south from Mount Ararat, which is today found in North East Turkey. We find that from the line of Shem, Eber his son, fathered Abraham, who fathered the Hebrew peoples. Some of Shem's sons and grandsons headed East (ref. Genesis 10:30), with their families, into the land areas today known as Iraq, Iran, Pakistan, Afghanistan, India, Burma, Thailand, Mongolia, Korea, Vietnam, China, Japan etc. Many Biblical scholars of anthropology believe the Americas, and American " Indians " originally migrated to this continent by way of the Aleutian Islands, and via the Bering Strait, during the many centuries Israel, and Western civilization nations developed. Apparently, these peoples relied upon their histories being passed from generation to generation by folk lore, and word of mouth, rather than written, or recorded history, as have the European peoples. These areas were overspread by the descendants of Shem. We find in Luke 3:36, that some called Shem, Sem, from which we derive " Semetic " peoples. From the line of Shem, though, came Abraham, the father of faith, which we will study in chapter ten. We say now that through the descendants of Shem God has spoken the most. Especially through Abraham's seed. The entire Old Testament is about God's activity, and work through Shem's great, great, great, etc. grandson Abraham. It is through the writings and speech of Moses, a grandson of Abraham, that the first five books [The Torah] of the Holy Bible came. Genesis 11:10-32 shows us the geneology of Abraham. Genesis 9:26 & 27 reveal to us that Noah prophesied that -*".. Japheth would dwell in the tents of Shem.. "* We can now see that this has come about by God providing His law through the children of Shem. This term -*".. tents.. "*, probably meaning spiritual housing, or protection. The protection of the knowledge of God's Word. The law of Judah has historically been a pattern for the seed of Japheth, or, the Gentile peoples. This is factual in that British common law, became the basis of American Federal

Law. Also, referred to by Christian Americans as the Judeo-Christian basis of ethics and law.

In Genesis 10:23, we see that a descendant of Shem, named Uz, is referred to as having had an entire land area called the land of Uz in the book of Job 1:1. Some say the book of Job may have been written even before the book of Genesis. This also shows that the Patriarch Job, also was a God-honoring man, who came from the line of Shem. And God worked in his life, and spoke, and yet speaks through him also. Those who take time to learn God's Word benefit.

We now conclude this segment on the fatherhood of Shem by stating that evidence shows us that God chose the line of Shem, specifically through Job, and Abraham, to be His oracle in the earth. God revealed His plan, and purpose, through the progeny of Noah's son Shem. For this reason, Noah's prophecy of Shem states, *" Blessed be the Lord God of Shem.."* - Genesis 9: 26.

THE PATRIARCH HAM

In our reflection on the life of Noah's second - born son, Ham, we find some serious problems in his fatherhood, and their evil effects on this world to this day. First, in our investigation of Ham, and his offspring, we look to God's Word in Genesis 9: 20 - 27.

20)   And Noah began to be a husbandman, and he planted a vineyard:

21)   And he drank of the wine, and was drunken; and he was uncovered within his tent.

22)   And Ham, the father of Canaan, saw the nakedness of his father, and told his two brethren without [outside].

23)   And Shem and Japheth took a garment, and laid it on both their shoulders, and went backward, and covered the nakedness of their father; and their faces

were turned away, and they saw not their father's nakedness.

24) And Noah awoke from his wine, and knew what his younger son had done to him.

25) And he said, Cursed be Canaan; A servant of servants shall he be to his brethren.

26) And he said, Blessed be the Lord God of Shem; And Canaan shall be his servant.

27) And God shall enlarge Japheth, and he shall dwell in the tents of Shem; And Canaan shall be his servant,..

[The Antiquitous Prophecies of Noah]

Webster defines *gossip* as: a person who indulges in idle talk, and chatter, about the private affairs of others. This specific sin of Ham was met with a severe prophetic pronouncement by Noah. We know now, that to drink fermented beverage to excess is wrong from Holy Scripture. Ephesians 5:18 (a) shows us that to drink wine in excess, and to the point of drunkenness, is sin. But Noah did not have this Scriptural light. Ham's activity of spreading private information greatly displeased his father. So much so, that Noah cursed the progeny of Canaan, his grandson. This started the principle of Exodus 20:5 in the world. With Noah as father of the New World. The sin of Ham was to flow from generation to generation. And, as we study further, we shall see that this took place. The curse of forced servitude was what Noah spoke from his mouth upon the son of Ham, Canaan. We are all servants in the world, but, to willingly serve is much easier than to be forced to serve. The power of the tongue is demonstrated here in this prophecy of Noah. This prophecy came about just as Noah spoke. We will talk more about this use of the tongue in chapter thirteen. Noah's negative curse against Canaan is hard to understand. The only things God cursed in the Garden of Eden was Satan, and the serpent he used, and the ground. The curse of Noah was against the progeny of a man made in God's image (ref. James 3: 8-10). We will see in the progeny of Ham's son, that this curse opened the doors to very much evil. And, Satanic activity.

It must have been devastating to Canaan to know his grandfather cursed him. This may have caused the seed of Ham to be given over to the wickedness it was (see Deuteronomy 7:1-5). But this slanderous disrespect for Noah, by his son Ham, did not need to be verbalized as shown by the maturity of Ham's two brothers Shem and Japheth (Genesis 9:23). Punishment for offenses in the early days after the flood were quite dramatic. As we saw previously, in the sons of Shem's judgment of Nimrod, who led a rebellion against God at the Tower of Babel, and in ancient Babylon [Masonic origins - Genesis 11: 1-9].

We will now look at some of Ham's descendants, and then elaborate on some of their activities after the deluge. Genesis 10: 1; 6-20.

1) Now these are the generations of the sons of Noah, Shem, Ham, and Japheth: and unto them were sons born after the flood.

6) And the sons of Ham: Cush, and Mizraim, and Phut, and Canaan.

7) And the sons of Cush; Seba, and Havilah, and Sabtah, and Raamah, and Sabtechah: and the sons of Raamah, Sheba and Dedan.

8) And Cush begat Nimrod: he began to be a mighty one in the earth,

9) He was a mighty hunter before the Lord: wherefore it is said, even as Nimrod the mighty hunter before the Lord.

10) And the beginning of his kingdom was Babel, and Erech and Accad, and Calneh, in the land of Shinar

11) Out of that land went forth Asshur, and builded Nineveh, and the city Rehoboth, and Calah,

12) And Resen between Nineveh and Calah: the same is a great city.

13) And Mizraim fathered Ludim, and Anamim, and Lehabim, and Naphtuhim,

14) and Pathrusim, and Casluhim, out of whom came Philistim, and Caphtorim.

15) And Canaan fathered Sidon his first born, and Heth,

16) And the Jebusite and the Amorite, and the Girgasite,

17) And the Hivite, and the Arkite, and the Sinite,

18) And the Arvadite, and the Zemarite, and the Hamathite: and afterward were the families of the Canaanites spread abroad.

19) And the border of the Canaanites was from Sidon, as you come to Gerar, Unto Gaza: as you go to Sodom and Gomorrah, and Admah, and Zeboim, even to Lasha.

20) These are the sons of Ham, after their families, after their tongues, in their countries and in their nations.

The first progeny of Ham we will look at is Canaan. This is a very interesting son of Ham in that the land of Canaan became God's promised land to the children of Abraham. We must keep in mind, through the study of the sons of Ham, that Noah cursed Canaan. This cursing literally turned the people of Ham, or Hamites, away from God. As you study these people you find all false gods. Polytheism originated with these peoples. Much immorality and iniquity developed among the Canaanites. Satan, and his demonic powers, literally took over the descendants of Canaan. So much so, that God ordered their lives destroyed by the Israelites under Moses, and Joshua. See Deuteronomy 7:1-5 -

1) When the Lord your God shall bring you into the land whither you go to possess it, and has cast out many nations before you, the Hittites, and the Girgashites, and the Amorites, and the Canaanites,

and the Perizzites, and the Hivites, and the Jebusites, seven nations greater and mightier than you;

2) And when the Lord your God shall deliver them before you; you shall smite them, and utterly destroy them, you shall make no covenant with them, nor show mercy to them:

3) Neither shall you make marriages with them: your daughter you shall not give to his son, nor his daughter shall you take unto your son.

4) For they will turn away your son from following me, that they may serve other gods: so will the anger of the Lord be kindled against you, and destroy you suddenly.

5) But thus shall you deal with them; you shall destroy their altars, and *break down their images*, and cut down their groves [asherah poles], and burn their graven images with fire.

We see here that God hated the life styles of these wicked Canaanites. Some historians say that immorality was so rampant in the land of Canaan the animals, and young children, were filled with venereal diseases. Beastiality and child molestation were part of their culture like we see today in the United States of America.

It is to be noticed, that God told Abraham to go to the land of Canaan. And, that He would give that specific land area of the earth to Abraham, and his seed, for an inheritance forever. (See Genesis 17: 8). The overthrow, and destruction of the Canaanites, took place under Joshua's command (refer to the book of Joshua).

God knew that the Canaanites would refuse to learn God's way from the Israelites. But rather, would become a vexation to them. We see this in Numbers 33: 50 - 56 -

50) And the Lord spake unto Moses in the plains of Moab by Jordan near Jericho, saying,

51) Speak to the children of Israel, and say to them, when you are passed over Jordan into the land of Canaan;

52) Then you shall drive out all the inhabitants of the land from before you, and destroy all their pictures, and destroy all their molten images, and demolish all their high places:

53) And you shall dispossess the inhab itants of the land, and dwell therein: for I have given you the land to possess it.

54) And you shall divide the land by lot for an inheritance among your families: and the more you shall give the more inheritance, and to the fewer you shall give the less inheritance. Every man's inheritance shall be in the place where his lot falls; according to the tribes of your fathers you shall inherit.

55) But if you will not drive out the inhabitants of the land from before you, then it will come to pass, that those which you let remain of them shall be pricks in your eyes, and thorns in your sides, and shall vex you in the land where in you dwell.

56) Moreover it shall come to pass, that I shall do to you, as I thought to do to them.

We can see that terrible conditions developed in the children of Ham here in this section of God's Word. But much more evil transpired than this though. Earlier than this time in the history of Ham's descendants, we see that God had to wipe out two entire cities called Sodom and Gomorrah. From which the word: sodomy, originates. Homosexual profanities, child molesting, and gay lifestyles, were the culture of these corrupted cities of the descendants of Canaan. God sent two angels to destroy the cities, and deliver Lot, and his two daughters. The immoral confusion of Sodom, probably inspired Lot's daughters to have intimate relations with their father, and therefore brought forth Moab. Who's children (the Moabites) caused much trouble for the nation of Israel (ref. Genesis 18:16-33; 19:1-38).

The final progeny of Canaan we review are those peoples that occupied historically, what today is still known as the Gaza strip, the Philistines. Today we know them as Palestinians. The most radical of which are the P.L.0. [Palestinian Liberation Organization]. There are two well known accounts of these people in Judges 16:1-31, and 1st Samuel, chapters four through thirty-one. They have always been the enemies of Israel. And, when Israel sinned against God, the Philistines were sovereignly used to correct Israel. Psalm 83:1-12 shows that their hatred for God, and Israel, has been perpetual. And, that hatred will not be content unless Israel no longer exists as a nation.   The next son of Ham is Cush. The Word of God tells us that Cush fathered Nimrod. Who organized open rebellion against God, in building the Tower of Babel, and then the wicked City of Babylon. We have already discussed the evil perpetrated by Nimrod, and his mother Semiramis, in chapters two and eight. Cush is the father of Egyptian origins, and Ethiopian origins. Some time in the propagation of the seed of Cush these people's skin turned black. The word niger, or negro, which originated in Latin, means: black. Some have said that Nimrod was a black man. It is at this point of the progeny of Ham we must say that the Cushites, or Hamites, continued to move into the African continent. The Persian (Shem), Greek, and Roman empires (Japheth) all entered into this continent of Africa to take slaves of the black race. The European nations also purchased criminal blacks as slaves out of the African nations. This taking of black Cushites, or Hamites, as slaves was in fulfillment of the prophetic utterance of Noah in Genesis 9:25-27. In the which, Noah declared three times that,

"..Canaan would be the servant of servants to his brethren..."

The words of Noah were carried out even as he said. As citizens of the United States of America, we all know that our nation in its founding also used the African black man as slaves. It was by the administration of Abraham Lincoln, who was a Christian president, that our bloody Civil War released the blacks from slavery through the Emancipation Proclamation. The Southern slave owners all used the curse of Noah on Canaan, as the Bible text which allowed for slavery. It was a political move in our nation by Abraham Lincoln to break this curse of Canaan by New Testament Bible principles. This shows us a distinct Christian influence in the development of our nation. A *"..setting of the captives free.."* if you will (see Isaiah 61: 1).

The next descendant of Ham we will speak of is Asshur. Asshur we are told in Gen. 10:11, went out of the land of Shinar, and built the city of Ninevah. The idolatrous, and profane Nimrod, also had certain influences in the building of this wicked city through Asshur (see Gen.10: 10-11). The book of the prophet Jonah tells us that Ninevah was a cruel and wicked city. Historians say they would skin alive their captives, and stack them like cordwood. Jonah the prophet hated them so bad he did not want to obey the Lord to command them to repent. He had to take a ride in a smelly whale's belly to think about it a while. It is interesting though that Ninevah repented at Jonah's preaching. They even made their horses and animals put on sackcloth, and ashes, in repentance. Finally, we speak of Raamah who fathered Sheba and Dedan. Sheba (also Saba) fathered the people from which the Queen of Sheba came (ref. 1st Kings 10:1-13). The people of this land area are said, in Ezekiel 38:13, to be going to be involved in the verbal questioning of the people in Gog and Magog, i.,e., Soviet Russia's Military forces coming down to attempt a take over of the nation of Israel in the Middle East of the last days. Another Bible reference of a Sheba and Dedan, are the children of Jokshan, who was one of the sons of Abraham, through Keturah, one of Abraham's wives after Sarah died. At any rate, Sheba and Dedan are those peoples to the South, and East of Israel.

THE PATRIARCH JAPHETH

Noah's third-born son was Japheth. The name Japheth means: " enlargement ". As we proceed, we will see that Japheth was the father of some special people. Genesis 9:27 shows us some insight into this youngest son of Noah's future.

> 27) And God shall enlarge Japheth, and he shall dwell in
> the tents of Shem; and Canaan shall be his servant.

In Noah's prophecy about Japheth we see three aspects. First is the fact that God would enlarge him. There are two ways to take this enlargement. That the enlargement was in relation to the actual physical stature of his progeny, or that the actual number of his progeny would be enlarged. Or, both. Historically speaking, both the physical stature, and the number were the case. Secondly, the prophecy states that Japheth, or his progeny, would *"..dwell in the tents of Shem.."* We covered this somewhat in our discussion of Shem. The fact that through Shem came the Word of God in the Judaic, and Christian ethic. That the sons of Japheth embraced the laws of God which came through Israel, specifically Judah. We see this relationship, even to this day, in the association between Israel, the United States, and European peoples. Yet, at this point in history, there are anti-God, anti-Christ forces, at work in the European nations, and the United States of America, to destroy the basis of law, and morality, the Holy Scripture provided for Japheth's seed. Should we say, the tents of Shem are wearing out? And getting holes in them! This wearing out of the tents of Shem could be prelude to what kind of condition the world system will be in at the rise of Satan's Anti-Christ. That the Anti-Christ is described as *"..a man of lawlessness and wickedness."* (read 2nd Thessalonians 2: 3-12). Israel, as God's channel, did provide a "covering" for Japheth's progeny. And, there has been a special brotherly relationship between the children of Shem, and the children of Japheth. It seems also, that God through the direction of the movement of true Christianity, has respected this special relationship in reaching out so much to the seed of Japheth, or, the Gentile race, with the Gospel of Christ Jesus our Lord & Saviour (ref. book of Acts 15:3-18).

The last aspect of this Noahic prophecy about Japheth, is that *"..Canaan shall be his servant.."* also. Historically this transpired. The Greek and Roman peoples, who were the seed of Japheth, took slaves from the African continent. Also, the European nations, and the early American nations took the seed of Canaan [Ham's seed] into slavery in fulfillment of Noah's prophecy about Japheth.

We now conclude this segment on Japheth by citing the direction in which Japheth, Noah's son, went after the flood. The plot of the movement of this progeny. Genesis 10:1-5 says. -

1) Now these are the generations of the sons of Noah, Shem, Ham, Japheth: and unto them were sons born after the flood.

2) The sons of Japheth; Gomer and Magog and Madai and Javan, and Tubul, and Meshech, and Tiras. 3) And the sons of Gomer; Ashkenaz, and Riphath and Togarmah.

4) And the Sons of Javan; Elisahah, and Tarshish, Kittim, and Dodanim (Rodanim)

5) By these were the isles of the Gentiles divided in their lands; everyone after his tongue, after their families, in their nations.

As we said before, Noah's Ark rested on Mount Ararat. Which is located today in the North Eastern area of modern Turkey. Throughout history there have been reports of a large ship like structure in the Ararat Mountain area . Presently, the Soviet Union [Russia] has forced the Turkish government to stop any exploration of Ararat by saying that those who say they are explorers, are really spies, attempting to get information on Soviet activity in the area. Chances are that Noah's Ark still rests on Ararat. It would also be quite a blow to their previously held atheistic Communism to actually find the Biblical Noah's Ark. Satan would seek to obstruct its discovery.

We say at this time that the sons of Japheth were, and are known, as the Gentile race of mankind. The progeny of Japheth are the white, or Caucasian race of people. There is still a geographical area called the Caucasus Mountains. Which lies between the Black, and Caspian seas, Northeast of Turkey. This is one of the directions the sons of Japheth took after the flood. It is highly probable that " Gomer " and " Magog " headed North, and West, after leaving Noah. Biblically speaking, the Gog and Magog of Ezekiel 38:1-23 & 39:1-12, are in fact the sons of Japheth. Which headed directly North. Or, into the North parts (see Ezekiel 39:2). The " ..Chief prince.." of Meshech and Tubal, is the evil spiritual principality which rules under Satan in that land area. Meshech being in modern translation " Moscow ". Tubal was the father of the people of Tubalsk. Which occupied the Russian area of mankind. Today, we know this area as the Soviet Union, or Russia. Prophetically speaking, these peoples are said to be going to form a confederation with Iran (ancient Persia), Ethiopia, Libya, Gomer (Germany) and Togarmah (modern Turkey) "..of the North quarters.." The confederation will be to attempt to destroy the nation of Israel, and control the Middle East. It is significant today, that these nations, at this time, rule by proxy for the Soviet Union [Russia]. And receive their military arms from them. God's Word declares that they will be destroyed when they move in an attempt to destroy Israel. Ezekiel 38:21 speaks of *"..mountains.."* Which in

Holy Scripture usually refers to governments of the world. God will call to other Gentile governments to defend the tiny struggling nation of Israel for Him. And, as Ezekiel 38:22 says, He also shall join in, to help Israel survive. The other direction the sons of Japheth took was a Westward course. Togarmah, probably being the son which occupied the ancient land area of Turkey. Ashkenaz, the son of Gomer, is known to historians as the progenitor, or father, of the Germanic tribes. The sons of Javan; Elishah, Tarshish, Kittim, and Dodanim (Rodanim) most likely fathered the Greek, Roman, Spanish, French, Anglo, Saxon, Danish, and Norsman peoples. Since Genesis 10:5 speaks of *"..The Isles (or islands) of the Gentiles.."* And these peoples occupy the geography of these areas of modern European nations. Especially the British isles are known as island nations. Some Bible scholars lean toward Ezekiel 38:13 as speaking of these European nations as being *"..the merchants of Tarshish.." "with all the young lions thereof..."* Which will verbally protest the move of Russia, and its confederacy of Arab nations, from their evil thought to move to overthrow Israel of the last days. *".. All the young lions thereof..."* being the nations of the United States of America, and Canada. Which broke away from these "..Isles of the Gentiles.." England, France, and Spain. And, are also "..merchants.." and pirates of the sea. These nations and Isles sailed the seven seas.

We close this segment on the progeny of Japheth, by referring to the prophecy of Simeon in Acts 15:13-20. Which shows us that God purposed to send the Gospel of Jesus Christ through the Gentile European nations after the religious leaders of the nation of Israel rejected Christ, and forced the Romans to crucify Him.

13) And after they had held their peace, James answered, saying, men and brethren hearken to me:

14) Simeon has declared how God at the first did visit the Gentiles, to take out of them a people for His name. [The Church]

15) And to this agree the words of the prophets, as it is written,

16) After this [after he is finished taking out a people for his name-the Church] I will return, and will build again the tabernacle of David, [the nation of Israel] which is fallen down. And I will build again the ruins thereof, and I will set it up:

17) That the residue of men might seek after the Lord, and all the Gentiles, upon whom My name is called, saith the Lord, who does these things.

18) Known to God are all His works from the beginning of the world.

19) Wherefore my sentence is, that we trouble not them, which from among the Gentiles are turned to God.

20) But that we write to them that they abstain from pollutions of idols, and from fornication, and from things strangled, and from blood. [emphasis added]

This early Council of the Church Age knew that God would begin to build His Church with the Gentile peoples. Another aspect of the sons of Japheth dwelling in the tents of Shem. What is exciting about this passage of God's Word, is that after God is about finished calling out of the world, the people who shall make up His Bride the Church, He will move to rebuild the tabernacle of David. Which has fallen down. Speaking of a rebuilding of the nation of Israel in the closing days of the Church Age. This rebuilding began after World War 2, when Britain made the Balfour Declaration, establishing Palestine as a homeland for the Jew. In 1948, God moved in the hearts of the Gentile nations, to allow Israel to become a nation in the land area God promised to Abraham. Promised to be an everlasting possession (Gen. 17:8). This act signaled that God is preparing to wrap up the age of grace [Church Age] by the rebuilding of Israel. Romans 11: 13 - 36 also shows that the blindness of the Jews, has opened the door to salvation for the Gentile world. Luke 21:24 states that, "..Jerusalem, [Israel's capitol], shall be trodden down of the Gentiles *"..until.."* the *"..times of the Gentiles be fulfilled.."*. The entire spreading of the Gospel of Christ, has been given over to Japheth's progeny, the Gentiles. We conclude this segment with the assurance that, as we see the nation of Israel become more and more independent of Gentile nations, we can conclude that the Lord God is very soon going to remove the true Church of Jesus Christ from the earth. And, begin His awesome judgments, contained in the book of Revelation, against those who have rejected Christ's love and forgiveness. And also, begin to work to bring Israel to repentance (see Matthew 23: 37-39).

In conclusion, careful study of the prophetic book of the Prophet Daniel, would be useful in gaining the prophetic history of all nations of the world. The book of Daniel, chapters 1-3, and 7 reveal the history of the world from the Lord God's perspective. The great image dreamed about by the wicked King of ancient Babylon Nebuchadnezzar, who was the progeny of the wicked and idolatrous Nimrod and Semiramis [who brought forth the profane offspring Tammuz - see Ezekiel 8:14 - 18], was the history of world powers, and governments, down through the history of mankind. The idolatry ending up with an eventual ten nations, ruled by three religious entities [Judaism, apostate Catholicism, and Islam].With the Beast heading up the final idolatry according to Revelation chapter 13. Daniel chapter 2: 44 - 45 speaks of the advent of our Lord Jesus Christ, and His mighty work to build His Church during the times of the world governments developing, and coming into existence. The phrase, *" ..without hands.."* found in verse 45, manifests that God Himself will be creating His eternal kingdom during the contrary building up of secular, and antiChrist world powers. The *"..stone.."* *cut out of the mountain,* will strike the contrary self worshiping governments at their very roots. Christ is the supernatural *Rock, or, Cornerstone* spoken of by the prophet. Though Japheth has hearkened to the Biblical council of Shem, he has also embraced the idolatries of

Ham's descendants through the Masonic Orders previously discussed in this book. American Masons and Shriners refer to Syria [ancient Assur] in their initiations. And, on their symbols. They have spread Nimrod and his mother Semiramis' religion even into the United States Capitol. And, into each and every State of the Union to date. " Mystery Babylon..." is no longer a mystery as " ..the finger of God.." His eternal Word & Holy Spirit is the Spirit of all Revelation of things hidden - read the Gospels of Luke chapter 8 verses 16 & 17; Mark 4 verse 22; and, Matthew 10 verses 26 - 28.

The Lord Jesus Christ shall be totally victorious over all His foes. All kingdoms, and interests, shall one day fully submit to His lordship (see 1st Corinthians 15: 24 - 28). We are wise to do it now.

The audio message - Noah's Ark, by: Kelly Seagraves, may be requested from Light Eternal Publications by calling 206. 497. 8553. The audio title provides great facts and details of the Genesis account of God's destruction of the world by water. It is available in CD formats. Or, by reading the book - The Genesis Flood - By: John C. Whitcomb & Henry M. Morris - Baker Book House

CHAPTER 10

Father Abraham

In beginning our review of the Patriarch Abraham, we refer to the fact that he was from the progeny of Shem, first born son of Noah. This fact is found in Genesis 11:10-31. At this point we reveal that Abraham's name, prior to receiving God's promise that He would give to him and his wife Sarai a son, was " Abram ". The name Abram means: " father is exalted ". The entire working of God in the life of Abraham was in relation to the bringing about of an increased awareness of the duties and responsibility of being a father. The purpose also for which this book has been written.

The intimate word: " Abba " found in Romans 8:15 came from the name Abram. It means: father or daddy. We find out that immediately after the flood of Noah's day, Satan, went to work in the life of the man named Nimrod, the father of the Masonic orders, and a great grandson of Ham through Cush. Genesis 10:8-10 & 11:1-9, shows us the attempt and success of Satan to use Nimrod to organize the world " politically " into a one-world system, instead of, and against God's will. Genesis 11:10-32 shows to us that God is not at all pleased with the earth being organized into a world, or global, satanic system headed up by one man. But rather, He is interested in the obedience of each man, as individual fathers. Fatherhood, we will see, is God's major area of interest in man as we proceed in our study of the patriarch, and father Abraham. Obedience to the principles God has laid down in the covenant agreement in the Garden of Eden (Genesis 2:15) is the desire of the heart of our heavenly Father God. Since then, the Lord God has given us many more insights as to His will in Holy Scripture. But, most men, that are fathers, are too busy being fascinated with Satan's alternatives to the Words and ways of their Creator. Marriage and family failures are the result!

God began His work in Abraham's life through his father Terah. By putting it in his heart to move out of Ur of the Chaldees to Haran (see Gen. 11: 27 - 32). God called Abraham to leave his family, which resided in Haran, and begin to allow God's Holy Spirit to lead and direct his life (Gen. 12: 1 - 9). It was in God's plan to use the life of Abram to speak to the nations about His will for the earth. The workings of God are very distinct and manifest that God desires to be intimately involved in every father's life. The covenant God was to make with Abraham was for the express purpose of manifesting God's care for fathers and their families. Genesis 12: 3 states -

3)   And I will bless them that bless you, and curse them that curse you: And in you (and those you father] shall all families of the earth be blessed.

The majority of God's Word has to do with the fatherhood of Abraham. Even the New Testament began with the life of the Lord Jesus Christ, and His twelve disciples, who all were offspring and children of Abraham. Most of the writers of the Old and New Testament books came from the family line of Father Abraham. All the prophets of the Old Testament came down from the fatherhood of Abraham. The majority of God's Words to man have proceeded from the seed of Abraham. So the next time you encounter a Jew, or Israeli, or, Christian, take God's advice in Genesis 12:3, and bless them! History shows us that these people have been the object of Satan's vicious attacks. Satan hates the Jew and Christians mainly due to their connections with God's Word. For this reason we should love and bless them. It is most likely because of this people being the oracle, or mouthpiece of God Himself, that they have gone through so much trouble on the earth.

Yes, Father Abraham has lived up to his name by being the father of a great multitude of great people. But that is not the only reason God chose to work through this man's life. No, Abraham was not a perfect man. He made a big mistake by following his wife Sarah's suggestion to have a child with Hagar, because of her lack of patience, and faith in God's Word to them both. We are told in Holy Scripture that there is no man without sin, or that is righteous (see Romans 3:10). But he almost always followed God's directions when He spoke to him. But this was not the only reason God chose Father Abraham. There is a very special reason God chose to use the Patriarch Abraham, and his children. The reason was what we will now explore. It will grant us greater understanding of parenthood.

THE FATHER OF FAITH

1) And it came to pass after these things, that God did test Abraham, and said to him, Abraham: And he said, behold, here I am.

2) And He said, take now your son, your only son Isaac, whom you love, and you get into the land of Moriah; and offer him there for a burnt offering upon one of the mountains which I will tell you of.

3) And Abraham rose up early in the morning, and saddled his ass, and took two of his young men with him, and Isaac his son, and clave the wood for the burnt offering, and rose up, and went to the place of which God had told him.

4) Then on the third day Abraham lifted up his eyes, and saw the place afar off.

5) And Abraham said to his young men, you abide here with the ass; and I and the lad will go yonder and worship, and come again to you.

6) And Abraham took the wood of the burnt offering, and laid it upon Isaac his son; and he took the fire in his hand, and a knife; and they went both of them together.

7) And Isaac spake to Abraham his father, and said; my father: And he said, here I am, my son. And he said, behold the fire and the wood: But where is the lamb for a burnt offering?

8) And Abraham said, my son, God will provide Himself a lamb for a burnt offering: So they went both of them together.

9) And they came to the place which God had told him of; and Abraham built an altar there, and laid the wood in order, and bound Isaac his son, and laid him on the altar upon the wood.

10) And Abraham stretched forth his hand, and took the knife to slay his son.

11) And the angel of the Lord called unto him out of heaven, and said, Abraham, Abraham: And he said, here am I.

12) And he said, lay not your hand upon the lad, neither do anything to him: For now I know that you fear God, seeing you have not withheld your son, your only son from me.

13) And Abraham lifted up his eyes, and looked, and behold behind him a ram caught in a thicket by his horns: And Abraham went and took the ram, and offered him up for a burnt offering in the stead [place] of his son.

14) And Abraham called the name of that place Jehovah-Jireh (meaning: God will provide for me): As it is said to this day, In the mount of the Lord it shall be seen. — Genesis 22:1-14

It was in the obedience to God to take Isaac, his beloved son, and sacrifice his life as a burnt offering, that the plan, and purpose of God the Father was demonstrated and glorified. The faithful obedience of Abraham honored God. Though this test of Father Abraham was long before the coming of the Lord Jesus Christ, this obedience to God provided for man a demonstration of what God was planning to do to rescue mankind from sin, and, death, and hell.

This account of the great test of Abraham is prophetic in nature. It was to give to man a preview of what God would allow to happen to His own Son for the sake, and redemption of mankind. There are a number of similarities between Abraham's test of faith, and God the Father's actual provision of salvation for man.

First of all we cite the similarity of Isaac being supernaturally conceived by Sarah in her old age (refer Gen. 21:1-4). Sarah was long past the ability to bear a child, yet God intervened. Jesus Christ was supernaturally conceived of the Holy Spirit, in a virgin named Mary. (refer Matthew chapter 1:18-25).

The next likeness of Abraham to God the Father was in that he was required to take Isaac, his only son whom he loved greatly, and sacrifice his life as a burnt offering to honor and glorify God. John 3:16 tells us that God the Father gave up His only begotten Son, to be sacrificed to manifest God's love. And, provide salvation and redemption for the whole world of mankind.

Another similar, and possibly prophetic likeness to the actual work that God the Father did through Christ, was in the place in which Abraham was shown by God to offer up his son Isaac. That place was in the land of Moriah. Specifically, on Mount Moriah. Mount Moriah, we learn from 2nd Chronicles 3:1, was on the outskirts of the City of Jerusalem. The crucifixion of Jesus Christ, God's Son, also took place just outside Jerusalem. It could have very well been the exact same place God commanded Abraham to offer up Isaac. Genesis 22:6 says that Abraham laid the wood for the burnt offering upon Isaac to carry, much like the cross of wood, the Lord Jesus Christ would carry to the place of His death by Crucifixion as God the Father's sacrifice.

The final similarity is seen in the question of Isaac. It said to his father that everything is available for the burnt offering but the lamb. "..Where is the lamb we must sacrifice?.." Abraham replied with one of the greatest statements of faith ever spoken by a man. " ..My son, God will provide Himself a Lamb for a burnt offering! " There are two ways that statement can be understood. One, God will provide (for) Himself a lamb. Or, God Himself will be the Lamb to be sacrificed to pay for sin. Both are true. God the Father, gave His Son Jesus Christ, to be the payment for man's sin. And, Jesus Christ, gave Himself as a sin offering to God His Father to pay for man's sin. (ref. Revelation chapter 6: 15-17 & 13:8 & 17:14). Abraham was willing to sacrifice Isaac his son. And, Isaac was willing to allow himself to be sacrificed by his father in obedience to God.

It is in Abraham's obedience and faith in God that he manifested God in the earthly setting. It is for this reason God has declared Abraham the father of faith. And, as we learn from Hebrews 11:6, no man can please God without faith. Galatians 3:6-14 shows us that God so honored the faith and obedience of Abraham, that even all those who put their faith in Jesus Christ, become the children, or seed of Abraham by this same faith.

Abraham was so obedient to God's voice, even to the point of not withholding his own beloved son Isaac, God has used Abraham, and his children, to speak to the world of the kind of life that pleases God the Father. The life of faith in Him, and His Word, the Holy Bible.

Not all the progeny of Abraham have chosen to keep this covenant.

THE ABRAHAMIC COVENANT

Abraham, because of his faith in, and obedience to, God the Father, received some tremendous promises from the Creator. These promises were not for Abraham himself alone, but covered every child Abraham, and his sons fathered. These blessings of fatherhood are despised and hated by God's enemies. It is downplayed by Satan and his angels. This is so because God's enemy's main objective is to make humanity think God does not keep His promises. That God really does not care about man, and has forsaken him. It is in Satan's plan to put thoughts such as these into the minds of men, women, and their children in order to exalt himself as god. To ridicule and criticize God's love, and promote himself, is the objective of our enemy. These evil devices can be defeated with the truth.

We say this because it is in the Word of God, the Holy Scriptures, that we can see God's great love and care. God's faithfulness to His Word is made manifest in the account of the Abrahamic Covenant. God has made His promises good. God has provided for man's salvation, deliverance, and healing through the seed of Abraham. Luke 3:23-38 manifests, that through the seed of Abraham, Jesus Christ the Lord, every family on earth can be blessed (Gen. 12:3). God has provided for us all whether Jewish or Gentile.

The Abrahamic Covenant has two aspects to it. The covenant promises, and stipulations, are both unconditional, and conditional. Unconditional meaning, *that no matter what is done by the man to whom the covenant is entered into with, the promises will remain in force.* Conditional meaning, *that if the conditions set forth in the covenant are not met, death shall be the result.* Death meaning always: *the separation one experiences from the person with whom the promises have been agreed to with.* We say, at the beginning of our review of the Abrahamic Covenant, that the majority of it was unconditional. Because of Abraham's faith in God, the promises and blessings of God came to him. The beginning of these promises and blessings appear in Genesis 12:1-3.

1)   Now the Lord had said to Abram, get you out of your country, and from your kindred, and from your father's house, unto a land that I will show you:

2)   And I will make of you a great nation, and I will bless you, and make your name great; and you shall be a blessing.

3)   And I will bless them that bless you, and curse them that curse you: and in you shall all families of the earth be blessed. [emphasis added]

This first statement of God to Abram was unconditional. It was entirely up to God to carry out this covenant with Abram.

The second aspect of the Abrahamic Covenant is the aspect that holds the offspring of Abraham responsible to keep the covenant with God in order to stay in fellowship with the same God of their father Abram. We see in John 8:31-59, that the Jews of the time of Jesus Christ, claimed to be children of Abraham. But they hated and despised Jesus Christ. This caused them, though they were the physical seed of Abraham, to be spiritually children of Satan. This war is prophesied of in Genesis 15:1-18.

1)   After these things the word of the Lord came to Abraham in a vision, saying, fear not, Abraham: I am your shield, and your exceeding great reward.

2)   And Abram said, Lord God, what will you give me, seeing I go childless, and the steward of my house is this Eliezer of Damascus?

3)   And Abram said, behold, to me you have given no seed: and, lo, one born in my house is mine heir.

4)   And, behold, the Word of the Lord came to him, saying, This shall not be your heir.

5)   And He brought him forth abroad, and said, look now toward heaven, and tell the stars, if you be able to number them: And He said to him, so shall your seed be.

6) And he believed in the Lord; and He counted it to him for righteousness.

7) And He said to him, I am the Lord that brought you out of Ur of the Chaldees, to give you this land to inherit it.

8) And he said, Lord God, whereby shall I know that I shall inherit it?

9) And He said to him, take Me a heifer of three years old, and a she goat of three years old, and a ram of three years old, and a turtle dove, and a young pigeon.

10) And he took to him all these, and divided them in the midst, and laid each piece one against another: But the birds divided he not.

11) And when the fowls came down upon the carcases, Abram drove them away.

12) And when the sun was going down, a deep sleep fell upon Abram: And, lo, a horror of great darkness fell upon him.

13) And he said to Abram, know of a surety that your seed[offspring] shall be a stranger in a land that is not theirs, and shall serve them; and they shall afflict them four hundred years;

14) And also that nation, whom they shall serve, will I judge: and afterward shall they come out with great substance.

15) And you shall go to your fathers in peace; you shall be buried in a good old age,

16) But in the fourth generation they shall come here again: for the iniquity of the Amorities is not yet full.

17) And it came to pass, that, when the sun went down, and it was dark, behold a smoking furnace, and a burning lamp [Hebrew = a flaming torch] that passed between those pieces.

18)   In the same day the Lord made a covenant with Abraham, saying, to your seed [children] have I given this land, from the river of Egypt to the great river, the river Euphrates:

This prophecy of God to Abraham, was to reassure him, that he would be a father of a great multitude of people (Genesis 15:4 & 5). Verse six shows that Abram believed in God, and God credited his account with righteousness. But it was in the offering of the sacrifices, verses 7-18, that the conditional covenant is manifested. The dividing of the sacrifices (vs.10) probably is prophetic of Israel and Judah warring and dividing into two separate kingdoms (see 2nd Samuel 2:1-10). Verse eleven of Genesis 15 is probably prophetic of Satan, and his demonic powers, attacking the seed of Abraham. Fowls in Holy Scripture, often refer spiritually to Satan's angels (refer to Mark 4:4;15). It is symbolic of Abraham to "..drive away. " the spiritual enemies of his children's lives. We should do this also by intercessory prayer for our children. Verse 13-16 prophesy of the children of Israel's bondage in Egypt, and the Exodus of the nation of Israel under the leadership of Moses. It is prophetic of God's judgment and destruction of the wickedness of the Amorites by the army of Israel as led by Joshua as they entered God's promised land (vs.16-18).

Verse seventeen shows us the eternal faithfulness of God to keep covenant with Abraham's children.

The next to last aspect of God's covenant with Abraham is found in Genesis 17:1-21.

1)   And when Abraham was ninety years old and nine, the Lord appeared to Abraham, and said to him, I am the Almighty God; walk before me, and you be perfect.

2)   And I will make my covenant between me and you, and I will multiply you exceedingly.

3) And Abraham fell on his face: And God talked with him, saying,

4) As for me, behold, My covenant is with you, and you shall be a father of many nations.

5) Neither shall your name any more be called Abram, but your name shall be Abraham; for [because] a father of many nations have I made you.

6) And I will make you exceeding fruitful, and I will make nations of you, and kings shall come out of you.

7) And I will establish my covenant between Me, and you, and your seed after you, in their generations for an everlasting covenant, to be a God to you, and to your seed after you.

8) And I will give to you, and to your seed after you, the land wherein you are a stranger, all the land of Canaan, for an everlasting possession; and I will be their God.

9) And God said to Abraham, you shall keep my covenant. Therefore, you, and your seed after you in their generations.

10) This is my covenant, which you shall keep, between me and your seed after you; every man child among you shall be circumcised.

11) And you shall circumcise the flesh of your foreskin; and it shall be a token of the covenant betwixt Me and you.

12) And he that is eight days old shall be circumcised among you, every man child in your generations, he that is born in the house, or bought with money of any stranger, which is not of your seed.

13) He that is born in your house, and he that is bought with your money, must needs be circumcised: And

My covenant shall be in your flesh for an everlasting covenant.

14)   And the uncircumcised man child whose flesh of his foreskin is not circumcised, that soul shall be cut off from his people; he has broken my covenant.

15)   And God said to Abraham, as for Sarai your wife, you shall not call her name Sarai, but Sarah shall her name be.

16)   And I will bless her, and give you a son also of her: Yea, I will bless her, and she shall be a mother of nations; kings of people shall be of her.

17)   Then Abraham fell upon his face, and laughed, and said in his heart, shall a child be born to him that is a hundred years old? And shall Sarah, that is ninety years old, bear?

18)   And Abraham said to God, O that Ishmael might live before you!

19)   And God said, Sarah your wife shall bear you a son indeed; and you shall call his name Isaac: And I will establish my covenant with him for an everlasting covenant, and with his seed after him.

20)   As for Ishmael, I have heard you: behold, I have blessed him, and will make him fruitful, and will multiply him exceedingly; twelve princes shall he beget (father), and I will make him a great nation.

21)   But My covenant will I establish with Isaac, which Sarah shall bear unto you. At this set time in the next year.

In this section of God's Word we see a repeat of God's covenant promises to Abraham and his offspring. We see also His promise to give the entire land of Canaan to Abraham's progeny through Isaac. Something the P.L.O. [Palestinian Liberation organization] refuses to acknowledge. We see in Genesis 26:1-35, that the perpetual hatred began against Isaac, and his son Jacob [Israel] long ago.

We also see the beginning of the ordinance of the sign of God's covenant with Abraham's progeny. Circumcision of the male children's fountain (see Proverb 5:18) or instrument of generation. It is significant that the source of the seed, or semen of Abraham and his children, was that place where God placed the sign of the covenant. The male source of the seed of physical human life in the procreative marriage covenant. It is now known by medical science, that at the eighth day of the male child's infancy, the blood-clotting elements of the male child's blood rises quickly to the level to clot, and stop the bleeding. That is why God told Abraham to wait until the eighth day before circumcising the man child's foreskin (Genesis 17:12). The omniscient Creator is Lord of all matters.

This sign of the covenant of Abraham was probably designed by God to be a reminder to honor Him in marriage, and the subsequent procreation of children. Something the men in our nation need to start doing, and faithfully teach their sons to do. Honor God in marriage, and the fathering of their own sons and daughters!

In verses 15-19, God again reaffirms His purpose, and desire for women. As Eve, in Genesis 3:20, was to be " ..the mother of all living.." So also, Sarah was to function in this her place of God's ordination. America's mothers need to focus on this reality.

Verses 18, and 20, show that God respected Abraham's son to Hagar, Ishmael. And, that he would become a father of a great nation. Probably the nation of present day Saudi Arabia. Yet, God's covenant was to be established in Isaac. The child born to Abraham's wife Sarah when she was way past menopause. Saudi Arabia still refers to its leaders as " Princes " (ref. Genesis 17:20).

Before we go to the next segment, we should cover the account of God's destruction of the cities of Sodom and Gomorrah. Genesis 18:1-33 and 19:1-38. Genesis 18:17-19 show us that God trusted Abraham to teach, train, and command his children to obey God's

Word. God, foreseeing the corruption the people of Sodom and Gomorrah would propagate, decided to destroy them all except Lot, and his two daughters. We see in this account that Sodomy, or in today's vernacular, homosexual, or gay life-styles, are exceedingly wicked in God's sight. Abraham, in Genesis 18:22-32, interceded for Sodom and Gomorrah, but as we see in the remainder of the account, God could only spare three souls out of the multitudes of those cities from destruction. Even Lot, and his two daughters in Genesis 19:30-38, sinned by fornication and incest, and brought forth the children of Moab and Ammon who hated Israel, and Israel's God.

12 Sons - 12 Patriarchs -12 Tribes

Before we continue in looking into the twelve sons of Jacob (Israel) and grandsons of Abraham, we must affirm the fact that God, in His covenant with Abraham, and Abraham's children, manifested His love and care for man. The covenant was designed by God to insure that all men, whether children of Abraham, or of any father in the entire earth, would keep their covenant with God (please meditate in Deuteronomy 4:1-10). It is a very displeasing thing in the eyes of God, for any father of children, to not only refuse to acknowledge God in his life, but to keep and hinder his children from knowing, and loving God. This book has been written for the express purpose of causing fathers in our nation to return to God. The true and living God. And devote themselves to His Word. So that they may have the capacity to teach their youngsters of the Lord God, and work at building a good relationship with Him. This is good for us as fathers. It is what God requires of us. This is needful in our children's lives. This is pleasing in God's sight.

Before we study the twelve sons born to Abraham's grandson Jacob, we would be thoughtless to neglect to review the love and care Abraham had in the choice of the woman who would be his son's - " help meet " (ref. Gen. 2: 20). The woman who would help Isaac.

Due to the great length of the Biblical passage of Genesis chapter twenty four, we will only quote here the first ten verses. It is encouraged that the chapter be read in its entirety. Genesis 24:1-10-

1) And Abraham was old, and well stricken in age: And the Lord had blessed Abraham in all things.

2) And Abraham said to his eldest servant of his house, that ruled over all that he had, put, I pray you, your hand under my thigh:

3) And I will make you swear by the Lord, the God of heaven, and the God of the earth, that you shall not take a wife unto my son of the daughters of the Canaanites, among whom I dwell:

4) But you shall go unto my country, and to my kindred, and take a wife unto my son Isaac.

5) And the servant said to him, peradventure the woman will not be willing to follow me to this land: must I needs bring your son again to the land from whence you came?

6) And Abraham said to him, beware you that you bring not my son thither again.

7) The Lord God of heaven, which took me from my father's house, and from the land of my kindred, and which spake to me, and that sware to me, saying, to your seed will I give this land; he shall send his angel before you, and you shall take a wife unto my son from there.

8) And if the woman will not be willing to follow you, then you shall be clear from this my oath: Only bring not my son there again.

9) And the servant put his hand under the thigh of Abraham his master, and sware to him concerning the matter.

10)   And the servant took ten camels of the camels of his master, and departed; for all the goods of his master were in his hand: And he arose, and went to Mesopotamia, to the city of Nahor.

This twenty fourth chapter of the book of Genesis is a most beautiful picture of servanthood in all the Word of God. It is also a most excellent picture of fatherhood. And, the love and care of a man for his son. All the fathers in the United States of America can learn simple yet excellent truths of God by meditating in this portion of the Bible. The message of fatherhood, servanthood, daughtership, motherhood and in-law relationships, are perfectly displayed in this great chapter. The contents of this chapter are desperately needed in our land today. It is our refusal to follow the simple truths found here that many of the destructions our nation is suffering from are coming upon us.

The first Biblical truth we wish to explain is the strange request of Abraham, " The Father of Faith ", of his trusted servant. It is found in Genesis 24:2(c) & 9(a). These are two, of the three verses in God's Word, which refer to " ...putting a hand under a father's thigh ". It was an extremely solemn act that Father Abraham initiated. It was for the purpose of providing spiritual protection of a father's offspring. It was a solemn oath, that we, today in the United States of America, could benefit from observing in the face of so much adultery, promiscuity, premarital relations, and abortion of the unborn.

The actual act represented here was the placing of one's hand, a trusted man, upon, or, near the procreative members of a father's body. It actually meant that the father was putting a sacred trust in another man's hand to protect his seed (offspring). It was truly a sacred and honorable transfer of authority from the father to an especially honored and trusted man. Genesis 47:29 speaks of Jacob, Isaac's son's commitment to the covenant promises of God, in relation to God giving to Abraham's seed the land of Canaan for an everlasting possession. It was a reminder and reaffirmation of the

185

covenant relationship between God, Abraham, Isaac, Jacob (Israel) and all their sons forever. A very special thing. With all the " sowing of wild oats" in our land, we definitely could be lifted higher morally by observing some ordinance similar to this benevolent and sacred transaction of godly men. Who honor each other and the Father God in heaven. Another important factor to be recognized is the problem Jacob's brother Esau had. We speak this in relation to the premature premarital relations many young people in America are indulging in. Holy Scripture calls it - fornication. It is a sin that carries serious and damaging effects on the individual who is deceived into practicing it (please read 1stThessalonians 4:1-9). It is basically allowing your fleshly desires to take priority over maintaining a God-honoring disposition in any area of your life.

Genesis 25:29-34, shows to us that Esau valued more his carnal needs, than the precious birthright of being first born. His belly of flesh was more important, than his honoring of God in his life. This disposition is rampant among the teenagers in the United States. The sad thing about it is that the parents allow and encourage such wickedness in their children's lives. Having done so themselves.

The Los Angeles Unified School District, under the direction of the School Board Directors, will attempt to provide pregnancy prevention, and abortion services, without parental consent. Because of the despising of God's marriage covenant principles. As said in the segment on " the wickedness of pornography " in chapter eight, the demonic activity in the life of these young people's fathers and mothers, has opened up their children to evil spirits of lust, promiscuity and evil concupiscence. Their parents "... sowed the wind..." of immorality, and their children will ".. reap the whirlwind.. " of destroyed morals. And the destruction of unborn children by abortion.

Esau, Jacob's brother, from the first of his adult life despised his father's, and mother's, moral and spiritual principles by marrying women of Canaan (Genesis chapter 26: 34-35). We can see in Hebrews 12:16-17, that the profane act of Esau is equated with the act of fornication. This shows that God views both as acts of dishonor toward His person. We, as fathers, are to work at building hedges in, and around our sons, to protect them from the moral destruction of their lives by immorality. It is a form of insanity to laugh at these evils.

In Genesis 28: 1-5, we observe that Isaac commanded his son Jacob to go to the land of Rebekah's brother; Laban the Syrian. Jacob was strictly prohibited to take a wife of the daughters of the land of Canaan. Today, in America, some would consider that principle of Abraham's children bigoted, or, discriminatory. But God knew that the daughters of the Canaanites would spiritually corrupt Abraham's seed (ref. 1st Kings 11:1-10). Canaanites were idolaters.

Jacob went to his Uncle Laban, the Syrian, and sojourned with him for twenty long years. In the account we see that Jacob fell in love with Laban's youngest daughter Rachel. So Laban contracted with Jacob to work for seven years to receive Rachel to wife. Jacob served Laban for the agreed upon time, and on the night of his reward of Rachel, after seven long years, Laban deceived Jacob by sending Leah, his first born daughter, into the tent. Can you imagine Jacob's disposition when he woke up the next morning? Not to mention Leah's feeling of rejection. So Laban made Jacob serve another seven years for Rachel.

We should also point out that both Leah and Rachel were given a handmaid by Laban. Leah's handmaid was Zilpah. Rachel's was Bilhah. The Genesis account shows which woman bore which of the twelve sons of Jacob (Israel). But Leah constantly strived to gain more attention from Jacob, knowing he loved Rachel more. All Jacob's sons were named by Leah and Rachel. The names they gave to each son reflected their striving for Jacob's attention and love. Not the best situation in which to raise children.

During the duration of Jacob's sojourn with Laban the Syrian, there were agreements made. Both Jacob, who through his mother Rebekah's counsel, had been encouraged in the art of deception. And Laban the Syrian, worked at out-smarting each other. Needless to say it got out of hand eventually. And forced Jacob to return to Mamre, in the land of Canaan (Gen. 35:27). Jacob's treachery in the accumulation of cattle gained him much prosperity. It is interesting the method Jacob used to increase the birth of " *spotted* " cattle (see Gen. 30:25-43). This treachery between Laban the Syrian, and Jacob the father of the nation of Israel, could very well be the reason for the strife, and enmity, that exists between these two nations today in the Middle East. The events of Genesis 31:1-42, caused a division between the two, and the events have not been forgotten by their children throughout the ages. Genesis 32:24-32 shows to us the event of God's wrestling with Jacob throughout the night. Which could be prophetic of God's wrestling with the nation of Israel throughout the dark history of mankind. Jacob would not release God's messenger unless he blessed him. Showing the desire of Israel [the nation] to have God to bless them. It is at this point in history that the nation of Israel was born. The nature of the Jewish people, and the people of Israel, is manifested. God changed Jacob's name from Jacob to " Israel " which means: " A prince with God and man ". Jacob now became Israel. And Israel, Leah and Zilpah, Rachel and Bilhah, Reuben, Simeon, Levi, Judah, Dan, Naphtali, Gad, Asher, Issachar, Zebulun, Joseph, Benjamin, and Israel's daughter Dinah, would band together as the seed of Abraham. A family that God would use to speak to the entire world. A people out of which kings and prophets would arise. A people out of who's seed the Messiah, Jesus the Christ, would come - read the Gospel of Matthew chapter 1 verses 1 - 25. A people who would be considered God's oracle, or mouthpiece, in the earth (ref. Romans 3: 1 & 2). A people who would be the object of God's enemy, Satan's, unrelenting attacks from the inside, and outside, of their nation in perpetuity - see - Ezekiel chapter 35: 5.

We continue to observe the beginning of the nation of Israel by seeing the strife stirred up among Jacob's sons by his favoring of Joseph; the son of his old age (ref. Genesis 37:1-36). Joseph's life, at this point, became symbolic of the Lord Jesus Christ. And the treatment he received at the hands of the leaders of Judaism in post-captivity Israel. The envy of all Jacob's sons of Joseph, drove them to sell their brother into the Ishmaelite's hands to be sold as a common slave in Egypt. As you meditate on the verses of Genesis 37:23-36; 39:1-23, and throughout the remainder of the Genesis account, you see Joseph's relationship with God gave him much wisdom and skill in life. Probably the greatest aspect of the character of Jacob's son Joseph's life, was his ability to forgive totally his brothers, for their terrible rejection, and cruelty. This reflected the likeness of Jesus Christ, in that salvation from physical famine was God's provision through Joseph, and salvation from eternal famine, and destitution was God's provision through the Lord Jesus Christ.

We learn from the book of Exodus, through the book of Deuteronomy, that God reorganized the children of Israel, which dwelt in the land of Goshen in Egypt, under the leadership of Moses. A son of the tribe of Levi, who was rescued from the Egyptian Pharoah's infanticide of all Israelite male children. God's judgment on Egypt, began as the result of its practice of killing male babies to control the population of Israel (see Exodus 1:8-22; 2:1-10). For Israel developed into a mighty nation in the land of Egypt. Some believe that the numbers of the Israelites were in the millions at the time of the Exodus out of Egypt. There were so many, that the Pharoah of Egypt became fearful of them. The promise of God to make Abraham's seed".. as many as the stars of heaven and as the grains of sand on the seashore.." had begun (ref. Hebrews 11:12). It should be said at this point, that the ten plagues God brought upon Egypt under Moses' command, all related to each of the many false gods the Egyptians feared. God said in effect, " you like frogs? " etc. God mocked their fears and superstitions.

After the Exodus from Egypt, God had Moses organize Israel into each respective tribe. Each of the twelve sons of Israel were representative of each tribe. In the book of Numbers, chapter one, we see that God, under Moses' leadership, turned this mighty nation of

Israel into "a mighty army of warriors " to bring His judgment upon the Canaanites for their great wickedness against Him. In the process, God would fulfill His covenant promise to give to Abraham's children the promised land of Canaan. God worked for forty years to get the corruptions of Egypt out of the children of Israel, before they could be fit to execute His judgment against the occupants of the land of Canaan. Much like the process God uses today to prepare His children to speak to those who are without Jesus Christ.

The book of Joshua shows us the mantle of authority and leadership, was transferred from Moses to Joshua. Deuteronomy 34:9 shows us that ".. by the laying on of Moses' hands .." the anointing was transferred over. The book of Joshua gives us a bird's eye view of the warfare of Israel against their enemies. Also, the allotment of land for each of the twelve tribes of Israel.

The next book we come to in our observance of Abraham's children is the book of Judges. It is in this book we see the desire of the nation of Israel to only have God as their king. But, as stated previously, Satan and his people, continually attacked the nation, causing the need for a National leader to direct the affairs of state. It should be learned though that God spoke through the Judges of Israel to remind Israelites of His will. This is definitely something that the US Supreme Court judges of our nation could learn from.

Gideon, one of the judges of Israel, manifested a great amount of understanding of God's will for Israel. He, as the other judges, first dealt with the sins of God's people. Then, went after their enemies. Each judge had to demonstrate a number of important qualities. First, a great love for God. Second, a great love for their nation. Third, a great hatred for sin. And fourth, an ability to overwhelm, and overthrow, the nation's enemies by God's direction. Needless to say the United States of America could use some leaders with these credentials. We now close this segment of the twelve tribes of Israel by saying that God has chosen to speak through His people Israel. The Holy Bible is all about God, and His workings in the life of Abraham, and his children. God's will is manifested to every man. Every father in Holy Scripture. The Old Testament is unique, in that it shows us both the good, and, the evil. And God's dispositions toward both. If it were not for God's working through the seed of Abraham, we all would be without any ability to know, and do God's will. We all would be totally given over to our enemies. We all should be very thankful to God and Abraham, the father of faith, for providing for us the contents of the Holy Bible to direct our activities today.

We would be remiss to explain that the nation of Israel sinned greatly against God in history past. Their sin was met by God's judgment. The prophets of the Old Testament, who were children of Abraham, have given us prophecies that say Israel would be scattered throughout the entire earth for their sins, and be hated by the nations they were scattered to (ref. Ezekiel 36). Ezekiel 37:1-28 tells us that God at the end of the world as we know it, would regather the children of Israel into their land. In 1948, after World War 2, God, through the Balfour declaration of Great Britain, began that process. To this day God has been bringing the children of Israel back into their land as promised.

God, through the prophet Zechariah, has told us that the state the nation of Israel is in today, is prelude to the end of the world as we know it (ref. Zechariah 12:1-3). Israel today is ".. a cup of trembling.. " because of her enemies. Acts 15:13-18 shows us that after the Church is complete, and every soul has had opportunity to receive God's eternal salvation through His Son Jesus Christ, the Great Tribulation, or time of ".. Jacob's trouble .." shall begin. God will, through the deception of Satan's man Antichrist, give Israel their desired " political messiah ". Whoever this false political messiah is, he will be well received by the nation of Israel (see Daniel 9:20-27; 11:21-45). For three and a half years, he will deceive the nation of Israel, into believing he is their messiah. Then, when he claims to be God, (Revelation 13 & 2nd Thessalonians 2: 3 -12), Israel will reject him. And many will die in Israel when the AntiChrist turns all his power against them. It will only be by the power of Jesus Christ our Lord, and Michael, God's chief warfare angel, that the seed of Abraham will survive (please read John 5:39-47; Matthew 23:37-39; Daniel 12:1-13; Revelation 7:1-8; 19: 6-21; 20:1-3).

The great " seven year " tribulation [also known as the Prophet Daniel's " last week " of the Seventy Weeks of Daniel chapter 9: 24 - 27] is to accomplish two specific purposes. First, to bring God's judgment upon a wicked, God-hating, Christ-rejecting world. And, secondly, to bring the nation of Israel to repentance. When the re-gathered nation of Israel is driven to desperation by all the nations coming against them. And, then the hellish attacks the Antichrist will make upon them. They will then cry out to the Lord to deliver them. When it is revealed that our Lord Jesus Christ is their Deliverer, " a nation shall be born in a day..". They shall see the nail scars in His hands and feet. Then shall they know Jesus Christ is ".. the only wise God.." and " their " Saviour!

For additional insight into the twelve sons, and subsequent twelve tribes of Israel, a review of Genesis 48:1-33 would grant more under-standing to the reader. Which records the prophecies of Jacob [Israel] concerning each son. These prophecies are still coming to pass.

THE HISTORIC FAILURE OF ISRAEL & HER FUTURE JUDGMENT & GLORY

The Lord God Almighty has spoken specific things concerning the children of Abraham that must come to pass. He has attempted to make Israel His light to all nations of the earth. Israel has grievously sinned against God's purpose and calling for them. They have failed to live up to the grand purpose of the Lord of life.

But God will keep His eternal Word of righteousness to these people. As the Lord God has turned to the Gentiles with His offer of salvation, so will He also return to rebuild the nation of Israel which has fallen from His intended purpose and glory. Repentance is the call of God to all peoples, whether Jew, or, Gentile [see Romans chapter 1: 16]. The Church of Jesus Christ is now reaching out to the people of Israel, though they are too proud and stubborn in their religious beliefs, to be capable of seeing their utter need for salvation from the Lord [Greek - κυριω- Kurio] Jesus the Greek translation from the [Hebrew - יְהוֹשׁוּעַ Joshua - Hosea - meaning - the Lord God is our salvation]. Christ [Greek - χριστω -Kristo - God's anointed Mes siah].

We must be faithful to "..Pray for the peace of Jerusalem.." and seek to "..save the lost sheep of the House of Israel." As our Lord Jesus Christ has said, "..The Lord is not willing that any perish, but that all come to repentance.." Those lost in their religious pride need to be loved out of it if possible.

The work of God in the life of His servant Abraham shows us how faithful God is to those who are faithful to Him. The account of the Holy Bible is our access into that Testament to how the Lord God responds to faithful men, and fathers. America has been under very similar attacks as the nation of Old Testament Israel. We have much more revelation than the people of Israel did. For this we will be held more accountable than they were. Our judgment will be greater. United States policies have been so far favorable to regathered Israel of these last days. If we see that change, we will quickly see the same judgment God poured out on Israel, and Judah, for their sins.

As we continue into the next part of this book, we will be teaching specific commandments God has issued to every man who becomes a father in the earth. Since women and mothers are intended by God to cooperate together with the husbands they choose to marry, we teach that both genders of parents must learn about and obey these commands set forth by our Creator God. Our nation's current political correct anti - Bible philosophies of feminism and pornography have been destroying harmony and oneness of purpose between fathers and mothers. Our land has been overthrown in so many ways due to both the ignorance of these commands, and, our disobedience.

The Lord our Maker will bless our obedience. And, our families will be blessed as the Abrahamic covenant has promised. Even us in this our day. " God is no respecter of persons..".

PART 4

Spiritual Practical matters for Effective Parenting

Light Eternal Publications, USA

- Biblical Light for America's Christian Families -

Mountlake Terrace, Washington 98043-2913

CHAPTER 11

Fatherhood & Gahvad

Throughout the first ten chapters of this writing our focus has been to give an historical, developmental and prophetic account of fatherhood as it relates to the United States of America, and also Biblical accounts of this important, yet neglected subject. The very condition of our nation is directly connected to the success, or failure of men in this their place of responsibility, and God-given authority. Not all, but many women in our nation, and Churches today, have deep bitterness and resentment in their hearts. Because of men who have been ignorant of, or, in open rebellion to, God's eternal commands to those who become fathers. Hebrews 12: 2-17 instructs us to look to Jesus Christ who has authored and finished our faith. It also admonishes us to *"..look diligently lest any man [or woman] fail to receive the grace of God; lest any root of bitterness springing up trouble you, and thereby many be defiled.."* [emphasis added]

Our land has been a vicious war-zone of whoredoms and playboy mockery of God's holy standards of moral principle. In the aftermath there are wounded, defiled, damaged and bitter women, and, children. God says to not allow this to take place. If the fathers of this nation rebel, and refuse to respect God's commands. And, refuse to allow them to be passed down to their offspring, Satan will gain power over their sons and daughters. This is the *"..land becoming full of wickedness.."* we already covered in chapter 8 on the wickedness of pornography. For we must understand that the moral atmosphere of a nation is created by obedient fathers and mothers. This provides a spiritual covering of protection for our children. God, will one day, judge each, and every parent for their obedience, or, lack of obedience, in this critical area. The remaining eight chapters of this treatise will be devoted to the practical details, and outworking of the principles God has laid down concerning this most important subject of fatherhood. All United States calamities exist due to ignorance of God's eternal commands.

In order to provide the reader with an illustration. And, describe what our objective has been thus far. And, what we propose to do, we would use the illustration of the doctor and surgeon. Just as when an individual must acknowledge, that there is something seriously wrong with his physical health. And, must submit to a medical authority to give an examination, and prognosis of a serious problem with their physical health. So we, as the fathers in our nation, must submit to the authority of God's Scriptural revelation of fatherhood. Found in His Word, the Holy Bible. The serious problems and destructive elements that exist in our nation have been partially addressed. This should give us a basic description of the kinds of cancer which are destroying the spiritual health of the families within the United States. It will take each father's diligent efforts to first acknowledge the enemies of their families. And, then work to bring God's deliverance and healing to each family unit. The humility a patient has before his surgeon is what we as fathers must have before God. We must trust in the Word He gives to us. That has the power to restore health. If we apply it. The confidence we would place in our surgeon, is the kind of trust we must place in our Creator. Just as the surgeon comforts and assures his patient, that he has in fact identified the specific area in need of surgery. And, that the operation will be over in no time. Also, that his complete recovery is assured. So, God provides comfort. And assures the fathers in the United States, that if they trust, and submit to God's surgery they shall see God's hand of skill, compassion, and healing manifested in their homes. Malachi 4: 1- 4; specifically verse two, shows us that God desires to bring His healing to our families.

2) But to you that fear [reverence My name - the Lord Jesus Christ] shall the Sun of Righteousness arise with healing in His wings; and you shall go forth, and grow up as calves of the stall.

FATHERS AS SERVANTS

As we now consider the many practical aspects of being effective fathers, we start at the basic foundation God established in the Garden of Eden, and build from there. We explain that every creature God made, He designed basically as a servant. To serve in a specified capacity. The most powerful angelic beings, the arch-angels, were to function in their specified, and ordained place. Lucifer we studied in chapter six, had the most powerful place before God as a servant. His sin was, that he decided he should be served, rather than be a servant of God. It was that basic form of iniquity he defiled the Garden of Eden with (refer to Genesis chapter 3).

Probably the most beautiful expression of God, in the life of His Son Jesus Christ, was that of Philippians 2: 5-7 which declares:

5) Let this mind be in you, which was also in Christ Jesus: 6) Who, being in the form of God, thought it not robbery to be equal with God: 7) But made himself of no reputation, and took upon him the form of a servant, and was made in the likeness of men:

In other words, Jesus Christ, who was God manifested in the physical body of a man (please refer to 1st Timothy 3:16). Of the seed of Abraham, humbly gave to us a perfect example of being a servant. Even though He was God Himself! He claims to be our example.

In this chapter, Fatherhood and Gahvad, we will explain God's basic principle of servanthood. The basic principle originated in this Hebrew word transliterated - gahvad. This basic Bible concept, found in Genesis 2:15, is hated in our nation today. Especially in the areas where men and women must inter-relate. It has been the fountain-head of much pride and strive in the work place. This area is also an area which a gymnastics with semantics has taken place. Such as a change of the words servant or slave; to the word - employee. This has been done to take away the negative connotation associated with the designation servant, or slave. We will, in this chapter, speak of the Hebrew and Greek words associated with God's primary principle of servanthood. We state at the outset, that this principle of gahvad, is the most important and basic mentality and spiritual attitude God demands from us as fathers. For we are to be His examples in the earthly realm. The very first place young children are to see this principle demonstrated is in their parents. It is interesting that in John 13:1-17, and, Mark 10:35-45, even the very men God would use to spread the Gospel of the Lord Jesus Christ, first struggled with the self-pride of being greater than others. And, not being a servant. God's way in this area is diametrically opposite of Satan's world of pride, and self-promotion system. The struggle to be above, and over others, is even found among God's own people. If you find yourself entertaining ideas of how great you are, you may be having a fiery dart of Satan fired into your mind! We contrast that Satan's kingdom of darkness is inspired by him to strive to get into the place of *" power, or, authority "* so you can have others serve you. God's kingdom of light is that you are pleasing to Him as you see yourself as being used by Him to help and assist others. God's Word admonishes even pastors to watch their attitudes [please read 1st Peter 5: 2-3]. We will now review Mark 10: 42 - 45, to get into the Holy Spirit, as we enter this beautiful subject. Hated by the world, but, loved by God.

42)   But Jesus called them [His disciples] to him, and said to them, you know that they which are accounted to rule over the Gentiles exercise lordship over them; and their greater ones exercise authority upon them.

43) But so shall it not be among you: But whosoever will be great among you shall be your minister [servant].

44) And, whosoever of you will be the chiefest, shall be servant of all.

45) For even the Son of Man came not to be ministered to [served], but to minister [serve], and to give His life a ransom for many.

The entire life of the Lord Jesus Christ was a life that exhibited God's principle of *gahvad-servanthood*. Whether in laying His hands on the physically diseased, and thereby bringing the administration of God's healing to them. Or, laying down upon the cruel Roman cross, and having spikes driven into His physical body, Jesus Christ was God's ultimate servant for mankind. He continually spent *His* energy helping others. Serving the needs of others. He was, and is still, God's perfect example to men of the principle of gahvad in the New Testament. We must learn to follow His example.

The two Biblical words, which are the basic words for servant are, first, the New Testament word [Gk. δουλοσ] transliterated: doulos. This New Testament word means: to be a servant, or a slave. Usually, in the septuagint (LXX), which is the Old Testament translated into the Greek language, the word found for servant, or slave is translated from the [Hebrew - עָבַד] transliterated gah-vad. Wigram's Concordance and Gesenius' Hebrew- Chaldee Lexicon, page 887, lists this Hebrew word under # 5647 as *an infinitve verb*. This means that the Lord God originally established this principle to be practiced throughout the existence of mankind. An eternal Word to be honored, and obeyed, from generation to generation! Since our desire is to see the basic purpose of God for fathers, and men in general, we will concentrate on what exactly the original purpose was prior to Adam's fall in the Garden of Eden.

In Genesis 2:15, the actual Hebrew word translated " dress " contains God's purest explanation of servanthood. There are two specific job descriptions for fathers in this verse of God's Word. In this chapter we shall cover the first word - gah-vad. In chapter twelve we will explain the other - shah-mar. After the Lord God formed man out of the dust of the earth (See Genesis 2: 7). And, breathed into him His very life, He placed him into the Garden of Eden. God put man on the earth in the garden He created to perform two specific functions: Genesis 2:15 -

15) And the Lord God took the man, and put him into the garden of Eden *to dress it* and to keep it.

#1 command and function: "...to dress it..." [Heb. עָבַד] transliterated - gahvad. The Holy Spirit of God inspired this Word, gahvad, to be the first anointed principle for man to follow in his oversight of God's garden. In the Hebrew the meaning of this word Adam found God's direction for activity on the earth. He was also instructed to obey God by assisting his sons and daughters to learn these God-given principles [see Genesis 1:28]. The Hebrew word transliterated *" mah-lah "* in Genesis 1:28, means to fill up certain containers with specific substances. Jesus Christ re-affirmed this original purpose and direction of God in Matthew 5:6. Today, most ministers only communicate this passage of God's Word, as an historical record of past events. Instead of seeing it as God's eternal commands given to be obeyed throughout eternity. Gahvad is released into the earth by the obedience of each man who becomes an obedient father. The literal Hebrew word carries the following aspects of servanthood:

A). To worship God.
B). To be the King's minister.
C). To serve in a specific capacity. With authority, and responsibility given to carry out assigned duties.

D). To administer that which has been provided, to that which is needed, in care of another's goods and property.

This Hebrew word gahvad we see has tremendous meaning. We all, as fathers, must know and understand that God's basic will for men has never changed. God created the earth, and man for a specific, and beautiful purpose. It has never, and will never, change. It must be understood that Adam, before the fall, was inwelt by the Holy Spirit of God. All the characteristics, and manifestations of God's Spirit, operated in Adam's life. Eve, and Adam's sin, brought death to this purpose of God. But, praise be to God, Jesus Christ came to bring God's will back to man. By pouring out His blood to forgive the sin of man. Adam, the first earthly father, was created to manifest God's likeness on earth. This was, and is, the glory God gave to man. Adam could not perform this without the power of God's Spirit. Neither can we. Jesus Christ came to earth to manifest God's will to man. His death and resurrection has provided for us the ability to again receive the Holy Spirit of God to perform these functions. Christ was the second Adam (please meditate on John 20:21-23) and (Romans 5:10-21). Jesus Christ came to restore to man the very dignity and authority he lost by obeying Satan's lie, rather than God's commands. When we, by faith in the person and work of the Lord Jesus Christ, enter into sonship with the Father, we receive from God the Father the capacity and ability to be like Jesus Christ (ref. John 17:17-23 & Luke 3:16) and (John 4:10; 14; 23-24).

FATHERS AS WORSHIP LEADERS

John 4:23 & 24 shows us the first aspect of this word gahvad in that we are to worship God in the Spirit. And, as we allow His Word to enter our hearts, and minds, by meditation. The Holy Bible is God's source for learning the numerous ways He has ordained for us to worship Him. Satan, the Arch-angel charged by God to lead in worship originally, now opposes all efforts of mankind to read and study God's Word, the Holy Bible. Due to this reality, men must go to war. And, resist, all efforts that distract them from this source of the Lord God for spiritual guidance and instruction. By the way, the Greek word " amuse " has the prefix "a" which causes the word to mean: to not muse. Amusement is actually an antiChrist alternative for God's first command to study and learn His commands and orders from heaven. Meditation, and musing upon God's Word, is essential to educate your mind with God's commands for your life. To ignore God's Word, and submit your mind to worldly alternatives, will leave you incapable of carrying out your intended purpose.

FATHERS AS THE KING'S MINISTERS

The second aspect of gahvad is carried out in us as fathers as we fill our hearts and minds with God's Spirit (see Luke 11:15) and His Word. And then, we begin to start allowing it to flow from our lives, and mouths (see John 4:14 & Proverbs 10:21). To be the King's minister is His will. Every human being is designed to be a minister. If they do not minister God's things, they will end up ministering the Devil's things. Our Lord Christ said there is no middle ground.

FATHERS AS SERVANTS & RULERS

The third aspect of God's purpose for us fathers concerning gahvad is found in Matthew 28: 18-20. In verse 18, the Greek word which is translated " *power* " is the word transliterated - *exousia*. Which literally means - authority. What Jesus Christ says here is that as fathers and servants of Christ, we are to go in the authority, and in the name of Jesus Christ. Christ operates by proxy in our lives. As He would lead a man, woman, or child to Himself, we are to do it. As He would lay his hands on a sick individual, or a family member,

204

we are to do it in His name. As He would cast out a demonic spirit, or spirits, in a victim's life, we are to do so in His name. We are to, as gahvad directs, *" serve in a specific capacity, with authority and responsibility given to carry out assigned duties. "* This is substantiated also in 1st John 2: 5 & 6. Memorize, study, and meditate this passage.

* Recommended Reading: ***IMPROVING YOUR SERVE*** - by: Charles R. Swindoll [9]

5) But whoever [this includes parents] keeps [obeys] His Word, in him truly is the love of God perfected: Hereby we know [realize] that we are in Him.
6) He that says he abides in Him ought himself also walk, even as He walked. [1st John. 2: 5 & 6].

FATHERS AS CARETAKERS

Just about everyone in the United States has been dismissed from the presence of a family member or friend with the statement *" take care of yourself "*. Also, a sad aspect. And, indictment against us, is that our young children, or, as the sociologists call them " latch-key children ", are today being told by those who are commanded by God to care for their children, " take care of yourself ". The economic crisis [judgment] on our households, and satanic feminism, is creating this wickedness. The generation of youngsters growing up under this evil situation will grow up being, and feeling, stolen from. And rightly so. God holds both fathers, and mothers, responsible for the care and nurture of their children. We must give account of this stewardship to God in the day of judgment. It is in the caring and nurturing of fathers and mothers, that children come to know, and understand, that God cares for them. If this is denied in a young child's life, since it

9   Recommended Reading: *THE SERVANT WHO RULES & THE RULER WHO SERVES* - by: Ray C. Stedman

205

is through us children learn about God, they will see our neglect as God's disposition toward them. This can have the effect of turning them over to Satan, and his demon powers. It is in the caretaking of fathers and mothers, that children feel protected, and secure. Many emotional disturbances can plague children into their adulthood, because of a curse of neglect by their parents. We are commanded by God Himself to provide a covering of loving care over our offspring's lives. Severe problems in our children's marriages can be caused by a failure to adhere to God's commands in this important area. We should also understand that our children learn that God cares for them, when we do. Our sons, and daughters, learn from us how to care for their children. We are to care for their spirits. We are to care for their souls. And, we are to care for their physical bodies (refer to 1st Thessalonians 5:23). It is evident that nature tells us these are facts to be observed in the challenges of parenting.

In review, as we saw in chapter three on " Wheat and Tares " -

Tares become tares when nobody cares!

We close this segment with the exhortation: *" take care "* of your children fathers. It is God's eternal command!

FATHERS AS ADMINISTRATORS

The word gahvad has at its core this final aspect we review. The aspect of *administration*. Fatherhood demands the administration of all that is needed, in the care of another's goods, and property. In 1st Corinthians 12: 5 & 6, we see that the Holy Spirit gives us the capacity to carry this out.

5)   And there are differences of administrations, but the same Lord.

6) And there are diversities of operations, but it is the same God which works [energizes] all in all. [emphasis added]

This is energized in us by our sensitivity to the various needs that come up in our family. To carefully study 2nd Corinthians 1: 3 & 4, we may learn of various kinds of comfort that could be applied to the principle of being good parents. Ones who are attentive to those under their care. We are to allow God's blessings to flow through our lives to the different members in our family. We are to administer God's love to each member of our family. We are to administer God's healing as we see a need. We should bring God's salvation through Jesus Christ to each member. Refer to Hebrews 2: 3; Acts 16: 30 & 31. We are commanded in God's Word, and must be filled with the Holy Spirit of Gahvad.

Fathers are to administer God's kindness. We are to minister God'sknowledge, wisdom, and His Word to each loved one. We are to administer God's correction (Proverbs 19:18; 22:6 & 15; 23:13 & 14). Memorize these passages. We are to administer God's reproof, and His instruction in righteousness (2nd Timothy 3: 14-17). As God's servants we are to administrate our households for Him. It is in the actual administration of all God's provision, whether spiritual, psychological, or physical, that our children learn how to also be servants. And, to function in the Holy Spirit, as outlined in the concepts and principles of gahvad. Faithful fathers are proactive overseers in family life. Faithful help - meets, and mothers, must energize together in a cooperative teamwork husbandry following this primary principle of gahvad.

When fathers and mothers. Men and women. Husbands and wives, start obeying this primary purpose of serving. Rather than pridefully seeking to compete and dominate one another, God is given first place. He will is being done on earth. Satan is cast out. Our children gain an example to learn from, and follow. The Lord Jesus Christ is honored and glorified. Let us be about our heavenly Father's business!

Recommended reading:

WHAT MEANETH THIS? - by: B. R. Hicks, 1980. Published by: Christ Gospel Churches Int'l., Inc. P.O. Box 786, Jefferson, Indiana 47130.

The Mind of Christ - By: T.J. Hunt, 1994.

Your Inner Child of the Past - By: W. Hugh Missildine, M.D. © 1963. Published by: Simon & Schuster, NY

* Improving Your Serve - By: Charles Swindoll, Copyright 1981 - by : Word, Inc.

* The Servant Who Rules & The Ruler Who Serves - By: Ray C. Stedman, Copyright 1976 by: Word Books, Waco TX.

CHAPTER 12

Fatherhood & Shahmar

It is very interesting that the two Hebrew words gahvad and shahmar [dress & keep] are placed together in Genesis 2:15 by the Holy Spirit of God. God did this to show man that both aspects of His will concerning our function in the earth as fathers are important to Him. Both are to be observed and obeyed by us as His earthly fathers. This is the second aspect of His job description for all male parents. This chapter should prove to be a very enlightening one indeed. We wish to communicate that it is because of a failure to do this basic command of God that all the wickedness and abominations exist in the United States of America. The atrocities committed are to be attributed to an ignorance and disobedience in this area. God's deliverance will begin to be manifested as we start to observe God's will for us in this concept of Shahmar. Our children desperately need for us as fathers to walk in the Spirit of Shahmar. For it is God's Spirit who has inspired it to be practiced in our families, and other realms of earthly authority.

As crewchief, and aircrew member, for United States Navy aircraft, I was trained in various methods of defense to protect the U.S. Constitution. Also, to assist in the development of weapons used in various strategies of electronic, and missile systems warfare. This was to protect the nation from all enemies opposed to its state. Now, I wish to explain the shahmar concept God gave to protect the family from all enemies opposed to the state God desires it to be in. First, we will explain the various meanings found in our meditation on the Hebrew word *shahmar*, and then proceed to elaborate on the many various ways to observe this important principle of God. God, after He created the first father, Adam, He placed him in the Garden (Genesis 2:15) to " ..care " for [gahvad - dress] it -

15(b)   "...and to keep it." Actual Hebrew (שָׁמַר) transliterated - shahmar - Wigram's Concordance & Gesenius' Lexicon # 8104.

There are important matters to observe in the interpretation of the Hebrew word - *shahmar*. The Holy Spirit had it written down to reflect a number of various concepts, which gave mankind specific direction, in the carrying out of God's commands. In the Hebrew meaning of Shahmar, as the infinitive future tense reveals, the latter half of the command as being, that which has been established by God, and should continue on into infinity. Gesenius page 837, and George Wigram's Englishman's Hebrew Concordance page 1300, establishes this to be a Kal.— *infinitive*. This means the command was delivered once. And, was to be obeyed down through each successive generation of male children into infinite eternity.

The Holy Spirit inspired it in these five aspects:

a). To keep a watch [spiritual oversight] over it.
b). To preserve in its original state.
c). To take, or receive command, or charge over.
d). To set up a garrison of protection, as in a military sense.
e). To guard, and protect, from all enemies opposed to the spiritual state in which God created it.

We can definitely see in a close meditation of the five aspects of this Hebrew word *" shahmar "* that the first father, Adam, definitely failed and sinned against this basic principle God gave to him to run the Garden of Eden. For the despotic fallen Lucifer did propose by his words through the serpent (see Genesis 3:1-5) to change the original state of the Garden. And, in his success with Eve (the mother of all living) and Adam, God's appointed authority in the earth, brought into this earth new negative spiritual principles opposed to the spiritual state in which God had created the Garden. As we affirmed in chapter seven on the person and work of the Lord Jesus Christ, one of God's major purposes in what He commanded Christ to do was to destroy the works of the Devil (ref. 1st John 3:8(c)). This must mean in every area of this earth. Luke 10:17-20 shows us that Christ has in fact given to us an anointing of power and authority to also destroy Satan's works and activities anywhere they exist (ref. John 20:21). From the author's experience and observance, the activity of Satan, and his powers, seems to be very much a part of the American home, and family. This is a seat of authority (see Ephesians 6:12 (e) in the realm of fatherhood and motherhood, in which anti-God, anti-Christ and anti-family powers "...wrestle.. " for control. In order to destroy God's work. Without being deceived into a fanatical mentality of - *"casting demons out of the door knobs "* of our homes, we need to find a balanced and realistic position in this area. Only God's Holy Spirit can give this to us. For, it is in our failure to be sensitive to God's Spirit that our enemies gain their control. We will see as we proceed further, it is only through the spiritual weapon-gift of *".. the discerning of spirits "* that we can ever be capable of overthrowing our enemies. The flesh of man cannot discern spiritual beings (ref. 1st Corinthians 2: 7-16). It is in this passage of God's Word, in 1st Corinthians 2: 7-16, that we learn that we receive the mastery over the works of God's enemies only through our fellowship with God's Holy Spirit. And, our diligent meditation in the Word of God. Which is in fact " ..the mind of Christ ".

At this point we wish to illustrate this point of our need to keep in constant fellowship with God, and His Holy Spirit. And, master God's Word. The illustration we cite is in reference to the training of the Federal agents who specialize in recognition of counterfeit currency. The Federal Bureau of Investigation [F.B.I.] utilizes a specific technique in training their officers in the Treasury Department of our Federal government. The method they use is that they blow up, and enlarge to gigantic size, a *" genuine "* bill. Usually the bills of the denomination most often counterfeited. And, place that bill up on a giant screen. And then " study the details " of a genuine twenty, fifty, or hundred dollar bill. They also learn the details of the process used to make the bill. Also, they learn about the kind of ink used in their production. When their training is finished these agents have memorized every line, symbol, squiggle mark, and design of a genuine piece of money. Then, almost the very split-second a counterfeit bill comes across their eyes, hands, or even smell, they immediately spot it. After their study of " the genuine ", they are masters at discerning a counterfeit! This is why God has admonished us in His Word to meditate day, and night, in His Holy Word, the Bible. The less you know of the genuine truth, the greater your possibility of being deceived by Satan, or his demons. The more you know and understand God's Word (His mind) the greater your capacity to discern spiritual things, and powers (see Hebrews 5:12-14, and 1st Corinthians 2:14-16). It must be said, that as this age closes, more convincing, and lying counterfeits will arise under Satan's direction to deceive mankind into " believing " his lies (ref. 2nd Thessalonians 2:11 & 12; Matthew 24:3-5). We are to study God's truth. Not Satan's myriad of cults, heresies, and counterfeit religions.

FATHERS AS WARRIORS

Men, do you consider yourselves as being a warrior as a male parent of children? Have you ever considered yourself an American fighting man? The United States of America desperately needs its fathers to develop the spiritual and mental attitude that a warrior possesses. Our nation would be in greater spiritual health today if the previous fathers in our nation had been taught this Biblical principle before they became fathers. We will, in this chapter, prepare your mind and spirit-man with the capacity to know and understand your God-given responsibilities. And, authority in this area which has been an area of great neglect. This neglect has produced horrendous conditions for our children to grow up under. So, " ATTENTION ON Deck! SNAP TO! " You shall now receive your spiritual military orders. You will begin to view yourself as God's fighting machine against your enemies. And, His. You will no longer fear Satan, or any of his principalities, or powers (ref. Joshua 1: 7-9). You will consider yourself as God's mighty man of valor. You will see yourself as a " bruiser on the head of Satan ". (ref. Romans 16:20) -

20)   And the God of peace [cessation of againstness] shall bruise Satan under your feet shortly. The grace of our Lord Jesus Christ be with you. Amen.

Have you ever considered yourself as a bruiser on Satan's head? If you have not, you shall from this day forward! After you learn what follows in this chapter, you shall know your enemy, and his various stratagems against you. You will learn all your weapons of warfare, the great *" God who is a man of war.. "* has provided you with (Ref. Exodus 15:3, 14:23-31). You will consider every place you set your foot as holy ground unto the Lord our God to be conquered in His name. For the Lord God has given you the city! Fear of any spiritual power, other than God's Holy Spirit, is an abomination to your very soul! Fear, wherever it exists, is to be cast out (violently thrown out) in the almighty name of the Lord Jesus Christ for His glory! (See Philippians 2:9-11). You will renounce "..your grasshopper complex." (see Numbers 13:28-33). You will become vicious against the unseen enemies at war against us in our homes, cities, states and national governmental leaders [Ephesians 6:10-18]. Your mentality shall be in accordance with 1st John 4:4 & 1st John 2:27) -

4:4)   You are of God, little children, and have overcome them: because greater is He that is in you, than he that is in the world.

2:27)   But the anointing which you have received of Him (see Luke 3:16 & 17) abides in you, and you need not that any man teach you: But as the same anointing teaches you of all things, and is truth, and is no lie, and even as He has taught you, you shall abide in Him.

In other words, outside of the triune God-head, you are the hottest commodity in God's universe! You are powerful in God's Spirit. You shall master each of God's many weapons of spiritual warfare. In a spiritual sense Rambo will look like a whimpish caspar milk-toast in comparison to you when God places His hand of approval upon you as being His warrior in the earth. You will scatter away all evil with your eyes (see Proverbs 20:8). Satan's powers will cringe when you enter any area. They will say, " lookout, boys, we have big trouble now." Just your presence in God's Holy Spirit will cause them to tremble. You will conquer Satan's forces of darkness in major cities, and set their captives free [study Isa. 61:1-3]. You will use weapons you have never used. These weapons you shall find are more powerful than the greatest physical military weapon man has ever developed. You will learn to master the chief weapons of the Most High God! Those who have been wounded by the enemy, you will bind up their wounds. Those who are in the prisoners of war camps you will set free. You shall receive from the Commander in Chief, the medal of valor. The purple heart for your wounds received in your battles. You will be an integral part of God's mighty army of the end of this world as we know it (ref. Joel 2:1-12). We must understand that with God there is no middle ground. Every man, woman, male, or female child has only two choices to decide from in relation to their future lives. You are either a citizen of the kingdom of light, or, of the kingdom of darkness (ref. Colossians 1:12-13). Jesus Christ affirmed this fact in Luke 11:23 -

23)   He that is not with Me is against me: And he that gathers not with Me scatters.

By way of illustration we refer to a member of organized crime who would come to a key member of a football, baseball, or basketball team, and offer him a bribe. The team favored to win would be the object of attack by those who wished to throw the game. The bribe would not be to get the team member to not play at all. No, the plan would be to get him not to play his best. What is sad about the majority of God's people today, is that they are mostly divided into two groups. The first being the nominal believer who is content to watch, and observe the activity of diligent children of God doing His work. The other group are *" The Red Flag "* warriors of God in this world. These Red-Flag warriors are marked believers. Satan, and his evil angels, know who they are. It is these Red-Flag warriors who do the most damage to Satan's kingdom of darkness. It is these Red-Flag warriors who are working, and fighting, to bring new people out of Satan's kingdom into God's family. These warriors are active delivering those Satan has bound in chains of sin and iniquity. It is these Red-Flag warriors who are bringing God's healing power into the lives of those Satan, and his angels, have deeply wounded and made sick. It is these Red-Flag warriors who are the object of Satan's most vicious attacks. If you are not a Red-Flag warrior, please, at least intercede in prayer. And, be supportive of those men, women, and even youngsters you know that are. Do not just sit on the fence observing! Everybody must be an active member of God's army. Each of us must find the place in which we are found to be the most effective. And, do our best in that place.

THE WEAPONS OF OUR WARFARE

Have you ever tried to use a tool, or weapon, of which you knew little about? You may have found that your attempts to use the specific tool, or weapon to be quite awkward. Or, even down-right dangerous to yourself, or others. By way of illustration we are taught by those who are masters of fire arms to never leave a gun loaded where another man may come along, and pick it up, believing it to be empty. The author recalls an experience in which one night, when he was a young teenager, he was alone in the house, when he heard noises outside like someone trying to break into the house. He loaded his shotgun. And, prepared to confront the would-be intruder. The noises stopped. And so he stuck the shotgun loaded under the living room sofa, and went to sleep. The next day he went to school forgetting to unload the shotgun, and return it to the gun rack. His uncle and cousin from Pittsburgh, PA, had come down for a visit, and saw the barrel of the shotgun sticking out from under the sofa. His cousin pulled it out, and aimed it playfully at his dad. As his dad tried to warn him not to point a gun at anyone. You never know whether, or not, it is loaded. His cousin said, " Its empty, watch." He lowered the gun, pulled the trigger, and boom! He blew a big hole in the carpet. And, just about gave his dad a coronary. We first refer to 2nd Corinthians 10:3-5 in learning about our weapons against Satan.

3)   For though we walk in the flesh, we do not war after the flesh:

4)   For [because] the weapons of our warfare are not carnal, but mighty through God to the pulling down of strong holds.

5)   Casting down imaginations, and every high thing [idea-thought] that exalts itself against the knowledge of God. And, bringing into captivity every thought

to the obedience of Christ. [meaning, or, emphasis added]

We explain, at this time, that the word *" mighty "* in verse four is the Greek word [δυνατα] transliterated - " dunata " from which we get our English word - dynamite. This tells us that God's weapons have explosive power to destroy Satan's strongholds if applied. We say at this time that it is also *the kind of faith* we place in God's weapons, that gives us the proper appreciation for their power. If we think lightly about the weapon of - *the name of the Lord Jesus Christ* it will be to us, and our enemy, like a B-B Gun in its effectiveness. But, if in strong faith, we see the name of Jesus as a double-barreled, sawed-off 12 gauge shotgun, we visualize in our imagination, that the name blows back Satanic-demonic powers. And does great damage to them! When we truly know, believe, and understand, the authority, and tremendous power God has given to that name: (ref. Philippians 2: 9 - 11). The next important aspect of this preliminary study of our weapons, we observe the word translated- " thought ". In the original Greek, the word [νοημα] is transliterated- *" noama "*. Which means literally, *a thought, purpose, or, design*. This word is also found in 2nd Corinthians 2:11. In which, the same basic word is used in a different declension, and translated *" devices "*. What we learn from this study, is that our major warfare is centered around what takes place within our minds, and thought life. Apparently, Satan, and his demons, have power to place evil thoughts within our minds. It is a very intimate, close warfare, we are waging with the powers of darkness. This is the reason God requires us to learn, and, meditate, upon His thoughts. Which are found in His Word. The Holy Bible (ref. Isaiah 54: 6 - 11).

Ephesians 4:23 reaffirms this basic weapon against Satan, and his powers.

23)   And be renewed in the spirit of your mind;

As we said in the first part of chapter eight, as we studied the fact that God had in *His* mind what He proposed to bring into existence, before He did. So, we also, having been created in God's image and likeness, are given the power and ability to operate much the same way on earth. Satan works to put thoughts into our mind to seduce us into violating God's principles of life. But we can gain the mastery over Satan's devices [thoughts] by placing God's thoughts faithfully into our hearts, and minds. Then, they will be available to use, against Satan. And for the Lord God. The fact that God had a basic thought in His mind, prior to the actual creation, is evidenced by all we now see in His created world. Everything we see in the world man is creating today is also evidence that God, and man, can have an idea in their mind, and then bring that idea into actual existence by using substances to create it. Those whose occupations are engineering, or architecture, really know this principle exists. All we see in the world, whether God, or man made, began as a thought in the mind of someone. In the next chapter thirteen, we are going to delve deeper into this area by examining where our thoughts, and words, originate. And the power they carry. Both good and evil. Suffice it to say at this point, that our greatest, and most effective weapon in our arsenal is our mental grasp of the knowledge of God's Word. Found in the sixty-six books of the Holy Bible! You are, in fact, going into war without your major weapon to defeat the Devil, by failing to saturate your memory banks, and heart, with the entirety of God's Word. His complete revelation about Himself, and who you actually are, in your relationship with Him. As good fathers, it is our responsibility, along with mothers, to fill up our children's hearts, and minds, with God's mighty weapons in His Word. If we fail in this important task, it is like a United States Marine Corps. Drill-Sergeant sending a man to the front line of combat without any training, or weapons, to fight with. In 2nd Peter 3:18, we are exhorted to "..grow in grace *and knowledge* of our Lord and Saviour Jesus Christ." It is also the responsibility of all parents, to assist their sons, and daughters, to do the same. We observe another exhortation concerning our minds, and our children's minds, in 1st Peter 1:13(a).

13(a) Wherefore gird up the loins of your mind...

We learn, that ***to gird up the loins of our minds***, is to fill it up with all the counsel, and instruction, of God's Word. This activity, on our part, will prepare us, and our children, to have all the chief weapons of spiritual warfare readily available to employ at a moment's notice. The fertile young impressionable minds of our children are ready to be programmed with the Word God has given to us. It is not just to be put on a coffee table to make guests think we are religious. Most of us as adults need to flush out the corrupt worldly philosophies we have been brain-washed with, by the submitting of our minds to the anti-Christ forces behind our National education systems, radio, television, movies, books and magazines. The failure of the nation's past fathers and mothers to do God's command here in the concept of shahmar, has provided for Satan, and his demons, beach-heads in our minds. Our failure to *"..love God with all our minds.."* has made it possible for the enemy to gain access into our minds to paralyze them. This makes it more difficult for us to understand. And, then carry out God's will in the earth. The minds of many fathers in the United States are " bound " by Satan's powers by sports, and other deviations of the enemy. We are to " loose " these minds by the Word of God. And, the power of God's Spirit (see Matthew. 18:18-20). Jesus affirmed this in John 8: 31-32.

31) Then said Jesus to those Jews which believe on him, if you continue in My Word, then are you My disciples indeed;

32) And you shall know the truth and the truth shall make you free.

Our minds are free only to the extent that we allow the Word of God into it. And, appropriate it to each, and, every area of our lives. At this point we wish to explain that all of the gifts of God's Holy Spirit, are in essence, weapons of warfare against Satan's powers of darkness. We will contrast the ministry of the Holy Spirit, in His activity in our lives, with the enemy's deceptive works - read 1st Corinthians chapter 12 verses 1 - 11 to follow the contrasts to God's Weapon- Gifts.

The Weapon-Gift of the Spirit vs The Works of Satan

1. The " Weapon-Gift " of Prophecy: gives to the believer God's purpose and direction for his life, or direction for the life of another believer. To know specifics about God's will, and plan for his, or her life. To speak of future events in God's plan. Note: prophetic utterances must line up with what has already been written down in God's Word, the Holy Bible [ref. Jeremiah 29:23 & 23:16-36 & Isaiah 8:20].

Verses

Astrology and horoscope, psychic ability, divination (fortune-telling), ouji boards, crystal ball, tarot cards, palm reading, tea leaf reading, water witching, etc. (all based on satanic lies. And, half-truths [sometimes wrongly called " white-lies "]).

2. The " Weapon-Gift " of faith: gives the believer the capacity to see God, understand His power, and use it for His glory. Faith finds its fulfillment in obedience to God's Word.

VS

Satan's perversion of faith = fear. Satan's despotic and destructive force. Presumption also - see James 4:13-17. Fear is the primary force used by Satan to destroy men. And, he utilizes it in various forms to overthrow them. Examples = phobias, i.e., Acrophobia.

3. The " Weapon-Gift " of healings: the ability of God through the life of the believer, to produce the supernatural healing of spirit, soul (mind, will, or emotions), or physical body, and life systems. Ref. Luke 10:9; Mark 16:18(d).

VS

Sickness and disease of spirit, soul and body by evil spirits of infirmity. Ref. Luke 8:2. Psycho-somatic illnesses caused by evil spirits.

4. The " Weapon-Gift " of miracles: The ability of God, through the believer, to produce supernatural results without which the object of the miracle would remain in its natural state. Ref. Exodus 10:12-23 & Acts 4:13-13-16.

VS

Counterfeit miracles designed to deceive man into following Satan (Ref. Exodus 7:9-12; 2nd Thessalonians 2:9; Revelation 13:12-15). Magic also, and magicians.

5. The " Weapon-Gift " of speaking in tongues: The supernatural ability to allow God's Holy Spirit to flow through your spirit and give an utterance that natural knowledge does not understand (ref. 1st Corinthians 14: 14 & 15; Romans 8:26-27). Also, the ability to bring a message to an assembly, which must be interpreted by another individual who has the gift of the interpretation of tongues (1st Corinthians 14:5). The supernatural ability to communicate God's Word in a language unknown to you [ref. Acts 2:1-22].

VS

Satan's use of the tongue to slander, gossip, and evil speaking. False-teachings, and heresies, mocking tongues. Which are designed by Satan to bring confusion about the true gift. Counterfeit tongues.

6. The " Weapon-Gift " of the word of wisdom: The ability given to an individual to speak in such a way as to bring clarity and understanding to God's Word. Using practical illustrations to explain application of spiritual truth (parables), etc.

VS

Wisdom twisted, and used to produce confusion, and deception. Ezekiel 28:17; James 3:15-16; 1st Corinthians 3:19 & 20.

7. The " Weapon-Gift " of the word of knowledge: All knowledge is God's knowledge. The ability to speak, or write, a specific amount of the knowledge of the mind of God. Each man of God, who wrote each book in the Bible, had this weapon-gift. Any ability to know about any person, place, or thing supernaturally.

VS

Satan's use of knowledge to deceive through lies. The use of ignorance to gain control over anyone. The use of half-truths to deceive. Deception means: saying something is true, when in reality, it is false. Psychic words of knowledge are used to bring glory to the psychic. Which reveals evil spirits to be operating in the person to deceive. And bring people under their control. When the Lord Jesus Christ is given honor for revealing an unknown matter, it is a manifestation of God's Holy Spirit! [Ref. Genesis 41: 16; Daniel 2: 17-23]

8. The " Weapon-Gift " of the discerning of spirits: The supernatural capacity for a believer to discern demonic powers active in a person's life. The purpose of which is to identify the kind of spirits operating in a victim. And exactly what those spirits are doing in a victim. And to cast it, or, them out. See Mark 16:16-17; Acts 16:16-18). Example: a spirit of lust, spirit of adultery, a lying spirit, a spirit of jealousy, a spirit of fear, a spirit of divination - ref. 1st Samuel 28: 7-9.

VS

Satan's demonic power structure (ref. Ephesians 6:12) i.e., spirits of whoredoms, a lying spirit, spirit of hate, murder, jealousy, envy, pride, the perverse spirit, etc. Worldly counterfeit forms of exorcism.

9. The " Weapon-Gift " of giving & generosity: A capacity to be sensitive to the needs of others whether, spiritual, psychological, or physical. And giving to meet those needs as God's vessel.

VS

Greed, covetousness, and poverty. Also, the use of gifts to bring glory to self. All true Spirit -led gifts bring honor to God the Father [see James 1: 16-17; Matthew 5:16] and His Son, the Lord Jesus Christ.

10. The " Weapon-Gift " of administration: The capacity given by the Spirit of God to petition others, who have certain abilities, and direct them in such a way so as to accomplish God's purpose.

VS

Confusion and disorganization. Disorder [ref. 1 Cor. 14: 33].

11. The " Weapon-Gift " of out-going love & concern.

VS

Hate and indifference. Apathy.

12. The " Weapon-Gift " of the blood of Jesus Christ (Ref. Revelation 12:11). Has power to heal all manner of disease and expel demons trespassing in the souls, or, bodies of people.

VS

Impurity, sin, and iniquity. Spiritual defilement.

13) The " Weapon-Gift " of the name of the Lord Jesus Christ (Mark 16:17 & Philippians 2: 9-11).

AntiChrist Satan, or any of his principalities, or powers.

THE WEAPON OF PRAISE

When we speak praise to God the Father, and His Son Jesus Christ, in the power of the Holy Spirit, it is a powerful weapon against the powers of darkness. Since Satan, and his angels, are looking for worship, they despise it when God's children sincerely and faithfully worship and praise God. They cannot stand to hear genuine praise to God. We refer to a few examples of this in the book of Psalms.

Psalms 149: 1 - 9 -

1) Praise ye the Lord. Sing to the Lord a new song, and His praise in the congregation of saints.

2) Let Israel rejoice in Him that made him: Let the children of Zion be joyful in their King.

3) Let them praise His name in the dance: Let them sing praises to Him with the timbrel and harp. [Our dancing brings glory to God].

4) For the Lord takes pleasure in His people: He will beautify the meek with salvation.

5) Let the saints be joyful in glory: [The Holy Spirit]. Let them sing aloud upon their beds.

6) Let the high praises of God be in their mouth, and a two-edged sword in their hand;

7) To [for the purpose of] execute vengeance upon the heathen, [Satan's powers] and punishments upon the people;

8) To bind their kings [rulers] with chains, and their nobles with fetters of iron;

9) To execute upon them the judgment written: this honor have all His saints. Praise ye the Lord.

This passage shows us that when the high praises of God come forth out of our mouths from our hearts, and, we praise God with musical instruments, and dancing. Satan's powers are punished, receive vengeance, and are bound with chains and cords of iron. This spiritual activity, we have the honor of performing, raises havoc against the forces of Satan. It is a mighty weapon against the kingdom of darkness. Psalms 8: 1 & 2 also reveals to us that Satan's works are stopped in their tracks as we. Praise God's name! DO IT NOW! Come on. You can do much better than that. That's a little better. Practice makes perfect!

Psalm 8: 1 & 2 -

1)   O Lord, our Lord, how excellent is your name in all the earth! Who has set your glory above the heavens.
2)   out of the mouth of babes and sucklings have you ordained strength [praise - see Mt. 21:16] because of your enemies [Satan and his angels] that you might still [stop] the enemy and the avenger.

A careful study of praise reveals the reason God's enemies are so disarmed and rendered powerless. It is found in Psalm 22: 3.

3)   But you are holy, O you that inhabits the praises of Israel [your people].

Psalms 9:1-3 also shows us the reason.

1)   I will praise you, O Lord, with my whole heart; I will show forth all your marvelous works.
2)   I will be glad and rejoice in you: I will sing praise to your name, O you Most High.
3)   When my enemies are turned back they shall fall and perish at your presence.

Our praise brings God's presence. And God's presence causes Satan and his powers to be overthrown and disarmed. Refer to Acts 16: 25 -33. It also drives out evil powers from in, or, around our lives or, those who are being oppressed by him. Psalms 34:1 instructs us to allow God's praise " to continually flow " from our mouths. We are to offer up to God.. - refer to Jeremiah 33:11 - " the sacrifice of praise." That means we are to be active in praising God even when we do not feel like doing so! The true practice empties us out of selfish attitudes and creates a place of access for God to fill us up!

THE WEAPON OF MUSIC

In beginning our study of this powerful weapon of spiritual warfare we say that music originated with God. God created music. It is His creation. It was originally created for the purpose of assisting in the worship and praise of God. Job 38:3-7 shows that music was part of the beginning of the creation of God. Genesis 4:20-21 shows us how God started music in the earth. A man, by the name of Jabal, had a son he named Jubal [the root derivative of the word jubilee]. Leviticus chapters 25, and 27, gives God's orders concerning a time of expressive celebration of His people. Jubal fathered, or originated, the creation of instruments of sound to create music in the earth.

Something the average believer in Jesus Christ is ignorant of is that Lucifer [Satan] was created specifically with the ability to produce music. Ezekiel 28:13(c) states:

> 13(c) ...The workmanship of your tabrets [drums with accompanying musical sound producers] and of your pipes [horns] was prepared in you in the day that you were created.

In God's creation of Lucifer he built into his spiritual body the capacity to make music. In the " anointing " (see Ezekiel 28:14)

God gave Lucifer, he was made to be the perfection of the ability to produce worship and praise to be administered with instruments of music. Lucifer, the created and anointed cherub, stood as God's prime minister of musical worship and praise to the Lord God his Creator. It was in this powerful, and strategic place of creating and presenting exquisite worship and praise to God his Creator, that he began to entertain desires to be worshiped himself. Instead of the Lord God Almighty [refer to Isaiah 14:12-16]. Isaiah 14:11 records the first kind of musical instrument Satan has mastery over. The " viols " are six stringed instruments, that are representative of all stringed instruments. The word " tabrets " found in Ezekiel 28:13(c) is an obsolete French word, from which we derive the word tamborine, or tabor. It basically speaks of a percussion musical instrument. A drum with accompanying features to produce musical sounds. This is the second type of musical instrument. The " pipes ", being the third kind, refer to various horns, or trumpets. The whole family of wind instruments. So, for all those saints who have been deceived into thinking, and led by wrongly inspired artists to believe that Satan, or, the Devil has " horns "; the horns are not the kind the artists portray as protruding out of his head! These kinds of artists, also made people believe God's angels are little fat babies, or, look like women. They also have made pictures of what they want people to think Jesus Christ looks like. A long-haired effeminate weakling. Those who want to see what He really looks like, should read and meditate in Revelation 1:12 -19. It is just like those who serve Satan, to try to create these kinds of perverse ideas about God through pictures. Yet, we all would be startled at the amount of money made by selling such pictures of deception. Now back to music. Prophetically speaking, the direction, or, should we say orchestration, of Satan's anti-Christ system will, without a doubt, utilize the mastery of music to lead the masses of humanity to worship him through the Beast (ref. Revelation 13). Contemporary songs like John Lennon's " Imagine " or, the multi-rock star composition "

We are the World ", are the beginning of this orchestration of Satan through the perverse use of music.

The prophetic description of all Gentile nations, kingdoms, and empires, were manifested in Nebuchadnezzar's great image-statue. (refer to Daniel chapters 2 & 3). The conclusion of the Gentile rulership of the earth will relate prophetically to the book of Daniel the prophet. It should be recognized that in Daniel 3:4-6 the king of Babylon demanded all peoples to fall down and worship his image-statue. And, the " *cue* " to let all the people know when to worship was...

4)   Then a herald cried aloud, to you it is commanded, O people, nations, and languages.

5)   That, at what time you hear the sound of the cornet, flute, harp, sackbut, psaltery, dulcimer, and all kinds of music, you fall down and worship the golden image that Nebuchadnezzar the king has set up:

6)   And whoso falls not down and worships shall the same hour be cast into the midst of a burning fiery furnace.

We say this, and remind our readers of this prophecy to reveal the ultimate purpose of Satan behind the recent " *world* " moves of certain rock music stars to produce global-political change. This use of music to produce world manipulation will proceed in the direction to organize a " *Global one-world religious - political system* ". Headed up by the Anti-Christ at the end. Music will move the nations to cooperate in the bringing of Satan's world leader to power. Satan, before his fall, was a master musician. He still possesses musical power. And he uses it to train those who will work to bring him worship as this age closes. Beware! Shadrach, Meshach, and Abednego could handle the heat of peer rejection by their faith, and not submit to idolatry [musical, or any other kind]. Can you? Just because it sounds good, does not mean, it is good. Master musicians can be demon possessed.

But, just because Lucifer is now corrupted, does not mean God has given up on music. Remember that God created music. 1st Thessalonians 4:16, shows us Satan only gains power over this earth, and its Christ rejecters, after God's trumpet sounds. And signals the removal of true marriage supper participants! The entire book of Psalms was designed by God to manifest to us, His people, how we are to learn to worship and praise the Lord God, His name, and His Word. There are around fifteen verses in Holy Scripture with the actual word " music " in them. The word - *" music "* was derived out of the Greek language. The Greek god " Muse " represented a deep prolonged thought upon a specific subject. It represented the art of meditation. Joshua 1:7-9, and Psalms 1, and other passages inform us, that God richly rewards those men who take time to muse, or meditate, in His Word. It is in the use of, and implementation of, musical instruments to assist in exquisite worship and praise of God. And, His Word, that is the perfection of music. It is probable that Lucifer, assisted the creation to worship and praise God, with his anointing of intimate knowledge about God, and His Word. As fathers, and mothers, we should encourage our children, who have abilities in music, to master, and use them, to assist God's people in worship of our Creator. Some examples of the use of music in warfare are found in the Old Testament. Music, in times of old, was for the purpose of celebration. Triumph and victory over an enemy was usually the cause of musical celebration.

In Judges 7:15-23, God directed His anointed leader "Gideon" to organize three hundred warriors, to assemble at night around the Midianites. Who had a far greater host of warriors than Gideon. The three companies of warriors were ordered to blow their " trumpets " at a specific time, in unison. Break their pitchers, raise their torches, and cry out, " The sword of the Lord, and of Gideon ". This method God inspired Gideon to use, totally set the enemy forces in confusion. So much so, that they turned upon each other, and destroyed one another. We must learn how to use these Biblical tactics of warfare to destroy the enemies we face in our households and families. In 1st Samuel 18: 5-16, we see that music was used to manifest God's choice of leadership of His people. 1st Samuel 16: 14-23 manifests to us that demonic powers can be removed from a person's life by employing music. Depending on how music is played. And, the spirit and attitudes behind it, music either attracts evil spirits, or, repels them. We all need to develop skill, and discernment, as it relates to music. We must understand that each, and every musical instrument, can be used either to produce an attitude of worship to God, or lead people in worship of other false gods. Music has the capacity to produce an infilling of God's Holy Spirit. Or, it can open up lives to demon possession. Music is a gift. And, also, a weapon.

The three elements that compose music are directly connected to each area of man's being. They also relate to each member of the triune God-head.

Triune God-head:	1) Father	2) Son	3) Holy Spirit
Man's being:	1) spirit	2) soul	3) physical body

[man's soul has mind, will, & emotions]
3 Elements of music: 1) melody 2) harmony 3) rhythm

Music must be understood to be the most potent force of spiritual warfare. By way of illustration, I am reminded of a specific time while stationed at the Pacific Missile Test Center, Naval Air Station at Point Mugu, CA. We were assigned to a mission to test a new form of electronic warfare actually called, " The music." We flew with the device hooked up inside the H-46 helicopter just off the coast of the Los Angeles basin. As we turned the *" music "* on, it is my understanding that all radar, and radio transmissions, in that huge area were blacked out. As fathers and mothers we should provide music to assist us in leading our families to worship God. We should be very interested in promoting all music that brings joy and praise in the worship of God. We should be interested in finding ways to use music against the kingdom of darkness. As we do, we may find tactical ways of blacking out the Devil's efforts to sow strife, hate, confusion and contention in our homes. We close this segment on the use of music as a weapon of warfare by reviewing one of the greatest examples of God inspiring the use of music to destroy his people's enemies. The account is that of the king of " Judah " [means: God's praise] Jehoshaphat's prayer for the deliverance of his people.

2nd Chronicles 20:12-23 -

12)   O our God, will you not judge them? For we have no might against this great company that comes against us; neither know we what to do: but our eyes are upon you.

13)   And all Judah stood before the Lord, with their little ones, their wives, and their children.

14)   Then upon Jahaziel the son of Zechariah, the son of Benaiah, the son of Jeiel, the son of Mattaniah, a Levite of the sons of Asaph, came the Spirit of the Lord in the midst of the congregation;

15)   And he said, hearken you, all Judah, and you inhabitants of Jerusalem, and you king Jehoshaphat, this says the Lord to you, be not afraid nor dismayed by reason of this great multitude; for the battle is not yours, but God's.

16)   Tomorrow you go down against them: Behold, they come up by the cliff of ZIZ; and you shall find them at the end of the brook, before the wilderness of Jeruel.

17)   You shall not need to fight in this battle. Set yourselves, you stand still, and see the salvation of the

231

Lord with you, O Judah and Jerusalem: Fear not, nor be dismayed; tomorrow go out against them: For the Lord will be with you.

18) And Jehoshaphat bowed his head with his face to the ground: And all Judah and the inhabitants of Jerusalem fell before the Lord, worshiping the Lord.

19) And the Levites, of the children of the Kohathites, and the children of the Korhites, stood up to praise the Lord God of Israel with a (loud)   voice   on high.

20) And they rose early in the morning, and went forth into the wilderness of Tekoa: And as they went forth, Jehoshaphat stood and said, hear me, O Judah, and you inhabitants of Jerusalem; * believe in the Lord your God, so shall you be established; * believe his prophets, so shall you prosper.

21) And when they had consulted with the people, he appointed singers unto the Lord, and that they should praise the beauty of holiness, as they went out before the army, and to say, praise the Lord; for His mercy endures forever.

22) And when they began to sing and to praise, the Lord set ambushments against the children of Ammon, Moab, and Mt.Seir, which were come against Judah; and they were smitten.

23) For the children of Ammon and Moab stood up against the inhabitants of Mt. Seir, utterly to slay and destroy them: and when they had made an end of the inhabitants of Seir, everyone helped to destroy another.

The Biblical account here shows us that when God's people are willing to be obedient in this area of His Word, that tells us to believe Him. And unite in concerted worship and praise, it permits Him to do what is necessary to defeat our enemies. Even to the point of attacking each other! If all the true Christains, in the different denominations of Church fellowships, would repent of the pride associated with their specific denomination, and quit bad-mouthing other Churches, Satan would be in very serious trouble! He loves to "..sow discord between the brothers." But, he could not do it without human mouths to do it! If all true belivers will turn their mouths against the real enemy, we could do very powerful things for God. And, set people free. Oneness of heart in the whole fellowship of saints will allow Jesus Christ to exercise His Lordship, and defeat the Devil. We must fasten our eyes on Him. And learn all about Him, so praise can be expressed toward Him. If we all start bad-mouthing the work of the Devil in spreading pornography all over our land, he would be seen as the real problem, and this would give us a great national victory. Because our mouths and words are God's weapons of our warfare.

Recommended reading - THE REBIRTH OF MUSIC; BY: Lamar Boschman, Manasseh books, 1980. Recommended cassette tape - ROCK-A-BYE-BYE BABY; by: Pastor Gary Greenwald.

THE SWORD OF THE SPIRIT

17) And take [receive the ... sword of the Spirit, which is the Word of God:

— Ephesians 6:17(b)

Swordsmanship is pretty much an out-dated activity among men in our day, but it is an essential skill in any attempt to do warfare against Satan, or his powers. When most people think of a sword they think of a large Roman soldier-type broadsword. But a careful study of the word " sword ", which has been translated in Ephesians 6:17(b) is a little misleading. The actual Greek word here is (Gk. μάχαιραν)

233

transliterated - machairan. The Greek word - " machairan", speaks of a large knife, or poniard. Which is a dagger held in the fist. It speaks of being a weapon utilized in close mortal combat. This is precisely why the apostle Paul in Ephesians 6:12 states that we are " wrestling " with spiritual beings of wickedness. Usually, when you are wrestling with an opponent, you are wrapped around each other in an attempt to overcome your adversary. This machiaran of God's Spirit is a very handy weapon to be used in a close, wrestling conflict. It can even be used to attack Satanic, or demonic thoughts placed in our minds, or hearts, by our enemy. The next aspect of this passage on the " machiaran " of God's Spirit, is what is found in the latter part of the verse. " The *machiaran* of the Spirit - which is the Word of God." There are two different Greek words used in the New Testament for *the word* -" word ". The one is (λογοσ) transliterated logos. Which means: the " literal " Word of God. Jesus Christ, in John 1:1, is the Logos - the actual Word of God. The Bible is also the logos, or written down Word of God. But, in this verse of Ephesians 6:17, we find a different word. The Greek word -ρημα - transliterated " RHEMA ". This word - rhema - is also found in Romans 10:17. It means: specific words proceeding out of the mouth of an individual. In the purest sense it means: from the mind, down through the heart, and out over the lips. A specific utterance of the actual, literal Word of God. Let us put all this information together now to produce a working definition of this weapon of our warfare. " The sword of the Spirit, which is the Word of God is: " The machiaran " [little knife, or dagger] to be used as we wrestle with our spiritual enemies. Is when we have taken time to place God's literal Word into our minds. And by faith, have learned of its power over Satan, and his angels. And, allow God's Word to flow down into our hearts [our will, and emotions]. And, then come up and out of our hearts through our tongues. And, then out of our mouths. This is the sword-Machiaran-Rhema of God's Spirit. It is a powerful weapon when a man has prepared himself to use it effectively. It should be understood, that as Romans 10:17 shows, that faith in God comes to us, and our families, in proportion to the amount of " Rhema ", specific utterances about God's Word, that we hear. Our households must be allowed to hear us speaking it as God's Spirit gives us direction at opportune moments! Example: Speaking God's Word of agreement overthrows strife!

OUR WARFARE STRATEGY

As fathers, in the United States of America, it is our responsibility to provide a covering of protection for every person in our family. With all the blatant and subtle attacks upon the minds and lives of our family members, our job is becoming increasingly difficult. The messages, and allurements of Satan, and his angels, come at our family members through current music, television programming, various books and magazines, Internet, the corrupted aspects of our Public school systems, their unbelieving friends at school and work, and the direct attacks by Satan on their hearts, and minds. Unless we, as alert fathers, understand the importance of our protection and influence in our children's lives, they will be left at a disadvantage in enemy territory. Our knowledge, and understanding of God, and His Word, is the key to success as fathers (ref. Joshua 1:8 & 9). Our submission to the Lordship, and likeness of Jesus Christ, can give us the needed edge against our enemies. There are three Bible passages which we will close this important chapter on Fatherhood & Shahmar. The first is found in Matthew 4:1-11. The deep spiritual truths found in this section of God's Word are our example to follow. In it we find that Jesus, as a man, had to experience all the temptations any of us as fathers must face. It shows us that Jesus was led by the Spirit of God. It reveals to us the importance and guidelines for fasting. That the practice of fasting puts down the fleshly carnal man Satan likes to manipulate. And, allows the spirit-man to arise, and be strong in God's might. In verse 3, we see that Satan likes to challenge us on whether, or not, we truly are the sons of God. To doubt our relationship with the Father. He works to make us take matters into our own hands, when pressures increase upon us. In verses 3-5 Satan's attack was upon Christ's physical needs. In verses 5-7 Satan attacked the psychological (mind, will and emotions) of Jesus Christ. In verses 8-11 we see Satan's deceptive appeal to the Spirit of Christ. The exchange of all the powers of the kingdoms of the entire world, in exchange for His loyalty to God the Father. As fathers, we all will struggle with each of these same areas Satan tried to deceive Jesus Christ the Lord with. Our children also, will need us to help them to discern Satan's tactics against their lives. It is very important that we study every response of Jesus Christ in this passage of Matthew 4:1-11. We must see that every response of Christ against the Devil's allurements and attacks was a " rhema " of God's Word. In verse 6, we see that the Devil knows God's Word, and in certain instances, uses it to deceive mankind. All false religions, and cults, are evidences of this use of Holy Scripture by Satan, and his demons. For this very reason it is imperative that all parents gain a mastery of all that is in God's Word. Verse 4 shows us the method of developing a mastery of the Bible. We are to eat it. We are to digest all its contents into our spiritual bodies, and souls. To assimilate the entire Biblical revelation. Usually U.S. military personnel eat real good. So must God's army eat all the best spiritual foods. It brings health and strength to our spirit-man. We are commanded by God to feed this spiritual nourishment to our children. To provide for the natural part of man only, is just half the job. Our next strategic weapon is found in Luke 11: 9-28. The passage centers around God's Holy Spirit filling the lives of our children. This is a major key to keep out demon spirits from being able to enter their lives. This passage gives us discernment concerning the evil activities of the Devil, or his demons. It is the father's job to be discerning if the enemy is getting an advantage over his children. And then, do warfare whenever they try to gain access into his son, or, daughter. We are then charged by God to fill the house [our children's lives] with God's Holy Spirit. Luke 11: 9-13 manifests that it is our responsibility as fathers to administer the Spirit of God in our family. To encourage faith in His power!

To give an illustration to how demons may gain access to a daughter, we know current magazines, such as are directed at young women, try to encourage them to violate moral standards in their dress. If the young woman is wanting to be attractive to young men, she may be seduced into receiving a spirit of whoredoms, which will cause her to dress in a whorish fashion. This will cause young men to lust after her. And, set up the conditions for violating moral standards of purity for both the daughter, and the young man. This is the main cause of women being forced into getting abortions. Opening her eye-gate to seductive magazines allows demons of lust to enter. Fathers and mothers must speak out against such whoredoms by the secular Teenage magazine Media! Luke 11: 9-13 manifests, that it is our responsibility as fathers, to administer the Spirit of God in our family. We will cover this in more detail in chapter fifteen on husbandry. The verses we want to study at this time are Luke 11: 21-22.

21) When a strong man [original Greek = strong *" one "*] armed keeps his palace [the people of the earth] his goods are in peace:

22) But when a stronger than he shall come upon him, and overcome him, he takes from him all his armor wherein he trusted, and divides his spoils.

In this part of God's Word, Jesus Christ explains that, the " strong one " [Satan] has certain strategies to protect his kingdom. The " goods " spoken of here are the men, women, sons and daughters of this world. The *" palace "* is this world system. Christ tells us that Satan is *" armed "* with certain weapons. Verse 22 shows us that if we would be stronger, we must know the armor Satan uses. Ephesians 6:11 shows us that Satan uses *" wiles "* [cunning devices]. Ephesians 6:16 tells us he uses *" fiery darts "*. These are evil spiritual thoughts he fires into our hearts and minds to confuse, or corrupt us. Fear, and hate, are two other pieces of Satan's armor. A lack of love [compassion: going out of your way to help others] is another piece of armor Satan guards his palace with. Ignorance and disobedience to God's commands is another piece of armor we are to take away from the strong one. This means that our enemy is only as strong as we let him be. As verse 22 of Luke 11 shows us, we are, as God's warriors, to take away all the armor Satan, and his demons, are trusting in. It is in our failure as fathers to practice God's principle of " Shahmar " that the enemy gains his beach-heads, or foot-holds, in the lives of our children. We are commanded by our Commander-in-Chief to obey His commands found in Genesis 2:15. Any refusal to obey could very well cost our lives, or, the lives of our children.

Lastly, we turn to Exodus 6:14-26 & 7:4; 12:17 & 51, to explain how the Lord of all the earth, actually views our families as armies! Fathers and mothers are to train themselves, and their children, in the principles of warfare. Very few, if any, Christian people know this principle of God's Word. So we want to make it known. God says, "...bring forth My families,...bring forth My armies." Both the Church, and the family, are supposed to be preparing warriors for the purposes of Almighty God. In closing we say that in the founding of the government of the United States of America, the framers of our U.S. Constitution considered the protection of the nation from outside enemies, a major priority. Since then, it has spent literally trillions of dollars to provide military superiority over all foreign enemies. Our nation is literally armed to the teeth. But, my dear reader, we must know, and understand, that our greatest enemies are not outside the boundaries of our nation. Our greatest threat is found inside our land. It is the spiritual beings of immorality, that through pornography, are working to turn our daughters into whorish women. It is the whoremongering spiritual powers of Satan, leading our sons to be irresponsible in their relationships with women. And causing the destruction of our offspring by abortion. It is the demon powers of greed and covetousness, that cause us to see material possessions more valuable, than our precious children. These are some of your enemies, fathers of America. They exist within your borders. Not outside. It is the evil attitudes and demons of our hearts. It is these real enemies in our land, that will turn God, the Almighty, against us. And, if He is against us, all the sophisticated weapondry we are working to invent, will not be capable of defending us from His mighty hand of judgment. The seldom read book of the prophet Habakkuk shows us that God will use nations of greater wickedness than us, to destroy us, if we refuse to repent of our own National wickedness. We, as fathers, are to not allow ourselves to be deceived by the forces of Satan. Our greater responsibility is to provide for the care [gahvad] and protection [shahmar] of our families. When we stand before God, we will give account to Him, of these commandments. We have covered just about every weapon God has provided us with to annihilate our enemies. It is now our job to be God's mighty warriors in the earth. For His honor, and glory. Below are listed some books which can increase our discernment relating to spiritual warfare.

Recommended reading:

1. *War on the Saints*; by: Jessie Penn-Lewis, Lowe Press, New York, 1984.
2. *The Invisible War*; by: Donald Grey Barnhouse, Zondervan Press, 1977.
3. *Chains of the Spirit*; by: Tim Timmons, Canon Press, 1973.
4. *Pigs in the Parlor*; by: Frank & Ida Mae Hammond, Impact Books, Inc., 1973.
5. *The Saints at War*; by: Frank Hammond, The Children's Bread Ministry, P.O Box 789 Plainview, TX. 79073.
6. *Born for Battle*; by: R. Arthur Mathews, 1978. Published by: Overseas Missionary Fellowship - 404 S. Church St., Robesonia, PA. 19551.

7. *Principles of War*; by: James I. Wilson, published by: Random Press, 1983.

8. *The Symposium on God's Deliverance*; By: Michael D. Juzwick, Light Eternal Publications, ©1999 - Phone 206. 497. 8553.

CHAPTER 13

Fatherhood &
The Use of the Tongue

21)   Death and life are in the power [authority - direction
        under the supervision of] the tongue: and they that
        love it [life or death] shall eat the fruit thereof. —
        The Book of Proverbs 18:21

We begin this study of the use of the tongue by saying that it is
in our mastery of our ability to use words that we achieve victory in
our own lives, and in the lives of our sons, and daughters. For in this
Proverb 18:21, we can observe some important principles. First, we
see that death is a life force. It is the negative use of God's positive
life force. This negative principle was introduced and released into the
Garden of Eden (ref. Genesis 2:16 & 17; 3:1-24) under the deception
of Satan. The negative force of death *"..was."* in the hands of the
Devil. Hebrews 2: 14 -

14)   Forasmuch then as the children are partakers of flesh
        and blood, He [Christ] also Himself likewise took
        part of the same; that through death He might destroy
        him that had the power of death, that is, the Devil;

Revelation 1:18 shows that Jesus Christ, in His death, and resurrection, took back the keys, or authority, of the death principle
from Satan. We also see that in Romans 10:8-9, it is when an individual "..believes. And confesses with his mouth, that Jesus Christ

is Lord..." that Proverbs 18:21 comes about. The man, that by his own words acknowledges Christ to be Lord, transfers his life from Satan's kingdom of death, to God's kingdom of everlasting life. This is the starting point for us all. The transfer of our lives out of Satan's kingdom of darkness, and into God's kingdom of light only accomplishes eternal salvation. We know that there is much to be done in our lives after this. Depending on our lives prior to salvation are we made aware of the changes God, through the working of the Holy Spirit, and ourselves, must make.We should make a careful inventory of established thought patterns, and habitual practices, we exercise that are contrary to God's purposes for our lives. The fact that Satan, his demonic powers, evil men and women, and this evil world system has literally brain washed our hearts,and minds, to think and live according to their ways must be understood. If we wish to go anywhere from our present state. There are three specific portions of God's Word that manifests His will for us in this important area. Romans 12: 1 & 2; Ephesians 2: 1 & 2; Ephesians 4:23. Since it is in the heart and mind of man that every action is conceived and brought to fruition, we must come to a basic understanding of what actually dwells inside our multi-faceted heart. What resides inside the corridors of our minds. As we said in our chapter on fatherhood and Shahmar, unless we, as fathers, understand that we are commanded by God to protect our minds and hearts, and the hearts and minds of our sons and daughters, Satan and his demon powers can place their evil devices, or thoughts, in our minds, and hearts. This can cause us to act, or react, in ways contrary to God's will.

The words that proceed out of our mouths through the vehicle of our tongues originally come from our minds and hearts These words can bring about certain positive or negative results in our lives, or in the lives of those within our sphere of influence. As we said earlier in the writing, both God and Satan must have a medium through which to manifest their will and purpose within the earthly setting. This also means either of them must also have *a mind - heart - mouth system* to speak through. We all must understand this basic principle on earth. We must learn to discern whether truth, or error, is being spoken by the mouths we hear daily speaking to us. We need to learn why certain words are spoken by certain individuals. What are the motivations behind a man, or, woman's, communication. We must learn to discern our own hearts and minds and those of others and gain the capacity to know if the words proceeding from the lips of others are originating from God as their source, or, Satan, or, his angels. For there are only two spiritual kingdoms on this earth. All men, women, boys and girls are representatives of one, or, the other. It must be understood that each and every human being on the face of this earth is a minister. Everybody ministers something. It is a deception for us to believe that only a man who speaks from a pulpit is a minister. ***We all are ministers of God, or, of Satan.*** (See 2nd Corinthians 11: 13-15). Both God, and Satan, desire to utilize our hearts, minds, and mouths to bring things to pass in this earth. It is within our decision to allow God, or, his enemy, to use us to accomplish their will. As fathers and mothers we must seriously study this reality. It is our responsibility to help our children to understand these deep truths.

A SMALL MEMBER - JAMES 3

1) My brothers, be not many masters [teachers], knowing that we shall receive the greater judgment.
2) For in many things we offend all. If any man offend not in word, the same is a perfect - mature] man, and able also to bridle the whole body.
3) Behold we put bits in the horse's mouths, that they may obey us; and we turn about their whole body.
4) Behold also the ships, which though they be so great, and are driven of fierce winds, yet they are turned about with a very small helm, whither so ever the governor desires.

5) Even so the tongue is a little member, and boasts great things. Behold, how great a matter a little fire kindles.

6) And the tongue is a fire, a world of iniquity [a great source of sin in the earth]: So is the tongue among our members, that it defiles the whole body, and sets on fire the course of nature; and it is set on fire of Hell. For every kind of beasts, and of birds, and of serpents [creeping things], and of things in the sea, is tamed, and has been tamed of mankind:

8) But the tongue can no man tame; it is an unruly evil, full of deadly poison.

9) Therewith we bless God, even the Father; and therewith we curse men, which are made after the similitude (likeness] of God.

10) Out of the same mouth proceeds blessing and cursing. My brothers, these things should not be so [happening].

11) Does a fountain send forth at the same place (origin] sweet water and bitter.

12) Can the fig tree, my brothers, bear olive berries? either a vine, figs? So can no fountain yield both salt water and fresh.

13) Who is a wise man and endued with knowledge among you? Let him show out of a good conversation [behavior] his works with meekness of wisdom.

14) But if you have bitter envying and strife (quarreling] in your hearts, glory not (do not be proud, and lie not against the truth.

15) This wisdom descends not from above [does not originate from God], but is earthly, sensual, and demonic.

16) For where envying and strife is, there is confusion, and every evil work. [Satanic and demonic power is present].

17) But the wisdom that is from above [derives its source from God] is first pure, then peaceable, gentle, and easy to be entreated, full of mercy and good fruits, without partiality, and without hypocrisy. 18) And the fruit of righteousness is sown in peace of them that make peace. [Emphasis added]

It is very interesting that James 3 states, that we should be very concerned about *" the fountain "* or, origin of the words that proceed from our mouths. That, in verses 2 - 6, our tongues are given credit for the direction of our lives and our world. That, this can, in fact produce destruction in the earth. That, in verse 6, "..being set on fire of Hell." Is that Satan's authority in the earth rests in the words spoken by men, and women. We see that though all types of animals are able to be trained by man, man, without God's supernatural assistance, is helpless to bring his tongue under control. We see that it is possible for a believer to have both God's spiritual water come forth as a fountain out of his mouth. And then, bitter, or demon inspired words, to come out of his, or her heart and mouth. We see, that in verse 9, God expects us to honor His likeness in the lives of men. We are not to go to church, and praise and bless God. And then, with the same mouth, go out and curse and abuse people. God shows us in verses 13-18, that there are in fact two sources of wisdom " ..water and life.. ". God has wisdom, and it has certain characteristics (James 3:17 & 18). Satan has wisdom, which is twisted and perverted (Ezekiel 28:17). It is in the words that we speak, and the " way " in which we speak them, that God's nature, or, Satan's nature, is demonstrated. We are told by James, that our lives are a direct manifestation of either of these two natures. The epitomy of hypocrisy is when both natures are manifested in the same *" fountain "*. God says we cannot have this. Our work is to only be a fountain of God's blessing into the lives of others. That, when we allow the Satan-inspired hurts, and attacks of others, to release bitter water out of our mouths — we must check our plumbing to see if we have tapped into a source contrary to God's everlasting fountain of living waters. We must understand, that God can use our tongue to produce understanding and healing. And, Satan can use the same tongue to produce destruction and disease. It is our responsibility to "..steer the helm..". It is our responsibility "..to bridle and guide the horse..". It is our responsibility to allow and permit God through the ministry of His Holy Spirit, and His Word to order our words and speech. It is through our example, instruction, and guidance that our children learn to be wise with their words.

AN IMPORTANT WARNING
CONCERNING YOUR TONGUE

33) Either make the tree good, and his fruit good; or else make the tree - corrupt, Original Greek — σαπον (transliterated - Sapon) [defined - depraved, vicious, foul, or impure] and his fruit corrupt: for the tree is known by his fruit.

34) 0 generation of vipers, how can you being evil, speak good things. *For [because] out of the abundance of the heart the mouth speaks.*

35) A good man out of the good treasure of the heart brings forth out of his mouth good things: and an evil man out of the evil treasure of [his heart] brings forth evil things.

36) But I say to you, that ever idle word that men speak, they shall give account thereof in the day of judgment.

37) For by your words you shall be justified, and by your words you shall be condemned. - Gospel of Matthew 12:33-37) [Emphasis added]

The first three verses of Jesus Christ spoken here are designed by Him to produce discernment in our lives. Again, it is our work to investigate, and evaluate, which kind of " ..tree.. ", or "..treasure..", we are. This allows us to work at producing change in our "..trees.." and our "..little sprigs..". God instructs us to "..make.." the tree, and it's fruit good. It is in our hands to do this. This is precisely God's instructions in Genesis 2:15. To Gahvad (care for) and Shahmar (protect) our gardens. But the nourishment of a tree proceeds from " a source ". The sap of a tree provides for its nourishment. God created all people " trees " to need, and be filled, with His Word and Holy Spirit. This makes the tree good and it's fruit (children) good. The proverb *"you don't have to look too far from the tree to see its fruit"* is well stated. But, in the United States of America — since our seeds (children) are scattered across our nation that becomes difficult. It is this broken down " hedge " of father-mother, and son and daughter accountability, that has, in some cases, produced evil fruit in our land. In Matthew 12: 33 - 37 - we find one of the greatest warnings to all men and women. He warns here, that "..every.." idle word that proceeds forth out of our mouth.." will be brought into account. A C. P. A. [Certified Public Accountant] is certified to account for all accounts receivable, and expenditures, their clients are responsible for. It is not clearly known how God will do this - "..every idle word spoken..". Some have witnessed, in " out of the body " temporary death experiences, that their lives passed before them. Some have believed that our brain has a " recorder " type mechanism, which records all we say, and do. That, after death, the " taped " recording rewinds. And God, at His seat of judgment (ref. 2nd Cor. 5: 10 & Revelation 20:11-15) will play back our lives, and words, to Himself, and us. At any account, Jesus Christ assures us we all must give account to Him, of all our words, which we permit to come out of our hearts, and through our tongues. We all will most likely be very embarrassed in that time of reckoning with God for our loose tongues. There is a proverb in the United States Navy, " Loose lips, sink ships!"

THE ATROCITY OF DIVORCE
& THE USE OF THE TONGUE

In this segment, we wish to bring understanding to fathers in relation to the horror of divorce in our nation. How it is bringing untold ruin to America, one family at a time. We speak not of divorce among the unbelieving community, but mainly of the scandal of treachery within the ranks of American Christianity. Our desire, and prayer, is that what is spoken in this book will deal a death blow to this area of Satan' s activity in this critical area. As we have said again, and again, both the Lord God and Satan, and his many evil powers, must have access to our tongues to produce effects and results in the earth [our physical world]. Please refer to chapter two again to review the definition of " earth ".

To start this important segment we ask the reader to muse and meditate in Matthew chapter 18 through chapter 19:15. The Holy Spirit of God, in His supervision of the writing of this text of Holy Scripture seems to have ordered these five basic elements to be understood in the Church and family.

1 - His judgment against abuse of children (Matthew 18:1-10).

2 - God's desire to rescue lost & abused people (Mt. 18:11-14).

3 - The united force of two believing people (fathers & mothers) in God's Spirit of agreement (Matthew 18:15-20).

4 - Forgiveness vs unforgiveness (Matthew 18:21-35). The release of God, or Satan's powers in our lives (and our children's lives).

5 - Divorce. And, its source (Matthew 19:8). Its damaging effects on children, since we are their examples in life.

These two chapters in Matthew are in essence power chapters. They show us how we are the vehicles to release spiritual forces in the earth. This relates with James 3:6, in that the very course of " nature ", or, earthly elements, are controlled by our tongues. This is an extremely important principle to understand. And learn to cooperate with God's Holy Spirit and Word in respecting. At this point we wish to refer to an important book which explains this " power-authority " principle. The book is titled: *Authority in Three Worlds* by: author Charles Capps.[10] The principle he speaks of in chapters four and eight is that through eating of the tree of the knowledge of Good and Evil (ref. Genesis 3) Satan gained access into this earth by using the *" tongue "* of the serpent. After that was accomplished, he then had been given by Adam [father of the earth] an authority to use physical bodies to do his works through. The first work he did after the fall is found in chapter four of Genesis. He energized in Cain, ' an unbelieving man, to " murder " his brother Abel (Ref. John 8:44). The principle Charles Capps brings out in his chapter on " The Keys to Understanding the Bible " is that in the eating of the tree of the " Knowledge of Good and Evil ", Adam, and his progeny had " learned " how to produce - evil - (Hebrew- רַע - pronounced - RAG). It is interesting that this word in the Hebrew meaning, refers to words of the mouth that produce evil, calamity hurts, wickedness, noxiousness (poisonous substances). Refer to chapter 3 under " Wheat & Tares ". This refers to the destruction of God's creation in the earthly realm. With the *words* [good or evil (RAG)] which proceed out of our hearts, and through our tongues, these powers [God's, or Satan's] are released into this earth. By way of illustration, we cite the process Satan, and his demons, use to break up a marriage. We must understand, that the break up of every marriage, begins in the heart of each spouse. Jesus reminded us of this truth in Matthew 18: 21 -35 and 19: 7-8).

They say to him [the religious Pharisees], why did Moses then command to give a writing of divorcement and to put her away? 8) He said to them, Moses, because of the hardness of your hearts, allowed you to put away your wives: but

---

10   Authority in Three Worlds, Charles Capps, Harrison Publishing House 1980.

from the beginning [God's original creation intent] it was not so. [Emphasis added]

"...Because of the hardness of your hearts..." This is why divorce is so rampant in our land. It is because Satan's destroying force of unforgiveness is practiced by those pursuing divorce. Rather than God's life restoring force of forgiveness. We all know that if two people dwell together there will be disagreements and offenses. It is the spiritual maturity, or immaturity, marriage partners practice that produces God's successes, or Satan's destruction in relationships. But the author wishes mainly to explain that it is in our failure to be mature enough in God's likeness to forgive in every situation no matter how hurtful to us personally, that Satan gains control over our lives. The author is speaking of those who are true believers. We should not expect unsaved, or unbelieving people to walk in God's ways. The main area that Satan launches his demonic attacks in our hearts, as believers, is when we fail to receive God's grace through Holy Spirit forgiveness. And refuse to let go of the offenses of both knowing and unknowing sins in our partner's life that are against us. It is here in the bonds of marriage that we are given many opportunities to prove we appreciate God's forgiveness, when we give it to our life partner. If we are truly God's child, it could be that God may be allowing certain offenses to come against us to assist us to learn to be like Him, in His great forgiveness of us for our offenses that have been committed against Him. Even our failures to forgive every time someone wrongs us, is an offense to God. If God would forgive adultery or murder, who are we to not do so? He grants us the ability to forgive the worst sin, and wickedness of anyone. And, God did not " wait " until any of us " deserved " to be forgiven, to provide it for us. Praise his magnificent grace and mercy!

We conclude this segment by stating that Satan uses our hurts to cause us to begin using evil (RAG) words concerning our relationship with our marriage partners. We speak evil (calamity) (Noxious) and negative words like: " he does not ever help me." " We cannot communicate anymore." " We have irreconcilable differences." " He does not care for me? " " He does not really love me." " She is always uncooperative with me. " " She is always unsubmissive in our relationship. " " He does not ever take time for the children." " She always nags me." "He never listens to me."

You notice the continual emphasis on the words - " always " and " never ", reveal the evil (RAG) disposition of always magnifying the negatives in the other partner's life. These are Satan's weapons to destroy a relationship. It is these " confessions " that "..set on fire the course of nature..", that bring "..deadly poison.." into a marriage. It is in the permitting of Satan, and his demons to incite and inspire us to speak out of our mouths, these kinds of statements that produces destruction in our lives. Marriages are destroyed only by the kinds of words we speak about our partners. In our hearts, or in our voices. They also are made strong as a fortress by the kinds of words we use to describe them. It is important for us as fathers to grasp this important concept of the authority and power of what we say. Our example sets the standard for, or against, our children.

It is also very important to help our children to understand these principles for the good of their lives. We are to cultivate the speaking of faith inspired statements. We refer to Hebrews 11:1, to explain this.

1)   Now faith is the substance of things hoped for, the evidence of things not seen.

In other words we are instructed by God to use our faith to produce results for us. This is explained by saying " I do not " see " kindness and consideration in my husband, but, " by faith " I can see it. And I will begin to speak it into existence by the words of my mouth. A statement like this brings God on the scene. Because, in Hebrews 11: 6, God is pleased with words like this! Another example of a practical outworking of this faith principle is: " I may not see, at this time, an ability to really communicate between my husband and me, but, by the powerful faith God gives to me, I speak free-flowing, positive communication into existence between us "..now..". Hebrews 11:1 says "..now..". Faith is released immediately at the place, and point, of our speaking it. This is confirmed in Romans 10:6 -9. Faith is, speaking into existence with our faith-filled words, those things that are "..hoped for..." or desired. Because of the reality of Satan's power, it may take a certain amount of time for it to manifest. But God will have respect. And honor your faith-filled confession, and words, you release through your tongue. Hebrews 11: 3 shows us that God used His Words, mixed with faith, to bring into existence every single thing we see in the creation. Genesis 1 - 2 shows us that "..God said.." and specific things came into existence. This applies to all of us, as having been created in God's image, and " likeness..". We are to imitate God by speaking certain things, that do not exist, into existence. Especially those things which are lacking in our marriages. And in our children's lives. Faith honors God. And God honors faith! Try it out.

It will be at the point of our maturity in Christ, that we will know, and understand, this powerful principle of God. We shall see some mighty things accomplished by our words as we obey.

THE SPIRITUAL STATE OF THE HEART

11)   " Does a fountain send forth at the same place, [opening] sweet [fresh] water and bitter? "

How would you like to be extremely dehydrated and thirsty, and run up to a drinking fountain, and when you turned the knob to release the water, find out that both good clean and fresh water came out? But, also, at the same place, polluted, noxious and smelly water came out? It would be very weird to find both kinds of " water " coming out of the same fountain. We, as fathers, must understand that God sees us all as little fountains walking around on His earth. Our children are, in fact, little fountains in the making! It is in our permitting of the polluted elements of our nation to propagate the filth of Satan, by secular media, that the little fountains, we are responsible to God for, take into their minds, and hearts, this noxious material. They become poisoned. And therefore, become fountains of poison. To be used by Satan, and his demon powers. The spiritual-state of the heart is be cultivated by us as fathers and mothers, in the development of our children's little lives (fountains).   What we permit to " flow " in through the " eye-gate " or, " ear-gate " fills their little hearts up with some kind of " water ". We are the " gate keepers " in their lives, until they have hopefully matured enough to keep their own gates. It is necessary to refer to two contrasting verses of Holy Scripture that speaks of " gates ". The first is found in Psalms chapter 24: 7-10)

7)   " Lift up your heads, 0 you gates; and you be lifted up you everlasting doors; and the King of Glory shall come in.

8)   Who is the King of Glory? The Lord strong and mighty, the Lord mighty in battle.

9)   Lift up your heads [the place of authority] 0 you gates; even lift them up, you everlasting doors; and the King of Glory shall come in.

10)   who is the King of Glory? The Lord of hosts, He is the King of Glory. "

This invitation comes to each and every man, and woman. Each of us who receive Jesus Christ the Lord, become His gates, or doors into this earth. It is through these gates, or doors, that God, His Word and Spirit " flows " through us into the lives of our children, and others. Revelation 3: 20, in some translations, the word - " door " is also translated " gate ". It means: a place of access into another world, or, area. In contrast to this view of people's lives being gates, or, doors for God, we see Satan's counterpart in using certain men, women, or children in Matthew 16: 18 - 25 -

18)   And I say also to you, that you are Peter, [original Greek - Πετροσ transliterated Petros - little stone] and upon this rock [Greek - πετρα transliterated -petra - strong foundation stone] I will build My Church; and the gates of Hell shall not prevail against it.

These ".. Gates of Hell.. " are those fountains under Satan's control. Those people who reside inside the kingdom of darkness. Those who have become inhabited by the demonic powers of darkness. Those who have not entered into God's kingdom by the New Birth (Ref. John 3:1-8). Genesis 22:17 speaks of Abraham's seed (Ref. Galatians 3: 29) possessing the " Gate " of his enemies. Which most likely speaks prophetically of the evangelization of Satan's gates (people) by us who believe, and reach out to those who are in the enemy's hands. Our love, and care, for those without God. And a free flow of God's waters of life, opens these " gates ". And causes us to possess the gate of God's enemy. The spiritual state of our hearts, and those of our children, is under the guidance, care, and protection, which we as fathers and mothers provide for them. As explained in the proceeding chapters of this book there are many sources of polluted, obnoxious waters of bitterness, attempting to flow into our lives. And those of our offspring. We are commanded by God " to protect the gates ". " to guard the doors ". Make sure " the fountains " are not polluted by God's enemies. We are to practice the principle of Shahmar. In Matthew 12: 34, we have learned that "...out of the abundance of the heart our mouth speaks..". This instructs us to watch carefully what " flows into the heart through the eye, or, ear gates ". As manifested in Genesis 2:15, God's principle of Gahvad commands us as fathers to administrate the Words of God, and His Holy Spirit, into our hearts. And those of our children. It is in the abundance of these precious substances that our mouths, and those of our sons and daughters shall speak. It is when this is done that these proverbs shall come to pass.

Proverb 4: 24 -

" Put away from you a froward mouth,
and perverse lips put far from you."
Proverb 10:13(a)

" In the lips of him that has understanding wisdom is found:."

Proverb 10:21(a)

" The lips of the righteous feed many..."

Proverb 10:32(a)

" The lips of the righteous know what is acceptable..."

Proverb 14:3(b)

"...But the lips of the wise shall preserve them."

Proverb 15:7(a)

" The lips of the wise disperse knowledge..."

All this knowledge, wisdom, health, acceptable things, food, understanding, etc. proceeds from a source. A fountain if you will. That fountain, or source, is our hearts. We must first have inside of us the knowledge of God's will (His Word) before we can speak and do His will. This is why Colossians 1: 7-13 uses the word - " filled

" in verse 9. This is our assignment from God. The cultivation and planting into our hearts and minds. And of our children's minds of God's Word, and the flow of God's Spirit causes the " trees " to grow and bring forth fruit that can feed those who are hungry. Mankind is under such deception and delusion by Satan, and his powers, they do not even recognize fruit, or, food that is good to eat, from that which is evil (RAG) and produces perversity and destruction. To hate the good Word of God, and love Satan's garbage, is normal for the unregenerate carnal mind and heart. In recognizing this we see how desperately we need God's mighty deliverance in our lives. That, without Him, we truly can do nothing. That, without His care, we shall surely perish. We close this segment by referring to two areas of God's Word. The first is Matthew 5: 8 -

8)   " Blessed are the pure in heart: For they shall see God. "

It is in our cleansing out of our hearts that our eyes begin to be able to focus, visualize, or, see God. James 4:8 instructs us " to purify our hearts ". 2nd Timothy 2: 21 speaks to us of our part with God of "..purging ourselves.." of the defilements of Satan's world system. That, as we do, we become fit, or clean enough for the Master to use. Ephesians 5:17-29 manifests to us that as husbands and fathers it is in our administration of filling the vessels with the " water " of the Holy Spirit. And utilizing the Word of God to cleanse hearts and minds, that the state of the heart is strong and healthy. It is in our failure and disobedience to this life principle that corruptions and pollutions from God's enemy enter the heart and mind. Psalms 24:1-5 shows us that those who have prepared "... a pure heart.. " shall enter God's presence. Cleansed out of all the defilement of the enemy. The spiritual state of the heart of our lives, and those under our authority as fathers and mothers, is becoming increasingly difficult to maintain. It takes much, much more than a Sunday morning each week in a church service. The forces of the gates of Hell shall intensify as the end nears. We shall see more and more blatant control of all media sources by Satan, and his demons in the future. This will be to produce the anti-christ, one-world or New Age system. Proverbs 4:1-2; 20-23 is our mandate to overcome it, and be victorious.

1) Hear, you children, the instruction of a father, and attend to know understanding.

2) For I give you good doctrine, forsake you not my law [covenant].

3) My son, attend to my words; incline your ear to my sayings.

21) Let [permit] them not to depart from your eyes; keep them in the midst of your heart.

22) For they are life to those that find them, and health to all their flesh [including children].

23) Keep [Hebrew- שָׁמַר - shahmar] your heart with all diligence; for out of it are the issues [spiritual forces] of life.

Proverbs 4:23 shows us God's area of deep concern. The spiritual - state of our hearts. Because it is from this source everything in the earth comes into existence. Psalms 53:1-6 shows us that "..the fool " says in his heart " no " to God, and consequently that heart produces evil, calamity, and destructions in the earth. In the Book of Hebrews 4:12 we observe another revelation from God on improving the spiritual state of our hearts.

12) For the Word of God is quick, [alive and powerful] and sharper than any two-edged sword [lit. Greek. μαχαιραν - Machiara] piercing even to the dividing asunder of soul [lit. Greek. Psyche and spirit, [lit. Greek - Pneuma] and of the joints and marrow, and

257

is a discerner [lit, Greek. - κριτικοσ - Kpitikos - Criticizer] of the thoughts and intents of the heart.

Here we see again the " Machiara " spoken of in Ephesians 6:17, as we studied in chapter 12. The little hand-held dagger used to get into small areas. The small areas of our hearts and minds. The Greek word - krino " discerner " is the word we get critic, or criticizer. God's Word is to be used as a little dagger in our hearts and minds to be a critic of our " thoughts " and intents (motivations) of our hearts. This reveals our dependence on God, and His Word, to keep, and Shahmar our hearts and minds from evil (RAG) thoughts and intents. This is the focal point for all warfare. You control the heart and mind of a man, woman, boy, or girl you control their entire lives. God desires, and even commands us to permit His Word - to rule - [literally umpire] inside our hearts. Colossians 3: 12 - 16. The parable of the sower in Luke 8: 11 - 21, should also be meditated upon.

SPEAKING YOUR MIND VS SPEAKING GOD'S MIND

"sticks and stones may break my bones;
but words will never hurt me."

So goes the childhood poem we are taught to use to counter unkind hurtful words spoken against us. But what does God say about this crucial area? Proverbs 15:1 -

" A soft answer turns away wrath;
but grievous words stir up anger. "

That childhood poem does nothing to turn wrath away. If any-thing, it stirs up a more intense desire to inflict wounds in the one speaking it. It is, therefore, a lie. Here is another revelation where spiteful words spoken out of the mouth do damage. Proverbs 18: 8 -

" The words of a talebearer are as [like] wounds, and, they go down into the inner most parts of the belly."

Here we see that words produce wounds inside the victim's innermost parts of their belly. Inside their heart and emotional part. This verse is repeated in Proverbs 26: 22. It does not seem natural, or normal, but God does not always direct us in ways that " seem " natural and normal. We see this in this next proverb. Proverbs 25: 15 -

" By long forbearing [enduring verbal attacks] is a prince persuaded, and a soft tongue breaks the bone."

Now we know God's way. We repay unkind, and hurtful words with kind, and healthful words. For God knows that behind every unkind word, is an evil (RAG) spirit, working to do damage, or produce destruction. Usually a person cutting, and chopping on someone less strong, is seriously suffering with their self esteem. Cutting words usually are designed to make the one speaking them " seem " superior. To use our words of kindness, and help build our offender's self esteem " ..breaks the bones.." of the evil spirit behind the verbal abuse! Praise be to God for His wisdom! To look for any good qualities in our offender, and compliment verbally those qualities, destroys Satan's power in that person's life. And causes him to become your friend. You have to be built up in God's Spirit of forgiveness to be able to do this, but God will always honor it. They may walk away even ridiculing your kindness in the midst of their abuse, but that act of your's will go into their hearts, and produce good eventually. You must pray, and intercede for that enemy. Even thank God for him, or her (Ref. 1st Timothy 2:1-6). If you, by God's Spirit, discern a demon spirit is inspiring the abuse, cast it out of him in the name of the Lord

Jesus Christ (Ref. Luke 10:17-20). We say this because, the natural way we normally respond, is contrary to the way God would have us respond. We see this in Isaiah 55: 6 -11. -

6)   Seek you the Lord while He may be found, call you upon Him while He is near:

7)   Let the wicked forsake his way, and the unrighteous man his thoughts: And let him return [check in] with the Lord, and He will have mercy upon him: and to our God, for He will abundantly pardon.

8)   For My thoughts are not your thoughts, neither are your ways My ways says the Lord.

9)   For as the heavens are higher than the earth, so are My ways higher than your ways, and My thoughts than your thoughts.

10)   For as [like] the rain comes down, and the snow from heaven, and returns not back into cloud form, but waters the earth, and makes [causes] it to bring forth and bud, that it may give seed to the sower, [farmer] and bread to the eater:

11)   So shall My Word be that goes forth out of My mouth: it shall not return to Me void, [without fruit] but will accomplish that which I please, and it shall prosper in the thing whereto I sent it. "

God says what comes out of His thoughts, and then, His mouth always succeeds. When we understand that in our sonship relation-ship with the heavenly Father, we are to develop " our " minds into minds " like " - God's mind. And our hearts are to become like God's heart. Then, our mouths, hearts, and words will be lined up with God's Words. This will cause us to see God's power manifested in the earthly setting. Jesus told the twelve disciples this in Matthew 6: 9 -13. Specifically verse 10:

10) "Your kingdom come your will be done in [the] earth, as [like] it is in Heaven."

It is in this earth that God's will is not obeyed. It is in the physical beings of the earth's hands to do God's will, or not. Therefore, fathers and mothers are to speak God's kind of words in this earthly setting. We are to follow His ways. This principle is reiterated in 1st Corinthians 2:10-16. The last phrase of verse 16 says - "..We have the mind of Christ. ". Our minds are to be duplicates of the mind of God in the earthly setting. The image, and likeness of God in man commands for this to be so. The greatest reason for the lack of vigor among God's people is because a small portion of their minds are given over to God's instruction and likeness. And the majority of it is filled with the programming of Satan's philosophies and ideologies. James 1: 5 -8 shows us the cause of this serious problem.

5) " If any of you lack wisdom, let him ask of God, that gives to all men liberally, and upbraids not; [does not throw your lack of it up in your face] and it shall be given to him.

6) But let him ask in faith, nothing wavering. [absolutely no doubts] for [because] he that wavers is like a wave of the sea driven with the wind and tossed.

7) For let not that man think he shall receive anything from the Lord.

8) A double-minded man is unstable in all his ways."

We cannot expect to receive from God anything unless our minds are transformed to be like God's. It is interesting that the condition psychologists call schizophrenia - Greek - διψυχοσ - transliterated - diphukos, means: having two minds, or personalities, is being double-minded, and therefore unstable, or unreliable (Ref. Psalm 12: 2). The Bible confronts this as sin to be repented of by men and women. Not only mental illness to be treated with powerful and debilitating pharmacuticals. The psychiatric diagnosis of multiple personalities disorder could be in reality demonic possession. Though licensed mental health professionals cannot diagnose a condition of this kind. Christ has commanded believers to cast out demons. We are, as Romans 8: 29 and 12: 1 - 2 says - to be conformed to the image of God's Son. We are to have one mind, united with God's mind. God's mind is revealed in Holy Scripture. We are to flush out our minds, and pour in God's mind, about everything. When we have properly reproduced God's mind in our lives, then, in the power of His Spirit, we can " speak " His mind in the earth.

Because our world is now at war with our Creator, we must cut off the sources of Satan's lies and falsehoods. The TV, radio, and Internet medias are full of corrupting and defiling influences in our day.

RULING BY YOUR WORDS

The Book of Genesis reveals to us that all we can see in the physical universe came into existence by God speaking it into existence. We also know that all the stars and planets stay in their courses because God commanded it to be so. Everything on the earth stays on the earth because God said for this to be so. Sir Isaac Newton gave a name to it. He called it gravity. God has ruled everything by His Word. Not so long ago, the Wright Brothers learned how to use aeronautic principles in order to overcome God's Word concerning gravity. Now, we see the amazing transportation of people all over the earth by aircraft. Genesis 1: 26 shows us that God, in His creation of man made him to function in the earthly setting " like " He rules the universe. Adam, and all subsequent men, were created to rule over this earth in the same way God has given example of. By His words. It is in our knowledge of God's wisdom [the principles of His creation] that we are able to rule in this earth as God has ordained. Both God, and Satan, know that man can produce specific results in this earth by the words of his mouth.   This is the purpose God has provided us with the Holy Bible. It is our guide to run the earth God's way. It is in our diligent study of God's mind that we gain God's ability to be like He is. It is in our failure to do this that Satan, and his powers, gain entrance into, or, over our lives.

If I, as a father, speak to my son, and convince him to follow a certain course of action he may greatly benefit from it. If he refuses my instruction, he may get into serious trouble. Man is the only creature that God has given the privilege of being like Himself. Like Himself in using words to produce specific results. Like Himself in fathering new beings like ourselves. Made in God's image. The author encourages further study, and research, on the words in the Bible, that speak of *the tongue, mouth, lips, speech, voice, heart, ears, eyes, and mind*. Through this pursuit we will gain further ability to rule in righteousness over God's creations in the earth. We, with God's understanding, and power, can produce miracles with our spoken words. Mixed with God's power of faith. God's salvation, deliverance, and healing will be administered through our lives, to the lives we, as fathers and mothers, have brought into existence in this world. This is God's glory created in man. To be like Him. To love like Him. To care like Him. To heal like Him. To think like Him. To feel like Him. To speak like He would speak. These things would glorify God (Ref. Isaiah 61:1-3). Psalms 119: 169 -172 -

" Let my cry come near before you, O Lord: Give me under-standing according to your Word. Let my supplication come before you: Deliver me according to your Word. My lips shall utter praise, when you have taught me your statutes. My tongue shall speak of your Word: Because all your com-mandments are righteousness. "

And, Proverbs 23: 15 -16 -

" My son, if your heart be wise, my heart shall rejoice, even mine. Yes, my reins [heart] shall rejoice, when your lips speak right things. "

THE SPIRITUAL POWER OF WORDS

" And Jesus answering said to them, have faith in God. [Have God's kind of faith]. 23) Because truly I say to you, that whosoever shall say to this mountain, you be removed, and you be cast into the sea, and shall not doubt in his heart, but shall believe that those things which he says shall come to pass: he shall have whatsoever he says. 24) Therefore I say to you, what things soever you desire, when you pray, believe that you receive them, and you shall have them.' — The Gospel of Mark 11: 22 - 24

In this area of God's Word, we see that Christ confirmed that man has the capacity to operate in the same powerful principle of faith as God. That, which we say, when genuine faith and understanding is mixed with it, will produce miraculous results. By way of illustration the author must give testimony to the glory of God to heal, and deliver from demons, in a number of examples in his own life which took place. The first was when my son, Justin Wyatt, was 1 -1/2 years old. He developed a viral infection in his mouth. Large blisters were all over the inside of his mouth, and it was bright red. He had an accompanying high fever. God led me to take authority over it, in the name of Jesus Christ. I laid my hands upon his head. Prayed. Then I spoke directly to the viral infection, and commanded it to dissipate and be destroyed. The fever immediately left. The blisters grew smaller and the redness grew normal. It took a little longer for the blisters to totally disappear. Praise be to God our healer! By being his father, I had authority to speak over my son, and see God's Spirit produce healing. God is pleased to see healing take place. We minister His Word in the earth for Him. The second situation was when a fellow worker in California wanted to be delivered from his addiction to heroin. The demons destroyed the glass ash tray by turning it into powder as he burned his needle, and remaining heroin in it, as they departed out of his life. Praise God for the Word of God! When we allow God's power, and Word to flow from our lives, the natural must give way to the supernatural. This is what God is pleased to see take place. I could speak of other mighty events that took place.

Another area that shows the spiritual power of words is found in John 6: 63)

" It is the Spirit that quickens: [makes alive] the flesh profits nothing: The words that I speak to you, they are spirit, and they are life. "

Whenever anyone speaks to us, their mouth and tongue move, but do we " see " words coming out? No. Because spoken words are spiritual. They cause things to happen in the spirit - realm. This is the reason those who preach God's Word are very important. They release the knowledge of God's will into the earth. If they all stopped preaching, it would not be long before Satan, and his demon pow- ers, and principalities gained total control over the earth. This will be manifested when God removes the true Church off this earth (Ref. John 14:1-6 & 1st Thessalonians 4:13 -18; 2nd Thessalonians 2: 1 -12). But, at this time, we are to be working with God to rescue those held captive by Satan, and his demon powers. We say this now because it is in the Spirit - anointed use of our tongue, and words, that demon spirits are "..cast out.." of their victim's lives.

Many of God's people do not know how to cast out spirits of evil. Much wickedness and evil now exists in the lives of people because of ignorance, neglect, and disobedience in this vital area. Many cases of spiritual, emotional, mental, and physical illness and sickness have demons behind them. The Lord Jesus Christ has given, and vested us who believe, with His all powerful name. We need to see a great move of God's power being exercised by us who truly believe, and love Him. Fathers and mothers must glorify God by seeing that Matthew 8:16 reveals this important truth.

> 16) When the evening was come, they brought to Him [Jesus] many that were possessed with demons: [evil spirits] and He "cast out " - literal Greek - εκβαλαιν - transliterated - ekbalain - which means: to violently throw out] the spirits with His Word, and healed all that were sick. "

Many Christians are not exercising their faith in Christ's blessed words of power. Even though Mark 16: 17 informs us that this very ability to remove demons would be a true sign, of a true believer in the Lord Jesus Christ, this vital, and desperately needed ministry, is usually neglected and ignored. It is very interesting that in Luke 11: 20, Jesus equated the use of the tongue to cast out demons as -

"...the finger of God.."

When we, as believers, use the Words of God, to allow God's Holy Spirit free reign (ref. 1st Thessalonians 5:19) to flow out of us, into those in need, we also can be used to "..put the finger on.. " demon powers. And, we too can cast them out with " our " words! At certain times, mental and physical sickness and illness can have wicked evil spirits behind it. They must be removed before God's healing can occur. Many spend their hard earned money for harmful drugs to get cured. When the exercise of faith, and love, through the laying on of hands would restore health to those who suffer various illnesses, sickness and maladies. - see the book of James chapter 5: 13 - 16. Medical authorities can be helpful to bring healing, but,

Jesus Christ is the Great Physician, and, our ultimate Healer. Sadly, in this time of our nation's history, greed is behind the big push to sell pharmaceuticals. And our food sources are being poisoned and altered with GMO [Genetically Modified Organisms] by those only interested in their own profits at the expense of our physical health. Shame be upon them for it !

CONFESSION FOR HEALING

I am the body of Christ, I am redeemed from the curse, and I forbid any sickness, or disease, to operate in this body. Every organ, every tissue functions in the perfection to which God created it to function. Every organ, every tissue, will function properly. For greater is He that is in me, than he that is in the world. Based upon the book of Exodus chapter 15 verse 26 - obedience to God's Word.

- Charles Capps: The Tongue - A Creative Force

CHAPTER 14

Fatherhood and Hedgework

Believing, and understanding, that we live in a spiritually hostile environment is the first step in securing a trustworthy system of protection in, and around, our family's lives. Any father, who refuses to acknowledge that there are spiritual forces, which are out to defile and destroy that which God loves, is in fact under the deception of the enemy Satan. Deceiver of the whole world [see Revelation 12: 9].

So, as we proceed into this strategic chapter, we will study the many aspects of providing the spiritual, not physical, protections God has ordained for our lives. And, the lives of our sons and daughters.

As fathers, we are commanded by God to utilize every mean available to us to halt, and hinder, any advancement by the enemy into our lives. Or, those who are placed under our care by God the Father. A refusal to do this is a direct disobedience to God's known will (ref. Genesis 2:15). It is, in fact, an abominable dereliction of duty. We are communicating not only of hedgework protection to surround the lives of our sons and daughters, but of the real center of battle and warfare; their hearts and souls.

This treatise on Fatherhood and Hedgework provides the understanding of this often neglected need. And some of the knowledge of what kind of materials to use in erecting protection in, and around, those we are caring for. And how to construct them. It is the work and labor of each and every father and mother that brings about these forms of protection for the benefit of our households.

Before we enter into the various aspects of hedgework, we will first review the way God has indicted men for their refusal to do this work in the past nation of Israel, and their subsequent destruction by God's judgment. The Lord God Almighty sought to utilize the pre-dispersion people of Israel and Judah to be an example of His will and desire for all nations of the earth. But as we review the words of the prophet Ezekiel, we can see they became an example of His wrath and chastising hand rather than an example of how God can bless those who obey His commands for the earth.

FOOLISH PROPHETS VS. NATIONAL HEDGEWORK

3) " This says the Lord God; woe to the foolish prophets, that follow their own spirit, and have seen nothing!

4) O Israel, your prophets are like the foxes in the deserts [waste places].

5) You have not gone up into the gaps, [broken places -broken marriage & family relationships. Generation gaps] neither made up [or repaired] the hedge for the house of Israel to stand in the battle in the day of the Lord." (Ezekiel 13:3-5)

The first condemnation of God against Israel's prophets was that they *"..have seen nothing! "* and *"..follow their own spirit,.."* In Old Testament times a prophet was also called a " seer ". The place a seer held, was to bring God's answers to perplexing problems men and women were surrounded by. When God indicted Israel's false seers, or prophets, it was because they sought the vision, or veiwpoint of other sources, rather than the Lord God. Jezebel, in 1st Kings 18:1-22, had eight hundred and fifty false seers or prophets that were giving occult information through the spirit of divination.

This was the communication of demons to the head witch of the nation of Israel, the queen of Ahab, Jezebel. Elijah was given specific instruction from God on how the nation could recover from being overthrown by the wicked, but the witch Jezebel used the authority of Ahab, king of the nation, to destroy God's true seers. She even desired to kill Elijah after God gave him victory over all her false prophets. In America today there are many more than eight hundred and fifty false prophets and prophetesses that also *"..eat at Jezebel's table.."* [ref.1st Kings 18:19]. Astrologists, psychics, tarot card readers, palm readers, therapists ect. all give their professional counsel, for at times very large sums of money, but their advice is received from occult sources. Many today even use the name of Jesus Christ to deceive with occult information [see Matthew 24: 4 & 5]. The English word- " therapy " is the Biblical Greek word - θεραπεύετε for healing transliterated. The word " psychology " means: word, or study of the soul. God's Word was written to give mankind a way to examine themselves and see their great need for the Lord God. Yet, those who occupy powerful places of authority over men and women's lives, reject the pure Word of the Creator and derive large sums of money even from U.S. Federal and State treasuries. The antithesis is the shabby ways those who teach and minister God's Word are financially cared for! To bring this into today's vernacular it would be said this way. These prophets (preachers) follow their own human programs. Rather than God's hedgework program. They follow their own desires and ignore God's desires for His people. Verse four is descriptive of spiritual leaders who act like "..foxes.." scavengers in the waste places. They are not doing the things God has ordained to protect or strengthen God's people. But rather they are taking away the little strength that is there. In effect, they are doing more for God's enemy than for God.

The Lord God's next criticism is that they *"..have not gone up into the " gaps..."* This speaks of the divisions between fathers and their children. Divisions between men and women being created by gender pride and self-centered attitudes. The wars that rage to destroy peace, harmony and cooperation between husbands and wives. The generation gaps that block the passing on of vital information for success in life from fathers and mothers to their needy offspring. Communication gaps between God's people in families and Church. They are busy dividing the sheep [criticizing other Churches and ministers] rather than " seeing " the destruction Satan is bringing into families with pornography. And wicked divorce courts. They are refusing to do what God expects to be done. They do not stand up in the gaps where Satan is bringing in his wickedness and destruction.

" Neither made [built] up the hedge " for the house of Israel.."

This is the work of the ministry for God's true spiritual leaders. Those who know God's Word are to be active in the building of hedges. If they are not doing this they are useless to God and His people. They are foolish prophets. Isaiah 56:10 & 11 describes these foolish ministers also as we can review God's Word through him: -

10)   " His watchmen are blind: They are all ignorant, [ignore the dangers to God's nation] they are all dumb dogs, they cannot bark; sleeping, lying down, loving to slumber.

11)   Yes they are greedy dogs which can never have enough, and they are shepherds that cannot understand: they all look to their own way, every one for his gain, from his quarter."

A good watch dog will guard his master's house in either of two ways. He will either be silent until an intruder enters the property and attack viciously, or, he will bark viciously, to warn the intruder that the cost of advancing further will be to be met by an attack. This is the work of the prophets in any nation. Including our nation called the United States of America. God has ordained that His prophets be the instruments of warning to wake people up before it is too late. The evil and wickedness we see existing in our nation today exists because there is a great lack of prophets who " bark ". Speak out the warnings of God's judgment against wickedness. The very preaching out against various forms of evil builds hedges by warning others of spiritual danger to their lives. What kind of bark do you have?

Next, are some of the things God wants spiritual leaders to manifest. And what happens when they refuse to be the right kind of leaders in a nation. Our reference text is in Ezekiel 22: 26 -31.

26) " Her priests have violated my law, and have profaned my holy things: They have put no difference between the holy and profane, neither have they showed difference between the unclean and the clean, and have hid their eyes from my sabbaths, and I am profaned among them.

27) Her princes in the midst of her are like wolves ravening the prey, to shed blood, and to destroy souls, to get dishonest gain.

28) And her prophets [preachers] have daubed them with untempered mortar, seeing vanity, and divining lies to them, saying, this the Lord God says, when the Lord has not spoken.

29) The people of the land have used oppression, and exercised robbery, and have vexed the poor and needy: Yes, they have oppressed the stranger wrongfully.

30) And I sought for a man among them, that should make up the hedge, and stand in the gap before me for the land, that I should not destroy it: But I found none.

31) Therefore have I poured out mine indignation upon them; I have consumed them in the fire of my wrath:

Their own way have I recompensed upon their heads,
says the Lord God."

It is extremely interesting that in Ezekiel 22:25 God says that
there was *" a conspiracy "* among the spiritual leaders within Israel
before God's judgment came on them. They all refused to speak out
against the wickedness and atrocities the National leaders, and the
common people were doing. God wanted to warn the nation of His
coming wrath against them. But, those He was supposed to be able to
speak through, were involved in an evil and greedy conspiracy to get
"..treasure and precious things." from the people. They were "..greedy
dogs that could never get enough." (Refer to Isaiah 56:11). Their
materialistic greed blinded them from seeing God's anger against
the nation and His forthcoming destruction. Rather than speaking
out against the things that were about to bring God's destruction of
the nation, they compromised God's standards of holiness. If they
would have rebuked sin fearlessly, and stood against those propagating
wickedness in the land, they would have forfeited monetary gain and
treasure. Their silence allowed wickedness to continue unhindered.
And allowed the profanity of God's holy things (vs. 26). The conspiracy was that these spiritual leaders were bought off to keep them
quiet. How many spiritual leaders and pastors in the United States of
America have fallen in this way! If they led God's people into true
holiness and righteousness they would lose most of their congregation. Especially in the area of God needing mothers to care for their
own children vs. day care centers [review Ezekiel 23: 39]. If a woman
has a child, God expects it to be nurtured by its mother. Some of the
real reasons women leave children to be cared for by others is pride.
Look at the big shot woman who has servants do what she should be
doing! They literally sacrifice the needs children must receive from
their mothers so they can be big shots taking over the place of men
in the business world. They will look real stupid at the judgment seat
of God Almighty! No self promotion glory matters there!

Usually those things pastors are afraid to speak out against are the areas that need the most attention. But Satan, and his demons, sow fear of losing money if they " make waves ". And do not keep their mouth shut. Money is needed to do God's work. But it should not ever be the deciding factor in the content of preaching for those who deliver His Word! We are to fear and please God in our speech. Not men, or women! Amen.

It is interesting that all the true prophets of the Old Testament were ostracized and killed by false prophets and leaders in Israel prior to God's judgment. Jezebel and Ahab, with all their prophets of Baal [Satan] one case in point. God's love and forgiveness was attempting to reach out before His wrath came. God's prophets were His voice of warning. But the nation refused to listen, and repent. God had no other choice but to do what Ezekiel 22:31 says. It is very important to observe that God, in vs. 30, looked for a voice in the nation to speak through. " That should make up the hedge " around the nation. To stand in between God and the people for His, and their benefit. He did not find a hedge builder. Therefore, He had to destroy the nation.

The work that has been poured into this writing is from God, through the author. It is in response to the need in the United States of America for someone to " stand in the gap." "To make up *" the hedge "* in this nation. If our nation's parents refuse to heed God's warning and instruction from this writing, it will be destroyed by God's judgment. Every man who claims to be one of God's spiritual leaders should be preaching this same warning. If they do not they are foolish. And false prophets. And should be known as such. Jeremiah 49:3, and Nahum 3:17, also describes God's judgment on those in authority. Who occupy the place of spiritual leadership. It is very interesting that the Hebrew word for fool is transliterated " nabal ". The word means: to be a moral defective. This seems to be an indicator of why moral principle, and the practice of righteousness, is held in such low regard in our land. Even inside many of our Christian fellowships. True Christians must hold the leaders of their Church to the standard of God's Word. To call them to account should they neglect any part of the Holy Bible. Servant Eldership [see 1st Peter 5: 1 - 3] not super stars!

WHAT IS A HEDGE?

There are seventeen references to hedges in God's holy Word. They are under three specific noun, and verb classifications. The three words are:

1) Hedge (N.)
2) Hedged (V.)
3) Hedges (N.)

There are seven variations of this word in the original Hebrew language. Hebrew word- שָׂכַר transliterated-gah-dar', the verb form for " hedged ". We will explore some of these as it pertains to our subject. In New Testament Greek, the word used is (original. Greek-φραγμοσ transliterated - phragmos), from which we get our English word " fragment ". This implies that a hedge is usually made up of pieces of a certain kind of material. Spiritual hedges pertain to Isaiah the prophet's direction for educating the Lord's people in Isaiah 28: 9-10. Planting faithfully verses and sentences of God's Word. Placed in their hearts and minds. Then, parents plant them in the children.

First, we will define the word hedge as it is found in Noah Webster's dictionary of the American language. Noah Webster defines hedge as:

[... Wickerwork, wickerwork pen, whence L. caulae sheep-fold: Basic sense " woven fence, enclosure "]. 1. A row of closely planted shrubs, bushes, etc. forming a boundary or fence. 2. Anything serving as a fence or barrier; restriction or defense. 3. The act of, or an instance of hedging - adj. 1. Of, in, or near a hedge - vt. hedged, hedging. 1. To place a hedge around, or along; border or bound with a hedge. 2. To hinder or guard as by surrounding with a barrier (often within) - vi. 1. To hide or protect oneself, as if behind a hedge. Under Hedgehog - 3. Military sense.

a) Any of several defensive obstacles set up to slow the enemy's advance. b) Any of a series of defensive fortifications capable of continued resistance after being encircled.

In studying the various aspects of the definition of what a hedge is, we first see it in the sense of being a wickerwork, or a wicker pen, i.e. a sheepfold. We will study wicking, or wickerwork further in the final two segments. Now we observe that the wickerwork of a sheepfold has a dual purpose. First, to keep out wolves, lions or bears from entering into the sheepfold and devouring the sheep. But the same wickerwork is designed also to keep the sheep inside the sheepfold and from wandering out into unprotected areas.

This relates to our little ones under our care and protection. The wolves of satanic rock stars, drug promoters, procreation deviants, etc. are all are hungry for our offspring. They drool with desire to eat up our children's life substance. Their spiritual, moral, financial and physical well being. We need to provide wickerwork to not just keep the wolves out, but also to keep our children from wandering out away from God's protection for them. This means instructing their hearts and minds. Fathers and mothers are His first line of defense.

The definition further shows that a hedge is a number of closely planted shrubs, or bushes, which form a boundary, or fence. We will discuss this further in the segment on spiritual hedges.

We find in Webster's definition a number of synonyms for the word hedge. They are: Wickerwork, fence, boundary, enclosure, barrier, restriction, defense, hindrance, guard, obstacle, fortification, border or, resistance. These all may be utilized by fathers and mothers to produce their mindset in regards to this important work: the spiritual protection and defense of our family and home.

We will now produce a working definition of these words to aid in our understanding.

#1   Wickerwork - to wick - to weave, knit together fabric. A thin bundle of threads designed to absorb fuel by capillary attraction. Wicker - to bend, 1. A thin flexible twig; withe. 2. Such twigs, or, long woody strips woven together, as in making baskets, or furniture. [author - taking sentences and phrases of God's Word, and then weaving - wickering them into the hearts and minds of your children.]

#2   Fence - 1.Orig., a protection; defense. 2. A barrier, as of wooden, or, metal posts, rails, wire mesh, etc. Used as a boundary or means of defense or confinement - hence - a barbed wire fence.

#3   Boundary - Any line or thing marking limit; bound; border.

#4   Enclosure - something that encloses, as a fence or a wall etc.

#5   Barrier - 1. orig., fortress, stockade, etc. for defencing an entrance, or, gate. 2. A thing that prevents passage, or, approach obstruction. 3. Any- thing that holds apart, separates, or, hinders.

#6   Restriction - 2. Something that restricts; A limitation.

#7   Defense - 1. The act or power of defencing, or guarding against attack, harm, or danger. 2. The fact or state of being defended. 3. Something that defends; means of, or, resources for protection. b.) A plan, or system of defending.

#8   Hindrance - To keep, or, hold back. 1. To keep back restrain, get in the way of, prevent, stop. 2. To make difficult for, thwart, impede; frustrate.

#9   Guard - 1. To keep safe from harm; watch over and protect. Any device that protects against loss, or injury.

#10   Obstacle - Anything which literally, or, figuratively stands in the way of one's progress.

#11   Fortification - 1. The act, or, science of fortifying. 2. Something used in fortifying esp., a fort, or defensive earthwork, wall, etc.

#12   Border - A dividing line between two countries, states, [or, spiritual kingdoms - author].

#13   Resistance - 1. The act of resisting, opposing, withstanding, etc. 2. To oppose actively, or, work against. The power, or capacity to resist an opposing force, or power.

As we learned in chapter twelve we have many different kinds of weapons to use against the powers of Satan. It is in our mastery of these weapons that we gain a powerful advantage against his activities to overthrow us, or, attack our families. It stands to reason that since our warfare is not against " flesh and blood " [ref. Ephesians 6:-10-18] but rather against unseen spiritual entities, we must know and understand how these spiritual forces operate in order to effectively counter their attacks.

Anyone who has labored in the work of building physical fences knows that it takes much labor to complete the arduous task. A physical fence is designed to keep that which is on the inside of a specified area inside. And, it is designed also to keep anything outside this specific area outside. Spiritual fences, or hedges, are also designed to do this.

MAKING UP A HEDGE

As fathers, it is our duty before our Creator, to be practicing the needed work of making up hedges for our children and families. There are numerous techniques each of us can develop by using our God-given imagination. We should draw from the creative resources of our minds to create protection in the lives of each family member. Since every one of our children are different in their personalities we must design our protection according to the specific need in each life under our care.

Making up a hedge can be very difficult. But, also, very rewarding. To know that something, or someone in your care has been provided protection from all possible destructive forces produces a sense of fulfillment and security in our lives as fathers. And, also, in the lives of those in our care. As we will learn in the next chapter, both fathers and mothers should work together to make up hedges of protection for their little ones. This most important task begins by fathers and mothers utilizing the power of their example to train their children about how to be successfully married and effective parents. A child's memories of the husband and wife relationship is designed by God to plant His ways of marital behavior and principles of parenthood in youngsters to draw upon when they enter adult living. These things are intended by God to flow from generation to generation as God has given commandment in Genesis 2:15.

Making up hedges is only accomplished in the flow of our life-times. It takes diligence and faithfulness to accomplish. You cannot see the enemies approaching and then in a panic say " I've got to build protection against them." No, it takes a steady, faithful, persevering disposition to always be in the process of making up hedges. We must have foresight to be successful. We cannot procrastinate this work until it is really necessary, but rather, we must understand that it is necessary to always be active in this area of building spiritual defenses. May it be said of us as it was of the honorable patriarch

Job, "..thus did Job continually.." [ref. Job 1: 5]. We must understand that as long as we exist in this world, Satan and all his forces will be working to destroy us, our marriages, our families, and our children. The author believes America is a particular target of the Devil's war against the Lord God. It is not a matter of will he attack, but rather, of when, and how [ref. 1st Peter 5:8-9]? Hedgework is our work before God.

Our diligence and intelligence in making up effective hedges will give us insight in knowing where and how to make up various defenses. It will be our team work with God the Father, through the Holy Spirit's earthly ministry, that will give us the needed edge.

One of the most important examples of hedgework is the account of the life of the Patriarch Job. In the book of Job 1:1-5 we are give an insight to examine.

1) " There was a man in the land of Uz, whose name was Job; and that man was perfect and upright, and one that feared God, and eschewed [avoided, kept away from, shuned and abstained from] evil [רַע - RAG. - calamity].

2) And there were born to him seven sons and three daughters.

3) His substance also was seven thousand sheep, and three thousand camels, and five hundred yoke of oxen, and five hundred she asses, and a very great household; so that this man was the greatest of all the men of the East.

4) And his sons went and feasted in their houses, every-one his day; and sent and called for their three sisters to eat and to drink with them.

5) And it was so, when the days of their feasting were gone about, that Job sent and sanctified them, and rose up early in the morning, and offered burnt

offerings according to the number of them all: for Job said, it may be that my sons have sinned, and cursed [renounce] God in their hearts. Thus did Job Continually."

Job was a man God was pleased with. He was a father of seven young men and three daughters. He was the greatest man in the eastern country in relation to wealth. But, he hated evil. And, was a man of integrity (ref. Job 2:9). He stood for God, and His righteousness. Job was a man who stood in agreement with God. He did his best to be a good father, and reflect God in the earthly sphere. For this reason he became the object of Satan's numerous attacks.

One of the most important aspects of Job's life was that he was a man of intercession (ref. 1st Timothy 2:1-6). He was an interceding father. He would deny himself, and would "...rise up early in the morning..." to worship God. And stand in the gap between his children, and their Creator. He worked together with God to build hedges around his household. He was one of God's best earthly representatives. A true servant on the earth. Job 1:6-10 gives us access into listening in on an important conversation that took place many years ago in God's Heaven between His, and our enemy.

6)   " Now there was a day when the sons of God came to present themselves before the Lord, and Satan came also among them.

7)   And the Lord said to Satan, where have you come from? Then Satan answered the Lord, and said, from going to and fro in the earth, and from walking up and down in it.

8)   And the Lord said to Satan, have you considered my servant Job, that there is none like him in the earth, a perfect and an upright man, one that fears God, and eschews evil?

9) Then Satan answered the Lord, and said, does Job fear God for nothing?

10) *Have you not made a hedge about him, and about his house, and about all he has on every side?* You have blessed the works of his hands, and his substance is increased in the land."

Yes, Job was the talk of Heaven. When all God's sons were gathered together in Heaven, the subject of discussion was God's earthly servant Job. This shows us that what goes on in the earth is God's concern, and our behavior is being observed. Verse 10 of Job chapter one shows us that God, and Job, worked together to build, and make up hedges around all Job had been entrusted by God to care for and protect. Job was a good steward of God's property. God blessed all that belonged to Job because of his faithfulness to the Lord. It is important to see that protection was provided "...on every side ? " Satan had no access into that which was in Job's care. A very important thing to see. That this very reality was acknowledged, and complained about by Satan himself, says volumes! We all, as fathers, must ask ourselves the question. " Have I secured adequate protection around those in my household and under my care? "...on every side ? "

The Hebrew word for the phrase here in Job 1:10, "... made a hedge about..." is the word [שׂוּךְ - transliterated - sooch]. It has the meaning of erecting, or putting together a system of protection, or defense. Job worked together with God in the putting together of his household's system of spiritual protection. He, as an Old Testament Patriarch, is a good example of faithful hedgework by a father in the earth.

A contrasting portion of God's Word is in Isaiah 5:1-7. But, in verse 5, the Hebrew word for " hedge " is [מְשׂוּכָה - transliterated -m'soo - 'chah]. This speaks of a hedge made of briers and thorns intended to keep out destructive elements.

1) " Now will I sing to my well-beloved a song of My beloved touching His vineyard. My well-beloved has a vineyard in a very fruitful hill:

2) And he fenced it, and gathered out the stones thereof, and planted it with the choicest vine, and built a tower in the midst of it, and also made a wine press therein: And He looked that it should bring forth grapes, and it brought forth (wild) grapes.

3) And now, O inhabitants of Jerusalem, and men of Judah, judge, I pray you, between Me and My vineyard.

4) What could have been done more to My vineyard, that I have not done in it? Wherefore, when I looked that it should bring forth grapes, brought it forth (wild) grapes?

5) And now listen to me: I will tell you what I will do to my vineyard: I will take away the hedge [transliterated - m'soo-chah] thereof, and it shall be eaten up; and break down the wall thereof, and it shall be trodden down:

6) And I will lay it waste: it shall not be pruned, nor digged; but there shall come up briers and thorns: I will also command the clouds that they rain no rain upon it.

7) For the vineyard of the Lord of hosts is the house of Israel, and the men of Judah His pleasant plant: And He looked for judgment, but behold oppression; for righteousness, but behold a cry. "

This section of God's Word shows us that He views, or sees, nations to be like vineyards, plantings, gardens, trees, etc. And, that there are certain elements that are needed to provide proper care and protection of them. This spiritual description of Israel as being a vineyard that belonged to God is interesting. It reveals that God provided everything He could possibly provide in the care of this vineyard except two things. Those two things we find in Genesis 2:15. What are they? Do you know now? If you do, this writing has been successful in your life, and in your family's life. God needed two things done in His vineyard. There were plenty of men to do this specific work but as history shows us they did not do these two commands of God. Gahvad - care for it. - " administer to the spiritual needs of it. " And, shahmar - protect it - " from all enemies opposed to the spiritual state in which God created it." It is important to see in Isaiah 5:5 that inside the nation was evil and corruption and still a "..hedge and a wall.." was around the land. God said He could take away its protection. This is because it no longer was bringing glory to Him. It was a stench in His nostrils. It was a vineyard of rotten " wild grapes." It developed into such a state only because the husbandmen given authority in it did not function as godly husbandmen. They failed to function in the Spirit of Gahvad and Shahmar as God has given His men commandment.

Another interesting fact about this Isaiah 5:1-7 is that in verse 6 God says that "..thorns and briers.." shall come up in the vineyard. These same thorns and briers is what the hedge of protection (m'soo -chah) once was. In other words the hedges will be in the wrong places. Instead of securing and protecting the vineyard, it would be obnoxious by being a nuisance to those it used to protect. By being in the wrong places, it would puncture and offend the people with thorns and briars [God's hedgework materials]. Rather than being seen as a good source of protection. The same sword that could have destroyed the enemy forces now becomes a sword of judgment against a sinful people refusing to do God's will. This is now happening in the United States of America as we continue to turn the sword of our national word against our offspring in our abortion atrocities. That same sword will be turned against us in God's wrathful judgment against our wickedness. As Ezekiel 22:31 warns He will return our own ways upon our heads. In our nation, godly leaders wrote moral laws for our land. Satan, and his evil men and women, have been very militant, and active in the past one hundred years of our history to destroy and knock down these hedges of National protection. Many good hedges were destroyed with the advent of birth control pills, and devices. Hedges of morality, i.e., the consequences of premarital relations, were almost torn completely down by the 1973 Roe vs. Wade judicial decision to provide the wicked and immoral in our land the " right " to Federal, and State taxpayer-funded murdering of God's unborn children. The new president-elect Clinton has promised to pass an abortion rights act in congress. This will overthrow all the efforts of many Christians who influenced the Republican party from 1980 to 2008. This effort was to bind the blood-lust demonic powers of abortion on demand [Molech child sacrifice - see Leviticus 20:1-5] that has, since 1973, been loosed upon God's offspring in the womb [ref Ezekiel 23: 36-39]. Do you realize the unborn belong to God?

Note that the word " right ", as used in politics today, is a perversion of the word it was derived from. That word is the Biblical word " righteousness ". These perverted, and demon inspired feminists, say it is their " right " to destroy their children if they so choose to do so. Hence, you see the perversion of righteousness. Can you see Satan, and those who serve him, destroying these God-ordained hedges of spiritual protection for the unborn? We can, and we must, be working with God to reconstruct these hedges. And quickly. Or, else, suffer the consequences. If we work to re-establish State and Federal laws regarding all forms of pornography, we will, in essence, be making up a hedge of moral protection in our Cities and States. It must be understood that a careless, or tolerant attitude in our lives, actually invites demon powers to enter our cities and homes. We provide a legal entrance for these enemies by being indifferent (ref. Matthew 16:19). God says we are expected by Him to "..bind it,..to stop it " on earth. Hedges are made up in these ways. It is a spiritual activity. And, therefore, it takes faith to bring it to pass. Not the idle faith that hypocritically says " I believe in God." (ref. James 2:19). It takes God's kind of faith. Faith that makes us say - " yes, I believe in God". " But, I believe also that Satan, and his demons exist. And are out to destroy life. And the life of my family. I am determined to do all God requires to protect the family." This is the making up of hedges. The work begins by becoming consumed in our relationship with God through the ministry of the Holy Spirit. And, continually meditating in, and throughout, the entirety of God's holy Word.

In reference to this we see another important section of God's Word in 1st Chronicles 4:23. -

> 23) " These were the potters, and those that dwelt among plants and hedges: There they dwelt with the king for His work."

This verse is in reference to a certain sect of the tribe of Judah [praise] out of whom came God's laws [ref. Genesis 49: 9-12]. It is very interesting that in the midst of the tribe of Judah there were those special people known for their association with with "..plants and hedges..." the place and source of God's Word in the earth was known as having an affection and positive disposition toward "... plants and hedges..."

SPIRITUAL HEDGES

In our previous studies we have acknowledged that we as fathers cannot do any harm to spiritual beings without spiritual weapons. It has been said that in the life of Martin Luther, the 15th century re-former, there was times of spiritual attack on his life by the enemy. It is reported that at one time Martin Luther became so angry at the Devil he threw his ink well at him. Angry acts like this does nothing to hurt the Devil. It probably only made him laugh! No, the only way to hurt Satan, or his spiritual powers, is with weapons ordained by

God's Holy Spirit. Only spirit can bring an attack against spirit. Flesh, in no way, can attack personalities in the realm of Satan's kingdom of darkness. Only spiritual power can oppose spiritual power. As we learned in John 6: 63, the Words God speaks are spirit. And, they can produce life [ref. Proverbs 18: 21]. God has created us to operate on the same faith level as He. This faith operates in the earthly setting. As God speaks in Heaven, we are to say the same thing on the earth. For those who doubt that God has created us to function on the same faith level as He does, we cite two Biblical verses to confirm this. Matthew 19: 26 & Mark 9: 23.

26)   " But Jesus beheld them, and said to them, with men this is impossible; but with God all things are possible."

Mark 9:23 -

23)   " Jesus said to him, If you can believe, all things are possible to him that believes."

This shows that those who honor God, and His Word, can enter the super-natural realm, and produce miracles by releasing God's kind of faith into certain areas. It is interesting that Mark 9:23 is a passage that reveals the account of a distraught father who's son had become inhabited by a demonic power. Jesus Christ attempted to raise this father's faith to the level of being able to deliver his own son and would have liked to see the man exercise spiritual authority for his family member. The man did not have a clue to what deliverance was. Jesus would have liked the father to be able to cast the demon out, but he did not know how to release the faith necessary to do it. He may have even been to see the therapists and psychologists of his day and been told his son had a " mental problem ". When, in reality, a demonic power was possessing his son's life. In verse 25 we see that Jesus spoke directly to the demonic personality, and commanded it to come out. Jesus Christ the Lord released His faith through His mouth. With the words that proceeded out of His spirit, and through His tongue, he forced the wicked spirit out of the young man's life. The father had the authority to do this because he was his father. And, his words could have kicked the demon out. The context of the passage shows that the faith needed to accomplish this act of warfare against Satan's kingdom was lacking in this father.

We have said these things because it is impossible to even think about spiritual hedges, let alone build them, without using faith. Because God tells us in Hebrews 11:1 this is so.

1) " Now faith is the substance of things hoped for, the evidence of things not seen."

In other words spiritual hedges will not be visible to the physical eyes of men and women. But there will be " evidence " that they are in place. That evidence will be that those who have faithfully built spiritual hedges in, and, around their children's lives will find their children bringing glory to God in their lives.

There are many kinds of spiritual hedges. On the National level, we have US Federal laws designed to " protect " the people in our land. When certain people break these laws, or work to take them out of our system of justice, they do what Ecclesiastes 10: 8 says -

8) " He that digs a pit shall fall into it; and whoever breaks a hedge a serpent [serpent here refers to evil spirit powers] shall bite him. "

Satan, and his powers, look for, and wait, to find the areas that have had the hedges destroyed to gain their entrance. This is why we must all insure there is some system of judicial accountability to hinder, and oppose, any law-making legislative body in our nation from

288

nullifying the laws regarding morality in our nation. As we examined in our appendix at the end of this book, the first US Supreme Court justice, John Marshall, presided as one of America's powerful Masons over the planting of the secret Masonic asherah-grove [Washington's Monument] in America. And, thereby, set an immoral tone in the judgeships throughout our nation's judicial history. Specifically regarding perverse pornography. As we find in all the many Bible references we listed in that appendix, the Lord God directed His prophets to call the leaders to repentance. And tear down the source of Satan's power to profane the nation. If we would see the Lord's deliverance in America, we also must obey His Word, and destroy these occult items of masonry. The moral face of America will change if this is carried out. As President Ronald Reagan told Mikhail Gorbachev to tear down the Berlin wall, so I call on the current President and United States Congress of Representatives to tear down the secret Masonic asherah in Washington,D.C. and its counterpart female idol in New York Harbor - perversely renamed - The Statue of Liberty. To get rid of these objects that give Satan legal power to spread profanity is a preliminary step to overthrow his established authority in our land. This is also building spiritual hedges. Refusing to purchase certain products. Or, patronizing stores, or businesses that are found to be a conduit for pornographic materials is a great way to build hedges. If you do this, you must also inform the owners of the business the reason you are not going to do business with them any longer. And give them the opportunity to change policy. If they are hard-nosed, and act indifferent to your legitimate concern, take your money to a more worthy place that will maybe even get money into God's people's hands to carry out His work! Amen. Demons do use the evil use of money to bite people with! Deuteronomy 8:15-18, instructs us to use wealth to help those who are active establishing God's Word in the lives of people! I would appreciate your help.

Another spiritual hedge that could be erected is in relation to God's special agents. His angelic hosts of warfare. We see God's first use of this kind of hedge in Genesis 3:24 -

24)   " So he drove out the man; and he placed at the east of the Garden of Eden cherubim, and a flaming sword which turned every way, to keep [guard] the way of the tree of life. "

This was an " angelic firey hedge " God placed to stop Adam, or any other human being, from eating from the tree of life. In Psalms 104: 4, we can see that God can make His angels turn into a flaming fire. We see God doing this in the hindering of the chariots and horsemen of Egypt from recapturing the children of Israel in the Exodus [ref. Exodus 13:21-22 & 14:19-20]. This is also seen in the overthrow of the wicked cities of Sodom and Gomorrah [Genesis 19: 1 - 24].

An important thing to understand is that we also may be able to join together with God to request the help of His angels to do this work of building spiritual hedges. Psalms 103: 20 shows us that God's angels move out, and are released- *"..at the voice of His Word."* It could very well be that if we are filled with, and are under the direction of God's Holy Spirit. And are filled with the knowledge of His will i.e., His Word. We can, by faith, dispatch our angelic allies, and friends to help do what God has impressed on our hearts needs to be accomplished. We can release their mighty power in the name of Jesus Christ the Lord. Hebrews 1: 14 bears this out. Speaking of God's angels -

14)   " Are they not all ministering spirits, sent forth to minister for them who shall be heirs of salvation? "

The key word in this verse is the word " ..for.. " . It does not say that these angels are sent forth " to " minister to these heirs of salvation. But rather, " for " the heirs of God.

Another spiritual hedge is one which is very powerful in the spiritual realm. It is put into place by faith in its powers to overcome the powers of Satan. Revelation 12:11(a) -

11(a)   " And they overcame him [Satan] by the blood of the Lamb..."

The magnificent power of the forgiving, and purifying blood of Jesus Christ, can be considered as a spiritual hedge. As Leviticus 17:11-14; Matthew 26: 28, and John 6: 53-63 reveals, the life of all physical beings is in the blood. Since Satan majors in the negative spiritual principle of death, the " blood-hedge " of the Lord Jesus Christ can be repulsive to his powers. It was the blood of Jesus Christ that has destroyed Satan's works in all those who have exercised faith in His blood (ref. Romans 3: 25). We should lay our hands on our children's minds and speak the blood-hedge of Jesus Christ to be upon them, and, around them. Our words carry God's power to deliver.

The last of the spiritual hedges we will discuss will be the spiritual hedgework of God's holy Word. It is here that we again review what wicking, or, wickerwork is -

#1 Wickerwork - wick- to weave, knit together, fabric. A thin bundle of threads designed to absorb fuel by capillary attraction. Wicker - to blend, 1. A thin flexible twig; withe. 2. Such twigs or long woody strips woven together, as in making furniture, baskets, or a wicket fence.

[Author - taking sentences and phrases of God's holy Word and weaving them together into the hearts and minds of our children].

Fatherhood and hedgework is just this: " Knitting together and weaving God's eternal Word into our children." This builds spiritual hedges of protection into their very lives. If this is done well, every time Satan, or any of his powers attack, or, try to even get near our children, they will be punctured and stabbed with the " machiara " sword of God's Spirit. Our children will be a thorny hedge that the spiritual out-laws of our nation would rather just avoid, than attempt to bother with at all. Hallelujah! Praise be to God our Lord!

Concluding this important chapter we say the effective wicker-working of weaving God's Word into the minds and hearts of our sons and daughters demands a commitment to God, and His Word. It will take faith in God's Word. And careful, and appropriate placing, and knitting of the Holy Scriptures into the lives under our care. It will take a diligence in spirit to continually be about this business the Father has given to us as earthly fathers to do. This very important activity should continue to flow from generation to generation [ref. Psalms 145: 4]. Both fathers, and mothers, can be active together. And involved in this wickerwork of the Holy Scripture. We have the mind of Christ and must transmit it to the children.

Fathers would have more insight in weaving those parts of God's Word into their son's lives regarding men, sons, brothers, husbands, and fathers in preparing them for battle [Deuteronomy 6: 5 - 9]. Mothers would have greater effectiveness in weaving the many por-tions of God's Word relating to daughters, sisters, future mothers, and women [please see Titus chapter 2: 3 - 5].

Fatherhood and hedgework demands a faithful, and diligent, at-titude in our lives as fathers in authority over our households. Spiritual hedges provide protection and strength for our children. The absence of hedges allows for destruction from the enemy. And, the polluting of God's sanctuaries. We are to view our lives, and our children's lives, as God's dwelling places (ref. 1st Corinthians 3:16 -17). Our work is to protect them. And keep them pure. Free from every kind of defilement the enemy can throw at them. As we see in Psalm 127, it is the Lord God's delight to assist us in doing this work. And it is impossible for us do it without Him.

As Ezekiel 22: 30 has shown us God looks for men. Men who should "..make up the hedges.." These men are special men to God. They are fathers of faith, and His Word of righteousness. Fathers in whom God is well pleased!

Other Bible references to hedges not covered in this chapter:

Proverbs 15:19; Hosea 2:6; Micah 7:4; Mark 12:1; Job 3:23; Lamentations 3:7; Matthew 21:33; Psalms 80:12; Psalms 89:40; Jeremiah 49:3; Nahum 3:17; Luke 14:23.

CHAPTER 15

Fatherhood & Motherhood

In the beginning God created Adam the first man to rule and reign over all God's creation in the earth. He created him a spiritual being, but created him to have a physical body wonderfully made out of the dust of the earth (Genesis 2: 7). Adam, and all men procreated after his likeness, were designed by God to manifest the nature and likeness of God (Genesis 1: 26). Each subsequent man-child was to be nurtured and discipled to manifest God's likeness in the earthly setting. Adam, as we have learned, was commanded by God in Genesis 2:15 to operate in the authority and responsibility of making sure this creation of God remained in the spiritual state in which He created it.

God also designed Adam to be like Him in that nature of being a father. To father spiritual and physical beings like himself. This is the glory of God in man. God's nature manifested in the earth. God designed this glory to flow from generation to generation [see Psalm 145: 4 & 13]. This is what fatherhood is all about. Keeping God's glory flowing as each subsequent generation of man and woman comes into being through God's procreative covenant of marriage. The fact that men have this glory of God in bringing beings into existence is found in Exodus 1: 5

"And all the souls (Lit. Heb. - נֶ֫פֶשׁ - NEH-PHESH) that came out of the loins of Jacob were seventy souls: For Joseph was already in Egypt."

This is confirmed in Hebrews 7:5 & 10; Genesis 35:11.

As we said in our preface, *"fatherhood is not a mere biological function; it is an extremely important spiritual responsibility"*. Something is out of order when the Los Angeles County Unified School District finds that a substantial number of young women are becoming mothers out of wedlock. Many of which are destroying their babies by abortion. Of course with their parent's consent. There are major hedges torn down that causes this serious problem. God holds the parents of these children responsible for these things. They will give an account to God for allowing the violation of His womb, and the murder of unborn children. The school system is not responsible to provide birth control to our children. It is a direct violation of the parental authority God ordained in the family. But we say this to show the abuse of this holy ordinance of God; father and mother. Psalm 2 records for us the state many quarters of our nation are in. Men and women out of fear of divorce refuse to marry. This is an established stronghold of Satan and his demon powers in certain quarters of our land. It began with demonic attack on marriages and homes in the nation. The hatred and strife released by quarreling fathers and mothers left a bad taste for God's ordained state of marriage in the lives of children raised in these "war zones" of the American home.

The minds and hearts of young children are extremely impressionable. The memories of children and growing up are designed by God to give strength to our children as they enter marriage. If they have been raised up in bickering and strife they most likely will be concerned with avoiding it when they come into adulthood. This is Satan's use of parents to destroy respect for marriage in the hearts and minds of their offspring. This very thing should be considered by us as God's warriors as a major stronghold of Satan's to be destroyed by fervent intercessory prayer and deliverance (Ref. 1st Timothy 2: 1- 6).

Yes, before we continue in our work of explaining the relationship between fatherhood and motherhood, we must first understand the fact that our nation, the United States of America, has been, and is now, a spiritual war zone. Satan wants this nation! He wants to steal the glory God has given it as being " One Nation Under God ". This nation has been under spiritual attack from its beginning. There have been, and are at this time, many hundreds of little children who have become victims of this evil onslaught of satanic and demonic attacks. It has occurred inside our homes and families. Families in America's Christian Churches have not been immune to this horrible plague. Sometimes worse in that demographic. It has been designed by Satan's works to overthrow God's glory in the family unit and produce a contrary spirit of global citizenship. A system of not being loyal to God's design of marriage and family. But a one-worldism under which Satan's Anti-Christ will ultimately receive control and authority. Our nation, because of its Biblical roots, has been a fountain-head to powerful forces in the earth. The massive systems of multimedia alone has great power to mold and persuade the minds of the entire world.

Yes, prophetically speaking, Satan and his powers have great interest in these United States of America. But we, as fathers and mothers, who are in authority over the hearts and minds of our young ones, are God's real power in this nation. Do you believe this?

Satan and his powers are totally impotent when we unite together in the Holy Spirit of God, and submit to His holy Word. It is in the outworking of fatherhood and motherhood that God, or Satan, receives control in our children's little lives. This very fact is the basic foundation of parental authority and responsibility. No work of Satan enters a life of a human being unless it is either allowed to enter by parents, or it is invited in by the individual. As fathers and mothers, we have the authority to be the "gate-keeper". Our spiritual covering of authority is designed by the Creator to protect our children. The men and women in our nation must understand this spiritual truth of God before they marry and become fathers and mothers.

TEAMWORK HUSBANDRY

We must see a spiritual revival of knowing God's purpose in *teamwork husbandry* if we would see God's deliverance of our nation from the powers of darkness. We all must re - evaluate ourselves in light of this important concept of the Creator God.

God created Adam to be His husbandman in the earth. All men procreated subsequently were also to function in this spiritual ordination of God. In chapters 11 through 14 we have studied out the specific details of what actually basic husbandry God's way is all about. We are to study these things and give ourselves to obediently carry them out in service for our Creator. He designed us for this very purpose. In order that He might be glorified in the earth (see Isaiah 61:1-3). Men and women must unite in agreement for this to occur.

In producing a mindset that glorifies the Lord God, we must break from what we should consider the "concrete jungle mentality" we all have grown up in. We must divorce our minds from the world system of thinking. And return to God's mindset which He has designed for us. That mindset relates with everything else in God's creation. As we have studied and learned God likes to view nations of people as *vineyards*, (Ref. Isaiah 5:5) *plants and trees* (see Isaiah 61:3) *flowers*, (see 1st Samuel 2:33; 1st Corinthians 7:36; James 1:10) *and gardens*, (see Genesis 2:8 & 15; Job 8:16; Song of Solomon 4:12-16; 6:2; Ezekiel 36:33-35; Luke 13:19). Bible word studies in each of these areas should be done by us as fathers and mothers if we desire to have the mind of Christ on this subject of husbandry. We must view our little families as little gardens God has given us to care for and protect. That the children we generate in the procreative covenant of God are little plantings of the Lord and us. As a father who has assisted in delivery of my son, Justin Wyatt, I have seen God's glory of child bearing. Every father should, if at all possible, help in bringing their sons and daughters into the world. There are special creation bonds that are made in the process of childbirth. This is part of the beginning of child care and husbandry. Fathers need to take an active part. It is one of the most blessed times of a man or woman's life to become a father or mother. To see the wonders of God's creation unfold before your very eyes is one of the most precious times we can experience in God's world. The beautiful relationship God designed to exist between men and women is only known in the obedience to God's principles of husbandry. When fathers and mothers submit to God's ways, and in love serve Him, each other, and their children. Yes, serve their children. Because a child's best example of servanthood is what they see in the behavior of the closest people to them. God's overseers. Husbandry team.

ADMINISTRATIONS OF THE HOLY SPIRIT

In our study of the team work of fatherhood and motherhood we must close some gaps. In Genesis 2:18-25 & 3:20 we find God's ordination of women. It is in this area God manifests to us the only reason for the creation of woman. Her ordination is all centered around helping man. In our previous writing - •[11] Satanic Feminism vs. the American Home - we explained that this basic purpose of the woman is under Satanic attack in our land. We also explained the reasons this is so. But both fathers and mothers together must be in total agreement in their relationship as it relates to their ordination. Amos 3:3 speaks of this basic principle of relationships between men and women. It does not matter what Satan's world system is propagating for women to do. It is God's ordained commandments that are to be obeyed. God definitely has a structure of authority to be observed in the earth. Before we continue in this explanation we say that we first handle this area under the administrations of God's Holy Spirit because God's Spirit operates only in the power of agreement and harmony with God's Word (i.e. - His will and ways). The " Satanic Feminism

---

11 • Recommended Reading - *Satanic Feminism v. The American Home* - Call to Order @ Ph. 206. 497. 8553..

" propagated in our nation is a major stronghold Satan is working to establish in our households. It is a major area of strife and division brought in by satanic power. It is designed by God's enemy to reject God's ways and look to a one-world global system. We speak this prophetically. There are key verses that show us God's order in His creation. The term *" glory "* is synomonous with the Holy Spirit in God's Word. This relates to men, women, and children in the earthly creation of God. 1st Corinthians 11:3; 7-9 & Proverbs 17:6 shows us God's creation order.

1st Corinthians 11:3; 7-9 -

3)   "But I would have you know, that the head of every man is Christ; and the head (authority) of the woman is the man; and the head (authority) of Christ is God.

7)   For a man indeed ought not to cover his head, forasmuch as he is the image and glory of God: But the woman is the glory of the man.

8)   For (because) the man is not of the woman; but the woman of (from) the man.

9)   Neither was the man created for the woman; but the woman for the man."

Proverbs 17:6 (b) "...And the glory of children are their fathers."

These sections of God's Word reveals to us God's flow of *glory* and authority. There is manifesting an animosity to these basic principles of God even inside many churches in our nation. This Satanic display of power is to be bound and cast out by us as God's warriors in the earth. It is designed to overthrow and cause confusion among God's people. Strife and division in the home and church. The two areas our children should be able to see God's ways on display for them to follow. Mothers hold an extremely important place in the outworking of husbandry. There must be a spirit of humility and cooperation flowing between husbands and wives. Satan and his powers are able to manifest in the absence of this key principle of God. It is in this area the powers of Hell gain their control, or, lose it. In the mighty power of agreement! It is interesting that Jesus Christ the Lord reaffirmed God's principle of agreement in Matthew 18:18-20.

18) "Truly I say to you, whatsoever you, [can apply to fathers and mothers] shall bind [stop] on earth shall be bound [stopped] in Heaven: and whatsoever you shall loose [release] on earth shall be loosed [released] in heaven.

19) Again I say to you, that if two of you shall agree on earth as touching anything that they shall ask, it shall be done for them of my Father which is in heaven.

20) For [because] where two or three are gathered together in my name, there am I in the midst of them."

God's power is stopped, or bound by us, or, it is released, or, loosed by us as fathers and mothers. The promise of the Lord Jesus Christ is that when only two of us on this earth are gathered together in one spirit of agreement God's mighty power is present. It is available to us to do whatever we discern needs to be done. Whether it is salvation, healing, miracles, or deliverance from demons, God's anointing is right there wanting to work along with us to do God's will. We know that the Spirit of God does not operate unless it is in agreement with God's Word. Neither does God's Word function in a given situation without the anointing of the Holy Spirit. It is *the work of husbandry* to understand and cooperate in these principles. God's anointing flows with God's work. John 3:34 shows this. John 14:12-14 shows that as we grow in likeness to Jesus Christ we also will find God's ability operating in our lives. We will glorify God the Father by being like His Son Jesus (Romans 8:29).

FATHER & MOTHER DELIVERANCE TEAMS

We were going to consider naming this segment "Spiritual Pest in your Garden", which would be appropriate to the subject. But we want to major on the authority God gives to fathers and mothers.

One of the greatest strongholds of pride Satan operates in is in this area of some fathers, and especially mothers, refusing to admit and acknowledge a demon power, or powers, have entered into their son or daughter. The reason this is difficult to accept is that it shows a failure on their part as parents. Demon powers love this area of strongholds because they can continue their works in the child as he, or she grows older. They can establish a strong hold in the life of their victim. It is sad that this is sometimes so because God has provided everything we as parents need to keep our offspring clean and free of all of Satan's power. (Ref. Luke 10:17-20). They only gain entrance by our neglect of the principles of " Gahvad and Shahmar " or, our ignorance of our spiritual authority. God shows us as fathers and mothers how to bring deliverance to our children's lives in the example of Jesus Christ. The work and ministry of the Lord Jesus Christ shows a number of encounters with parental situations where demons were inside their children's lives. We will cover two of the Bible references to children in need of deliverance. The first is Mark 7:24-30 -

24)　"And from there He arose, and went into the borders of Tyre and Sidon, and entered into a house, and would have [liked for] no man to know it: But He could not be hid.

25)　For a certain woman, whose young daughter had an unclean spirit, heard of Him, and came and fell at His feet:

26) The woman was a Greek, a Syro-Phoenician by nation; and she besought [begged] Him that He would cast forth the demon out of her daughter.

27) But Jesus said to her, let the children [of Israel] first be filled: For it is not fitting to take the children's bread, and to cast it to the dogs.

28) And she answered and said to Him, yes, Lord: yet the dogs under the table eat the children's crumbs.

29) And He said to her, for this saying go your way; the demon is gone out of your daughter.

30) And when she was come to her house, she found the demon gone out, and her daughter laid upon the bed."

This account of child deliverance is very important in that it showed that God would turn to the Gentile peoples with salvation and deliverance after His work with the nation of Israel. This is seen in the phrase *" ..the children's bread.. "*. He speaks of the children of Abraham. The children of Israel. It is interesting that Jesus correlated deliverance from demon power with bread. He is speaking of spiritual bread. God's Spirit and His Word. The humiliated place this Gentile woman placed herself; "..under the table eating the children's crumbs..", moved the heart of Jesus Christ to give her her request. Sometimes a father, or mother, who is too proud to admit " their " child is demon possessed, will need to take on this extreme attitude of humility for God to permit deliverance to occur [refer to James 4: 6 - 8].

The next reference in God's Word we will cover is in Mark 9:17-29. This account shows a father whose son had become inhabited with a demon power.

17) "And one of the multitude answered and said, Master, I have brought to you my son, which has a dumb spirit'

18) And wheresoever he [the demon] takes him, he tears him: [convulses - produces epileptic seizures?] and he foams, [at the mouth] and gnashes with his teeth and pines away: [loses strength] and I spoke to your disciples that they should cast him out; and they could not.

19) He answered him, and said, O faithless generation, how long shall I be with you? How long shall I put up with you? Bring him to me.

20) And they brought him to him: And when he saw him, immediately the spirit convulsed in him; and he fell on the ground, and wallowed foaming.

21) And he asked his father, how long is it ago that this [demon] came to him? And he said, of a child.

22) And often it [this demon] casts him into the fire, and into the waters, to destroy him: [a spirit of suicide] but if you can do anything, have compassion on us, and help us.

23) And Jesus said to him, if you can believe [exercise God's kind of faith] all things are possible to him that believes.

24) And immediately the father of the child cried out, and said with tears, Lord, I believe; you help my unbelief.

25) And when Jesus saw that the people came running together, he rebuked the foul spirit, [by] saying to him, you dumb and deaf spirit, I command you, come out of him, and enter no more into him.

26) And the spirit cried, and convulsed him severely, and came out of him: And he [the child] was as one dead; insomuch that many said, he is dead.

27) But Jesus took him by the hand and lifted him up; and he arose.

28) And when he was come into the house, his disciples asked him privately, why could not we cast him out?

29) And he said to them, this kind [of spiritual power] can come forth by nothing, but by prayer and fasting. [emphasis added]

This is one of the most hellish accounts of demon possession in the ministry of Jesus. The account of the maniac at Gadara (Luke 8:26-40) seems rather mild in comparison. To meditate in this passage of the deliverance teaches us many important things. First, that in verse 19, Jesus manifested displeasure that this father was not functioning as a proper husband. He tried to encourage the power of faith in this boy's father. For, it was that father's authority that God ordained to do the work of husbandry. The father did not understand his authority and responsibility before God. Jesus tried to explain this to the father, but a crowd of people came running up to distract Christ's teaching. So, Jesus exercised authority in the place of the boy's father over the demon spirit in his son's life. Christians are woefully ignorant of this.

It is important to study the words of Jesus Christ to the demon power. For, we are commanded to do this work in the name of Jesus Christ (see Mark 16:17). Jesus said that certain demon powers come out by "prayer and fasting". Jesus had God's power operating continually in His life because He was continually in communion with His Father through prayer and fasting (see John 4:31-34).

If we, as fathers and mothers, are active in the work of husbandry, there is no reason for evil spirits to enter our children. It is in our failure and disobedience that they may gain entrance.

There are two basic things to understand in the administration of the Holy Spirit by us as parents, and demonic activity in our children's lives. First is the fact that we must see our children as little vessels, or containers for the Holy Spirit to fill up. A glass that is totally filled cannot hold any other substance in it. If we have been faithful in administering God's Holy Spirit by praying and speaking it into their lives, and we have been faithful in the wickerwork of building hedges in the hearts and minds of our children, it is very unlikely an evil spirit power would even want to enter them. It is important that this be understood. We are the **gate-keepers** for our children until they are grown enough to keep their own gates. We are charged with protecting the little fountains, and keeping them clean. We are to assist our children through our relationship with Jesus Christ to look to Him as their source of " ..living water..": (see John 4:10-24; 7:37-39).

We conclude this segment on father and mother deliverance teams by encouraging our readers to carefully meditate in the eleventh chapter of Luke's Gospel. In this chapter is found important information about deliverance. It records an intense time of Christ's ministry. A time of His judgment against wicked religious leaders who oppose what God desired for fathers and mothers to do. The connection of the water of God's Holy Spirit with the problem of demon possession is seen in verse 24. Christ said that evil spirits walk through *"..the dry places.." "..seeking rest..".* The absence of God's Holy Spirit (water of life) produces dry places. It is here that spirits of Satan take up residence. They even claim the human being as *"..their house..".* Jesus gives us God's answer to this in Luke 11:9-13 -

9)   "And I say to you, ask, and it shall be given you; seek, and you shall find; knock, and it shall be opened to you.

10)   For every one that asks receives; and he that seeks finds; and to him that knocks it shall be opened.

11)   If a son shall ask bread of any of you that is a father, will he give him a stone? Or, if he ask a fish, will he for a fish give him a serpent?

12)   Or, if he shall ask an egg, will he offer him a scorpion?

13)   If you then being evil, know how to give good gifts to your children: how much more shall your heavenly Father give the Holy Spirit (to them that ask him?")

It is interesting that in Luke 10:17-19 Christ also used the analogy of "..serpents and scorpions.." in contrast to the Holy Spirit. This shows us, as fathers and mothers, that God wants us to give the Holy Spirit to our children. God has, through the shedding of blood, death, and resurrection of His Son Jesus Christ, returned to us as fathers and mothers the ability to receive God's Holy Spirit again. As Adam and Eve had before their sin and disobedience in God's Garden of Eden. We are to ask the Father, in Jesus' name, for the Holy Spirit, in order to have it in our lives to minister it into our children's lives. *This is God's husbandry*. This is the work God commanded us all as fathers and mothers to perform.

THE LAYING ON OF HANDS

The Biblical teaching of "..the laying on of hands.." is a very interesting, powerful, and blessed area of God's ways among men, women and children. In this segment we will study these ways of God operating in the earth. He rules in, and through, us.

The Biblical " *laying on of hands* " is only for those who know, love, and obey the Lord God through the direction of the Lord Jesus Christ. It is His ordination and gift to those who love Him. And those God loves. The Biblical credentials needed to administer this ordinance of God are found in Psalms chapter 24 verses 3 - 5:

3) Who shall ascend into the hill (Lit. Heb. הַר - HAR = mountain, or mount) of the Lord? Or, who shall stand in His holy place? (Lit. Heb. מָקוֹם - MAH-KOHM abode, habitation).

4) He that has clean hands, and a pure heart; who has not lifted up his soul to vanity, nor sworn deceitfully.

5) He shall receive (the) blessing from the Lord, and righteousness from the God of his salvation.

" Mountains" throughout Scripture refer to governments. The Hebrew word "HAR" is translated hill, mountain, mount, etc. in different verses in God's Word. They generally refer to God's government. His ways of operation. His lordship and administration over creation.

The Hebrew word for "Place" is MAH-KOHM which means: a dwelling place. It is interesting that from this same root word comes the Hebrew word for *"fountain"* or *"spring"*. MAH-KOUR is the variation. In other words, these verses explain God's credentials for the laying on of hands to impart His Holy Spirit. Verse 4 explains to us that there must be ***humility*** - vs. 4c. ***Clean hands*** - vs. 4d. ***A pure heart*** - vs. 4b. ***A tongue under God's control*** - vs. 4d. Do you qualify? If you do not, you cannot have verse 5. Obey God's requirements, and you will have access into the resources of God's blessing to flow from your life into your family. Through your lips and through your hands! Christ in you is the hope of glory.

It is important to see in verse 5, that those who meet God's requirements for the authority to lay on hands; *"he shall receive "* the *" blessing from the Lord,..."* to give to others. It does not say " a " blessing. It says ***"the"*** blessing to impart! If you are doing God's commands of husbandry properly, your children will also be flowing with God's blessings to benefit others. His fountains of blessings.

Now, for the remainder of this segment we will go over some of the verses in Holy Scripture relating to this subject, and comment slightly about them.

307

Genesis 24:2-4,9 -

2) "And Abraham said to his eldest servant of his house, that ruled over all that he had, put, I pray you, your hand under my thigh:

3) And I will make you swear by the Lord, the God of Heaven, and the God of the earth, that you shall not take a wife unto my son of the daughters of the Canaanites, among whom I dwell:

4) But you shall go to my country, and to my kindred, and take a wife to my son Isaac."

5) And the servant put his hand, under the thigh of Abraham his master, and sware to him concerning the matter."

As we said in chapter ten on the fatherhood of Abraham, this solemn act of placing the hand of his servant "..under his thigh.." [a euphemism] on, or near his procreative anatomy, meant an entrusting of his seed [offspring] into his servant's hand. A placing of the responsibility for the well-being of Abraham's progeny upon his servant. A very sacred trust. This honoring of Abraham's seed seems to have become a family tradition. For, in Genesis 47:29, we see it in Jacob's honoring his father's Isaac, and Abraham's, place of burial.

In Genesis 48:1-22 we find the account of Jacob laying his hands on Joseph's son's heads. Ephraim and Manasseh, through this laying on of hands, were brought into the number of completing the twelve tribes of Israel. It is important to see that as in the life of Jacob, he received the greater blessing than Esau. In this account of Ephraim and Manasseh, the younger son also received a greater blessing through the laying on of the hands of their grandfather - Jacob/ Israel.

Next, in Exodus 24:1-18 we see that in verses 9-11 God chose to "..lay his hand.." upon Moses, Aaron, Nadab, and Abihu to anoint them as leaders over the giant nation of Israel, but not upon the nobles.

Later on in Numbers 11:16-17, we see God spreading out leadership responsibility among seventy of the elders.

Next, in Numbers 27:16-23 we see God requesting that Moses transfer leadership authority over to Joshua (Moses' servant) by laying his hand upon him.

18) "And the Lord said to Moses, you take Joshua the son of Nun, a man in whom is the Spirit, and lay your hand upon him;

19) And he laid his hands upon him, and gave him a charge, as the Lord commanded by the hand of Moses."

In Deuteronomy 34:9 we see that because Moses had laid his hands upon Joshua, God transferred the Spirit of wisdom into him.

The next time we see God's power released by the laying on of hands is in Daniel 10:10, 18. Strength was given by laying on the hand.

We see the laying on of hands in the New Testament begins with the Lord Jesus Christ. It all started with a man who was diseased with the contagious disease of leprosy. Matthew 8:2-3 -

2) "And, behold, there came a leper and worshiped Him, saying, Lord, if you will, you can make me clean.

3) And Jesus put forth His hand and touched him, saying, I will, you be clean. And immediately his leprosy was cleansed.

Any place in the Gospels that the phrase "..Jesus put forth His hand..", "..touched..", "..reached..", "..laid his hand upon..", we see the miraculous healing power of God flowing out through the hands of Jesus Christ. The first New Testament resurrection took place at the request of a ruler whose daughter had died, asking Christ to lay his hand upon her in order that she might live again [Matthew 9:18-26].

Luke 4: 40- 41 shows that there were times that Jesus was willing to heal every disease. Every person who came to Him, He laid His hands on them, and they were healed. Verse 41 shows that demons would be expelled from the people as God's healing Spirit entered into their lives. The Lord wants us to go as He did (refer to John 20: 21).

The last reference we make to the laying on of hands in the ministry of Jesus Christ as He walked the earth is Matthew 19:13-15 -

13) Then there were brought to Him little children, that He should put His hands on them, and pray: And the disciples rebuked them [the parents].

14) But Jesus said, permit the little children, and forbid them not to come to me: for of such is the kingdom of Heaven.

15) And He laid His hands on them,..

It is important to know that in Matthew 18:1- 5, Jesus warned His disciples (those who had been following Him for years) that if they did not become converted to be like little children [in humble need of Him] they would not enter into God's kingdom. Adult pride was crushed by these Words of Jesus Christ. He said to us to learn how to be toward Him, and His heavenly Father, by observing how little children need help from their fathers and mothers.

In Mark 16:14-20 we find that Christ transferred the ordinance of "..the laying on of hands.." to any man, or woman, boy, or girl that believes. Exercising God's kind of faith permits us to see God energize the same miraculous healing power Christ Jesus demonstrated while on the earth. Mark 16:17-18 are the words of Christ to us:

"These signs shall follow those that believe; in My name [Jesus Christ] shall they cast out demons;...they shall lay hands on the sick, and they shall recover."

It is in our obedience to the command of Jesus Christ to believe and go that we will be able to see these supernatural things happen. Faith in putting into practice what Jesus Christ told us to do will manifest God's working through our hands.

In closing this discourse on the laying on of hands we say that after Jesus Christ ascended into Heaven to sit down at God's right hand, a revival of laying on of hands took place in the early Church. This is recorded in the Book of the Acts of "sent ones" under the Holy Spirit's direction. In Acts 3:1-12 we see Peter and John taking a lame man by the hand and "..in the name of Jesus.." telling him "..to rise up and walk.". In Acts 6:1-8, we see the transfer of authority and anointing imparted into Church leadership and serving. Acts 8: 5-17, we see Phillip being used by the Holy Spirit to do miracles and signs. Verse 17 shows the impartation of the Holy Spirit into the lives of believers. We also see Simon, the man who had occultic involvement with sorcery before joining with the Church, seeing God's power, full of a spirit of envy, desiring to buy with money God's supernatural gifts. He was bound with the chains of iniquity by Satan.

Acts 13:1-12 shows Barnabas and Saul called out to spread the Gospel in the Gentile regions. After a time of ministering to the Lord, prayer, and fasting, the Holy Spirit spoke and directed the anointing of Barnabas and Paul by "the laying on of hands" and impartation of God's Spirit. Verse 9 shows Paul was filled with the Spirit. We see that in verses 9-12, Paul ordered a wicked sorcerer named Elymas to be struck with blindness for a time, and it took place. Acts 19: 5-6 shows us Paul, after he had hands laid on him, and had been anointed with the Holy Spirit, he then had authority to do the same for others.

Before we close this segment we will need to close up some loose ends - 1st Timothy 4:14-16. We see the Apostle Paul's exhortation to one of the men he assisted in helping enter God's ministry. Verse fourteen shows us an important impartation by God through " laying on of hands".

14) "Neglect not the gift that is in you, which was given you by prophecy, (prophetic utterance by gifted spiritual leaders) with the laying on of the hands of the Presbytery."

So we see this imparting of God's spiritual gifts by the leadership of the church into future leaders. 1st Thessalonians 5:19 - 20 gives us commands concerning this working of God.

19) "Quench not the Spirit.
20) Despise not prophesyings."

Going back to the conclusion of the Apostle Paul's ministry in Acts 28:1-31, we find that after being shipwrecked in the waters off the isle of Melita, Paul, when assisting in building a fire was attacked by a large snake which was extremely poisonous, and deadly. All the men knew he should have dropped dead immediately. But he did not even get sick. Praise God! That was a miracle worked by God's Holy Spirit. Death cannot touch us until God allows it.

The last time we hear of God using the ministry of the laying on of hands in Paul the Apostle's life, is in Acts 28: 7-9:

7) "In the same quarters were possessions of the chief man of the island, [Melita] whose name was Publius; who received us, and lodged us three days courteously.

8) And it came to pass, that the father of Publius lay sick of a fever and of a bloody flux: [the intestinal disease of dysentery] to whom Paul entered in, and prayed, and laid his hands on him, and healed him.

9) So that when this was done, others also, which had diseases in the island, came, and were healed."

We conclude this segment on this ordinance of God, ".the laying on of the hands..", by making a few final statements of warning, instruction, and encouragement. First, God's warning in 1st Timothy 5:21-22:

21) I command you before God, and the Lord Jesus Christ, and the elect angels, that you observe these things [God's ordinances] without preferring one before another, doing nothing by partiality [showing a favoritism].

22) Lay hands suddenly on no man, neither be partaker of other men's sins: Keep yourself pure. [emphasis added]

How exciting to see God's Holy Spirit bringing His healing power into sick and diseased lives by the caring deed of laying on of our hands. Through our lives, He touches those in great need of love.

This is God's admonition. We are to care for the sickness of others, and impart God's healing into their lives. But only as God directs us to do so. We ask, how do we know where, and when, to lay hands on the sick to release God's healing power? This is an important question to ask. Careless actions can cause much pain, sorrow, and grief.

In John 11: 4 we find God's first explanation of how to discern His will in the area of sickness and disease.

4) "When Jesus heard that, he said, this sickness is not unto death, but for the glory of God, that [in order that] the Son of God might be glorified thereby."

Here, we see two ways to discern what to do in a situation of sickness:

#1)   "A sickness unto death" - ref. John. 14: 4 - 44 & 1st John. 5: 16

-- Is it God's time for the individual to leave life on earth?

#2)   "A sickness to the glory of God's Son Jesus Christ ?"

--Is the sickness for the purpose of demonstrating God's glory and power to supernaturally heal?

#3) "   A sickness unto God's chastisement"

--Is this sickness designed to be used by God to chasten the individual to produce change in character, or repentance? - see - 1st Corinthians 5: 1 - 13

We see this number three referred to in a number of places. It usually is designed by God to produce humility. In the Old Testament we see God using it in a number of places. One of the first was in Numbers 12:3-15:

3)   Now the man Moses was very meek, above all the men which were upon the face of the earth.

4)   And the Lord spake suddenly to Moses, and to Aaron, and to Miriam, come out, you three, to the tabernacle of the congregation. And they three came out.

5)   And the Lord came down in the pillar of the cloud, and stood in the door of the tabernacle, and called Aaron and Miriam: And they both came forth.

6)   And he said, hear now my words. If there be a prophet among you, I the Lord will make myself know to him in a vision, and will speak to him in a dream.

7)   My servant Moses..., who is faithful in all mine house.

8)   With him will I speak mouth-to-mouth, even apparently, and not in dark speeches; and the similitude of

the Lord shall he behold: Wherefore then were you not afraid to speak against my servant Moses?

9) And the anger of the Lord was kindled against them; and He departed.

10) And the cloud departed from off the tabernacle; and, behold, Miriam became leprous, white as snow: and Aaron looked upon Miriam, and, behold, she was leprous.

11) And Aaron said to Moses, alas, my Lord, I beseech you, lay not the sin upon us, wherein we have done foolishly, and wherein we have sinned.

12) Let her not be as one dead, of whom the flesh is half consumed when he comes out of his mother's womb.

13) And Moses cried to the Lord, saying, Heal her now, O God, I beseech you.

14) And the Lord said to Moses, if her father had but spit in her face, should she not be ashamed seven days? Let her be shut out from the camp seven days, and after that, let her be received in again.

15) And Miriam was shut out from the camp seven days: And the people journeyed not till Miriam was brought in again."

Moses, in verse 3, was considered by God as the most humble man alive on the earth. In other words, Moses would put up with an awful lot of problems before he would get angry. As we see in the behavior of the wandering children of Israel, God needed such a man. But God Himself stood up for the authority He gave to Moses. Miriam had to be the source of this attack on the authority of Moses, since God smote " her only " with leprosy, and made her an example of God's chastisement. The text says, Aaron spoke evil against Moses also, but he did not receive God's wrath against this rebellion. It may have been that Aaron was a priest for God's people, and God used this diseasing of Miriam to put him back in place under Moses' leadership, to pray for God's people, and intercede for them. Not try to lead them in competition with Moses. Verses 6-9 shows us God usually only prepares one man to lead His people. One voice. Not competing voices striving for recognition. God hates confusion. Parents must not be competitive because it causes strife and confusion.

It is very important what is found in verse 14. God said that "..if her father had but spit in her face..." A very hard word against this woman. This shows us that it is a father's responsibility to teach his daughters to be submissive to men as they function in God's authority. We will speak more of this in chapter seventeen.

This disease of leprosy God allowed Miriam to receive, was a ***"..sickness unto the chastisement of God."*** To humble her pride.

2nd Kings 5: 1-14 is a classic example of a humbling of a man named Naaman with God's cure through Elisha the prophet. 1st Corinthians 11: 27-32, and Hebrews 12: 5 -11, are important sections of God's Word to assist us in understanding whether, or not, a sickness, or disease, is a chastisement of God. To give us discernment.

Some sickness, and disease, is a result of improper nutrition in people's bodies. A failure of motherhood in our nation. We will cover this more in chapter seventeen on Daughtership - Teaching Motherhood.

The last laying on of hands is recorded in Revelation 1:17 -

17) "And when I saw Him, [Jesus Christ the Lord in His glorified state] I fell at His feet as dead. And He laid His right hand upon me, saying to me, fear not; I am the first and the last..."

With that, John the Apostle, received one of God's most powerful and prophetic books. The Book of the Revelation of Jesus Christ. This was one of the most powerful laying on of hands in all of God's eternity! Where Christ Himself reveals His final judgments.

We close to say that the combined authority of God's two member team of father and mother can bring God's healing power into all our homes in the United States of America. God's power to heal all manner of sickness and disease whether spiritual, mental, psychological (emotional), and physical rests in the hands of parental authority. This is not to say we do not need medical doctors to assist in bringing healing. Medical doctors have studied our bodies and learned healing arts to help us know more about our physical anatomy. Their knowledge and wisdom is valuable. Luke, who wrote the third Gospel, was a physician! Jesus Christ is the Great Physician though.

The father-mother husbandry team must function in this laying on of hands if it is to be complete. Chapter eleven on fatherhood and GAHVAD revealed this vital truth. God's commands are good.

We conclude this chapter by stating that there are various forms of child abuse and neglect manifesting in our nation. We say prophetically that this is all caused by an ignorance, or refusal, to function in God's husbandry by fathers, or mothers, or both. God intended for all children to be raised up as *"trees of righteousness that he might be glorified. The planting of the Lord."* (Isaiah 61:3) But God requires all fathers to be doing the work of the ministry of husbandmen. Together in harmony, love, and unity with the woman God has chosen for him to work together with. Within this beautiful covenant purpose of God. 1st Peter 3: 7-12, reveals this to be God's will. Also, Ephesians 5:17-33.

7)   "Likewise, you husbands, dwell with them [your wives] according to knowledge, [God's garden principles] giving honor to the wife, as to the weaker vessel [fountain for the Lord God] and as being heirs together of the grace of life; that [in order that] your prayers be not hindered."

Ephesians 5: 17-20, 25-29, 33 -

317

17)   Wherefore do not be unwise, but understanding what the will of the Lord is.

18)   And be not drunk [overindulgent] with wine, where-in is excess; but be filled (orig. Greek. πληροῦσθε - transliterated - PLARUSTHE - means: the filling of the wind in a ship's sail, i.e. empowerment to move by God's Spirit)with the Spirit. [The Greek aorist - imperative speaks of being continuously kept full of the Holy Spirit].

19)   [By] speaking to yourselves in [Old Testament] Psalms and hymns and spiritual songs, singing and making melody in your heart to the Lord;

20)   Giving thanks always for all things to God and the Father in the name of our Lord Jesus Christ.

25)   Husbands love your wives, even as [like] Christ also loved the church, and gave Himself for it; [for its redemption and forgiveness].

26)   that [in order that] He might sanctify and cleanse it with the washing of water by the Word, [of God] [in-ternal spiritual cleansing of soul and spirit with the Holy Spirit (water)   and the cleansing agent of God's Word.] [Administered by the words of our lips and actions of our lives]

27)   that He might present it to Himself a glorious church, not having spot, or wrinkle, or any such thing; but that it should be holy and blameless

29)   for [because] no man ever yet hated his own flesh; [wife, sons and daughters] but nourishes and cher-ishes it, even as [like] the Lord the Church.

33)   Nevertheless. Let every one of you in particular so love his wife [and children] even as himself; and the wife see that she reverence her husband."

The United States of America has degenerated, and now is apostate to these sound teachings of God's Word. Because they have departed from them by filling their minds with Playboy profanity and pornography via the TV & Internet. Because they have gone after the satanic inspiration of feminism, they are being overthrown in the gifts of marriage and family operations of Biblical child raising. God's husbandry.

CHAPTER 16

Fatherhood and Sonship

As we enter a study of fatherhood and sonship we say that the purpose and glory of God the Father has been darkened by the rebellion of Satan and his angels, and the transgression and sinfulness of each man. But God has intervened in the midst of His fallen creation. Man. God has taken the lead in reconciliation and restoration of His glory in man. We speak in relation to men, who in the flow of life on earth, become fathers of sons and daughters. God has dramatically spoken and acted with the very concepts of a father to son relationship. That very relationship being His own with His own Son our Lord Jesus Christ. Even though both God the Father, and His Son Jesus Christ, knew the great humiliation. Great infliction of torment. Great lacerating scourgings. Great beatings by strong Roman military soldiers. Extremely excruciating pain brought by having spikes driven into His hands and feet into the Roman cross. Hung between heaven and earth. The pouring out of His blood. And then having their eternal relationship severed by Christ actually becoming sin for us (See 2nd Corinthians 5:21). God, and " His Son " in their relationship, covenanted together to allow this all to happen in order that every man and woman could again enter into relationship with their Creator God. Without this great sacrifice on the part of God the Father, to allow His greatly beloved Son Jesus to be put to death for our sinfulness, we all would by God's righteous and holy justice be eternally condemned by our own sin. Yes, God the Father had to weep great tears of sorrow that His precious Son had to go through such suffering to save us from His eternal punishment for sin. Eternal death. God the Father gave His best for us. He sacrificed the very One who was most precious to Him. And, Jesus Christ His Son, obeyed God's will. And, laid down His life for His Father God. This is found in 1st John 4: 9 -10 -

9)   In this was manifested the love of God toward us, because that God sent His only begotten Son into the world, that we might live through Him.

10)   Herein is love, not that we loved God, but that He loved us, and sent His Son to be the propitiation [atoning blood sacrifice] for our sins.

It is through this main gate, or door, that we as fathers enter into our new relationship with God the Father. It is through acknowledging the great sacrifice of God the Father, and His Son Jesus Christ that we receive a restored relationship with God as our Father also. We also see through this great manifestation of the love of God, that he indeed wants a relationship with us. So much so that He would go to such a great sacrifice to provide for it. Praise and glory to His matchless grace and mercy!

I will forever lift my eyes to Calvary. To view the cross where Jesus died for me; how marvelous the grace that caught my falling soul; he looked beyond my faults, my faults, and saw my need. -- sung to the melody of *Dannyboy*

Fatherhood and sonship was on display throughout the work and ministry of our Lord Jesus Christ on the earth. We who are fathers will do well to study that relationship between that Father and Son. We can view special glimpses of that relationship as we meditate in each of the four Gospels: Matthew, Mark, Luke and John. John Chapter seventeen is a special place that shows some of that relationship in our redemption.

MADE IN GOD'S IMAGE

We have endeavored in this writing to establish in our hearts and minds that God has created us to manifest his likeness in the physical earth. God created us men to be fathers. Fathers of sons that will do His will. We have learned that we as fathers have a responsibility to guard the covenant God has established for life on the earth. This covenant of God is to be transferred from father to son. Understanding what exactly the image and likeness of God is comes only by intimate fellowship with Him. Failure to nurture and develop an intimate and strong relationship with God the Father, by faith in Lord Jesus Christ, only produces an inability to transfer that image into our son's lives. This is what sin is all about. This is what Satan deceived Eve with in God's garden " you will be like gods..." (Genesis 3:5). The genuine likeness to God comes only through our relationship with God through obedience to His Word and the workings of the Holy Spirit. Our sons, as God intended, in essence are disciples in our lives to train and develop into the true image and likeness to God. The character and life a father displays is "the" most powerful force to assist in the development of a father's son into a man that honors and gives glory to God's nature. It is in the process of time in which our sons are under our care that they develop into men. We know that the way our world is set up at this time it is extremely difficult to use this time wisely. But pressure is on us to be effective fathers. The heat is on to build into our sons all that God requires us to build into their hearts and minds before they launch out to find their place in the sun and become fathers themselves. Much of our time is taken up in the effort to make a living for our family. Other forces in our nation war for our attention. They steal from us that crucial time in which our sons need us to learn how to become men. It is in those times of intimate communion between a father and his son that a man-child develops into man. A young son develops a strong and secure personality through a wholesome and blessed spiritual relationship with his father. He learns how to be a man by observing and watching his father. The things a young man's father sees as being important, he values as important. The actions he sees his father doing he attempts to imitate in his little life. The words he hears his father speak, he learns to speak also. The entire father-son relationship is a transfer of identity and authority. God created it to flow from on generation into the next (see Psalms 145:4). But we find this important exchange is constantly under attack. There have been a couple excellent songs which have been written that speak of this opposition to father-son relationship and the results it produces. The first is a song by singer Harry Chapin, called -

Cat's in the Cradle

A child arrived just the other day; he came to the world in the usual way; but there were planes to catch and bills to pay;
He learned to walk while I was away. And he was talking before I knew it and as he grew, he'd say, "I'm gonna be like you, dad, you know I'm gonna be like you".
And the cat's in the cradle and the silver spoon little boy blue and the man in the moon.
When ya comin home dad? I don't know when, but we'll get together then. You know we'll have a good time then.
My son turned ten just the other day, he said, "thanks for the ball dad, come on let's play. Can you teach me to throw?" I said, "not today, I gotta lot to do."
He said, "that's ok". And he, he walked away, but he smiled up at him, and said, "I'm going to be like him, yea, you know I'm going to be like him."
And the cat's in the cradle and the silver spoon. The little boy blue and the man in the moon.
When ya comin home, dad? I don't know when, but we'll get together then. You know we'll have a good time then."

Well, he came from college just the other day, so much like a man I just had to say, "son, I'm proud of you, can you sit for a while?" He shook his head, and he said with a smile, "what I'd really like, dad, is to borrow the car keys. See ya later. Can I have them, please?"

And the cat's in the cradle and the silver spoon. The little boy blue and the man in the moon.

When ya comin home, dad? I don't know when, but we'll get together

then. You know we'll have a good time then."

I've long since retired. My son's moved away. I called him up just the other day. I said, "I'd like to see you if you don't mind?" He said, "I'd love to dad, if I could find the time. You see my new job's a hassle and the kid's with the flu. But it's sure nice talking to you, dad, it's been sure nice talking to you."

And as I hung up the phone it occurred to me, he'd grown up just like me. My boy was just like me.

And the cat's in the cradle and the silver spoon. The little boy blue and the man in the moon.

When ya comin home, dad? I don't know when, but we'll get together then, dad. You know we'll have a good time then."

This song is a perfect description of the major problem we face as fathers. It is addressed by God in Galatians 6:7-8 -

7) "Be not deceived; God is not mocked: For whatsoever a man sows, that shall he also reap.

8) For he that sows to his flesh [his own selfish desires] shall of the flesh reap corruption; but he that sows to the Spirit shall of the Spirit reap life everlasting."

You sow quality time with your son; you will reap quality time with him. You sow to your own desires and neglect the early childhood needs of your youngsters, you will reap their negligence of you in your old age. This is one of the reasons the social security system is so destructive to family love in our nation. God designed us to need our fathers and mothers when we are young. And he has given us commandment to return the favor towards our parents in Exodus 20:12 -

12) Honor [the authority and needs financially of] your father and your mother: that your days may be long upon the earth which the Lord your God gives to you."

Ephesians 6:2-3 confirms this basic command of God is to be obeyed by us today. It even adds something good for us if we do.

3) "That it may be well with you,..."

God commands us to care for our children, and then He commands a return by our children when, and if, we see them in need of care. God designed care to flow from generation to generation. A curse comes on our lives if we refuse to obey this basic command of God. We must see as fathers of sons that God designed His creation to be healthy and well by our obedience to His Garden of Eden covenant commands of GAHVAD and SHAHMAR. God has never recinded, or changed His command. We are expected to keep covenant with our heavenly Father and teach and train our sons how to do the same.
Psalm 145:4, 11-13 -

4) "One generation shall praise your works to another, and shall declare your mighty acts.

11) They shall speak of the glory [authority] of your kingdom, and talk of your power;

12) [In order] to make known to the sons of men his mighty acts, and the glorious majesty of His kingdom.

13) Your kingdom is an everlasting kingdom, and your dominion endures throughout all generations."

This is God's command for us as fathers. God created us to do this. It is time we stop thinking the wicked thought that only those who occupy the office of bishop or pastor in a church have the authority to speak God's Words to our family. We are commanded by God to fill the hearts and minds of our sons and daughters with God's Word and His Spirit. These are His covenant commands. We will not only be judged by God Himself at the resurrection for refusing to do this, but also we wickedly leave the generation we have brought into this world at a tremendous disadvantage in the fact of their enemies, Satan and his angels. Jesus Christ has warned us that "...every idle word that men speak, they shall give account of in the day of judgment. For by our words we as fathers shall be justified or condemned.". (Ref. Matthew 12:36-37). We must see our words to our sons as being life giving to them. They need to learn about God from us.

But we understand that the pressures of life steal away the best times to transfer God's ways into our son's life. This must be viewed as an enemy. We should, in the name of Jesus Christ, take authority over our time. We must manage our time wisely as Ephesians 5:15-16 orders us to:

15) See then that you walk circumspectly, not as fools, but as wise,

16) redeeming [ordering our daily time wisely] the time, because the days are evil."

Watching programs on the television or reading the sports section of the newspaper rather than obeying God's covenant commands is sin against God if it steals away from this important task God has given to us. There must be in our lives as fathers a faithful spirit to do all God requires us in relation to our children. We must understand that Satan and his powers will always attempt to persuade us that some other "program" other than God's program is what we should do. This very area is where the ministry of SHAHMAR actually begins. We must understand that God's way at first is not necessarily the easiest way. But, we as fathers, must learn to order our time wisely. And place value upon the times of the transfer of all the wondrous details of God's covenant into our son's lives. They learn from us how to walk as men of God upon the earth. They learn to function in the Spirit of GAHVAD and SHAHMAR by our example. They learn to be good husbandmen, and fathers, by observing it being obeyed in our lives. This is precisely what God is communicating in Proberb 17:6b.

6b) "...And the glory [example, authority, standard] of children are their fathers."

It is in the outworking of all the principles we have learned from God's Word that the transfer of this glory goes over into our son's life. That glory is diminished by our disobedience or enhanced by our obedience to God.

We wish to utilize three illustrations to bring a little more understanding to this transfer.

The first is the illustration of the members participating in a relay race. It can be in the actual way, method, and accuracy that each runner transfers the baton to the next runner that success and victory is known.

The second is seen in the transfer of the Olympic torch. In the 1984 Olympic games, held in our nation, we saw the torch travel half way around the circumference of the earth to its destiny of Southern

California. A tremendous accomplishment. But each individual who participated in carrying the torch knew he could only carry it so far. He or she had to relinquish it into the hands of the next individual responsible to assure its arrival at the games. As fathers we are responsible to insure God's principles are properly transferred and relinquished into the hands of the next individuals responsible. Our sons.

The third illustration is seen in the Star Wars series. Specifically "The Return of the Jedi". If you have seen it, the beginning is the scene of the young Jedi receiving crucial information from "Yoda" just prior to his death and glorification. The information gave the young Jedi the ability to overthrow the dark side of the force. There were powerful correlations between that movie and spiritual realities. The one being the finding out that Darth Vader was actually the young Jedi's father. Being used by the enemy. Also, that the evil emperor told the young Jedi by deception that the more he hated, the more power the emperor gained.

Though these illustrations may give some added insight into understanding this transfer of crucial information to our sons, we must realize that our sons become "made in God's image" and likeness through what is available to them from our lives. God designed the transfer of authority from generation to generation through father and son relationships. The knowledge of God's covenant commands and promises lay in our hands as fathers of the earth. This is fatherhood and sonship. The hearts and minds of our young children are created by God to receive from their fathers and mothers all the information they need to be pleasing to God. Our fountains are either filling them up with God's good things or filling them with polluted waters. We can only give out that which we have received. That is why Christ has admonished us as fathers to "make the tree good and its fruit [our children] good". (Ref. Matthew 12:33-35) Our sons and daughters [our fruit] do not naturally become good. It takes our tilling their ground [their hearts and minds]. It takes planting the seeds of God's Word in this fertile soil. It takes proper watering with love and kindness from the Holy Spirit water (Ref. John 7:37-39; Galatians 5:22-25). It takes keeping the spiritual pests out by functioning in the spirit of GAHVAD & SHAHMAR. Then we will find good trees growing and producing good fruit! We must view our sons as future trees which will bear fruit in the earth through marriage.

TEACHING GOD'S MARRIAGE AND PROCREATION COVENANT

In our nation we can see a myriad of avenues Satan is using to corrupt and destroy honor for God's marriage and procreation covenant. We also see the result: Rampant divorce, immorality, child abuse, child sacrifice by abortion, new social venereal diseases. God's covenants cannot be broken without serious consequences coming upon those who break them. It is sad but there are many object lessons of God's righteous judgments against rebellion to His will today in our land. A wise man, or woman, would take heed and learn from them.

As fathers we commanded by God to teach our sons God's covenant for marriage and procreation. The December 1985 issue of Time Magazine was about all these young teenage girls that are becoming pregnant without a foundation of responsibility. Which is marriage to a man who obeys God's covenant commands. Satan is using it to mock those opposing abortion on demand in our land. They say, "now you who oppose abortion, what do you say about this problem?" The answer is simple. But those who are filled with rebellion against God's ways will not listen to it. If you violate God's covenant commands there is a price to be paid. That price should not be placed upon the head of an unborn child by abortion. It should be placed upon the individuals and their parents who caused the situation! The teaching by fathers about God's marriage and procreation covenant is a little more involved than talking about the "birds and the bees"! There is much information to teach our sons in this area. We have worked at being as complete as possible in this writing.

We are commanded by God to teach our sons to honor the Lord God in their physical bodies. To allow the Holy Spirit to energize the fruit of the Spirit - "self-control" in their bodies (Ref. Galatians 5:22-25). We are to teach them to honor God their Creator in their view of women. To view them as " bearers of life " into the world. To honor the Spirit of SHAHMAR in protecting young women from the disgrace of immoral unwed childbearing.

We as fathers must teach our sons that their enemy, Satan, and his demon spirits have a way for them to go in relation to women but that way ends in God's judgment and death. They need to know the difference between God's way and Satan's and the consequences of both. They need to know how to view and possess their bodies in sanctification and honor (Ref. 1st Thessalonians 4: 1 - 8). To flee from and avoid the sin of fornication (Ref. 1st Corinthians 6:9-20). We as fathers are to work to produce holiness and purity in their minds and hearts toward young women. " Treat younger women as sisters..".

At this point we need to understand that our sons will be exposed to situations in our public school systems, and buddy relationships, that will challenge adherence to God's covenant principles. For this problem we need to build into their hearts and minds a discernment of what a fool is.

God defines a fool in Psalms 53:1 -

1)   "The fool has said in his heart there is no God..."

The words - *there is* - are in italics which means they were added by translators because they felt it needed them. But a fool is also a man who says no to God. One who says in his heart he will live his life the way he wants to. Despising and rejecting God's ways. We are to build into our sons God's warning about these kind of men. It is found in Proverbs 13:20 -

20) "He that walks with wise men [those who keep covenant with God] shall be wise: but a companion of fools shall be destroyed."

It is important to warn them to avoid these fools because they will bring destruction into their lives. Even though refusing to associate with the groups of these children given over to wickedness might bring laughter and scorn against them for following God's ways of purity and virtue. We must contrast the life style of those given over to Satan to propagate wickedness. And, those given over to the Lord God of hosts to propagate righteousness and holiness. This is found in Psalm 1 [memorize] -

1) "Blessed is the man that walks not in the counsel of the ungodly, nor stands in the way of sinners, nor sits in the seat of the scornful.

2) But [rather] his delight is in the law of the Lord; and in his law does he meditate [fill his heart and mind with] day and night.

3) And he [that man] shall be like a tree planted by the rivers of [God's] waters, that brings forth his fruit [children] in his season; [God's time for it] his leaf [the sustenance of his life] also shall not wither; and whatsoever he does shall prosper.

4) The ungodly are not so: But [rather] are like the chaff which the wind drives away.

5) Therefore the ungodly shall not stand in the judgment, nor sinners in the congregation of the righteous.

6) For the Lord knows the way of the righteous: But the way of the ungodly shall perish." [emphasis added]

We are to teach our sons that those who talk pornographic talk about women are under demonic influence. And a man is wise to avoid them. As fathers we are to prepare our son's minds and hearts to be repulsed by pornographic talk, literature, and pictures. If we have properly done our job, our sons will grieve in their spirits to see, or hear, such activity around their spheres of influence. This is an aspect of building moral hedges in our son's hearts and minds [review chapter 14].

YOUR SON AND THE DOCTRINE OF BALAAM

The two main potential enemies of our sons are Canaanitish (whorish & idolatrous) (Ref. Genesis 24:2 - 3, 9) women. And, or, money (Ref. 1st Timothy 6:6-11). We can see that this is so in the account of Numbers chapters 22-25 & 31:1-18. This area of God's Word is the greatest account that reveals to us that both money and/ or, women can be used by the enemy of our sons to corrupt them and/ turn their hearts away from God. Because of the length of these passages in Numbers, we will mention a few of the key verses explaining **Balaam's Doctrine**, but we will give an overview of the situation. It must be taught by all loving and caring fathers. The children of Israel were being prepared to do warfare against those who lived inside the promised land. Numbers 22 records that Balak, the King of the Moabites [review Gen. 19: 30 - 38], had received word that the armies of Israel were on the outskirts of the land of Canaan preparing to invade. Balak made his move. Numbers 22:1-20 show us that he knew that a man named Balaam had spiritual power with God to *" bless, or, curse "* God's people. He sent messengers to Balaam promising *a great wealth of silver and gold.* And, to be promoted to " very great honor " if he would speak a word of cursing against the children of Israel. The scenario continued by Balak to give greater and greater material wealth and greater honor if he would but pronounce a curse upon the people of God. Balaam developed *a compromising* *spirit* toward God's refusal to allow Balaam to speak a curse against Israel. This is first seen in Balaam's attempt to go to the princes of Moab in Numbers 22:21-22. God sent an angel to oppose Balaam in his effort to get the wealth from Balak. Even the jackass Balaam rode on knew he should not proceed. The ass even was trying to protect his master Balaam. Finally God opened the mouth of the jackass and gave it the ability to speak to Balaam. What a humiliation! To have a jackass tell you what you are up to is wrong.

Balaam continued to be enticed by Balak to curse God's people but Balaam submitted somewhat to God and gave prophecies of blessing toward Israel. Yet, he practiced duplicity, and spiritual hypocrisy.

In Numbers 24:10-11 we see that Balak got so angry he flew into a rage and told Balaam that God kept him back from wealth and honor. But in verse thirteen we see Balaam again slipping into compromise by placing a question mark on the statement of integrity to speak only as God commanded him to speak? Numbers 24:14-20 shows us the basic spiritual problem we as God's men must learn to handle. We, as fathers of sons, must teach them how to handle this problem. Verse 14 reveals the beginning of compromise by Balaam.

14)   "And now, behold, I go to my people: Come therefore, and I will advertise you [counsel] what this people shall do to your people in the latter days."

This beginning compromise of Balaam was to give God's enemies crucial information on how to weaken the moral fiber of the sons of Israel. First, we will explain what information Balaam gave to the Moabites. Then we will exercise the principle of Hermeneutics by bringing understanding to us by applying what it is to the United States of America. How it relates to us. And it certainly does! The information of Balaam to Balak is first found in Numbers 24:20:

20)   "And when he looked on Amalek, he took up his parable, and said, Amalek was the first of the nations; [the first that warred against Israel] but his latter end shall be that he shall perish forever."

This verse shows us that this *"Amalek"* was the first to give Israel trouble. Historically speaking Esau, Jacob [Israel's] brother, was the father of this people. Esau, who was more concerned with his fleshly needs and desires than his birthright[see Hebrews 12: 14 - 17]. Esau fathered a nation, Amalek, that also was fleshly-minded like their father.

God prophesied in Exodus 17:8-16 that this would be his major difficulty with his people.

8)   "Then came Amalek, [the flesh] and fought with Israel in Rephidim.

9)   And Moses said to Joshua, choose us out men, and go out, fight with **Amalek**: tomorrow I will stand on the top of the hill with the rod of God in mine hand.

10)   So Joshua did as Moses had said to him, and fought with Amalek: And Moses, Aaron, and Hur went up to the top of the hill.

11)   And it came to pass, when Moses held up his hand, that Israel prevailed: and when he let down his hand, Amalek prevailed.

12)   But Moses' hands were heavy; and they took a stone, and put it under him, and he sat upon it; and Aaron and Hur stayed up his hands, the one on the one side, and the other on the other side; and his hands were steady until the going down of the sun.

13)   And Joshua discomfited Amalek and his people with the edge of the sword.

14) *And the Lord said to Moses, write this for a memorial in a book, and rehearse it in the ears of Joshua. For I will utterly put out the remembrance of Amalek from under Heaven.*

15) And Moses built an altar and called the name of it Jehovah-Nissi:

16) For he said, because the Lord has sworn that the Lord will have war with Amalek **from generation to generation."**

This is a very important passage in God's Word to show us where our war, and the war of our son's lies. In verse 16 we see that God prophesied that he would have to *" war "* with Amalek [the flesh of men] *"..from generation to generation."*.

As fathers, we must recognize this enemy which continually wars against God in our lives. The spiritual principles of fasting and prayer weakens our "warring " flesh man and releases our spirit-man to gain domination. This is manifested in verses 9-12. When Moses lifted his hands in intercession and support of Israel they prevailed. When he grew weary of raising his hands in prayer and intercession, God's enemy Amalek [the flesh] gained strength to defeat God's people. The more we as fathers practice fasting and prayer and teach our sons to practice it, the less trouble we will have with **"Amalek"** in our lives. God warned us that we would have to go to war against it in "..each generation..".

We now return to Numbers 25:1-5 to show what Balaam advised Balak to do. It relates to Amalek in that it had to do with the men of Israel being seduced through their fleshly (or physical - carnal) desires.

1) "And Israel abode in Shittim, and the people began to commit whoredom [have forbidden relations] with the daughters of Moab.

2) And they called the people [God's] to the sacrifices of their gods: And the people did eat, and bowed down to their gods.

3) And Israel joined himself to Baal-peor: and the anger of the Lord was kindled against Israel.

4) And the Lord said to Moses, take the heads of the people, and hang them before the Lord against the sun, that the fierce anger of the Lord may be turned away from Israel.

5) And Moses said to the judges of Israel, slay you everyone his men that was joined to Baal-peor."

This is the doctrine of Balaam: Balaam was forbidden by God to curse Israel. So, rather than cursing them directly, he cursed them indirectly by "advising - advertizing " Balak to send to the men of Israel beautiful women of Moab. The entire Hollywood film industries, and all major high power advertisers utilize this wicked use of women. The daughters of Moab, whose patriarch came into being by Lot's daughters seducing their father to have immoral relations with them. The Moabites seduced them into committing spiritual and physical adultery and fornication with Baal-peor worship. A powerful spirit of immorality came into the children of Moab (Lot's illegitimate grandson) because of his daughter's immoral rebellion against God (Ref. 1st Kings 11:1-8). After God's destruction of Sodom and Gomorrah, the demon spirits and principalities that lost the host bodies of the Sodomites, were most likely seeking out new places of access in which to spread perversion and overthrow mankind. Balaam counselled Balak to use Amalek "the flesh" to corrupt Israel. And, therefore, God Himself would have to curse His own people. The curse comes when holiness is replaced by spiritual and immoral impurity and defilement. Very attractive women are utilized to accomplish this. **This is the Doctrine of Balaam.** Satan, and his demon powers, have used this spiritual principle throughout the history of mankind. Every nation that has ever fallen, has fallen by *the Doctrine of Balaam*. In the book of Revelation 2:12-16, Jesus Christ warned the Church to repent of this wicked Doctrine of Balaam.

12) "And the angel of the church in Pergamos [bad-marriage; i.e. marriage of the fallen Roman Empire with Christianity] write; these things says he which has the sharp sword with two edges;

13) I know your works, and where you dwell, even where Satan's seat is: [where he is exercising his authority through government leaders] and you hold fast to my name, and have not denied my faith, even in those days wherein Anipas was my faithful martyr, who was slain among you, where Satan dwells.

14) But I have a few things against you, because you have those there [in your church] **that hold the doctrine of Balaam**, who taught Balak to cast a stumbling block before the children of Israel, to eat things sacrificed to idols, [demons] and to commit fornication.

15) You also have them hold to the doctrine of the Nicolatanes, [from which we get St. Nicolas - these Nicolatanes were people who infiltrated into the Church, and called themselves Christians, and were not] which things I hate. [emphasis added]

Satan still uses beautiful seductive women to infiltrate into God's people and seduce them into fornication, and apostasy from God.

Today in the United States of America the doctrine of Balaam is being used by the Media to seduce our sons into committing fornication and adultery against God. The various New York Madison Avenue advertisers use sensuous and seductive women (the daughters of America that are immoral) to corrupt the moral fiber of our sons. We as fathers must see that these advertisers use subtle immoral suggestions to slowly corrupt, and break down our children's hedges, so that demon powers can enter their lives, and drive them into fornication and sin against God. We should all boycott those advertising com panies that use these immoral tactics to lead our sons and daughters into immorality. It is significant that Numbers 24:14 actually uses the word *"advertise"* in describing Balaam's Doctrine. It is still being used today to corrupt God's people into apostasy from God's way of purity and holiness.

As fathers, we must know this doctrine of Balaam, and warn our sons to forbid their souls to be corrupted by satanic use of money, honor, or, women. We are to instruct our sons to do two things to overthrow these enemies of their lives. The first is found in Deuteronomy 8:18 -

" But you shall remember the Lord your God: for [because] it is He that gives you power to get wealth, that [in order that] He may establish His covenant which He sware to your fathers, as it is this day."

We must instruct them that the money they make is to be used to establish God's covenant in the earth (refer to chapters 11-12). That God is the one who blesses them. And gives ability to gain wealth for His work.

The second is in Psalms 74:20 -

" Have respect for the covenant: [according to Genesis 2:15] for [because] the dark places of the earth are full of the habitations of cruelty."

If we, as fathers, train our sons to have a healthy respect for God's covenant they will avoid Satan's snares of using their abilities God gives them to do evil against God's covenant. They will respect the fact that they should avoid, and keep clear of women, who look outwardly very beautiful, but are tools of destruction in Satan's hands.

If we do not build the Biblical principles of God's authority and responsibility in their lives there will definitely develop *"...habitations of cruelty and dark places...".* If there is failure to transmit God's ways into our son's lives before they go out from us to start a life on their own we will rue the day we did not. And, we do not love them.

THE TRANSFER OF AUTHORITY

Authority in our nation, the United States of America, has generally been relegated to being found in the occupation our sons settle into. The kind of college, or university degree, gives to them their authority. Whatever subject they master gives to them their *authority*. This is true in the sense of earning a living. But we, in this book on fatherhood, wish to bring out **God's place of authority** among fathers in relation to their children. The place a father, and mother hold in their offspring's early childhood development, is the most crucial area in the transfer of the spiritual principles they will need to live as God has created them to live.

This book has been written because the author saw that in many quarters of our nation, these life-giving principles were not only not being transferred to each new generation coming into existence, but that these God-ordained principles were not even known by the majority of the fathers in our land. And, we all know that you cannot teach what you do not know yourself first! God promises us that if we seek Him with all our heart He will teach us of His ways. The ways we should walk in.

We say, at this point, that the transfer of authority and responsibility begins at the conception of our children. Fatherhood begins at the place of the actual generation of a new life through God's ordinances of the marriage covenant and procreative relationship of husband and wife. The transfer begins in the heart and minds of the father and mother of each child. The actual knowing that God created us to be like He is. To act, walk, think, and speak as God does. To reflect the image and likeness of God upon the earth in our earthly bodies. The single most powerful force in showing our sons how they should live their lives is the actual example we demonstrate before their little eyes and ears. The transfer begins here. As we flow in obedience to God's Word and move in the fullness of the Holy Spirit our children learn how to do the same. Every day is a learning experience for our sons and daughters. They absorb all kinds of information in the world around them. We, as fathers, and mothers, are to supervise that intake of information. We are to watch over their little hearts and minds. Their little fountains. We should work to keep them clean of the poisonous and noxious materials Satan endeavors to place into their hearts and minds through television and other forms of media. We are to fill their hearts and minds with God's Word, and Holy Spirit. Through music and dancing. By continually rehearsing God's words in their ears. By helping them to read books that tell them of God's ways. By showing them how to love and care. Showing them how to serve others. This transfer God has ordained to take place throughout a child's lifetime while under his parent's authority. This is what Proverbs 22: 6 means -

"Train up a child in the way he should go:
and when he is old, he will not depart from it."

That is God's promise to us as fathers and mothers. Great promise!

But, there is a certain time in which our sons are ready to leave home, and start one of their own. At this point we must have already given to them all the information they need to be successful. A military drill sergeant does not train his soldier half way, and then put him out on the battlefield. We, as fathers, must take this responsibility before God in our son's lives. Father, and son word studies in the Book of Proverbs would definitely assist in this process.

340

We conclude this chapter on - Fatherhood and Sonship - by studying the authority and responsibility in our family name. Proverbs 22:1 shows us something interesting about names:

"A good name is rather to be chosen than great riches, and loving favor rather than silver and gold."

God also shows us a contrast to this in Proverbs 10:7 -
" The memory of the just is blessed: but the name of the wicked shall rot." What do people think of when your name comes up? Is it a favorable thought, or, does dishonor accompany your name, or, your son's name? Is your name more valuable than great riches, or, is your name rotting?

When we marry, our wives receive our name for their own. The children born to our marriage also receive our last name. We should be concerned about what kind of name we are giving them to live with. Is it a good name?

Names in the banking, and financial world, strive to be recognized as a source of strength and stability. A signature loan is a loan that says your name placed upon a piece of paper can guarantee you certain monetary funds. Trust and reliability are found in your name.

In ancient oriental, and Jewish customs a man's name, and his word, were enough to seal an agreement, or, covenant. A man's name carried weight and power if it was honorable. The authority of a man's name was transferred to his son at the point in which he was old and mature enough to use his father's name. When that time came, that son could have the authority to speak in his father's name. He could use the credibility of his father's name to transact any business contract. It was as if his father was actually there speaking, or, signing his name, when his son was speaking, or, signing his name. He had the authority and responsibility to use his father's name. His love and respect for his dad made it so.

This transfer of power and authority is graphically seen in God the Father's name for His Son. Our Lord & Saviour Jesus Christ. Philippians 2: 8 -11 shows us the power and authority of God's name for His Son.

8) "And being found in fashion as a man, he humbled Himself, and became obedient to death, even the death of the cross.

9) Wherefore God also has highly exalted Him, and given Him a name which is above every name.

10) That at the name of **Jesus** every knee should bow, of things in Heaven, of things in earth, and things under the earth.

11) And that every tongue should confess that Jesus Christ is Lord, to the glory of God the Father."

Jesus Christ gave to His true believers His name to do His works in the earth. Matthew 28:18-20, and Mark 16:14-20, shows us all the kinds of authority and power that comes to us when we use His name responsibly. And with honor and dignity. The powers of Satan are bound and cast out by that Almighty name. The Spirit of God is released into our lives, and our children's lives *" in the name of Jesus Christ "*. Our access into God's presence is only through that name. And, as Proverbs 18:10 tells us -

" The name of the Lord is as a strong tower: The righteous run into it, and are safe."

Let us, as fathers, raise up our sons to honor and glorify the nature and likeness of God's image as was manifested in the life of His Son, our Lord Jesus Christ. Then there will be honor and dignity found in fatherhood and sonship in our nation. We see this is God's will in Romans 8:28-32 -

28)   "And we know that all things work together for good
        to them that love God, to them who are called ac-
        cording to his purpose.

29)   For [because] whom he did foreknow, he also did
        predestinate to be conformed to the image of his Son,
        that he might be the first born among many brothers.

30)   Moreover whom he did predestinate, them he also
        called: and whom he called, them he also justified:
        and whom he justified, them he also glorified.

31)   What shall we say then to these things? If God be for
        us, who can be against us?

32)   He that spared not his own Son, but delivered him up
        for us all, how shall he not with him also freely give
        us all things?"

This is fatherhood and sonship. God, in the beginning, created man
to be like He is. He sent His Son Jesus, to us to show us that likeness.
He has given commandment to be like He is (See 1st Peter 1:15-16).

Our work, as fathers on the earth, is to produce that likeness in
our sons by example and word. We are to plant the seeds of God's
Word in the hearts and minds of our sons. If we obey the Lord in this
administration, our sons will grow up to be "..the trees of righteousness.." Isaiah 61:3 tells us of. And the result will be "..that He will
be glorified.."!

We must, as fathers, take on the Spirit and concern of Father
Abraham in Genesis chapter 24. To protect our sons from marrying
a " *Canaanitish woman* ". A woman who would be used by Satan
to turn our sons from serving the Lord God our Creator.

Below are two informative books which clearly show the doctrine
of Balaam in our National Media sources, books, magazines, billboard
ads and Television Media manipulation. Also, now the Internet.

1. <u>Media Sexploitation</u> - Wilson Bryan Key, New American Library, 1976.
2. <u>Subliminal Seduction</u> - Wilson Bryan Key, New American Library, 1981.

Recommended reading:

1. <u>A Man's Touch</u> - Charles F. Stanley, S.P. Publication, Victor Books, 1977.
2. Character Sketches - Volumes 1 - 3 - By: Bill Gothard - Institute in Basic Life Principles - Oak Brook, IL, USA - Website URL - store. IBLP.org
3. 7 Basic Needs of a Wife - Institute in Basic Life Principles - Bill Gothard - Oak Brook, IL - Website URL - store.iblp.org/catagories/FAM/80
4. Bless Your Child - By: Dr. Kevin McDonald - Grand Rapids, MI - 1- 888 - 581 - WORD (9673)

CHAPTER 17

Fatherhood & Daughtership

We have endeavored in this writing on the excellent subject of fatherhood, to infuse into our hearts and minds the requirements God has laid down for His success in this area. In God's eyes we are either successful or failures as fathers depending upon our adherence to His covenant commands. God has established one way in which He has ordained both fathers and mothers to function in life on the earth. The way He has ordered is a blessed way. His way is the true way. We can be confident that the way God has established is the best way we can live our lives in service to Him. We can be confident that God's way is best for our children. Our sons, and, our daughters.

As we begin our study on the subject of fatherhood and daughtership we say that a lot of good reference material can be found in the book to which this is a sequel. <u>Satanic Feminism vs. The American Home</u>. As we said in the preface of that writing, the state of a nation is governed by the way in which the daughters in that nation are viewed and taught by their parents. That, if we permit a default in the payment of motherhood for our children, we will see a greater weakening of the state of marriage, and the family, within our nation. That these very important principles are the very fiber of our nation's strength. To allow them to be destroyed is in essence causing the destruction of our nation. As we have learned in this writing on fatherhood, it is our job to protect our nation from this kind of destruction in all ways possible. To provide God's excellent instructions in these crucial matters is a great joy. Obedience will complete it.

It is not in the hands of the State or Federal governments of these United States of America to administer these matters to our children. It is in the hands of the fathers and mothers in our land. Fathers and mothers will give an account to God in which He shall judge all the secrets of men's hearts according to our Gospel (Ref. Romans 2:16).

The beginning of our study will be in relation to the negative aspects of daughtership in our nation. We will endeavor to explain why these negative aspects have developed among our daughters. The remainder of our study will be to instill in our minds and hearts the ways God has provided to avoid and guard against these negatives in our daughters.

A Prophetic Word to the Fathers of Daughters

The disposition and mentality a father has toward women in general, and his daughters in particular, has a direct effect upon the spiritual state of the home, and nation. God has warned us that if we as fathers and mothers permit the existence of a certain thing it will turn our entire nation into a land of various kinds of wickedness. When God speaks to one nation, that Word He speaks, carries over to all other nations that are existing, or, that come into existence.

This means that every nation on the face of this earth is to adhere to the spiritual direction God ordains when He speaks to one nation. This means that if God instructs the fathers and mothers of one nation to obey a certain principle, He expects all others to follow suit. This includes the United States of America. Our nation. What God commands in one nation He commands to all nations. We say this in our opening statements to this segment because there are those elements who say that God only speaks certain things to certain nations. We speak of the main oracle of God in the earth since Noah's flood, the children of Abraham [the father of a multitude], the children of Israel, the nation of Israel. God commanded the parents of the

346

nation of Israel to be careful to not permit their daughters, or cause their daughters to be used a certain way. All the prophets of the Old Testament spoke God's righteous judgment against the oracle nation of Israel because they allowed this very thing to be done. God's anger and wrath was their experience because they allowed it. Our nation, the United States of America will also experience God's judgment unless we all as fathers and mothers put an end to it in our nation. This is God's command and warning to every nation.

Leviticus 19:29 -

"Do not prostitute your daughter, to cause her to be a whore; lest the land fall to whoredom, and the land become full of wickedness." It is very interesting that the next verse in Leviticus 19:30 also commands us to "reverence" God's sanctuary. In 1st Corinthians 6:15-20 we are allowed to know that God's sanctuary is not a temple *"made with hands"* but, rather, it is God's desire to dwell inside us. We are his earthly tabernacles. The major prophets Isaiah, Jeremiah, Ezekiel, and Daniel all accused Israel of *"defiling God's sanctuary"*. Polluting His dwelling place. The spiritual principle to be observed here is in relation to causing, or allowing, God's sanctuaries (our bodies, and those of our children) to be defiled. God warned Israel's fathers that *"the land"* (which also means the physical bodies of earthly beings) would become *"full of wickedness"* if they caused or allowed anyone in their nation to use their daughters in a prostituting way. The nation of Israel did this in the evil (RAG) worship of Baal-peor. And God's anger fell against God's own people. It is only because of God's mercy that we as a nation have yet to experience God's same judgment against us. Through this first segment we pray that God will bring His light to the fathers of our land specifically in this matter. As fathers we must catch a vision from God that our daughters are created by God to be the sanctuary of newly created spiritual and physical beings coming into the earth by procreation. We have been commanded by God to not permit the defiling, polluting, or prostituting of these *"sanctuaries"*. We speak at this point of our daughters. The author in meditation and prayer has been allowed to know that all the different kinds of wickedness we see, and are experiencing in our homes, cities, states, and nation all are in existence *"because"* of this very disobedience in our land. Divorce, fornication, adultery, sodomy (gay or homosexual behavior), child abuse and molestation, and child-sacrifice (abortion on demand), wife abuse, teenage pregnancy all are *"caused"* by our refusal to judge the flood of pornography coming out of California, and other states in our nation. The disposition and view of our daughters and the women in our nation has produced these various forms of *"wickedness"* against God. It is our job to force the legislators and judges, and law enforcement officials to root out and destroy each and every form of the expression of the prostitution of the daughters in our nation. Whether in Playboy-type magazines, evil romance novels, movie and video forms. We have been commanded by God to put a stop to it. As we said in earlier, it is our job as fathers and mothers to force the enforcement of National and State laws in this very matter! As the author, I wish to organize three hundred men (specifically fathers) in every City and State to organize themselves together. And demand these sources of wickedness be destroyed by those whose job it is to do so. Romans 13:1-7 instructs us as to who those individuals are! We are to have in our hearts and minds that the First Amendment to the Constitution of the United States, protects the freedom of pure and wholesome expression, not polluted and immoral expression. We are to guard our hearts and minds from the demonic phrase, ***"you cannot legislate*** *morality"*. Because, that statement is a wicked lie out of the pits of the damned. The author has been assured that if we all band together in defeating these destructive forces of pornography (all types) God will manifest a great revival within our nation. God's love and peace [cessation of againstness] will flow into our homes, cities, and states. The purity, and virtue, God desires us to know will be manifested. And the evil, and wickedness, will be annihilated without the shedding of anyone's blood. This is the reason Benjamin Franklin stated *"the pen is mightier than the sword"*. All we must do is use our democratic process to accomplish it. To the praise and glory of God! For the spiritual, moral, and physical health of our land! Amen.

BUILDING SPIRITUAL HEDGES IN AND AROUND OUR GIRLS

We have attempted to bring clarity to the fact that the treatment of women, and daughters in particular, has a direct connection to the strength, or destruction, of a nation. Therefore, as fathers and mothers we must understand that Satan, and his powers, desire to utilize our daughters for his purposes (Ref. John 10:10a) Satan is the first prostitute. He is the ruler over all the various forms of prostitution. He is the god of all whoremongers. Or, as we hear in today's venacular; king of pimps. God had a specific estate and position for Lucifer to occupy in God's creation. Lucifer literally has *"prostituted"* that position. Ezekiel 28:18 show us this.

18)   You have defiled [polluted] your sanctuaries by the multitude of your iniquities, by the iniquity of your traffic;..."

As we said in <u>Satanic Feminism vs. The American Home</u>, "..to use anything, or anyone in God's creation for anything other than God's original purpose for it, or them, is basic prostitution." The only way we as fathers can guard, and protect our daughters from this manipulation of Satan, is to build into them, and around them spiritual hedges. There are key materials God has ordained to perform this in our daughter's lives. Those hedgework materials are to be built in, and around, their hearts and minds. This is the work God has ordained fathers and mothers to do. The Spirit and ministry of Shahmar is to be released and exercised by fathers and mothers in their daughter's life. Satan will work to defile, and pollute, the sanctuary of our daughter's lives. Our work before God is to keep covenant and stop those *" advances "* of the enemy.

At this point we wish to express the ways we as fathers can allow the advances of Satan in the lives our daughters.

The very first is found in our very own attitudes and dispositions concerning women in general. These dispositions are developed in us as fathers in our relationships with our fathers and mothers in the homes we come out of. These dispositions are also formed in us in our "buddy" relationships at public schools. They also are formulated by our interfacing with our sisters and girlfriends as we grow into adulthood. The multi-medias of music and television, video and movie *"hearing"* and *"viewing"* also form our attitudes toward womanhood. This has a direct affect upon our relations with our daughters. We wish mainly to speak concerning our *"eyes"*. The eyes seem to be a major area of satanic and demonic activity in the earth. This has been so from the beginning as we see in Geneses 3:4-5 -

4)   "And the serpent [Satan's oracle] said to the woman, you shall not surely die:

5)   For [because] God does know that in the day you eat thereof, then your eyes shall be opened, and you shall be as gods,..."

350

The word **"as"** in verse five can also be translated **"like"**. Rather than God's Holy Spirit ruling your lives. ***"You shall be like gods."*** We know that Satan, and his demon powers, view themselves as, or, like gods. What Satan was communicating to Eve was that rather than being like the true God, they would be like him, and his angels. We say this here because it is in the way a father views his daughters that greatly influences their behavior. If a father has great difficulty keeping his "eyes" from wandering toward immorality and seductively dressed women, his daughters will receive a silent, yet real message, that men like women to be like that. Even men who are endeavoring to serve God in purity and holiness can have a difficulty with this. This is why we must follow God's admonition in Job 31:1-10.

I made a covenant with mine eyes; why then should I think upon a maid.

Verse 7 also refers to the connection of the "heart" and "eyes". We are not to allow our hearts to follow our eyes. It seems that daughters specifically observe their father's eyes. We need to observe Proverbs 20:8 -

A king that sits in the throne of judgment scatters away all evil with his eyes.

A father who is acting as God's prophet, priest, and king also will scatter evil by his eyes. It stands to reason that if you can scatter evil with your eyes, you can gather evil by them also. We as God's men are to scatter evil - see Romans 12: 21.

The looks, comments, and actions a father expresses greatly influences his daughters. God has built into women, even young women who are daughters, a desire to be pleasing to their fathers. This can be honored by us, or abused. It is in this crucible that they will develop into women who serve God's purposes, or turn to the prostitution program of Satan, and his demon spirits. This reality is seen in the great efforts our older daughters, and women, work so hard to look good to men. It is God's desire in them to have Dad's approval. But it can be perverted and abused just like anything else. It is in our hands as fathers and mothers to govern in this area.

THE ATTIRE OF OUR DAUGHTERS
AND THE WILL OF GOD

2) "For you know what commandments we gave you by the Lord Jesus.

3) For this is the will of God, even your sanctification, that [in order that] you should abstain from fornication:

4) That everyone of you should know how to possess his [or her] vessel **[physical body & future life partner]** in sanctification and honor;

5) Not in the lust of concupiscence, [evil lascivious desire] even as the Gentiles which know not God:

6) That no one [man, or woman] go beyond and defraud his brother **in any matter** [including dress] because God is the avenger of all such, as we have forwarned you and testified.

7) For God has not called us to uncleanness, but to holiness.

8) He therefore that despises, [this Biblical teaching] despises not man but God, who has also given us of His Spirit. 1st Thessalonians 4: 1 - 8 [emphasis added]

As fathers, we are to be very careful with the way we allow our daughters to be dressed. To add a little humor to this teaching, which may have spiritual implications, God did ask the first man, the first father to *"dress"* the garden (Genesis 2:15). And we are to view our young daughters as future potential gardens to be cared for and protected. Most of us have heard Satan's extreme remark given by those who "despise" these principles:

" What do you want us to do? Wear a burlap sack?!! "

We have all been blown back by the beauty that can be brought out of a woman by the way she is attired. We are not " throwing out the baby with the wash-water " here. But we are going to sound God's warning loud and clear.

The true Church of Jesus Christ, specifically the women in it, have been allured by the world's Media systems to violate God's standards for them. The main reason is that the old prophets have seemed to have fallen asleep, and are not *"..barking.."* [see Isaiah 56: 10].

We encourage a review of God's judgment on the daughters of Israel found in Isaiah 3:11-26. Verse seventeen specifically records that God Himself will reveal their "secret parts". This refers to the procreative anatomy of a woman. Women in the Church today are wearing pants so tight they literally are showing their "secret parts". They are in their indiscretion leaving nothing to imagine. They are in fact "creating lust" by their dress. They are defrauding their brothers by being indiscrete. Titus 2:5 instructs them: As fathers we are commanded by God to keep the garden from being like this. It is a disgrace to God, and us as husbands, and fathers. God will hold us accountable. God has given commandments to obey in 1st Timothy 2:9-15; 1st Peter 3:2-6; Deuteronomy 22:5. These commandments are to be known and obeyed in our families. It is the work of fathers and mothers to teach our daughters to observe God's way in the conduct of their physical bodies. We, as fathers and mothers, must understand that the way our daughters dress themselves communicates a silent advertisement to those they come into contact with. This principle is seen in Proverbs 7:10:

"And behold, [look] there met him a woman with the attire of a harlot, and subtle of heart."

God says certain garments are to be attributed to being the type of clothing a harlot-prostitute wears to entice her customer. God forbid any daughter who calls herself a daughter of God would even think of such activity. We say at this time that **" the doctrine of Balaam "** was centered around this principle to send in seductive and alluring women into the camp of Israel to corrupt them. The Madison Avenue, and world fashion designers, have been slowly corrupting God's own people in our nation this way. They **"advertise"** their immoral seductive attire to allure our daughters into buying them. Much of the new physical fitness push today in our land has, might we say, disgusting outfits for our daughters to wear to "really get into it" with. In Old Testament times women that showed their thighs were considered to be into harlotry. There are certain areas of a woman's body that should be reserved only for her husband's eyes to see. To our disgrace there are not too many areas at all that cannot be seen in various quarters of our nation. It is the defiled way for women to get the attention of men. Hugh Hefner's Playboy Magazine started out only with what we consider " modest " bathing suits worn by women. Today, the fashion designers of swim wear for women, have totally thrown out the principle of modesty in their designs. We must understand that if we as fathers have principles to give to our daughters in this area they most likely will desire to follow them. We must cultivate the respect for us as fathers in our daughters so they will seek our opinion regarding these areas rather than the corrupted world views. We, as fathers and mothers, should work to set the godly standards for our children to follow.

Before we close this segment we should examine something God calls *an abomination* [something to be hated and disgusted] among our daughters. Deuteronomy 22:5 -

"The woman shall not wear that which pertains to a man, neither shall a man put on a woman's garment: for [because] all that do so are an abomination to the Lord your God."

The workings of satanic powers have energized to cause us to do this in our nation. It began in the 1960's with the " unisex " movement. Then, it moved from there into the equal rights movement. Women started cutting off their hair to be like a man. Fashion designers started designing clothing for women to wear that related to the male counterpart. Fathers and mothers, God calls it an abomination to His eyes. It causes confusion in our children's eyes. God commands repentance of these wicked works against Him. God says we are manifesting rebellion in our family, or marriage partner.

We close by stating that there are beautiful things our daughters and wives can do in relation to their attire. The Holy-Spirit directed woman, or daughter, can receive a creative ability to be used to design fashions to put to shame the ungodly examples Satan works to raise up to deceive our daughters. Let us take the admonishment we find in Jude 23:

" And others save with fear, pulling them out of the fire; **hating even the garments** spotted by the flesh. [Garments that glorify the flesh; not God's Spirit]."

AFFECTION IN A YOUNG GIRL'S LIFE

This segment should be considered one of the most important in our discussion about our daughters. God designed physical affection to meet certain needs in all our lives. A new born baby desperately needs the affectionate words and touches of their father and mother. It builds bonds. And, a sense of security in a child who has arrived into a new world from their world within the womb of their mother. Studies now show that serious emotional problems can be caused by neglect in this area. Affection allows a new born baby to know all is well. My mother and father love me. They appreciate me. They care for me. God's care is manifested in and through our care of our children. The child abuse in our land is a manifestation of evil satanic power in our land. It is one of the forms of wickedness God warns us of in Leviticus 19: 29. We also have been warned in Romans 1: 31 & 2nd Timothy 3:3, that there will be an absence of " natural affection " among men. Colossians 3:5 warns us of " inordinate " affection. Webster defines inordinate as:

1. Disordered; not regulated.
2. Lacking restraint or moderation; too great, or too many; immoderate.

We can learn from this definition that affection is to be administered properly. The Spirit of Gahvad should be observed. It should be administered as God's Spirit directs. Specifically, as we as fathers see the need of it in our daughter's lives. At any age! We say at any age because it is in this very area that Satan gains place and advantage in our teen-aged daughters. A very real stronghold of Satan can be to take advantage of her vulnerabilities. Affection needs of a young-woman are established in our young daughter by her father neglecting this special need she has. The hugs, touches, kisses, and words of affection in a young girl's life, actually builds hedges in and around her life to guard against a young man who would use that very real need to violate her virginity before marriage. Love and affection needs in a young girl are to be met by her father and brothers until a commitment to her is made by a prospective husband. The affection need factor is transferred to her husband when her father says in the marriage ceremony:

" I do give her away to this man" and the minister officiating the marriage states, "Do you (name of husband) take [receive] her to have and to hold? "

We will cover this a little more in the last segment.

We conclude this segment by saying that God requires us fathers to provide affection for our daughters. If we fail to do so our daughters may seek this need to be met in the wrong way. A way that may bring disgrace upon you as a father. The author believes that the explosion of pornographic materials has caused the perversion of natural affection in our land. The impure, or evil thoughts in men who are fathers, can cause a distortion, and neglect of affection towards their daughters. Therefore, this can cause the young girl to seek affection in the wrong places. This can develop when his little girl starts developing into a young woman.

We close by saying that each and everyone of us needs affection. From cradle to the rocking chair. Babies, young children [sons and daughters], teenage youngsters, young men and women, middle aged men and women, husbands and wives, grandfathers and grandmothers all need the administration of physical and verbal affection. But we as fathers must recognize the need of **affection in our young girl's life**. To the glory and praise of God! Amen. Romans 12:10

THE BEARERS OF LIFE - TEACHING MOTHERHOOD

20) "And Adam called his wife's name Eve; because she was the mother of all living." — Genesis 3:20 God, in His creation of Adam, created him to function in a specific ordination. That ordination is found in Genesis 1:26-28; 2:5-7, 15. That ordination has never changed. Man has changed. God's ordination for man to operate in has never changed. It will never change.

God's will is perfect. It never needs to change. We, as men, need to change. And come into proper alignment with God's perfect will.

God also created the woman Adam named Eve to function in a specified ordination. That ordination is found in Geneses 2:18, 20-25; 3:20. This ordination also has never changed. Woman has changed. God's will for the woman has remained the same. Woman must be taught and instructed by her father and mother from the time she is a little girl until she grows into a woman. What our nation is saying a woman should be is not necessarily what God has already said she should be. We, as fathers, are in authority to speak into existence God's will as revealed in Holy Scripture. Our guide to help us know God's will for our daughters is not Satan's world Media system. Our guide is the Word of God, the Holy Bible. It speaks. We are to listen, and obey it. No questions. No rebellion. Just obey it.

God created the woman so Adam would not be alone. God said,

" It is not good for the man to be alone..."

This has not changed either. Even though there are men who are alone. And, there are women God created to meet the needs of men. Even so God created woman for this purpose. A thorough exposition of Genesis 3:20 would reveal the second purpose of God for our daughters. Genesis 3:20b -

"...Because she was the mother of all living."

God's design for our daughters is that they be " the bearers of life " into the earth. A peach tree bears peaches. An apple tree bears apples. A banana tree bears bananas. God created woman to bear fruit also. Psalm 127:3 -

" Lo, children are a heritage of the Lord: and the fruit of the womb is His reward."

There are numerous verses throughout God's Word that speak of this ordination God has for women. They are God's bearers of life into this world. This is why abortion on demand is so wicked. Life is being destroyed by the hands of men (Ref. Proverb 6:16-17). God requires the blood of these children at the hands of those who are destroying it. God will return this upon our own heads if we refuse to repent as a nation. The author cannot read anywhere in Holy Scripture where God says, "when you feel there are too many start murdering some before they are born." He has found that when any nation did this abomination God destroyed that nation! What is a great atrocity is that the wicked God-haters in our land have taken a perfectly righteous United States Constitution, and twisted its interpretation to accommodate their filthy life-styles before God their Creator. If we do not work with God to bring this nation to repentance it will be destroyed. The ordination of women to be the bearers of life is one of God's most holy places. Yet, this place has been allowed to be defiled by the fathers and mothers of our land. Let us intercede and petition God for a Spirit of repentance to come into our nation. Let us pray for peace: To cease being against God in this most holy place. Only God knows the beautiful and wonderful people who have been destroyed before their birth.

TEACHING MOTHERHOOD

The human body, as revealed in Psalms 139:11-19 is *" ..wonderfully and respectfully.. "* made by God. God makes our bodies within the womb of our mother. In the womb, the developing child needs and depends upon the nourishment he, or she receives from the mother. Pediatricians warn that smoking and drinking alcoholic beverages, and drugs can have negative affects on pre-born babies.

After being born, we find Genesis 49:25, and Psalms 22:9-10, shows us a reinforcement of a mothering principle. Psalms 22: 9-10 -

9) "But you are Him that took me out of the womb: you did make me hope when I was upon my mother's breasts.

10) I was cast upon you from the womb: You are my God from my mother's belly."

But motherhood does not end there either. We are learning, the hard way, that all the organs of our physical bodies need certain different kinds of vitamins, proteins, minerals, fibers, liquids, fruits, and vegetables to remain healthy, and functioning properly. The absence of any critical nutrition can produce a diseased state of the body. Someone needs to be in authority and responsibility over this important area of life inside the family cell. Genesis 3:20 tells us God showed Adam that his woman functioned well in this area. Teaching motherhood starts in our training of our daughters in how to be effective mothers. God, through the Apostle Paul, communicated that as His will in Titus 2: 1-5. Specifically 3-5 -

3) "The older [elder] women,..., teachers of good things;

4) That they may teach the young women to be [responsible], to love their husbands, to love their children,

5) ...to be keepers at home..."

Our daughters must be trained and taught to know all that is needed for the nourishment of their husbands and children. The end of verse 5 of Titus 2 says if this is not taught, God's Word will be *"..blasphemed."*. All the various facets of motherhood must be taught. No woman knows it all when she is born. Older women and mothers have failed to obey God's will if they do not work to help their daughters know all they need to before they enter marriage. They have caused God's Word to be blasphemed. Fathers should oversee this teaching. We close this segment by referring to an important song of God's Word. It is the song of Deborah and Barak. It should be meditated upon and sung by God's daughters in our land. Due to its length we will only refer to the basic thought of it.

"The enemies of God's people prevailed...until that I Deborah arose, that, I arose a mother in Israel." — Judges 5:1-31

FATHER AND SON-IN-LAW RELATIONSHIPS

"Who can find a virtuous woman? For her price is far above rubies." — Proverbs 31:10

What makes the value of rubies so high? And, why does God's Word say that a virtuous woman is worth much more? Let's study it a little. We will study the procedure of procuring rubies, then apply it to the fatherhood and daughtership interaction.

The first step in the acquiring of rubies is to locate where they may be found. We must know a little geography and topography. We must do some survey work. The best place to locate the virtuous kind of woman should be in the home and Church.

The next step in acquiring these precious jewels is the mining process. This is where labor and hard toil needs to be expended. Sometimes you must dig a short distance. Other times you must dig down deep into the heart of the earth to mine these gems. Sometimes you must bore through solid rock. At other times you only have to remove the dirt in the way. The hearts of our daughters are the same.

The third step after locating and mining these special creations of God is to clean them. The cleansing process is to remove all foreign debris from the actual ruby substance. This can take a chisel and special solvents and brushes. This relates to God's Word. The special soap and purifiers found in God's Word. They are applied with the water of the Holy Spirit of God. The blood of Jesus Christ is a special cleaning agent (Ref. 1st John 1:7). It is to be applied with loving care where ever necessary.

The fourth step is polishing. This is done with certain harsh to fine sandpaper and cloths. Coarse paper, and cloth for stubborn areas. The fine cloth for smooth refinement. This can be applied to the various kinds of interfacing a father, mother, sister or brother has with our daughters. My mother was sent to a - **Refining School** - in her day by her father and mother she once told me.

Cutting the prepared stone is the next step. This takes skillful hands. It is in the actual, and precise manner, a gem specialist cuts the raw stone that produces the specific magnificence and luster of the finished ruby. This applies to our daughters in the final cutting God must do in her life to remove areas that do not bring out His glory in her life. It takes the skill of the Master's hands.

The next to last step in the ruby making procedure is setting the finished ruby. A skilled gem specialist will search for an appropriate setting to place his finished product. The setting should enhance and bring out all the beauty and brilliance of the perfected stone. Gold or silver maybe. Sometimes platinum is utilized by the Gemologist. The setting for a daughter is where her father allows her to be placed. What kind of home and life her perspective husband will give her.

The last step in the acquiring of these gems is in the process of giving them away to someone. Some gems are so magnificent they are acquired by committee groups with vast sums of money. They are acquired by museums and studied by gemologists. Some are just as beautiful, and are placed in rings. Or necklaces, and given as expressions of deep love for someone special. This is the father and son-in-law relationship as explained in Proverbs 31:10.

We do not normally give anything away to anyone who would not be greatly thankful for the work and investment we have placed in preparing that gift. Neither would we give something away to someone special, someone that we love, that did not cost us to give it away. Daughters are like this. Son-in-laws should be like this.

But, we should always remember to Whom these special jewels belong. Malachi 3:17 -

"And they shall be Mine, says the Lord of hosts, in the day when I make up My jewels; and I will spare them, as a man spares his own son that serves him."

Ezekiel 16:17 -

"You have also taken your fair jewels of My gold and of My silver, which I had given you, and made yourself images of men, and did commit whoredom with them."

This shows us that our daughters are given to us by God. It shows us we can do with them that which is an abomination to Him. Cause them to be whorish. This is in the hands of the fathers and husbands in the United States of America. God will judge us in these specific areas in the end. Let us work in our father and son-in-law relationships to have that judgment of God be in our favor. May He say to us what is said in Matthew 25: 21 -

" His Lord said to him. Well done, you good and faithful servant. You have been faithful over a few things, [those jewels in the making in your home] I will make you ruler over many things: Enter you in the joy of your Lord."

Yes, God is deeply concerned with the little souls walking, running, and jumping around our feet. They are special, and precious jewels in the making, to Him. Let us, as fathers and mothers, have that same concern. And, let it also be deep. Because, this will cause our heavenly Father to be glorified in, and on the earth.

We close this chapter on fatherhood, daughtership, and son-in-law relationships with an appropriate poem from a dear and trusted friend.

<u>Waiting</u>

I don't know who you are, yet I'm waiting.
I don't know where you live, but I'm waiting.
I don't know what you are doing, but I'm waiting.
I don't even know if you know about me, yet I'm waiting.
I'm alone now, but someday I'll be with you.
I just know that, because I already love you.
I'm not sure what you look like,
but I know that you will be beautiful to me.
I'm not sure how you will act, but I know it will suit me.

I already know that the things
that bother you, won't bother me,
and you will feel the same way about me.

Until I meet you, I'm trying to
make myself the kind of person
I think you want me to be.

That in itself keeps me pretty busy
because you deserve the best.
I won't even try to find you,
because somehow I know that we will meet when it is time.

An when we do, I'll just know that it's you.

I love you, and I don't even know
who you are, yet I'm still waiting.

— Alonzo J. Fernandez 1980

Recommending Reading:

1. Rodale's Encyclopedia of Natural Home Remedies - By: Mark Bricklin
2. The Illustrated Encyclopedia of Healing Remedies - By: C. Norman Shealy, MD, PhD - Harper Collins
3. Natural Cures - They Don't Want You to Know About - Kevin Trudeau
4. Satanic Feminism versus The American Home - By: Michael D. Juzwick - order by phone - 206. 497. 8553
5. You Can Be the Wife of a Happy Husband - By: Darien B. Copper, Victor Books, 1977.
6. Where Have All The Mothers Gone? - By: Brenda Hunter - Zondervan Publishing House. 1982.

CHAPTER 18

What's A Grandfather To Do?

The common belief in the United States of America about grandfathers is that they are old grey- haired men who have retired from their various secular occupations. They usually sit around their house that cost them a lifetime to pay for, and rock in their rocking chair. They usually do this until they die. Sometimes they visit their children, and grandchildren, and give them candy, or toys, and horsey rides on their knee. Let us contrast this belief with the Word of God. Genesis 3:19 -

" In the sweat of your face you shall eat bread, until you return to the ground; for out of it you were taken: for dust you are, and to the dust shall you return."

It's hard to read any retirement program into this verse from God's mouth. This is not to say that a man should not have times of rest at life's end. And be able to enjoy the fruits of his labors. But you just cannot find a retirement program here. It is good and wise to make plans for the end of our lives. But what we do with our life's ending years is important to God. He has given certain commandments concerning our working and activities as grandfathers. He requires us to be good stewards all the way to the end of our lives on the earth. Wicked and ungodly statements like:

" We're spending our children's inheritance" and "I, being of a sound mind, spent it all" will cause a wickedness to prevail in our land. God does not think it is very funny. It is an abomination to Him. There is a need for a number of men to stand in the gap between generations in our families. It is sad to say, but the grandfathers and grandmothers in our nation need God's instruction on the various aspects of grandparenting God would be pleased to see taking place. Repentance is needed among the elderly generation. TV has replaced reading the Holy Bible! And, that has brought curses, not blessings!

We say, at first, that God requires all men who are fathers, or grandfathers, to keep, or guard, God's covenant among their sons and daughters. Deuteronomy 6: 5 - 9 commands this work in all generations. To refuse to function in this capacity, and ordination, is to open the gates and doors of our nation to the powers of Hell. We, as fathers, are to serve God on this earth "until we return to the dust.". We are to keep, and obey, His commandments of **" Gahvad & Shahmar "** until He calls us to Himself. The time we may be able to utilize at the end of our life, through wise planning of our finances, should give us a greater ability to help our children do more to bring glory to God in their homes and families. We see this to be true in Deuteronomy 6:1-2, 5-7 -

1)   Now these are the commandments, the statutes, and the judgments, which the Lord your God command-ed to teach you, that you might do them in the land whither you go to possess it:

2)   That you [parents, grandparents] might fear [rever-ence] the Lord your God, to keep all His statutes and His commandments, which I command you, and your son, and your son's son, all the days of your life; and that your days may be prolonged.

5)   And you shall love the Lord your God with all your heart, and with all your soul [psyche: mind, will, and emotions] and with all your might.

6)   And these words, which I command you this day, shall be in your heart: [not on a shelf in the Holy Bible collecting dust].

7)   And you shall teach them diligently to your [disciple
        ] children, and shall talk of them when you sit in your
        house, and when you walk by the way, and when you
        lie down, and when you rise up. [emphasis added]

If there is a retirement program God would approve of in the United States of America, this is it. As grandfathers we must catch a vision of how important the life-giving Words of God are for our children and grandchildren. The greatest testimony a grandfather, or grandmother could have after they leave this earth is that their children, and grandchildren, learned the important things of life from their lips, and lives. We must break away from the idea that some building called "the church" is where everybody hears the Word of God. We must break from the idea that only those who are **"ordained ministers"** are supposed to speak God's Word to us. God has ordained that every father, and grandfather, be a source of information about God, and His Word, to their children, and grandchildren. We are all ministers in our homes and families. It is a destructive lie to believe only **" a man of the cloth"** has God's authority to operate as a spiritual leader. Our families in the United States need the ministry of God's Holy Spirit, and His Word, to be ministered inside our homes. We all must see a transfer of authority into our homes if we would see the working of Satanic powers defeated there. It is hard for the enemy to defeat a large assembled body of faith - filled believers in a church building. But a small family, he can overwhelm, and destroy. We must recognize the authority God has to give to fathers and mothers (two in agreement - ref. Matthew 18:18-20) within the family domicile. That grandfathers and grandmothers, can join their faith to assist in the nurture and protection of our homes. We must understand that certain universal commands of God are for all nations, not just the nation of Israel. We Americans must obey Deuteronomy 6:1. God has commanded us as fathers to teach our families. The fathers in our nation have caused God's Word to be considered something to avoid, rather than loved, and obeyed. Our families and children are suffering because of this atrocity. Let us put an end to it.

God has asked us to love Him with our total being in Deuteronomy 6:5. He has given us as fathers, or grandfathers, a command to place His Words **" inside our heart "**. We are to allow the Words of God to grip our entire being spirit, soul [mind, will, and emotions] and body. Then we are to teach them to our children **"diligently "**. There are four places God would be pleased for us to teach them diligently to our children (Deuteronomy 6:7).

1. Talk of them when we sit in our houses: Relating the importance of God's Word in our families inter-personal relationships.
2. Speak of them when enjoying family recreation.
3. Before we retire for the night to sleep.
4. When we awake from sleep. Before we head out to work and school.

These four times of diligent teaching will greatly bless our wives and children, if we obey God's command. We must have a strong and healthy relationship with God to first desire to do it. And, then, to be effective in doing it. If we try to do God's commands without the power and ministry of the Holy Spirit, we will be a bore and uninteresting minister of God's Word. Our family may even resent what we do with God's Word. We must make it live as it comes out of our lives and mouths. 2nd Corinthians 3:6 warns us of not mixing faith with our words.

" Who has also made us able ministers of the New Testament; not of the letter [only], but of the Spirit, for the letter [of God's Word alone] kills, but the Spirit gives life."

Romans 2:27, 29; 7:6 shows us that God's Word, without the Spirit, bringing life to it, can kill, and be destructive. It is like trying to eat dry bread without any butter. And nothing to wash it down with. God's Word, and His Holy Spirit, operate as a team. Jeremiah 1:12 reveals this:

" Then said the Lord to me, you have well seen: for I will hasten [watch over] My Word to perform it."

We, as fathers, and grandfathers, are designed by God to be His channels of life, love, truth, and mercy into the earthly setting. God created us to be manifestations of His glory. This is the most powerful force in our nation. Our children and grandchildren are little fountains [see John 7: 37 - 39] waiting to pour forth God's waters into the lives of others. Our children and grandchildren are little tape recorders taking in, and recording our lives. They are our little disciples hungrily looking to us as examples of how they should live. God created the family to be His training camp. A spiritual boot camp to prepare our little ones for warfare against God's enemy, and theirs. We are designed by God to be His nurturing drill-sergeants to prepare them for our Commander-in-chief. The success of the army of God is all found in the success in raising our offspring in God's ways. This is the battlefield. The war that rages within the borders of the United States of America. If all the fathers, and grandfathers, will understand the power, authority, and responsibility God has given to them, we all together can destroy the works of our common enemies. And produce salvation, deliverance, healing, and strength in our families and homes. There is nothing the enemy can do to stop us if we commit to these principles. God desires these things in our lives. He loves us, and cares about us. But He demands our obedience.

THE POWER OF PLEASANT MEMORIES

We all can recall events in our childhood that brings joy in our lives as adults. Many in our nation have gone through traumatic experiences in their childhood, that causes deep problems in their adult lives. The ugly fighting and divorcing of fathers and mothers leaves deep scars and emotional difficulties in young children's minds and hearts. This, in effect, can produce a repeat in their lives when they marry, and start a family. A wise father and mother, grandfather and grandmother, will work to place good, and wholesome memories, in their children's minds and hearts. This activity on our part will be a source of blessing inside the marriages and families of our children. It will give a strong resource for them to draw from during difficult periods of marriage, and child development. God created the subconscious mind and emotions of man to be programmed with His good things. Blessings of the heart and mind. Our children depend upon us as parents, and grandparents, to build into our souls (mind, will, and emotions) these blessed memories. We are to create positive memories for them to draw upon in difficult times. This is part of effective parenthood. Our children, as Proverbs 31:28 says, will rise up and call us blessed, if we do this important work for their families.

The serious problems our nation is facing in relation to our overcrowded prisons is an indictment against us as parents. Our prison systems would be greatly affected if the parents and grandparents in our nation would see their failures as parents to these men and women, who are their sons and daughters, and pray and fast for their children's deliverance from the hands of the enemy. Most inmates in prison are there because of a miserable childhood, and improper spiritual guidance from their parents. We, as a nation, must repent of the wickedness of finding excuses to place blame on others, when we are to acknowledge our own failures before God concerning our children. This is not to say that if we have done all these things, our children will not ever do wrong, but we should be able to say to ourselves, and God, we have done all we could to guard against our children turning to evil. Even if we find our children being placed into prison, Matthew 25:36 instructs us to go to them, and minister to their lives. Jesus Christ identifies with those in prison -

"I was naked and you clothed me, I was sick, and you visited me: I was in prison and you came to me."

Due to my 5 years of ministry as a Chaplain assistant in the City of Pittsburgh's Allegheny County Jail Maximum Security Pod 7d ministering to men incarcerated for violent and sexual crimes, I can tell you that many in prison have need of having their past child-hood memories healed by the Word of God, and His Holy Spirit. We all know it is very easy to criticize, condemn, and complain about the actions of others. It takes a man, or, woman of compassion and understanding to set the prisoner free. To work with the Holy Spirit to produce change in a life. As we stated in Chapter 2 on " Wheat and Tares ".

Tares becomes tares when nobody cares.

INTERCEDING GRANDFATHERS

12) The Word of the Lord came to me again saying, son of man, when the land sins against me by trespassing grievously, then will I stretch out my hand upon it, and will break the staff of the bread thereof, and will send famine, upon it, and will cut off man and beast from it:

13) Though these three men, **Noah, Daniel, and Job**, were in it, they should deliver but their own souls by their righteousness, says the Lord God." - Book of Ezekiel 14:12-14

What is significant about these three men? For what reason does God refer to them in relation to the destruction of a nation? Is it not because they were leaders in the work of intercession? Is it not because their hearts grieved with God's heart to see the evil wickedness existing in their nation? Is it not because they prayed earnestly for their families, and the people of their nation? Hebrews 11:7 shows us that Noah was like this. Daniel 6:10-11; 10-21 reveals that Daniel was an intercessor. Job 1:5 shows us that the Patriarch Job believed in interceding for his family. 1st Timothy 2:1-6 reveals to us that the peace, [cessation of againstness] godliness, and knowledge of the truth of God is all centered around the intercessory work of God's people. Prayers, intercessions, and giving thanks to God for all men releases the work of God in a nation. This is the most honorable place a grandfather can function in. This office of intercession literally stops the workings of Satan in our nation, and families. It is the most important work to be done by any man who fathers children. It is our responsibility and authority in the earth. Much evil and wickedness is restrained and stopped by those men who do this work. It can literally change the course of historical events. Nations rise and fall on the basis of whether, or not, this work is done. It is the work of standing in the spiritual gap between God, and your children. It is the work of building hedges in, and around their lives. It is caring enough to lay down your own life to help your children, and grandchildren, bring glory to God. God seeks out fathers, and grandfathers like these as seen in Ezekiel 22:30 -

"And I sought for a man among them, that should make up the hedge, and stand in the gap before me for the land, that I should not destroy it: but I found none."

Let us all work to not allow this to be true of our individual families. Let us be the intercessors God seeks out. This is the work of fathers and grandfathers alike.

THE PROPHETIC MINISTRY OF GRANDFATHERS

We all know that a specific word spoken to us by our grandfather can have a profound effect upon our lives. We tend to value greatly what Grandpa or Grandma has to say about us. These words can greatly influence the success or failure of our lives. The words that come out of a grandparent's mouth have the capacity to be treasured and valued by our children. Therefore, we must guide our words to be in accordance with God's Words found in Holy Scripture [study 1st Peter 4: 10 - 11].

The greatest example of the prophetic ministry of a grandfather is found in Genesis 49:1-33. A very special and insightful look into the nature and character of the twelve sons of Israel, which is represented in the twelve tribes of Israel. We must see that Grandpa Jacob had to study, and observe his sons, to be capable of making these prophetic statements about their individual lives. A prophetic word has the power to direct a child's life. It should be exercised with wisdom under God's direction. It should be used to be a spiritual blessing upon our children's lives. A word that will provide strength and encouragement in their lives on the earth. It is a spiritual anointing that grandfathers should function in for the strengthening of their families. Avoid evil prophesies like - **" You'll never amount to anything ... you must be a blankity - blank.. etc."** Remember that we all will account for every word we let fly out of our lips - Gospel of Matthew chapter 12 verses 33 - 37!

The Patriarch Noah, in Genesis 9:25-28, also functioned in this prophetic office in the lives of his sons Shem, Ham, and Japheth. We must be very careful in this area, because it can bring both blessings, and destructions in our children's lives if we do not watch carefully what we allow to come up out of our hearts and minds then through our tongues and out of our mouths. It should be based upon God's purposes in the earth. A prophetic word from a godly grandfather can become a source of strength and encouragement throughout several generations long after we no longer live upon the earth. Our sons, and daughters, need Grandpa to operate in this special ministry for families. 1st Thessalonians 5:20 instructs us to hold this prophetic ministry in a high regard. It can cause great things to happen for the glory, and praise, of God. Genesis 48:1-22 shows that grandfathers can operate in the authority of *" laying their hands upon"* their grandchildren, and blessing them. An office in which God is well pleased to see taking place in the earth. It honors God, and respects His covenant with men, and their children.

We complete this writing with two words of instruction from God's Word. The first is Psalms 25:14, which speaks of God's condition for *seeing* His covenant. Another name for Old Testament prophets - **Seer**.

" The secret of the Lord is with them that fear Him: and He will show them His covenant."

The second admonition to grandfathers is in Proverbs 13:22:

" A good man leaves an inheritance to his children's children: and the wealth of the sinner is laid up for the just."

The true Church of the Lord Jesus Christ has been suffering many failures and defeats due to the failures of marriages and father/ mother relationships. Our spiritual hedges have been torn down. And, due to our willful ignorance, and neglect, not even placed and established in the hearts and minds of our dear children! Satan has had a grand old time *"..stealing, killing, and destroying.."* [see John 10: 10] God's people in their families. God's covenant, and Word of righteousness, when obeyed, and carried out, can utterly overthrow, and defeat our great enemy, and adversary. This book was written to bless your life and household.

Let us all observe to keep the covenant God has established in the principles of **GAHVAD & SHAHMAR** in our children's lives, and in our children's children's lives. If we will do this, we will be blessed grandfathers. We will leave our children, and their children, with an inheritance that will have the blessings of God upon it. And all God's people said, *" Amen "*.

We finish this treatment on the excellent Biblical teachings concerning - Fatherhood in the United States of America - with the awesome Word of God in the book of His prophet Malachi chapter 4 -

" For behold, the day comes, that shall burn as an oven; and all the proud, yea, all that do wickedly, shall be stubble: and the day that comes shall burn them up, says the Lord of hosts, that it shall leave them neither root nor branch.

But unto you that fear my name shall the Sun of Righteousness arise with healing in His wings; and you shall go forth, and grow up as calves of the stall.

Behold, I will send you Elijah the prophet before the great and dreadful day of the Lord:

And he shall turn the heart of the fathers to the children, and the heart of the children to their fathers, lest I smite the earth with a curse. "

— Malachi 4: 1 - 2; 5 - 6

Recommended Reading & Viewing:

1. The Holy Bible [King James Version].

2. Character Sketches Volumes 1 - 3 - By: Bill Gothard - Institute in Basic Life Principles - Oak Brook, IL - Website URL - http://store.iblp.org/products/C123/

3. The Power of Spoken Blessings - By: Bill Gothard - Institute of Basic Life Principles - Oak Brook, IL - URL - iblp.org

4. How to Honor Your Parents - By: Dr. James MacDonald - Walk in The Word.com - Grand Rapids, MI - Phone - 1. 888. 581. WORD (9673).

5. The Complete Life Works of Michael D. Juzwick - Light Eternal Publications, USA Phone - 206. 497. 8553 - Websites & URLs - lighteternalpublications.wordpress.com/ - and, https://openlibrary.org/authors/OL3837346A/Michael_D._Juzwick

6. Michael D. Juzwick YouTube Channel Videos - http://www.youtube.com/channel/UCUMByWgZHpXm75b4kwKykLQ

You may follow us also via facebook @ the web presence -

My " America Bless God!!! " Last Call to Repentance - National Movement

Please pray for the good success of this new book for the benefit of all the fathers, mothers, grandfathers, grandmothers, and, their children throughout the United States of America - And, the countries it may reach. Thank you!

PART 5

Appendix A

God's Word
on
The Grove & Ashtoreth

Light Eternal Publications, USA

- Biblical Light for America's Christian Families -

Mountlake Terrace, Washington 98043-2913

FORBIDDEN MASONIC OBJECTS
PLANTED
AS NATIONAL MONUMENTS
IN
THE FOUNDING OF
THE UNITED STATES OF AMERICA

- AN HISTORICAL ANTIQUITIES, BIBLICAL & PROPHETIC TREATISE -

ISBN 1-887412-05-0

An addendum from the book:
"Fatherhood in the United States of America"

By:
Michael D. Juzwick

FORBIDDEN MASONIC OBJECTS
PLANTED AS
NATIONAL MONUMENTS
IN
THE FOUNDING OF THE UNITED STATES OF AMERICA

PREVIOUS TITLE:

GOD'S WORD ON THE GROVE & ASHTORETH

First edition - 1985
Second edition - 1993
Third edition - January 1997
Fourth edition - July 2005

First eBook edition - January 2010
ISBN: 1-887412-05-0

 **Light
Eternal
Publications**
— Biblical Light For America's Christian Families —

CITY OF SEATTLE, WASHINGTON STATE **98115**

PRINTED IN THE UNITED STATES OF AMERICA

HOPE LUTHERAN CHURCH

2799 Old Washington Road
Upper St. Clair (Pittsburgh)
Pennsylvania 15241
412-941-9441

RE: A Review of the Book - "Fatherhood in the United States of America"

To Whom It May Concern:

The home is the heart of all relationships. The happiness of a Christian home goes with the members of that family to school, work, Church or wherever they may be. A contented home is a priceless possession that colors the life of those who dwell there. To be a father, mother or child in a Christian home where there is peace and harmony is to live in the forecourt of heaven. On the other hand, an unhappy member of a home where there is strife and open hostility, is handicapped in everything the person does.

The home is the focus of Michael D. Juzwick's book "Fatherhood in the United States of America." His heartfelt desire is to inspire fathers in particular to develop their spiritual leadership abilities and then pass on that vital baton to their sons and daughters. What a mighty task!

But note how tenderly Michael describes that fatherly concern, "...The effective wickerwork of weaving God's Word into the minds and hearts of our sons and daughters demands a commitment to God and his Word. It will take careful and appropriate placing and knitting of the Holy Scriptures into the lives of those under our care. It will take diligence in spirit to continually be about this business the Father has given fathers to do...The work of fathers is to protect their children and keep them pure and free from every kind of defilement the enemy can throw at them."

Michael is very conscious of a father's failure which can affect his little ones so dramatically. He writes, "...Our children and grandchildren are little tape recorders taking in and recording our lives. They are our little disciples hungrily looking to us as examples of how they should live . God created the family to be his training camp; a spiritual boot-camp to prepare our little ones for warfare against God's enemy and their's. The success of the army of God is all found in the success of raising our offspring in God's ways. This is the battlefield. The war rages within the borders of the United States of America. If all the fathers and grandfathers will understand the power, authority and responsibility God has given to them, we all together can destroy the works of our common enemies and produce salvation, deliverance, healing and strength in our families and homes. There is nothing the enemy can do to stop us if we commit to these principles!"

Will church people let the enemy march on unhindered? They cannot afford to do that! Rather, let the people of the Church take up a book such as Michael D. Juzwick's and continue to march to war against the enemy in the home and beyond.

God's Blessings On Our Homes,

Neville Mirtschin, Pastor

382

MT. LEBANON UNITED
PRESBYTERIAN CHURCH

Michael D. Juzwick
1134 Illinois Ave., Suite 2
Pittsburgh, PA   15216

RE: A Review of the Book - "Fatherhood in the United States of
      America"

To Whom it May Concern:

I sense two of the most abandoned relationships and commitments in
our society is that of a husband to a wife and a father to a son or
daughter. Men are confused as to their role and responsibility to
their wives and children.   For many men, their priorities lie
elsewhere than to their home and to the relationships within their
homes.

Michael Juzwick, in his book, grounded in biblically and
theologically sound writing, calls men to claim their God-given
roles as Christian husbands and fathers. Mr. Juzwick articulates
with passion God's call upon the family and God's design for the
family to be the main vehicle of the communication of His Truth.
He explores clearly the attack upon the American family and he does
not leave us hanging in despair, but gives to the reader a concise
statement how God intends for the family to be and to function. In
desperate times, he communicates with urgency and passion an
insightful message of hope and strategy.

Our society has lied to men on what is important and essential for
the living of our days. Mr Juzwick sets the record straight as he
himself has grounded himself in the words of the very author of
life and sets forth that truth.   I recommend this book to every
American male who is open to spiritual direction in the area of
husbandry and fatherhood.

Faithfully submitted,

Robert J. Maravalli

RJM/kmr

255 Washington Road, Pittsburgh, PA 15216   Phone: (412) 531-3387 FAX: (412) 531-3419

About the Author

Michael D. Juzwick was born September 7th, 1953 in West Palm Beach, Florida to Joseph D., and Georgianna M. Juzwick. He was raised there except for seven years in Pittsburgh, Pennsylvania during his youth. Upon graduating from John I. Leonard High School, in Lake Worth, Florida he entered the United States Navy. After Boot Camp at the Recruit Training Center in Orlando, FL, he received his formal technical training in aircraft powerplants and airframes in Millington, Tennessee. From there he was ordered to San Diego, California to receive training at Ream Field, Helicopter Rescue and Anti-Submarine Warfare base. Part of his training was received on the Naval Air Station at Corornado Island, CA. He became a Naval Search and Rescue swimmer, and was trained in the preliminary methods of S.E.R.E. [Survival, Evasion, Resistance and Escape] in the California desert. From here he was ordered to P.M.T.C. [Pacific Missile Test Center] Naval Air Station, Point Mugu. Located on the West Coast of California in Ventura County, Northwest of Los Angeles. Michael was initially trained to become a Plane Captain on H - 3 & H - 46 Sea knight helicopters. He received further training on H - 46 Helicopters at the Marine Helicopter Training airbase in Orange County, CA.

It was after this military training that he was approached by a fellow sailor by the name of Bruce Able who was stationed also at the Naval Air Station, Pt. Mugu. Having been a Roman Catholic from birth, Michael was unaware of his need for personal salvation, which Bruce Able shared from I John 5: 10 - 13, and invited him to join some other sailors in the Navy Barracks to their Church in Ventura. Some time passed until he turned 21 years old, and he recalls, after a lonely night on the base on his 21st birthday, he was reminded of the Christians next door. So Sunday morning was the next day when he went next door to see if he could join them for Church. Perry Robinson was the only sailor who was there, and was going to the last service that morning. Perry offered to let Michael join him on his trip to Ventura Baptist Temple. A Church that was 30 minutes drive from the Naval Air base.

Michael D. Juzwick came to receive his personal salvation that morning by believing in the Lord Jesus Christ September 8th, 1975 during his military service in the US Navy. After 21 years of being a Roman Catholic, he was born again. And his eyes were opened after hearing a clear Biblical sermon on each man's need for the new birth in Jesus Christ. The message was delivered by Pastor George Golden. Michael was then water re - baptized according to Christ's command. The Lord blessed him with some new Christian friends on the Naval Air Station who were part of the Navigators Christian Discipleship organization active in the United States Navy. They taught him to read, memorize and study the Holy Bible. He worked with Junior High youth and Sunday School bus ministry in Ventura County.

After these events he continued his military service serving as Aviation Machinist's Mate [Jet Engines], Aircraft Crew Chief on H-46, H-3 and finally H-1 Huey Gunships during his active Reserve service. While assigned to duty on board the Pacific Missile Center at Point Mugu; he assisted in the development of the very successful Navy's Tomahawk Cruise Missile now deployed throughout the world, and assisted in other classified electronic warfare military readiness exercises to keep America prepared for war. After his honorable discharge from the US Armed forces, he came to be very concerned with the need for fathers in our land to be more concerned with the spiritual and moral overthrow taking place inside America. The gender wars, accelerating divorce rate, child abuse and domestic violence. He graduated cum laude in 1981 from the Pacific Coast Baptist Bible College with a degree in Theology, Pastor's Major. He also received ministerial training at the Eagle's Nest Christian Fellowship of Santa Ana, CA in 1983. He is the founder of Light Eternal Publications, a Christian publishing concern dedicated to educating parents on effective Biblical principles in marriage and child development. He has served Sunday school children across America, conducted Bible Support Groups in the Maximum Security pod 7d for inmates in Allegheny County Jail 1995 - 2000.

Preface

Deuteronomy 16:21 & 22 -

>21) You shall not plant for yourself **a grove** (ashehrah) of any
>trees near to the altar of the Lord your God, which you
>shall make for yourself.
>22) Neither shall you set up for yourself any image; which the
>Lord your God hates.

The purpose for the following treatment is to allow the citizens of the United States of America to learn of certain occult activities that took place in the early stages of their nation. One of the favorite statements those who rule in the higher orders of Masonic degree make is, " What they do not know cannot hurt them." Which is only one of the many lies propagated by the secret orders of the Masonic art. We, however, wish to expose deception and allow the inerrant and eternal Word of Almighty God prevail in the face of satanic falsehood by those who serve the purposes of God's arch-enemy. The Lord Jesus Christ, in John 8:31-36 promises true freedom from all deception if one will be faithful to disciple themselves in His Word, the Holy Bible. The information that follows is Biblical truth that God has decided to have placed in the canon of Holy Scripture for our benefit. The revealing of the facts surrounding the history of these occult objects planted in America is difficult because the items exposed, are as greatly a part of historical Americana as the nation itself. Though, if we will but look around ourselves and observe the horrendous evil and misery caused by these sources of disobedience, we will see the reality that God, when He says something is evil in His Word, He means it.

The United States of America has developed into a mighty super-power by the hard work and intelligence of a people who have sought to follow Biblical principles for success. Its leaders have periodically invoked the blessing of God during times of distress and aimlessness. But, like when something is put into the kitchen garbage container that has the potential to rot and begin to smell up the whole house, so also, our beloved nation has allowed some items to be planted that God's Word clearly forbids to be planted. And we, as a people, are grievously suffering the consequences of having done so. Believe it to be so, that spiritually speaking, America has a putrefying condition that if anyone would seek to invoke God's blessing on the land, He would have to hold His nose to even consider doing so! A few of the big reasons this is so will be explained in the following treatise. Idolaters may minimize their sin against God or when not under scrutiny for it, magnify it.

In deciding to bring out the secret evil behind the objects discussed in following pages, I had great consternation, given the gravity of public opinion that may be against me in doing so. But, given the continual repeating of the cursed objects throughout God's Word, it forced me to be obedient in helping the people of this nation gain true freedom from the forces of Satan now so clearly evidenced in America. One thing that was not covered in the text was that the objects discussed also release the spirit of witchcraft by their very nature of being forbidden by God Almighty. Witchcraft is, in reality, the seduction or manipulation of someone, in order to get them to do your will. Rather than the will of the Spirit of God. It is trying to take the place of God in the life of anyone. To work to cause someone to follow a purpose that is contrary to the supreme will of God. This can pertain also to a nation. To speak from a Biblical perspective, this is, and always has been, the objective of our arch-enemy Satan. To trap a nation in disobedience and then lead its people into activities that would cause God to judge and destroy it is his primary motive. Realizing any delusion is key to full spiritual freedom and true liberty. God's Holy Spirit will be calling His people out of the exposed falsehoods in the following pages of this book.Let God's Word cleanse your minds as we continue. May we not be found in cruel bondage to any

385

of Satan's wiles and still claim to be "..One nation under God.." Any nation of people can claim to be under God. Those who truly are, will be exhibiting specific behaviors, such as being submitted and obedient to all His commandments. Even the Old Testament commandments regarding idolatry. Evil self worship is the very root of the sin Satan enticed and enslaved Eve and Adam with in the Garden of Eden. For either men or women, male or female to put themselves in a prideful position of considering themselves more superior than the other gender is one of Satan's weapons to destroy marriage and cooperative relationship under God's leading. But is this not the very evil spirit of our nation of men and women today? The curse of idolatry, in Colossians 3:5 -6, is equated with various kinds of sexual rebellion and immoral behavior. God strictly warns of horrible corruption that follows the setting up of satanic idols and images when people ignore His commandments in these vital matters. The book of Hebrews reveals to us the power of God's Word to assist in our ability to discern our hearts thoughts and intents. This includes His Word found in the Old Testament!

Deuteronomy 4:15-16:

> 15) Take you therefore good heed to yourselves; for you saw no manner of similitude on the day that the Lord spoke to you in Horeb out of the midst of the fire:

> 16) Lest you corrupt yourselves, and make for yourselves a graven image, the similitude of any figure, **the likeness of male or female,..** [Emphasis added]

- Michael D. Juzwick - Author/Publisher
LIGHT ETERNAL PUBLICATIONS

Introduction

America has reached a very serious point in its history. The electorate has placed Bill Clinton in the White House -- his key phrase during the campaign was, "It's time for a change." It is not surprising that the nation, as a whole, faces the future with a bit of apprehension. Drug abuse and violence continue to grow in our cities. Abortion is considered acceptable behavior. Sodomy is an acceptable " alternative life-style ", now being forced on even those who know God hates it, by corrupt judicial activists, bent on forcing its evil on others, even little children in public schools. Child abuse and domestic violence are on the rise as families are disintegrating. Why are we as a nation facing these problems? How can we restore America, and its people to health? Many Christians agree that sharing Christ is the answer. However, in reacting politically to these issues, Christians have neglected the weightier matters of " ...loving your neighbor..". An excellent illustration can be drawn from the abortion controversy. Christians march in protest to the murder of unborn innocents. They are led by conscience to do so. (This behavior is not wrong). However, what is wrong is neglecting to minister individually to those in disobedience. We attack the fruit on the tree and find that it is an endless, losing battle. We must turn and attack the root. Then, and only then, will the tree wither and die. What has been happening over the past decades in the United States of America, is the development of what is called " self-worship ". The source of self-worship is the rejection of the Creator God. Since it is basic human nature to worship something, man must replace the object of his worship with something else. And if it is not God, man thinks, the next best thing is himself. Michael D. Juzwick has written a startling and challenging piece of literature, which addresses the very roots of the problems we face as a nation. His basic answer is simple, America has rejected God. Ancient Israel, in her disobedience to the Lord God, erected obelisks (translated "groves" KJV) as part of her practice of Baal worship. Baal worship also involved child sacrifice. When the obelisks (which represent the phallus idol of the male organ of generation) were set up, they created a spirit of disobedience in the entire land. Michael Juzwick boldly parallels this practice in Israel to America's erection of the tallest obelisk in the entire world, located in the capital of our nation. In man's terms, it is called the Washington Monument. Here it is important to keep in mind that what is honorable in men's eyes is detestable before God. Could it be, that because men have placed this object up in direct disobedience to God, that the Courts of this land no longer stand for justice, but rather wickedness? The government removed voluntary prayer from public schools, as well as Bible study, and instead, have made the murder of unborn children legal? If man worships the flesh, they are at war with God [see James 4:4]. And what is the worship of man's organ of procreation, but the worship of idolatry, and self-gratification? Men who serve their bodies, rather than their Creator, find they are producing unwanted children, which must be discarded according to the law of self-worship: " Thou shalt not get in my way." As startling, and as controversial this treatise may be, I urge all Christians in this nation to carefully and prayerfully consider its message, and its implications. However, we must be careful, because only removing an object, while the people are rebellious, will do nothing. They will find other ways to rebel. So let us cling to the Holy Word of God as our guide to full obedience of not just removing occult sources of corruption. But also, discipling of Americans in God's ways that are absent in their lives. Jesus said in John 13:34-35,

> 34) A new commandment I give unto you, that you love one another; as I have loved you, that you also love one another.

35) By this shall all men know that you are my disciples,
if you have love one to another.

Let us, as His Church, love our neighbor, and bring those who are in darkness to His light by sharing the whole of the Gospel of the Lord Jesus Christ. Let us pray for revival in this land. That the Lord God would let loose His mighty Spirit, if perhaps He may bring this nation to repentence. Let us love those who are walking in disobedience as Jesus loved us. Let us stop wasting our time attacking the fruit on the tree of disobedience, and destroy its root.

- Michael E. Citriniti
Co-author of: The Original Intent of the First Amendment -
According to the Founding Fathers.

Writing on the behalf of Michael D. Juzwick, the author of the article entitiled " Forbidden Masonic Objects Planted in the Founding of the United States of America". My review of the book found it to be extremely well researched and thought provoking.

Michael has demonstrated scholarship in his approach to the research in the writing of the article. Through his approach, he has presented a thorough and convincing argument and has addressed spiritual dangers for our country.

Bruce G. Jackson - Executive Pastor
Allegheny Center CMA Church

Light Eternal Publications

— *Biblical Light for America's Christian Families* —

— ABOUT THE BOOK —

GOD'S WORD

ON

THE GROVE AND ASHTORETH

THE UNITED STATES OF AMERICA HAS BEEN UNDER SPIRITUAL ATTACK FROM THE KINGDOM OF DARKNESS SINCE ITS FOUNDING. THOUGH THE MAJORITY OF THIS NATION'S FOUNDERS WHERE CHRISTIAN MEN AND WOMEN SEEKING TO ESTABLISH A NATION UNDER GOD, THAT WOULD PROTECT THE UNALIENABLE RIGHTS BESTOWED UPON MANKIND TO WORSHIP AND SERVE THE CREATOR, SATAN HAS BEEN MILITANTLY ACTIVE IN CAUSING THE OVERTHROW OF THESE FREEDOMS AND LIBERTIES GUARANTEED BY OUR U.S. CONSTITUTION AND ITS FIRST AMENDMENT. THIS NATION, IS AT THE CROSSROADS OF DECISION, REGARDING ITS USEFULNESS TO GOD'S ETERNAL PURPOSES. WILL AMERICA TURN FROM ITS WICKED WAYS AND REPENT OF THOSE THINGS GOD HAS BEEN FORCED TO JUDGE AND OVERTHROW PAST NATIONS AND EMPIRES FOR? OR WILL SHE GO THE WAY OF ALL PREVIOUS CIVILIZATIONS WHO THOUGHT TO DEFY HIS ETERNAL STATUTES AND MORAL PRINCIPLES? GOD WILL BE FAITHFUL TO CALL US TO THE FORMER APPEAL OF HIS WORD.

GOD'S WORD ON THE GROVE AND ASHTORETH, WRITTEN BY MICHAEL D. JUZWICK, IS AN APPENDIX TO HIS BOOK BY THE TITLE - FATHERHOOD IN THE UNITED STATES OF AMERICA. IT IS A BIBLICAL REVIEW AND HERMENUTICAL EXPOSE' ON THE OVERTHROW OF MORAL PRINCIPLE IN OUR NATION'S JUDICIAL COURTS OF LAW AND OUR FEDERAL GOVERNMENT BY THE MASONIC ORDERS. IT COVERS THE BIBLE ACCOUNTS OF GOD'S WRATH AND JUDGMENT THAT CAME UPON OTHER NATIONS FOR DISOBEYING HIM IN THE ERECTION OF FORBIDDEN OCCULT OBJECTS. IT REVEALS HOW GOD'S ARCH-ENEMY SATAN, HAS BEEN GIVEN PLACE TO RUIN AMERICA BY GOD'S OWN PEOPLE. ITS ISBN IS 1-887412-05-0. THE RETAIL PRICE IS $9.95 + $1.75 S/H. THE BOOK IS A HISTORICAL STUDY OF AMERICAN OCCULT OBJECTS, AND CAN BE UTILIZED TO BRING GOD'S DELIVERANCE TO THOSE NOW UNDER BONDAGE TO THE EVIL POWERS ASSOCIATED WITH THE MASONIC ORDERS. ORDER COPIES TODAY TO GAIN A GREATER UNDERSTANDING OF OUR NATION'S DEEP SPIRITUAL PROBLEMS AND THE ONLY SOLUTION. FOR AN ORDER FORM CALL TOLL-FREE - 1-888-753-1776 TODAY.

" · · · For the perfecting of the saints · · · " Ephesians 4:7-14

1134 Illinois Avenue Suite 2   Pittsburgh, PA 15234-2539   (412) 531-3439

GOD'S WORD ON THE GROVE & ASHTORETH

(1) Genesis 21:33- Strong's exhaustive corcordance word # 815 is the Hebrew word transliterated (eh-shel) = grove.

> 33) And Abraham planted a grove (eh-shel) in
> Beersheba, and called there on the name of
> the Lord, the ever-lasting God.

eh-shel = A Tamarisk tree whose fruit contains an acid pulp used for preserves or in a cooling
laxative drink.

Gesenius' Hebrew-Chaldee lexicon, pages 90 & 91, records the occult object referred to in all
remaining appearances of the English word that was substituted for the Hebrew word [אֲשֵׁרָה]
transliterated - ashehrah - [KJV = grove]. The word is numbered in Strong's Exhaustive concordance of
the Bible as word # 842.

(2) Deuteronomy 16:21-22-

> 21) You shall not plant for yourselves **a grove** (ashehrah)
> of any trees near to the altar of the Lord your God,
> which you shall make for yourself.
> 22) Neither shall you set up for yourself any image;
> which the Lord your God hates.

Nimrod is held the father of the secret Masonic orders, and his mother - wife Semiramis, the
originator of the Biblical "..queen of heaven worship.." spoken of by God's prophet Jeremiah chapter 44.

The Biblical word [grove] is actually the English word substituted by the scholars of King James,
who used it to replace the Hebrew word transliterated [asheh-rah]. This occurred when they translated
our English version of God's Word, the Holy Bible, out of the received Hebrew text. The word grove
appears at least 39 times in Holy Scripture. Since the word is only a substitute to replace the Hebrew word
asheh-rah, it does create some confusion for us today, who refer to a grove as an orchard of land devoted
to a specific kind of tree. This confusion may have been caused in the translating scholars due to the fact
that the occult grove [asheh-rah], spoken of by the Lord, originally was made out of trees, as the idolaters
would carve their images out of wood and then "...plant.." or fix them in the ground. Refer to Jeremiah
7:18; 32:28-35 & 44:15-29. The female counterpart to Baal-Bel, was called the " **ashtoreth** or statue
to **Astarte** " as Gesenius explains on page 661 of his Hebrew lexicon. The Hebrew word [עַשְׁתֹּרֶת] the
Greek word [ʼαστάρτη] transliterated - *ashtarte* has been the Biblical names Post-Exodus Israel has
used to identify female goddess occult worship, originating at Nimrod and Semiramis' ancient Babylon.
This evil and forbidden sin is now overthrowing America. As we continue in our study of the antecedents
of these two cursed objects God has forbidden, we will also see the secret re-establishment of them in
this nation's founding. The secretive American version of the Masonic order, was very much a part of
the re- establishment of occult satanic worship in the United States, by high rulers in American
government. A very sinister picture of George Washington - with his occult Masonic apron donned - can
be seen in the Rotunda of the U.S. Capitol Building, in Washington, D.C. [District of Columbia].
American Masons will generally falsely report of these subjects due to the fact that they are sworn to not
disclose their satanic worship to non - members, or members of low degree.

A French member of the occult Masonic order by the name of Frederic Auguste Bartholdi [1834-
1904] must now be mentioned concerning the female occult idol or image that is the grove's counterpart.
In France, he built this object again and utilized the theme of the American Revolution to perfidiously
re-establish the wicked seduction of even Christian Americans. Bartholdi accomplished this by
capitalizing on the Christian themes of the founding of the United States of America. *Liberty* was

the cry of the new country soon to be called the United States of America. Christian American patriots were using the Biblical reference of Leviticus 25:10, which was placed on the " liberty " bell in Philadelphia, Pennsylvania. The Mason Frederic Auguste Bartholdi - 1834-1904 - decided to call his new image to Semiramis, or Ashtarte: *The Statue of Liberty*. Thereby, gaining acceptance, even by Christians, who are specifically warned in I John 5:21, to guard themselves from such idolatrous deceptions. Bartholdi carried this demonic contagion of Semiramis into his ashtoreth by using the Biblical term " liberty ". The specific occult idolatry was spread by Satan and his principalities through the secretive Masonic orders so prevalent today in America. The evil spirits associated with Masons or " Shriners " as some are called today, compel those who enter the Masonic orders to bring honor to Nimrod and Semiramis by building these occult idols, thereby establishing Satan's foothold in the nation. The idolatry originated out of the mystery religious systems concocted by the mother-wife of Nimrod. Semiramis and Nimrod devised this idolatrous worship under phases of God's judgment against them both for attempting to create and establish a world-wide occult system of religious self-worship. Nimrod began to build these occult systems at Babel in the plains of Shinar when he built the Tower of Babel and originated the occult system of astrology and star worship God had to warn His people about in Deuteronomy 18:9-14. Semiramis continued to devise various forms of occult image worship out of her anger toward the Lord God, whose judgment against her son Nimrod began decisively at the Tower of Babel. The anti-God, i.,e. anti-Christ kingdom Nimrod began to develop under satanic direction, began at Babel [please refer to Genesis 11:1-9 & 10:8-12]. Most Biblical historians of the antiquities report that after Nimrod built Babel and all the other cities in the plains of Shinar, which later became the land area known as Assyria [today known as the Middle East], God's judgment drove Nimrod and mother Semiramis to the land area at which time he proceeded to build the mighty and fortified city of Babylon. From this center of occult worship was exported the contagions of Babel; hence: the origin of the name Babyl-on. This etymological confusion seems to have also been similar in the origin of the term "oBELisk " since it carries one of the substitute names of Nimrod - " BEL " in it. Please refer to Daniel 1:7 & 4:8. Also, Jeremiah 51:35-44, especially verse 44. Both Nimrod and Semiramis continued to develop and propagate the mysterious religious occult systems began at Babel.

The great-grandson or grandmaster, as high-degree Masons would call him, Nebuchadnezzar ruled Babylon during Daniel the prophet's day as recorded in the book of Daniel. Chapters two and three specifically reveal the idolatry the kingdom of Babylon was in bondage to because of Nimrod and Semiramis their founder. Since the major efforts of Nimrod and his devotees related to the actual *building* of cities. It is held by many historians that Nimrod was the originator of the secret mysteries of the Masonic art. Which had areas devoted to the perfection of occult objects and idolatrous statuary. Images created to cause his worship and cultivate loyalty to his evil cause. Historians of antiquities report that after Nimrod's father Cush died, Nimrod actually entered into an incestual married relationship with his mother Semiramis. That the sons of Shem, Noah's youngest son, found out about this, and went and killed Nimrod, cut his body into pieces, and sent them throughout the then known world with a severe warning. That this same judgment would come on anyone else who did such acts of moral perversion against God. Semiramis continued though, and in her anger, continued to devise various objects of religious worship, to perpetuate the perverse honor and fame of her idolatrous son, who had been killed by the righteous seed of Shem. The mysterious Masonic orders, given by Nimrod and mother Semiramis, were to be propagated and perpetuated at the hands of [their devotees] and in memory of Nimrod and his mother-wife. This worship of the originators of occult masonry continued to be propagated by the secret orders of masonry. The names, as they were continued into each new civilization, were altered or changed to gain acceptance, and usually catered to the esteem, and pride of the new nation, empire, or civilization. The United States now hosts what is called: The Supreme Mother Council of the World based in Washington, D.C. From there is a constant effort to make members of the Masonic Order out of our political leaders when they come to our nation's Capitol after their election. This is a curse.

392

These wicked occult objects of idolatrous devotion were financed through perfidy and deception by Masons, who would use the themes, or individual founder's honor, to establish the occult objects as relating to the founding of the new nation, empire, or country, i.e. Washington Monument. This would provide a new beachhead for Satan to rule over the people of the new land area. Nimrod being represented in the **grove-asher-rah** and Semiramis worshiped in the **ashtoreth** [Gesenius' Hebrew-Chaldee Lexicon to the Old Testament page 661; word # 6252]. The true, yet secret meaning, as originating out of the mystery religious systems of Babylon, were usually disguised and modified to hinder disclosure of the idolatrous nature of the various objects devoted to the propagation of Semiramis' and Nimrod's religious and demonic self-worship. This deception has been acute due to the Biblical semantics and terms the Lord God Almighty has established in the Holy Bible to protect His people from falling into sin and disobedience in this very area against Him. The changing of names and terms is constantly used by Satan. This is an aspect of the manner in which the deceiver propagates his lies upon mankind. The truth of Holy Scripture is very necessary for us to gain relief from living under masonic delusions, and follow God's Holy Spirit leading revealed in Revelation 18:1-4: "..come out of her, my people..." Idolatry causes both spiritual blindness and deafness in those that entertain the demons that inspire the sin. Remember well Christ's words that - " That which is held in high esteem among men, is an abomination before God." Luke 16:15. Idolatry challenges God's demand for exclusive worship from man.

The following is an excerption of information out of the American Heritage series that refers to the establishing of the asheh-rah in the seat of our nation's federal government by masons. Most American citizens, even the Christian citizens, are totally ignorant concerning these ancient occult objects. An idol, is and idol, regardless of the use of even Christian terms being utilized to erase the stigma of it. This kind of diabolical perfidy was particularly sinister in the culture of the Israelites whose worship of the true Lord and God; Jehovah, was corrupted through the lascivious and immoral worship of Baal [Nimrod] and Ashtarte [Semiramis] which had been established in the land of Canaan before the entrance of the children of Israel under the leadership of Joshua [refer to the Book of Joshua]. Satan lost power over God's people Israel as they cleansed the land by following God's instruction to destroy all the objects of Baal [Nimrod] and Semiramis [Ashtarte] occult worship [refer to Numbers 33:50-56 & Deuteronomy 12:1-4; 13:12-18]. Later on, in the development of the nation of Israel, as recorded in the historical books of Judges, I & II Samuel, I & II Kings and I & II Chronicles; God had to send in His prophets to reveal to Israel the wicked sin of allowing these occult items to be planted in their land. As we continue and review some of those Biblical accounts, we will see God's great hatred for these Satan-inspired objects, that give the Devil dominion over a nation, to corrupt it with moral perversion, whoredoms, and child-sacrifice. Of all the evil corruption and curses now in clear evidence in our land, we must heed God's warning found in the book of Proverbs 26:2. We are foolish and useless to God's eternal purposes if we just continue to complain about all the evil problems of this nation. We will be wise to follow the admonishment of the eternal will of the Lord God, who never changes what His Word has declared. The following is an edited excerption of information adapted out of the American Heritage series that refers to the establishing of the asherah in the seat of our nation's federal government by Masons. Most American citizens, even the Christian citizens, are totally ignorant concerning these ancient occult objects, or their connections to past judgments in history.

AMERICAN HERITAGE - DEC. 1968 - VOLUME LXX # 1 PAGES 68 - 73:

".. In 1833 a concerted effort was begun to implement the dream of the Continental Congress and the vision of Major Pierre L.'Enfant. That year a group of citizens, exasperated by the failure of the two houses of Congress to agree on an appropriate memorial, organized themselves into the Washington National Monument Society, choosing Chief Justice John Marshall [whose background was related and mixed with the Masonic orders] as their leader. .... the society raised $28,000 and was sufficiently

393

encouraged to announce a design competition; it was won by [Masonic] architect Robert Mills, who conceived an elaborate pantheonic and statuary-cluttered pedestal dominated by a six hundred foot obelisk [asheh-rah]. [Ref. Ezekiel 8:3-6 & Judges 6:24-32]. Though this design was widely publicized, the society concentrated from the beginning on only the obelisk [grove-ashehrah] itself. Robert Mills [a member of the mysterious Masonic orders] style of obelisk [grove] won in 1835 over a Syrian-styled one, and an English Gothic, or romanesque one, by Colonel Thomas Casey. ...In just six years, the society had managed to push its grand design 152 feet into the sky, and everything seemed to be proceeding smoothly. Then, early on the morning of March 6, 1854, a group of [so-called] " know-nothings ", members of the " xenophobic " and anti-Catholic American party, broke into the premises, " stole " the slab sent by pope Pius IX from " Rome's " Temple of Concord, and presumably hurled it into the Potomac River. A number of American Party members [know-nothings] struck a second time by secretly joining the society itself. And thus making themselves eligible for elections as officers by surreptitiously inserting newspaper advertizements announced thesociety's annual balloting, were able to seize control at a private (and presumably illegal) predawn meeting. Congress, in disgust, recinded its promise of construction funds. The society applied for and was quickly granted a Congressional charter to eliminate any future rump elections, [they wanted no more hinderances to finish the erection of this occult object] but public confidence in the project had been shattered. ...Finally, on Washington's birthday 1873, a select committee of the House recommended a massive injection of federal aid for the purpose of completing the monument in time for the centennial of the Declaration of Independence. The ensuing furor in the press stung the patriotic instincts of many senators, and on July 5, 1876, a joint resolution to complete the structure was introduced and quickly carried without a dissenting vote. The figure finally agreed on was $200,000 in four annual installments [making an approximate total cost of one million tax-payer dollars]. The society gratefully deeded the thirty acre monument site back to the United States. Completion date was set at October 19,1881. The Army Corp. of Engineers took over the obelisk [grove -asheh-rah] construction in 1879. On December 6, 1884, in *a raging gale* [powerful wind] six men climbed precariously to a wooden platform, high atop the monument [ashehrah idol] carrying the largest piece of aluminum ever cast (100 ounces). Before this tip was set in place, it had been displayed in New York and Washington, where visitors frequently asked to be allowed to step over it, so they might claim to have stepped over what was then the world's tallest structure, and is still the world's highest piece of masonry. [end of adaptation from the American Heritage historical account].

From the beginning of America's colonial governmental establishments, numerous entities have been seeking out the validation and promotion of their own particular views and interests. Though American history has generally been written to put forth the best face to our nation's beginning and causes, the truth not usually spoken of is all the occult activities that occurred at the same time as those the Christian American patriots endeavored to establish. Most Americans may have heard that George Washington, Thomas Jefferson, and other major builders were Masons. But this truth is not usually spoken of, at the same time, when religious interests seek to promote the religious tenents of those same men. This duplicity is a major function of the Mysterious Masonic Orders way back into the historical antiquities. The official crest of the Scottish Rite Mason displays a falcon with two heads, this manifests the hypocritical operations utilized to deceive the simple-minded. Even the occult asherah and ashtoreth [i.,e. Washington Monument and Statue of Liberty] have been made into objects of deception by the duplicit and false renaming of these Biblically forbidden antiquitous idols. The Supreme Mother Council of the World, now based in the seat of the American Federal government, Washington, D.C., have sought to ensnare the men and women of the United States by their falsehoods and delusions. The leaders of American Masonic religious operations are not to be considered a bunch of simple brick-layers, as most might surmise of them. Doing so is itself delusional. There are leading Masons in most of the major industries of this nation. The curse of Astrology, which Nimrod - father of the Masonic art originated, has been re-propagated upon the American people in the major Automobile manufacturers by naming

394

of a number of models. Ford Motor Corp. has the " Taurus "; Dodge had the " Aries "; Lincoln Mercury the " Scorpio ". Christians should realize the delusion our government is under relational to the Book of the Revelation 18:5 - "..For her sins have reached unto heaven,.." which speaks to the use of American taxpayer monies going to finance high-minded, delusional efforts to go into space, rather than use those funds to establish God's eternal covenant in the earth, as is His commandment. Many families have been destroyed by punitive and arbitrary taxation by our Federal government, just to glorify the works, as amazing as they may be, of certain Masons working in NASA space programs. Remember, Satan has always sought to deceive, and lead mankind, into rebellion against God's will throughout the ages ever since the fall in the Garden of Eden. We do well to receive God's admonition in II Peter 3:1-11 and Revelation chapters 17 through 18 as we contemplate His determined end of these delusions of our lives.

Though it is seldom reported in the American media outlets, there are aggressive efforts to bring Congressmen, Senators and Presidents into Masonic agreement. Please review II Peter 2:14-22. One of the main principalities Satan employs in the Masonic religion, is the power of witchcraft. As we have revealed in other publications, witchcraft has also been cloaked in artistic delusional thoughts such as the caricature of an ugly old woman dressed in black, riding on a broom, stirring a cauldron of evil brew, and a black cat as a companion. Witchcraft is actually the utilization of anything to control another person. To lead anyone to deviate from God's will for their lives. The establishment of the asherah pole [Washington Monument] has been one of the Mason's greatest successes, in that it sets the spirit of witchcraft over the land specifically in regards to men's dishonor of God's procreative covenant in the face of intense profanity through pornography, and sexual rebellion. This has opened up women to the curse of the end results to this wickedness: child sacrifice, i.,e. abortion of the unborn [also an evil fruit of these idolatries rooted in Masonry].

BIBLICAL HERMENEUTICS & HISTORICAL INTEPRETATION

The preceding account of the events surrounding the occult ashehrah reveals some key points in the understanding of the evil nature of this wicked object. First, we see that a Major Pierre L'Enfant was given a vision to build this object. Both God and Satan use such avenues to accomplish their purposes. God gives visions to His servants, and so does the great counterfeiter, Satan [ref. Acts 2:16-19]. From the beginning, false prophets have been used by Satan to deceive and corrupt God's people. The men of Nimrod's mysterious Masonic orders have been his proponents and false-prophets to establish wicked-ness in every nation in defiance to the Lord God Almighty. Most American citizens know that George Washington was given assistance to defeat the British forces during our American Revolution. Most know the help came from the French. What they do not know is the fact that the leader of the French naval forces was this Major Pierre L'Enfant. They also do not know that he was a powerful French Mason. They also do not know he was given something in appreciation for helping George Washington defeat the British. Do you know what it was? It was the legal right to plan, and develop, the seat of our national federal government. Washington, District of Columbia. Named after both, the celebrated father [even though he never actually fathered a child of his own] of the United States, and the Roman Catholic Spaniard, who supposedly was first to discover America. It is very significant that Pope Pius IX sent a dedicated slab to establish Roman Catholic influence in the seat of this nation's government. It is also known that Masons do certain occult practices at night, during the beginning of the building of a new structure, that they dedicate the cornerstone to the god they worship, Lucifer. This is especially done at the commencement of building a place of rule or government. It is also carried out at the beginning of building a " Church" ediface. As beautiful as some cathedrals may be, little do most Christians know, the cornerstone of it was dedicated to the enemy the Lord Jesus Christ has declared war on [ref. I John 3:8]. Most of the idolatrous statuary of Roman Catholicism has its roots in these realities. It is also interesting that Jesus Christ did most of His miracles out in the open air and on hillsides. He seemed to avoid ministering inside religious man-made buildings. We must remember that Masons built Solomon's temple, and the Lord Jesus gave prophetic utterance to warn of the coming destruction of the rebuilt temple of His day [ref. Mt.24:1-2]. God is not impressed with what man can do. He is very impressed with what He can do through man if He is allowed to. We are warned about men's works in Revelation 9:20-21. Another important fact about the planting of the Washington monument was that the **xenophobic** and **anti-Catholic American political party** attempted to overthrow its establishment in a number of ways but failed to do so. These American party members were most likely Christian citizens that knew the evil this occult object represented. The sinister nature is made clear with the fact that the Roman Catholic Pope Pius IX, sent a slab from Rome, to plant the influence of Mystery Babylon's religious authority [Review Revelation chapter 17 and 18] in the founding of our nation's government. Later in the treatise we will see that this same object is found in the Roman Catholic world center of rule - The Vatican. It is very important to realize that the Devil has re- established all the perverse tenets to ancient occult Bel - Baal worship, in the United States at this time in its history: pornography, prostitution of women, and child-sacrifice [abortion]. Only one hundred years after Congress injected massive tax-payer finance into building this occult object, the nation's Supreme Court moved, under satanic direction (in Roe vs. Wade) to institute the modern form of the ancient occult practice of offspring murder, which today is called: **abortion on demand.**

Gesenius, in his Hebrew-Chaldee lexicon to the Old Testament, says "..that Asherah was the consort of Baal [Nimrod], who answered to the Venus and Hercules of the Greeks, and subsequent Romans [Roman-Madonna]. And was the granter of **" fortune and happiness "** if devotees continued to worship them. In the Holy Scriptures, Asherah is joined to the male counterpart idol to Baal. A statue-image made of wood or stone was said to be a pillar, which because of its great size, was planted or fixed in the ground [ref. Deut.16:21]. Ancient versions of the description of this asherah idol, a pillar was the partner of Baal at his altars. The English rendering by KJV scholars became the word **" grove ".** Among the contemporary interpretations of scholars, it is believed that the Asherah - idol is in fact the modern architectural " obelisk " which has been modified to " appear " to be an innocent design of architecture. And has been planted in the center of the federal government of the United States of America -- Washington, District of Columbia. Robert Mills, also a prominent Masonic architect, in the founding of the United States, was chosen by the first Supreme Court Justice of the United States of America , John Marshall, to design and supervise in the building of the largest [obelisk-grove-asherah] ever built in the history of the world at United States tax-payer's expense. " In honor of the celebrated father of the nation..." And secretly in worship to the god of Nimrod - Jah-bul-on [York Rite 17th degree]. The father of the occult Masonic deceptions.

Below, and on subsequent pages of this treatise, are the remaining appearances of this word "asherah " , translated " grove " in the King James version of the Holy Scriptures by his English Bible scholars in 1611 A. D..

3) Judges 6:24-32; Then Gideon built an altar there to the Lord, and called it Jehovah-shalom: [The Lord's way is peace] to this day it is yet in Oph'rah of the Abiez'rites. 25) And it came to pass the same night, that the Lord said to him, take your father's young bullock, even the second bullock of seven years old, and throw down the altar of Baal [Nimrod] that your father has, and cut down the **grove** [asheh-rah] that is by it: 26) And build an altar to the Lord your God upon this rock, in the ordered place, and take the second bullock, and offer a burnt sacrifice with the wood of the **grove** [ashehrah] which you shall cut down.; 27) Then Gideon took ten men of his servants, and did as the Lord had said to him: and so it was, because he feared his father's household, and the men of the city,

that he could not do it by day, so he did it by night. 28) And when the men of the city arose early in the morning, behold the altar of Baal [Nimrod] was cast down, and the grove [asherah] was cut down that was by it, and the second bullock was offered upon the altar that was built. 29) And they said one to another, Who has done this thing? And when they inquired and asked, they said, Gideon, the son of Joash, has done this thing. 30) Then the men of the city said to Joash, bring out your son, that he may die: because he has cast down the altar of Baal, and because he has cut down the grove [asherah] that was by it. 31) And Joash said to all that stood against him [Gideon], Will you plead for Baal [Nimrod]? Will uou save him? He that would plead for him, let him be put to death while it is yet morning: if he be a god, let him plead for himself, because one has cast down his altar. 32) Therefore on that day he [Joash] called him [Gideon] Jerubbaal, saying, Let Baal plead against him, because he has thrown down his altar

(4 1st Kings 14:15 & 23-24; For the Lord shall smite Israel as a reed is shaken in the water, and he shall root up Israel out of this good land, which he gave to their fathers, and shall scatter them beyond the river, because they have made their groves [asherah-obelisks], provoking the Lord to anger.

   23) Because they also built themselves high places, and images, and groves [asherahs-obelisks] on every high hill, and under every green tree. 24) And there were also sodomites [gay-homosexuals] in the land: and they did according to all the abominations of the nations which the Lord cast out before the children of Israel.

   5) 1st Kings 15:12 & 13; And he [King Asa] took away the sodomites out of the land, and removed all the idols that his father had made. 13) And also Maachah his mother, even her he removed from being queen, because she made an idol in a grove [asherah-obelisk]: and Asa destroyed her idol, and burnt it by the brook Kidron.

   6) 1st Kings 16:31-33: And it came to pass, as if it had been a light thing for him [King Ahab] to walk in the sins of Jeroboam the son of Nebat, that he took to wife Jezebel the daughter of Eth-baal king of the Zidonians, and went and served Baal [Nimrod], and worshiped him. 32 And he reared up an altar for Baal in the house of Baal which he had built in Samaria. 33) And Ahab made a grove [asherah-obelisk], and Ahab did more to provoke the Lord God to anger than all the kings of Israel that were before him.

   7) 1st Kings 18:17-19; And it came to pass, when Ahab saw Elijah, that Ahab said to him, Are you him that troubles Israel? 18) And he answered, I have not troubled Israel: but you and your father's house, in that you have forsaken the commandments of the Lord, and have followed after Baalim. 19) Now therefore send and gather to me all Israel to Mount Carmel and the prophets of Baal four hundred and fifty and the prophets of the groves [asherah-obelisks] four hundred which eat at Jezebel's table.

   8) 2nd Kings 13:6; Nevertheless they departed not from the sins of the house of Jeroboam, who made Israel sin, but walked therein: and there remained the grove [asherah-obelisk] also in Samaria.

   9) 2nd Kings 17:10; And they set themselves up images and groves [asherah-obelisks] in every high hill, and under every green tree:

   10) 2nd Kings 17:16; And they left all the commandments of the Lord their God, and made them molten images, even two calves, and made a grove [asherah-obelisk] and worshiped all the host of heaven, and served Baal [Nimrod].

   11) 2nd Kings 18:4; He [Hezekiah] removed the high places, and broke the images, and cut down the groves [asherah-obelisks] and broke in pieces the brazen serpent that Moses had made: for in those days the children of Israel did burn incense to it: and called it Nehushtan.

397

12) 2nd Kings 21:3; For he [Manasseh] built up again the high places which Hezekiah his fatherhad destroyed and he reared up altars for Baal, and made a grove [asherah-obelisk], as did Ahab king of Israel; and worshiped all the [evil & wicked] host of heaven and served them.

13) 2nd Kings 21:7; And he set a graven image of the grove that he had made in the house, of which the Lord had said to David, and to Solomon his son, " In this house, and in Jerusalem, which I have chosen out of all tribes of Israel, will I put my name forever . . ." [Compare with Ezekiel 8:1-18; 9:1-11].

14) 2nd Kings 23:4,6, & 7; And the king [Josiah] commanded Hilkiah the high priest, and the priests of the second order, and the keepers of the door, to bring forth out of the temple of the Lord all the vessels that were made for Baal, and for the grove [asherah-obelisk] and for all the host of heaven: and he burned them outside Jerusalem in the fields of Kidron, and carried the ashes of them to Bethel.

6) And he brought out the grove [asherah-obelisk] from the house of the Lord [ref. Ezekiel 8:3-6], outside Jerusalem to the brook Kidron, and burned it at the brook Kidron, and stamped it small to powder, and cast the powder of it upon the graves of the children of the people. [Probably the place all the sacrificed infants where buried after they had been murdered].

7) And he broke down the houses of the sodomites, that were by the house of the Lord's, where the women wove hangings for the grove. [The perversion of sodomy, (gay or homosexual activity) is one of the corruptions that apparently follows the planting of the asherah since demons gain access in the land through it].

15) 2nd Kings 23:14-15; And he [Josiah] broke in pieces the images, and cut down the groves [asherahs-obelisks], and filled their places with the bones of men. [Possibly to make a statement as to the destruction of human life that followed the disobedience of rearing up the occult object].

15) Moreover the altar that was at Bethel, and the high place which Jeroboam the son of Nebat, who made Israel [the nation] to sin, had made; both the altar and the high place he broke down, and burned the high place, and stamped it small to powder, and burned the grove [asherah].

16) 2nd Chronicles 14:3; For he took away the altars to the strange gods, and the high places, and broke down the images, and cut down the groves [asherahs].

17) 2nd Chronicles 15:16; And also concerning Maachah the mother of Asa the king, he removed her from being queen, because she had made an idol in a grove: and Asa cut down her idol, and stamped it, and burned it at the brook Kidron. [Holy Spirit directed King Asa had to wipe out his mother's idolatry to rid the nation of its evil influence].

18) 2nd Chronicles 17:6; And his [King Jehoshaphat's] heart was lifted in the ways of the Lord: moreover he took away the high places and groves [occult-asherah-obelisks] out of Judah. [Israel's sister nation Judah followed the corrupt leadership of the northern tribes. See Malachi 2:11].

19) 2nd Chronicles 19:3; Nevertheless there are good things found in you, in that you have taken away the groves [occult asherahs] out of the land, and have prepared your heart to seek God.

20) 2nd Chronicles 24:18; And they left the house of the Lord God of their fathers, and served groves and idols: and wrath came upon Judah and Jerusalem for this their trespass. [Note: putting up occult objects was the specific act that brought God's wrath on their nation].

21) 2nd Chronicles 31:1; Now when all this was finished, all Israel that were present went out to the cities of Judah and broke the images in pieces, and cut down the groves [obelisks] and threw down the high places and the altars out of all Judah and Benjamin, in Ephraim and Manasseh, until they had utterly destroyed them all. Then all the children of Israel returned, every man to his possession, into their own cities. [All the people from all over the land of Israel and Judah moved out to destroy all occult objects in the land and then went home. A national house-cleaning occurred].

22) 2nd Chronicles 33:3; For he [Manasseh] built again the high places which Hezekiah his father had broken down, and he reared up altars for Baalim, and made groves[asherahs-obelisks], and worshiped all the host of heaven, and served them.

23) 2nd Chronicles 33:19; His prayer also, and how God was entreated of him, and all his sin and his trespass, and the places wherein he built high places, and set up groves [asherahs-obelisks] and graven images, before he was humbled: behold, they are written among the sayings of the seers.

24) 2nd Chronicles 34:3 & 4: For in the eighth year of his [King Josiah's] reign, while he was yet young, he began to seek after the God of David his father: and in the twelfth year he began to purge Judah and Jerusalem from the high places, and the groves [obelisks], and the carved images, and the molten images.

25) And they broke down the altars of Baalim in his presence; and the images, that were on high above them, he cut down; and the groves [asheh-rahs], and the carved images, and the molten images, he broke them in pieces, and made dust of them, and strewed it upon the graves of them that had sacrificed to them.

26) 2nd Chronicles 34:7: And when he had broken down the altars and the groves [occult asheh-rahs], and had beaten the graven images into powder, and cut down all the idols throughout all the land of Israel, he returned to Jeru-salem. 26) Exodus 34:13: But you shall destroy their altars, break their images, and cut down their groves [asheh-rahs].

27) Deut.7:5: But thus shall you deal with them: you shall destroy their altars, and break down their images, and cut down their groves [asheh-rahs], and burn their graven images with fire.

28) Deut.12:3: And you shall overthrow their altars, and break their pillars, and burn their groves [obelisks] with fire; and you shall hew down the graven images of their gods, and destroy the names of them out of that place.

29) Judges 3:7: And the children of Israel did evil in the sight of the Lord, and forgat the Lord their God, and served Baalim and the groves [asheh-rahs].

399

30) Isaiah 17:7-8: At that day shall a man look to his Maker, and his eyes shall have respect to the Holy One of Israel.

8) And he shall not look to the altars, the work of his hands, neither shall respect that which his fingers have made, either **the groves** [obelisks], or the images.

31) Isaiah 27:9: By this therefore shall the iniquity of Jacob [Israel] be purged; and this is all the fruit to take away his sin; when he makes all the stones of the altar as chalkstones that are beaten in sunder, **the groves** [asheh-rahs-obelisks] and images shall not stand up.

32) Jeremiah 17:2: While their children remember their altars **and their groves** [asheh-rahs] by the green trees upon the high hills.

33) Micah 5:12-15: And I [the Lord God Almighty] will cut off witchcrafts out of your hand; and you shall have no more soothsayers [astrologers, psychics & false-prophets]:
13) Your graven images also will I cut off, and your standing images [such as the Statue of Liberty] out of the midst of you; and you shall no more worship [give any value to] the work of your hands.
14) And I will pluck up **your groves** [asheh-rah-obelisks] out of the midst of you: so will I destroy your cities.
15) And I will execute vengeance in anger and fury upon the heathen, such as they have not heard. [The most violent and destructive war man has ever experienced will pale in comparison when God Almighty's horrible wrath released because of these areas of open rebellion to His Word].

This review of the Biblical words for Grove and Ashtoreth is limited to those specific words found in the Holy Bible. The many references to the word " image " found throughout God's Word may also be an accounting of these forbidden objects that God hates. We find in the New Testament a reference to the object in Romans 11: 4 transliterated - "..the image of Baal." Regardless of the number of references, the occult Grove - Washington Monument; and Ashtoreth - Statue of Liberty, are forbidden " standing " images our nation has entertained to our spiritual peril, and established a curse upon our land.

[EXPOSITORY CONCLUSION ON NEXT PAGE]

An Expository Conclusion

In concluding this treatise, it is necessary for there to be an expository explanation of the extremely serious consequences of a nation, such as the United States of America, to allow both the ashtoreth - i.e. Statue of Liberty and the asheh-rah -grove i.e. Washington Monument, to be placed, or planted in our midst. Because of the spiritual and Biblical ignorance, found today in most American Christians relating to these occult deceptions of the mysterious Masonic orders, we will seek to assist in our reader's ability to comprehend matters relating to national bondage to Satan, and God's will for national freedom and deliverance. The most important principle to understand in proper spiritual discernment is the principle of total submission to the Lord God, who is also called by the name: the Lord Jesus Christ. We are expected by Him to be in total agreement with Him in regards to His view of occult or satanic objects. Because the average individual, believing or non-believing, usually cannot see the adversity and danger of such inanimate occult objects, it is therefore irrational for them to despise them as God does. The author has found that most of the Christians he has approached concerning this information did not believe these two occult national monuments contributed to the exceeding great wickedness in the land. As a Biblical scholar, it is necessary to bring about a clear understanding on this matter of national deception.

God's Word, the Holy Bible, records for us His eternal disposition and utter hatred for certain " **things** " or " **objects** ". This is recorded for our admonition in Deuteronomy 7:16-26. I Corinthians 10:1-14 shows us that we cannot say these matters only concern the Old Testament nation of Israel, or that the admonition is only for those under the law of Moses, as many in the Church educational fields do. The Lord God, who created the heavens and the earth, and man to rule over the earth, hated idolatry in the Old Testament, and He despises it in the New Testament. True Christians will love what God loves, and they will also hate what the Lord God hates. We, as true believers, are expected to be totally obedient to God in all matters of our hearts and minds. The corruption of images, and idols of so-called saints, and other forms of image worship in the Roman Catholic religion, has defiled humanity's view of the true Christian faith. God's Word tells us that there is a demon behind the making of every image or statue; whether or not people try to say it is a " saint ", or notable historical figure [ref.I Corinthians 10:19-22]. It is expected of us, as we enter God's kingdom of light, that we throw off all previous opinions of our own and totally submit to the likeness of God, which includes His viewpoint regarding certain objects. It has been revealed that Satan, through the self-pride of the father of masonry, Nimrod, originated occultic objects as part of his religious self-worship. Which is anti-God, and therefore, Anti-Christ. It has also been revealed that even today, in 1999, the mysterious Masonic orders Nimrod, and his mother-wife Semiramis gave to their followers; continue to be propagated even in this nation which claims to be "..under God..". The United States of America. What is needed now is to explain the reason God abhors these objects that, throughout the history of mankind, have been built and renamed by Masons and Shriners in league with Satan from the beginning. Their sin is idolatry and witchcraft.

Explaining the curses that come upon those who either willfully, or also ignorantly, defy God's commands concerning occult objects, is quite simple, yet difficult to understand. Deuteronomy 7:26 is God's Word to us today. And it is just as valid as the day the man of God, Moses, under the inspiration of the Holy Spirit, wrote it down. II Timothy 3:16-17 declares "..all.." Holy Scripture to be given by God to teach, reprove, correct, and instruct us in His righteousness. God is not ever going to change His mind on this subject. But rather commands us to have our minds renewed and transformed to align with our Creator's mind [see Romans 12:1 & 2; Ephesians 4:17-24 and Philippians 2:5]. We have previously

401

brought out the facts surrounding both the asheh-rah [Washington Monument] and ashtoreth [Statue of Liberty]. We revealed how these two occult objects have been built, and deceptively renamed, by certain members of the Masonic orders. This occurred during the founding of the Federal government of the United States of America. That, the French Mason, Frederic Auguste Bartholdi, had **a vision**. And wanted to build the largest ashtoreth-ashtarte ever built in the history of the world. That this Mason stated that he built it: *"..to have the face of his mother and the body of his mistress. "* Which said declaration reveals the " evil spirit " actually behind its construction. Because we learned, it was Nimrod, who originally tried to establish and exalt the wicked spirit of immorality and profanity, by his immoral incestuous relations with Semiramis the proposed occult *"queen of heaven".* The giving of this modern American version, of the ancient occult ashtoreth, the new name: **" The Statue of Liberty "** was the purest, [only if it can be called pure] form of deception possible. The cry for liberty in the founding stages of our nation, was the cry of believers in the Holy Bible. Believers, who were desperately attempting to work at establishing a nation, that would stop the persecution of those who worshiped and served the Lord Jesus Christ. And create a new nation without any hindrances to the free flow of God's Word as Christ had commissioned His disciples.

The early American Christian patriots claimed the blessings of God just prior to the war with Great Britain. They were, contrary to the lies of today's Secular Humanists, strongly, and well established in Biblical knowledge- Christian men and women. God provided a special celebration in Leviticus 25:10, which was to be proclaimed throughout the entire land of Israel by God's people every fiftieth year. This Bible passage was God's institution of a holy-day for Israel. The year of jubilee, during which - **liberty** was to be proclaimed, was then established for the express purpose of each man, that was a head of a household, may celebrate with his family the blessings and goodness of God to His people. This shows the specifically Christian character that surrounded our nation's establishment as a Christian Republic. It also would be a very good holiday for us to establish today, since the principle would affirm a sound family structure as the standard God has established in His Word. And given the utter disintegration of marriages and family life in America, the Biblical concept should be honored today. The Christian hymn, *The Battle Hymn of the Republic*, is still sung at presidential inaugurations, and was at President Bill Clinton's in January 1997.

The French Mason Bartholdi, heard word that the concept of " **liberty** " was the central theme of the founding of the United States of America. For this reason he seized upon it, and capitalized on it for his occult image. It is in the actual changing of the name of these satanic objects that masons throughout the history of civilization have won their acceptance in new establishments nations and government. It is also how Satan, and his principalities, gain their legal right [through man's disobedience] to exercise control over the moral condition of the land. This is the reason that in Ezekiel 8: 5 & 6, God says He departs from the area that the wicked objects are planted. Both Satan, and the masons who worship him know, God has established this moral rule concerning where He refuses to dwell. It is also understandable to see the reason America's Federal Justice system is so extremely tolerant to allow the wicked propagation of pornographic materials, even of innocent children, throughout our own land, and even around the entire earth. The Mason who was the nation's first Supreme Court chief justice, John Marshall, presided over the planting of the largest occult asheh-rah grove in the history of the world, using tax-payer monies to exalt Nimrod with the deceptive name-change to the Washington Monument. God vehemently hates this deceptive use of new names to overthrow righteousness in a nation's governmental seats of power. We must explain the prophetic warning the Lord Jesus Christ delivered to His Apostles and all His people in Matthew 24:4-5; i.e. that many evil individuals would arise throughout the Church age using His name to create deception of God's people. The Holy Spirit in I Timothy 4:1-2 has warned that those who followed the instruction of demonic powers would,"..speak lies in hypocrisy.." meaning: they would use the deceptive perfidy of words, honorable things, and certain names to deceive God's very own people. This has been very cleverly accomplished by those under the control of satanic powers, the founding Masons in the United States of America. For it has been a great abomination for the people of this land to embrace these two occult objects as symbols of national pride. As a source of dignity. It is actually the looking to, and dependence upon these wicked objects, that the Lord God who created the heavens and earth becomes most jealous and angry.

Pure worship of the true God is found in a nation's obedience to the Holy Spirit, and Word of God, the Holy Bible. Strong marriages, and spiritually healthy families, raising children to love and serve God in His righteousness, would be the manifestation of that reality. Outrageous idolatry and corruption is the sin of looking to, and honoring of these occult objects as being the source, or cause of American's freedom and liberty. But this is the evil treachery and perfidy Masons have utilized in each and every nation, empire, and civilization they have corrupted with idolatry. And overthrown spiritually and morally. Biblically speaking, it is in the planting of these forbidden occult objects, that rebellion and disobedience to God's revealed will is expressed by men. This specific rebellion opens the doors of a nation to Satan, and his evil principalities of idolatry, witchcraft, profanity, immorality, prostitution, and finally child-sacrifice (in America - abortion of the unborn).

True freedom and true liberty is found in a nation's obedience to the Spirit of God, and His holy Word the Bible. Outrageous idolatry is the sin of looking to any occult object as the source, or cause of our liberty and freedom. But this is the evil treachery, and perfidy, masons have utilized in each nation or empire they have overthrown spiritually and morally. It is in the planting of these occult objects that disobedience to God's known will is expressed. This destroys the barriers of a nation to Satan and his principalities of profanity, immorality, prostitution and finally child-sacrifice. For reinforcement of this spiritual principle of God, we direct our readers to Ezekiel 8: 6, which reveals to us that God refuses to dwell anywhere near occult objects. Therefore, reason tells us that, if God vacates an area because of His disgust. Then the one who is seeking man to worship erroneously would be free to enter that place. This same principle is most necessary in understanding demonology and God's deliverance. For in the case of a man or woman, son or daughter, that is in need of and seeking deliverance from the powers of darkness. The first step in casting out evil spirits, is leading the individual to take a careful, and thorough inventory of their lives and homes. To investigate any, and all activities, or materials, that are giving legal rights for spirits of wickedness to enter the victim's life is job-one. After a thorough inventory of the person, and their house is complete. And the person has destroyed the items of disobedience, then and only then, can the deliverance minister cast out the demonic powers, and declare the house, or individual [ref. Luke 11:24-26] totally given over to the Lord Jesus Christ and fully submitted to His Lordship, and kingdom. This exact same principle carries over to the deliverance of an entire nation, exactly in the same way it works for a house, or individual. This is seen in Ezekiel 8: 3 & 18. The principle to be observed is that God views nations, or entire empires, as or like houses. The " house " of Judah, and the ancient " house " of Israel were made up of millions of human inhabitants of that specific land area. By exercising the Biblical principle of hermeneutics and to prophetically close the gaps between the time periods of ancient Israel and Judah's occupation of the Middle East promised land where they disobeyed God in this matter. We would call our nation - " The house of the United States of America ". Into this national " **house** " those under satanic direction, planted [Deut.16:21 & 22] an Americanized version of the masonic occult ashehrah and ashtoreth, the Lord God condemns in His Word. This was cleverly accomplished in the midst of a world power " declared " to be "..One nation under God.." Prophetically speaking, it is likely that Satan licked his chops when that statement went on our national currency, along with the " all seeing eye of Lucifer " on the back left-hand side of the dollar bill. This is not to say the true God who has blessed us in spite of our ignorance about these occult objects, does not wish to rule over us. But that because of His eternal Word which will never change, prohibits His rule as already revealed in Ezekiel 8:5 & 6. Remember, these objects open the door of the nation to the principalities of Satan's kingdom because they are forbidden by God's Word. As revealed, the first Supreme Court

403

Chief Justice John Marshall, was in the strategic place as a powerful Mason, to rule over the establishment of the Washington Monument occult abomination in the Federal government. This fully explains the reason morality and moral principle are now continually mocked in our land, and righteous judgments against the wicked atrocities of pornography, whoredoms, epidemic divorce, child molestation, sodomy [homosexual deviate activity] and the horrendous murder of pre-born children by abortion are freely exercized by the people in the land. Our entire national courts have become bastions of demonic rulership because Satan has been given legal right in the nation's judicial branch of government by these perverse occult objects. Remember, that the Lord God's people only gained authority over Satan in Old Testament Israel, by the people obeying the voice of His prophets to destroy these wicked objects. Remember also, that abortion is, America's New Age version of evil Molech worship found in Leviticus 20:1-8. The current attempts at judicial activism of federal judges, to even force military courts to overthrow laws against the sin of sodomy, is also the manifestation of demonic destruction of America's moral laws. All of the manifestations of demon expression through human behavior is the ending fall-out to the planting of Satan's occult objects in America. For we have already revealed that specific evil principalities are allowed access into our nation's governmental seats of power and authority by these forms of open moral rebellion against the Lord God, who demands man's obedience, as he rules over God's earth. The spirits of wickedness enter, in order to bind the righteous order of governing, and they work to loose the practice of wickedness to prevail until God brings down His horrible wrath against the intense rebellion against His moral and righteous principles. This is the very reason, as if God who is to be obeyed totally needed one, He commanded His people to not allow or permit the planting of these wicked objects near the place where national governing, or rulership would be conducted for the land. We are given instruction in I Timothy 2:1-6 to pray for all who rule as authorities over us in the nation. According to God's Word, those who occupy seats of authority will become overwhelmed by the forces of demonic power, as long as these occult objects are allowed to stand in our nation. Ephesians 6:10-20 instructs us to know we are at this time in armed warfare with satanic powers. Because of these evil occult objects, we have not been able to see God's victory, and are witnessing further overthrow of our nation's moral laws in our national experience. This will continue until God pours out His wrath as long as we refuse to remove the ashehrah and ashtoreth as His Word instructs. Matthew 28:18-20 shows us that the Lord Jesus Christ has commanded us to teach all nations to observe "..all.." things He has already commanded mankind in His eternal Word. Some Christians in our day do not think He meant *all things* when He said it. It is this cursed disposition that gives Satan all the room he needs to overthrow the nation we are trying to raise our children in. God requires His true servants to obey His Word in totality. We are not to pick and choose what areas suit our particular views and prejudices.

It is because these occult objects are highly famous national monuments that the greatest difficulty in removing them would come. We refer to the words of the Lord Jesus Christ to overthrow this stronghold in our minds. Luke 16:15 shows us that things of earthly value are an abomination in the sight of God. The prophetic Word of God points to His demand that man will be forced to destroy these occult objects as His Word has directed. Whether we wish to remain a land of disobedience, and continue to shed innocent blood, and receive God's wrath, is what must be weighed by us. Any rational people would choose God's blessing rather than His curse, and destruction for doing all the wickedness America has been doing. From my study of the causes for America's curses, it is concluded that this nation has been smitten with moral insanity by Satan. Even those in high spiritual office in the nation seem overwhelmed by moral indifference, and a repulsion to true righteousness, as explained in Holy Scripture. This was very evident in the U.S. Senate impeachment trial of President Clinton. These things must change quickly before we see God's hand of punishment released to the hurt of all Americans.

We conclude with facts that should also be understood in that the Vatican in Rome is also in collaboration with the secret Masonic orders. A number of popes have been Masons throughout history. Especially through the Dark Ages. This is seen in that, by deceit, Pope Pius the ninth, sent the corner stone for the planting of this occult object to Washington, D. C. at the time of its commenced building. This exact same occult object is planted in the center of St. Peter's Square at the Roman Catholic Vatican. The wicked have attempted to " Christianize " it by putting a cross [symbol of Christianity] at the top of it. This ashehrah was transferred to Rome from Egypt by the obscene Emperor Caligula, who by historians was known as the most profane, and preverted, of all the emperors to rule as Ceasar over the ancient Roman Empire. These facts give further insight into the occult nature of these forbidden objects, and shows the spiritual associations with Satan's power, by those who use the name, and words of the Lord Jesus Christ to overthrow and deceive mankind. The motion picture industry in Europe some years back produced an account of the life of Emperor Caligula. It was so wicked and immoral of a film it was banned from entering the territory of the United States of America. Yet, we have seen such films as The Life of Brian, and Jesus Christ Super Star, designed to dishonor and blaspheme the Savior and Creator.

The asherah and ashtoreth have been called by Almighty God a cursed thing. Which He directly forbids to be planted in any nation. With this treatise on the subject, Americans are no longer ignorant as to these evil curses established in our nation's beginning by even " Christian " Masons. It is very clear to us all that the United States of America is at war with God Almighty in relation to His moral laws. God is not going to continue to tolerate the shedding of innocent blood, and other disgusting atrocities the citizens of this nation are now committing in defiance to Him. Deuteronomy 7:21-26 gives us all a very clear vision of God's disposition toward all objects and items of occult origin. He declares that we all, Christian or non-Christian, will become an accursed thing, like to the cursed nature of these objects, if we permit them to be planted in our nation.

For America to get relief from the wicked spirits now given legal right to defile and destroy our nation and families, we must determine and resolve to obey the Word of God. To facilitate this we will finally refer our readers to I Timothy 2:1-6. We see, in this area of God's Word, that it is His will that "..all.." men be saved and come to the knowledge of all the truth contained in God's Word, the Bible. The most important information we wish to communicate through this book, is that because of the lies surrounding the Statue of Liberty and Washington Monument, the flood of pornographic materials and profanity of the people in America is our experience. Please refer to Isaiah 59: 1-19, esp. verse 19, about the flood the enemy brings into the west , and what God will do about it. The principalities of wickedness under Satan's control have been unleashed against the moral precepts of righteous government because of this nation's disobedience and rebellion. Also,the profanity of God's holy ordinance of marriage and procreation of children is under a vicious and relentless attack from Satan's powers. The Lord Jesus Christ has already told us that He has given to us the keys of the kingdom of heaven in Matthew 16:19. That whatever "..we..", not Him, allow on the earth, would be permitted in heaven. And whatever "..we.." stopped on the earth, would be stopped in heaven. Also, in Luke 10:19, we are told that the Lord Jesus Christ has already given to us authority over "..all.." the power of Satan [including his power to keep the occult ashehrah and ashtoreth up in our nation]. What we as God's people must ask ourselves is this, " Are these two national occult objects more important to us than the deliverance, moral sanity, unborn offspring, and family restorations God would like to bless us with? Let us all resolve to do all the Master requires of us as His servants in the earth. Amen.

As God's judge, Gideon, of the nation of Israel was taught by the Lord God in Judges 6:24; Jehovah - Shalom means: " The Lord's way is peace ". Peace, from the Biblical perspective means: to stop being against God. The people of the Lord God Almighty must fully repent of their submission to these occult Masonic curses if we are to move ourselves into alignment with Revelation 18:4. The author has contacted CBN's Pat Robertson to stop using these American occult objects in his promotional efforts. Also, Coral Ridge Ministies Dr.D.James Kennedy. Others are currently using them to promote their respective ministries and deluding even Christian men and women. What an abomination to the true God, who demands exclusive worship, and complete repentance to enter His kingdom. Amen.

Forbidden Masonic Objects
Planted
As National Monuments
in
The Founding of
The United States of America

Addendum

The following information adds to the volume of facts surrounding the satanic occult Masonic asherah [Washington Monument & Statue of Liberty]. We find in the book of the Revelation of Jesus Christ, that there is *"..a " beast " that was* [existed in the past] *and is not* [the beast appears deceptively to be gone] *and yet is..* " [meaning it is still carrying on its abominations to this very day]. Refer to Rev. 17: 8 to confirm this matter. As stated previously in this treatise, Satan deceives by changing the names of his objects of idolatry in order to re- establish them in new empires or nations. This is his modus operandi to deceive the whole world (see Rev. 20: 10). We are sad to report that a major Christian leader, Dr. D. James Kennedy of Coral Ridge Presbyterian Church in Ft. Lauderdale, Florida, has fallen into the same trap as wicked King Manasseh in 2 Kings 21: 1-16. Ezekiel 8: 2 - 6 in his book revealed the Lord God's vehement anger for Israel's leadership to put up this abomination in His Temple at Jerusalem.

Whether, or not, Dr. D. James Kennedy is a mason [a number of " **pastors** " are] he should have read his Bible on this subject, and refused to promote this satanic image in his Christian ministries. Remember, King Manasseh put this object into Israel's temple and provoked God to anger. He was deceived into adding it to the temple's furnishings in defiance to the commands of God to Moses. Christian ministers in America are deceiving even God's people by their deluded promoting of evil images that the Lord hates! Kennedy did the same evil as Roman Catholic Pope Sixtus V [Felice Peretti 1585 - 1590] did as a past leader of that idolatrous religion. Our research reveals that - * *"..he deliberately reclaimed Rome's imperial past by moving the obelisk* [satanic occult asherah] *of Emperor Caligula* [that he had moved by ship from Egypt to Rome] *to the center of St. Peter's Square and crowned* [" **christianizing**" - making it into a new Christian symbol] *it with a cross. It took 800 men, 40 horses, and 40 winches..[to complete the task under penalty of death if it was dropped.. "* The antiChrist official policies of Roman Catholic Rome's idolatrous religion was to rename all pagan gods after something found in the Holy Scriptures. They did this with the Roman Madonna. Calling Mary of the Bible by that name! These deceptive practices are being repeated by false leaders in America when they attribute forbidden occult objects built by masons to be new symbols of Christianity. Just because the masons who are skilled in their lying wonders, put some Bible verses into the Washington Monument, does not now make it a Christian symbol. It does not matter how much alphabet soup [educational degrees] you have behind your name as a Christian leader. You are a deceiver of both saints and sinner alike, just like Pope Sixtus V did back in the Roman Catholic Dark Ages! We are stating this information in reference to the Coral Ridge Hour broadcasted 7.17. 2005. As evidence he included as America being a Christian nation in its founding - and in his book - One Nation- Under God. We pray he would stop his deluding of God's people in both America and the world by this misinformation and worship of the"..works of men's hands.." [see Rev. 9: 20 - 21]. "... Keep yourselves from idols, amen.." 1 John 5: 21.

* Source - **Saints & Sinners - History of the Popes - page 172** - By: Eamon Duffy c., 1997.
For more information contact Light Eternal Publications @ 1. 888. 753. 1776

Was The American Mason General/ President George Washington A New Age Nephilim?
By: Michael D. Juzwick, © 2007

The true people of the Lord God are told through the Apostle Paul in 1 Corinthians 14: 33, that ".. **God is not the author of confusion,..**" In that passage of Holy Scripture, orderly conduct in the Church is addressed. But, we have seen in this our day both religious and political confusion surrounding the subject of whether, or not, we were established as a " Christian Republic " or, **a new secular pagan Government**. The American one dollar bill was cast to honor the first president of the American republic. To examine the back of the " green back" would show a strange mystery, as the right hand side of the back has the Great Seal of the United States. While the left hand side has a very Masonic image with Latin words unknown to most Americans. Below the Masonic pyramid are Latin words that translate: **A New Order of Secularism**. Above it: *He favors our new conception*, or idea of Government. Defenders of the occult/ secretive religion of Masonry, use what is called duplicity (hypocrisy) to deceive the ignorant masses. The Masonic symbol for the Scottish Rite Mason Order uses a bird with two heads, and two tongues, which projects this aberration of false witness and lying. It should not be ignored that Satan has been called in John 8: 44, by our Lord Jesus Christ, "..**The father of lies..**" And, in other of my treatments of this underhanded religion of Masonry, we learned that those who serve the Devil, will take on his nature. The truth is that Masons use a perverse system of " double - speak." Meaning they will have one thing they tell non - members of their occult religion, and, to the " in - crowd" members, go the real meanings. Now let truth win.. The Lord Jesus Christ warned His disciples in Matthew 24 : 4 - 5; & 23 - 26, and us today, to not be deceived by those who come using His name (Christ - Christian). The native " Indians " nailed it when they declared - " White man speaketh with " forked tongue". Masons dominate America in many secret ways, and always have! They secretly worship "..the prince of the power of the air.." see Ephesians 2: 2 & Genesis 11.

George Washington was a phenomenal character. Political and religious scholars both clamor to own his image as their own. To the political promoter of American democracy, he is their standard bearer, and his name commands power worldwide. The main line Christian denominations hold Washington as " The Great Christian statesman " who single - handedly established this nation. Hardly the truth! Since many Christian patriots striving for religious freedom and liberty shed their blood to do so! With all due respect to George Washington's military skills. It must also be restated that all the religious sanctimonium over George Washington being **" The Father of the Nation"** is contrary to Jesus Christ's command in Matthew 23: 9 that no man be called specifically " *Father* "upon the earth. Yet, the American Christian televangelists have been instrumental in creating this great Biblical Nephilim.

The Hebrew word - נְפִילִים transliterated: nephee - leem', translated - " Giants " in Genesis 6: 4, conveys to us that principalities and powers - see Colossians 2: 15 - came down to the earth to possess mankind in order to create a world too evil for God to not "..destroy with a flood of waters.." - Genesis 6: 11 - 17. We learned in previous scholastics that the secret Masonic images of the Statue of Liberty and pornographic Washington Monument are both spoken of in the Holy Bible. And they are hated and forbidden by the Lord God - refer to Deuteronomy 4: 23 -24; 16: 22; 7: 25 - 26; Judges 2:13. We learned George Washington himself was a Mason, and laid the cornerstones of the Capitol of United States first governmental buildings in the Masonic ritual of satanism. We learned that these secret occult practices are employed in secret ritualistic fashion due to the opposition and persecution from the children of Shem - at Nimrod and Semiramis [his mother's] Tower of Babel, and ancient City of Babylon. They created the masonic secrets of the craft. And initiated star worship in the astrological Zodiac in defiace of the Creator. We learned that the New Age religion of Christian American Democracy is now being propagated by a " new " Mysterious Babylon that is making the nations to drink the wine of the wrath of her fornication - see Revelation chapter 17. True Christians had better obey Jesus Christ's command in Revelation 18: 4 - 6. And shake off these dust of Babylonish pollutions of soul and spirit, transformed into American democratic delusions. And we better get ready and obey the Bridegroom.

Since we now see what the purported " father " of American democracy has done with his " Christian" witchcrafts [another aspect of Masonry], is fill the world with American pornography. Fully protected by the first amendment to the US Constitution; taught the nations how to medically rip apart the unborn child in the wombs of God by child hating women [see Jeremiah 1: 4 - 5; 2: 33-34]. Destroyed souls by levying exorbatant costs upon the American dream of owning a house built by the Masons. Abusing our need for shelter for our families. Spread satanic feminism [Eastern Star] and worked to force it upon Muslim nations such as Iraq and Afganistan. Caused nations to abhor us [see Proverbs 24: 24]. Defiled and profaned the name of our Lord Jesus Christ - whose name is Jealous. He has warned mankind of daring to use His name in vain self promoting idolatries. They will not be guiltless when they stand before His judgment seat. And stand they will! They will give an account, as must each one of us. Every man, or woman at their best state is altogether vanity warns the Holy Bible. If we claim to be true " **Christians** " , we better humbly respect that Biblical fact declared by our Maker.

407

America's occult masonic ashehrah pole. Being the object the Lord God forbids, to be planted, it opens the nation's government to Satan's principalities of immorality, whoredoms and child-sacrifice (abortion).

Anti-abortion demonstrators on the Ellipse, with the Washington Monument in the background.

Thousands of Abortion Foes Rally in Capital

By LEE MAY,
Times Staff Writer

WASHINGTON—On an emotional day marking the 13th anniversary of legal abortion, thousands of opponents Wednesday marched on the Supreme Court, lobbied Congress and listened to speeches, including one from President Reagan, who vowed to help them "overturn the tragedy" of the high court decision.

Speaking by a telephone hookup to the crowd gathered on the Ellipse, behind the White House, Reagan asserted that advances in prenatal medicine have provided "dramatic confirmation" that a child in the womb is a "live member of the human family." He went on to say that he is "proud to stand with you in the long march for the right to life."

Meeting With Reagan

Later, two dozen leaders of anti-abortion groups met with Reagan, emerging seemingly satisfied with the President's support for their cause but sharply divided over the issue of whether presidential amnesty should be extended to militants who have been convicted of bombing abortion clinics.

The rally, an annual rite that was drenched in sunlight on a springlike day, attracted a broad range of participants, young and old, wearing everything from suits to jeans. Estimated at about 36,000 by local police, the crowd—many of whom carried signs and banners—was about half the size of last year's.

'I Love Babies'

Rose of Sharon Keel, 14, of Danville, Va., wearing lavender corduroy slacks and a cardboard box that invited signatures of those opposed to abortion, explained her reason for protesting: "I love babies and I don't want to see them murdered."

As previously revealed in this treatise, God has given specific direction concerning this wicked masonic image in His word, the Holy Bible. The prophets of God gave direction to the rulers of Israel and Judah to destroy this object to gain His freedom from the wicked spirits associated with its curse. America has been deceived by certain powerful masons, who worship Satan secretly, to allow this forbidden occult phallus object to be put up in defiance to God and His eternal word. America will only gain deliverance from the powers that this object represents when it is destroyed.

408

Pro-life rally

McClintock equates abortion with slavery

By Patty McCormac
S-FP staff writer

Calling members of the pro-life movement "20th century abolitionists" and quoting Abraham Lincoln, Assemblyman Tom McClintock, R-Thousand Oaks, addressed a pro-life rally and march Saturday at the County Government Center, Ventura.

McClintock, who is a candidate for the 21st Congressional District, delivered an emotional speech that equated abortion with slavery, saying the pro-life movement was similar to the first stirrings among Americans against slavery.

"Just such a moral crusade is crossing the land," he said. "The moral is clear and we are being heard."

"Abortion," he said, "is an issue that we can no longer ignore, no longer endure."

And like slaves who could not speak for themselves, those who are murdered have no say in the matter, he said.

"Experience tells us the road ahead is long," and, quoting Lincoln, he said, "The end is not doubtful, we shall not fail . . ."

The rally, sponsored by the Ventura County chapter of Crusade for Life, was attended by approximately 150 people — half the number who attended last year's event.

Organizers blamed the poor turnout on the fact that there were similar marches taking place simultaneously in Thousand Oaks and Los Angeles.

Beau Listi, 17 months, Ventura, clings to her mother, Corry Listi

The rally and march were scheduled to coincide with the 13th anniversary of the Supreme Court ruling, Roe vs. Wade, which legalized abortion.

Protest signs were in abundance.

One sign, taking a jab at the pro-choice side of the abortion controversy, read, "Choice? Who asks the baby if he wants to die?"

Another sign declared, "The best birth control is self control."

And a boy about 3 ran through the crowd with a sign that read, "I was once an unborn child — thanks, mom."

George Spingler, past president of the Ventura County Right To Life League, recited statistics to the gathering.

"Within the next 24 hours, 3,600 American babies will be killed. Before this hour concludes, 1,000 children will have died," he said.

He wondered aloud why there are laws to protect condors and whales, but none to protect unborn children.

Leon Suprenant, 26, Ventura, a student of the priesthood, echoed the feelings of most who attended the rally.

"Abortion is clearly wrong. As Christians, we're called to stand up for what's obviously wrong. I can't be proud of a country that kills babies," he said.

"I'm here to make a stand," said Curtis Martin, 24, Ventura, an industrial photographer. "It's unjust to kill the helpless — the unborn — especially if they are being attacked by people who should be protecting them most, their parents."

Speaker Lance Ralston, pastor of Calvary Chapel, Oxnard, challenged the Supreme Court decision on abortion.

"Did the one who would have provided us with a cure to cancer end up in a glass jar somewhere?" he asked. "Who cares what the Supreme Court says — they're wrong."

Justin Juzwick, 5, son of Michael Juzwick of Ventura, passes time swinging on a tree

Molly McLaughlin, 10 months, Oxnard, gets a free ride from her mom, Julie McLaughlin

409

Mr. Bush, Mr. Thornburgh:

Why did you side with the lawbreakers in Wichita?

AMERICA'S
ASHTORETH

Anti-choice extremists from around the country have descended on women's health clinics in Wichita.

Operation Rescue members have blocked doorways and sidewalks, thrown themselves under cars and police horses.

They have intimidated, harassed and abused patients and clinic staff and have made it impossible for the women in Wichita to exercise the fundamental rights granted them by the U.S. Supreme Court.

A federal judge ordered Operation Rescue to stop terrorizing women. Two thousand of their members have been arrested.

But now the Bush-Thornburgh Justice Department has intervened on the side of Operation Rescue, on behalf of lawbreakers who continue to blockade clinics in contempt of a federal court order.

A Wichita judge said he was "disgusted" by Attorney General Thornburgh's actions. We at NARAL-PAC agree.

It is a sad day for every American when Mr. Thornburgh's Justice Department sides with vigilantes and supports lawlessness instead of protecting our rights and liberties.

Kate Michelman, Executive Director,
NARAL-PAC, 1101 14th St. N.W. Washington D.C. 20005
Paid for by National Abortion Rights Action League-PAC

Kate Michelman, one of Satan's major voice-mediums (ref. Deut. 18:9-12), manifests her dependence on the evil principality Molech. This wicked spirit gains access by the masonic ashtoreth. The United States of America's Statue of Liberty deception by the mason Bartoli.

410

THE IMAGE OF ASHTORETH I.E,
TO AMERICANS IT IS CALLED - STATUE
OF LIBERTY - REF JUDGES 2:11-14; 3:7.

BUILT BY FRENCH MASON BARTOLI TO ERECT
THE EVIL WORSHIP OF MASONIC ORDER FOUNDED
NIMROD'S MOTHER - SEMIRAMIS SHE WAS AND IS
THE PAGAN FALSE GODDESS OR QUEEN OF HEAVEN SPOKEN OF
BY JEREMIAH THE PROPHET. REF. JER. 44: 15-30

ASHTOROTH = GODDESS OF WAR, LUST
AND FORTUNE.

AMERICAN CHRISTIANS HONOR IT,
GOD IN HIS WORD CONDEMN IT. DEUT. 4:6

411

Q: What role is rock music playing in the pressure we're seeing on this generation of teenagers?

A: It is difficult to overestimate the negative impact music is having. Rock stars are the heroes, the idols, young people want to emulate. And, when they are depicted in violent and sexual roles, many teens and pre - adolescents are pulled along in their wake.

What could possibly be wholesome about showing explicit sexual scenes — especially those involving perversions —to 12- and 13-year-old kids? Yet videos come into the home via MTV and other channels that feature blatantly sexual situations, or even depictions of sadism.

One study showed that more than half of all MTV videos featured, or, implied violence, and 35 percent revealed violence against women. A steady diet of this garbage will pollute the minds of even the healthiest of teenagers.

I believe that this perpetual and pernicious exposure to rock music is responsible, at least in part, for many of the social problems now occurring among the young, including the high suicide rate, the reported willingness of young men to rape women if given an opportunity, and the moral undermining of the next generation.

As a case in point, you may remember the flap that occurred in 1990 over the Rap group - **2 Live Crew** - and their album, **"As Nasty as They Wanna Be."** A Florida judge reviewed the filthy lyrics of this album and, for the first time ever, a judicial official declared a piece of " music " to be obscene and illegal.

Predictably, Phil Donahue, and, his cronies in the press, threw their usual temper tantrums when the news broke. "Censorship!" they cried from the roof tops. Virtually every newspaper in the country carried editorials and feature stories about the audacity of the judge who imposed his standard of morality on the rest of us.

Dan Rather, on his show " 48 Hours," made outlandish statements about our loss of freedoms in this era of oppression. And Geraldo Rivera risked getting his nose broken again by bringing - **2 Live Crew** - and their critics face-to-face on his television show.

What the media did not tell the Public, however, was the content of - 2 Live Crew's - album. They *censored* that information, choosing instead to talk abstractly about " First Amendment rights " and " right-wing fundamentalists."

Millions of words were spoken about the obscene lyrics to a single album, yet no one would quote them directly. *Why not? Because adults would be shocked, and, outraged by their filth and debauchery. This language, which was unfit to print, or, utter on television, was considered perfectly acceptable for the consumption of young minds.* That is the logic of Phil, Dan and Geraldo.

At the risk of upsetting our readers, let me list for you— as discreetly as possible—the words that appeared in the one album, "As Nasty As They Wanna Be." They included:

- 226 uses of the " F " word

- 117 explicit terms for genitalia

- 87 descriptions of oral sex

- 163 uses of the word for female dog

- 15 uses of " ho " (slang for whore)

- 81 uses of the " S " word

Remember, too, that youngsters buying this " music "— some only 8 to 10 years of age — typically listened to it dozens of times.

Continued On Next Page

Descriptions of oral sex and extreme violence against women were thereby memorized and burned into the conscious experience of kids barely out of elementary school [Children younger than this are encouraged to seek after the " Naughty music " also]. More than 2 million albums were sold, and with the exception of Florida, and a few other locations where it was banned, no restrictions were placed on its distribution. A child of any age could purchase it.

This is merely one salvo in an industry that has helped destroy the moral code of Western civilization. It has been accomplished methodically and deliberately during the past 30 years, in cooperation with television and movie producers. The damage has been incalculable!

Q: I don't believe kids are as easily influenced as you say. What they see does not necessarily determine how they behave.

A: Well, look at it this way. Do you remember when the movie " ET " was the rage 10 years ago? There was a brief scene in the film where the extra-terrestrial was given a few Reese's Pieces. The candy brand was not named, but children recognized it during its few seconds on the screen.

In the months that followed, the sale of Reese's Pieces went through the sky. Isn't that a clear example of a movie's influence on children's thinking? Why do advertisers spend billions of dollars to put their products before the people if what we see and hear does not influence our behavior?

Of course, we are vulnerable to what we witness! How much greater impact is made by dramatic, sexually oriented, no-holds-barred musical and theatrical presentations that are aimed at the hearts and souls of our kids? Who are we kidding when we say they are not harmed by the worst of it?

*Focus on the Family Magazine, August 1992, Vol 16, No8, ISSN 0894-3346. Copyright ©1992 Focus on the Family. All rights reserved. International Copyright secured

* Emphases added by the author - 2014.

* USED BY PERMISSION *   AUGUST 1992 / FOCUS ON THE FAMILY

First major snowfall in 14 years dusts worshipers leaving the January 6, 1985,

THE ASHERAH-GROVE IN THE CENTER OF ST. PETER'S? SQUARE AT THE VATICAN, ROME. TRANSFERED TO ROME BY PONTIFEX MAXIMUS CALIGULA FROM EGYPT. THE OBELISK CARRIES OCCULT SATANIC POWER AS DOES ITS COUNTERPART IN WASHINGTON D.C.

Diocese revises policy for priest misconduct cases

By Ann Rodgers-Melnick
Post-Gazette Staff Writer

The Catholic Diocese of Pittsburgh will soon hire someone — not a priest — to track complaints of sexual abuse and other misconduct by clergy and help victims through the church's bureaucratic process.

It has also established a pastoral team to help parishes devastated by charges of criminal sexual misconduct against priests.

These changes are revealed in a 10-page policy for responding to allegations of criminal sexual misconduct by clergy. Bishop Donald W. Wuerl gave copies to about 100 priests at a voluntary meeting Monday and sent copies to the remaining 400 active diocesan priests.

"We want it to be known that we are as concerned about the families [of victims] as we are about the priests," the Rev. Ronald Lengwin, spokesman for the diocese, said, of the decision to make the newly revised policy public.

The church established a policy in 1986 but never made it public, though parts of it were revealed in 1988 when three priests were arrested and charged with molesting two former altar boys. The policy has been under review since 1988, Lengwin said.

The policy drew mixed reactions from experts outside the church. A local advocate for rape victims praised it for increased sensitivity, but the Allegheny County district attorney criticized it for allowing the church to investigate itself.

"The church has a real conflict of interest," said District Attorney Bob Colville.

Pittsburgh's distribution of its policy is not isolated.

"Many, if not the majority, of [Catholic] dioceses are moving now to try to get plans on paper," said Jason Berry, a New Orleans journalist who has written a book* about diocesan cover-ups of pedophilia scandals nationwide. "That is an important shift, given all of the scandals and the scandalous way these matters have been handled in the past"

Because canon law leaves open the possibility that a convicted priest could win an appeal to the Vatican for reinstatement, Lengwin said, the policy says at least seven criteria must be met for such a priest to return to duty.

Among them is the requirement that, after extensive psychiatric treatment and approval from his psychiatrist, the repentant priest participate in continuing therapy and work in a place where everyone knows about his problem and where he can be monitored at all times.

A new facet of the diocesan plan is a Pastoral Support Team made up of diocesan representatives and mental health professionals that will "offer guidance and support to parishes or communities affected by the allegations," the policy said.

The diocese felt this was a weakness in response to the scandal in 1988, when priests from three parishes were arrested, Lengwin said.

An attorney for a man who has made abuse charges against a Pittsburgh priest whose civil trial is slated this month said a written policy was only half the story.

"It's certainly calculated to give the impression that there is a change an attitude. The proof in the pudding will be whether the enforcement of the policy is carried out," said Douglas Yauger. Yauger represents a man who accused the Rev. Anthony Cipolla of molesting him when he was a teen-ager.

(Continued on next page)

3 cases in 1988 revealed policy on priest abuses

The Catholic Diocese of Pittsburgh policies for handling accusations of criminal sexual misconduct by priests were first made public in 1988 when three priests were charged with molesting the same two former altar boys:

- The Rev. Robert Wolk, 52, former pastor of St. Thomas More Church in Bethel Park, is in prison. He is serving concurrent five-to-10-year sentences for involuntary deviate sexual intercourse after pleading guilty in both Allegheny and Washington counties.
- The Rev. Richard Zula, 52, former pastor of SS. Mary & Ann Church in Marianna, Washington County, is out of prison and living with his mother, according to the Rev. Ronald Lengwin, diocese spokesman. In 1990, he received a 2½-to-five-year sentence in Washington County for assaulting two boys and a concurrent one-to-two-year sentence in Somerset County for molesting one of the boys at Seven Springs Resort in 1984. In a plea bargain, Washington Country dropped 138 counts.
- The Rev. Francis Pucci, 62, former pastor of Our Lady of Lourdes Church in Burgettstown, went free after a Washington County judge ruled in 1991 that the statute of limitations had expired. Although 75 is the normal retirement age for priests, Pucci was allowed to retire for health reasons and lives in the diocese.

*Lead us not into temptation, by Jason Berry

Pittsburgh Post-Gazette: Thursday, March 11, 1993

Seattle Archdiocese to pay $12 million to settle child sex abuse claims: lawyer

Wednesday, June 25, 2014 6:27 a.m. CDT

By Eric M. Johnson

SEATTLE (Reuters) - The Archdiocese of Seattle has agreed to pay about $12.125 million to 30 men who alleged they were sexually abused as children and teens at two Seattle-area schools from the 1950s until 1984, their attorney said.

The men alleged in lawsuits filed in King County Superior Court that the Catholic district failed to shield them from known abusers at Seattle's O'Dea High School and at Briscoe Memorial School, in nearby Kent, plaintiffs' attorney Michael Pfau said in an interview.

The schools were operated jointly by the Christian Brothers of Ireland religious order and the Archdiocese of Seattle, which owned both schools, he said. The settlement agreement, which had been negotiated over the past year, was announced on Tuesday.

The agreement comes weeks after Pope Francis said the Roman Catholic Church had to take a stronger stand on a sexual abuse crisis that has disgraced it for more than two decades.

Media in the U.S began reporting in the early 2000s how cases of abuse were systematically covered up and abusive priests were shuttled from parish to parish instead of being defrocked and handed over to civil authorities.

The Christian Brothers of Ireland, Inc, and Christian Brothers agreed in a May 2013 settlement reached in U.S. bankruptcy court to pay $16.5 million to more than 400 adults who said religious leaders sexually abused them as children.

"I deeply regret the pain suffered by these victims," Seattle Archbishop J. Peter Sartain said in a statement on Tuesday afternoon, according to the Seattle Times newspaper.

"Our hope is that this settlement will bring them closure and allow them to continue the process of healing," he said.

The Archdiocese will make three consecutive payments in June, July, and August, Pfau said.

(Editing by Sofina Mirza-Reid)

The Children's Bread

PLAINVIEW NEW COVENANT CHURCH & WORLD OUTREACH CENTER, INC.

The Ministry of:
  Frank & Ida Mae Hammond
  Jay & Sally Lee

P.O. Box 72
Plainview, Texas 79073
806/293-7669

November 15, 1991

Michael D. Juzwick
Light Eternal Publications
826 Rockwood Ave.
Pittsburgh, PA 15234

Dear Brother Juzwick:
Thank you for clarifying your request as to informing your
readers about The Children's Bread Ministry. That will be
all right with us.

I agree with all you said about the errors and resultant
curses coming through involvement in Catholic idolatry.
We find it necessary to break these curses from the family
line thought confession of family sins, renunciation and
commanding evil spirits (those that gained legal right) to go
in the Name of Jesus.

A former Catholic priest who became a strong deliverance
minister told me, "Anything in Catholic practice that is not
biblical is demonic". That seems the best way to judge.

Sincerely in Christ,

Frank Hammond

Frank Hammond

Ye shall know the truth and the truth shall make you free — John 8:32

418

Mr. M. D. Juz .wick
Pacific Missile Test Center
Code 6741
Point Mugu, California 93042

Dear Mr. Juz .wick:

On behalf of President Ford, I am replying to your
letter of June 30 regarding the appearance of a particular F-4 aircraft attached to VX-4, located at the
Pacific Missile Test Range, Point Mugu, California.

Your comments concerning this aircraft's paint scheme
have been read with interest and duly noted. You appear to
express an objection to this aircraft's black exterior
and the white bunny profile on the verticle stabilizer.
Additionally, you allege that this aircraft represents a
conscious plot to promote smut throughout the United
States.

Unfortunately, you have seriously misjudged the
original reason for the color configuration of the aircraft, and its effect on the vast majority of the inidivid-
uals who come in contact with it. This particular F-4
received its black exterior in 1969 as part of an evaluation
of new plastic base paint. At the time the test was
scheduled, black was the only color of this specific paint
available in any quantity. Several months later when a
small quantity of the white paint became available it
was suggested to paint the rabbit head on the tail.
This suggestion was approved by the Commanding Officer,
and has remained in force for seven years. During this
period of time the black paint and rabbit profile have
become a squadron tradition.

The total effect of this aircraft's present exterior
has been extremely positive. The present Commanding
Officer and Executive Officer, consider this aircraft a
prime factor in unit morale. Additionally, the aircraft
has received wide publicity in NAVY TIMES, and has been
an invited guest at numerous air shows. Your expressed
opinion, no matter how intense, is decidedly in the
minority and does not take into account the vast amount
of goodwill this aircraft has gained for the United
States Navy. The general appearance of this aircraft,
as with all naval aircraft, rests with the Commanding

Note: The Secretary of the U.S. Navy carefully only refers
to the pornographic "Playboy bunny" as a white bunny in para.
#2 and "rabbit head" in para. #3. Thereby excusing its use
as not being a specific advertizement for Hugh Hefner's evil

Officer of the squadron, and this office has no intention of interferring with this officer's prerogative.

Thank you for sharing your concern with the President.

Sincerely,

Joseph T. McCullen, Jr.

Joseph T. McCullen, Jr.
Assistant Secretary of the Navy

REBUTTAL NOTE CONT': Playboy pornographic men's magazine. If the truth could be revealed, the chances are very high that certain high ranking Naval officers were involved in some monetary agreement with Hugh Hefner's Playboy pornography enterprises in exchange for the use of this national symbol and idol of the pornographic lust and whoredoms of men in the United States of America. A nation declared to be "...One nation under God.." The reality of the evil abuse of America's women and their abandonment by whoremongering men, including Naval "sailors" proves that Satan himself has even gained power over our United States military forces to destroy military men morally before their going into battle and binding them in the wicked sins of adultery and fornication which will send their eternal souls to hell for eternity- ref. Revelation 21:8.

Not only is this abomination displayed at Naval "Air Shows " to parade Hugh Hefner's wicked lifestyle of prostituting America's young daughters in his evil magazine, it impresses our nation's young men to adopt Satan's evil philosophy of whoredoms and encourages them to violate God's moral standards of purity and faithfulness in marital commitment. I have learned in my tour of duty in the United States Navy that men have violated and raped women in Viet Nam and during other wars the U.S has engaged in and much of the reason these evil atrocities took place against women in foreign lands is because of Hugh Hefner's playboy magazine. Many nations vehemently despise our nation and the reason they call America "The great Satan" is because of this very wickedness in our armed forces.

America's first president, George Washington, issued the following General Order on August 3, 1776 according to my sources: " The General (Washington himself) is sorry to be informed that the foolish and wicked practice of profane cursing and swearing, a vice heretofore little known in an American Army, is growing into fashion. He hopes the officers will, by example as well as influence, endeavor to check it, and that they both, officers and their men will reflect, that we can have little hope of the blessing of Heaven on our arms, if we insult it by our impiety and folly....(James 3)."

2

Light Eternal Publications

Biblical Light for America's Christian Families

420

This magazine started a revolution.

This magazine starts another.

Thirty-two years ago, a young actress named Marilyn Monroe waved hello from the front cover of a rough-edged, new magazine to an eager new generation of young men.

That first issue of PLAYBOY went on to inspire an editorial and social revolution. And for the past three decades, young American men have accepted PLAYBOY's message and spirit as their own.

This week, another revolutionary magazine hits the nation's newsstands. Again, its name is "Playboy,"

but it's a magazine for today—as different in look, feel and spirit as life in the '80s is different from the '50s.

Once again, PLAYBOY dares to be different: Perfect-bound. Bolder. Brasher. Wittier. Wiser. Smarter. Sassier. Sexier, yet more tasteful. And as a result, more compelling and contemporary than any other men's magazine.

In short, a magazine that another young male generation—today's—can truly call its own. Discover the new PLAYBOY for yourself at newsstands now.

September 21, 2000

Mr. Michael D. Juzwick
Publisher, Light Eternal Publications
1134 Illinois Avenue
Suite 2
Pittsburgh, PA 15216

Dear Michael,

Thank you for your letter and for letting me know your concerns about the spread of pornography in our country. Like most Americans, I am deeply disturbed by material that glorifies drug use, violence and irresponsible sexual behavior. Pornography has no place in a decent society.

As Governor of Texas, I have used the bully pulpit of my office to send the message that pornography is not welcome in the Lone Star State. The state of Texas has been committed to enforcing state anti-pornography laws. If I am fortunate enough to be elected President, I will insist on vigorously enforcing federal anti-pornography laws. But government alone cannot solve the problem. It will take each of us, working together, to rid our neighborhoods of the menace of pornography.

I am encouraged that you share my concern. As parents and leaders we have an important obligation to help keep pornography out of the hands of our children. Only if we are united and involved, can we protect our most precious resource – our children.

I appreciate your taking the time to write.

Sincerely,

George W. Bush

CHIEF COUNTY DETECTIVE
JAMES E. DREYER
(724) 548-3282

VICTIM/WITNESS ADVOCATE
KELLI A. WILSON
(724) 548-3486

COUNTY OF ARMSTRONG

DISTRICT ATTORNEY
SCOTT J. ANDREASSI

DEPUTY DISTRICT ATTORNEY
GEORGE R. KEPPLE

ASSISTANT DISTRICT ATTORNEYS
FREDERICK L. JOHN, II
CHASE G. McCLISTER
JENNIE K. BULLARD

Michael D. Juzwick
1134 Illinois Avenue
Suite #2
Pittsburgh, PA 15216-2539

Dear Mr. Juzwick:

I served as District Attorney here from 1978 to 1998. Today I am Deputy District Attorney working on a part-time basis only.

During my tenure and particularly during the last ten (10) years, I began to notice with some consistency that pornography was playing a role in many of our cases involving small children and adolescents. Investigations revealed that pornographic pictures, films, videos and sex toys were often used as part of a modus operandi to entice these victims to engage in unlawful sexual activity.

I feel certain that an average of 2 or 3 cases each year came to my attention where this methodology was used by the perpetrator. That would mean I have seen at least 50 cases.

This office has kept no record of these cases by category, although all of my files have been preserved. It would take literally weeks to peruse these files to ascertain precise information. Between my staff and I, however, we have recall of many such cases.

I hope this information has been helpful. I am sorry I cannot be more specific.

Sincerely yours,

George R. Kepple
Deputy District Attorney

GRK:ded
cc:

HOMER D. CRYTZER
CHIEF DETECTIVE

DENISE M. KUHN
VICTIM/WITNESS ADVOCATE

GEORGE R. KEPPLE
DISTRICT ATTORNEY

ASSISTANT DISTRICT ATTORNEYS
FREDERICK L. JOHN, II
BRADLEY K. HELLEIN
JAMES H. WRAY

DISTRICT ATTORNEY
COUNTY OF ARMSTRONG

August 4, 1993

Michael Juzwick
1134 Illinois Avenue #2
Pittsburgh, Pennsylvania 15216

Dear Mr. Juzwick:

Per your request, I will state my view as to the effect which illegal, hardcore pornography is having upon our society.

As District Attorney of this county for the past 16 years, it has been my experience in many, many child sex molestation cases that pornography plays a major role in convincing children to cooperate with the desires of that particular defendant.

I can cite many examples, if you require. Please do not hesitate to contact me if you have any further questions.

Sincerely yours,

George R. Kepple
District Attorney

GRK:ldw

COURTHOUSE, KITTANNING, PENNSYLVANIA 16201   (412) 543-2500

424

DAVID DREIER
CALIFORNIA

410 CANNON BUILDING
WASHINGTON. DC 20515
(202) 226-2305

112 NORTH SECOND AVENUE
COVINA. CA 91723
(818) 339-9078
(714) 592-2857

Congress of the United States
House of Representatives
Washington, DC 20515

BANKING, FINANCE AND
URBAN AFFAIRS
COMMITTEE

SMALL BUSINESS
COMMITTEE
VICE CHAIRMAN
SUBCOMMITTEE ON
ENERGY AND AGRICULTURE

TASK FORCE ON EDUCATION
U S -MEXICO INTERPARLIAMENTARY
CAUCUS
TASK FORCE ON POW/MIAs
JOINT TASK FORCE ON AFGHANISTAN

August 8, 1988

Mr. Michael Juzwick
497 Will Avenue
Oxnard, California 93030

Dear Mr. Juzwick:

Thank you for your letter. It is good to hear from you again and to know of your work on behalf of the family.

Regarding pornography, you may be interested to know that I am a sponsor of the "Child Protection and Obscenity Enforcement Act," which stems in part from the 1986 recommendations of the President's Commission on Pornography. The legislation is intended to update a 1984 child pornography law and address loopholes and weaknesses in existing obscenity statutes.

Like you, I feel we must do everything we can to halt the sexual exploitation and abuse of our nation's children. The Child Protection and Obscenity Enforcement Act permits civil and criminal forfeiture proceedings against child pornographers and violators of obscenity laws, and makes the transmission of obscene materials over cable, subscription television, or telephone wires, a federal crime. The House Subcommittee on Crime held a hearing on April 28 and on June 16. I expect further hearings will be scheduled as several other witnesses have requested to testify.

Again, thank you for contacting me. Please let me know if I can be of any future assistance.

Sincerely,

David Dreier
Member of Congress

DD:kc

425

INTERCESSORS FOR AMERICA

NEWSLETTER

March 1986   Vol. 13 No. 3

A CALL FOR CHRISTIANS TO UNITE IN PRAYER AND FASTING FOR AMERICA

Freemasonry: A Personal Testimony

by John Metcalfe

During the past year, IFA has received reports of intercessory groups and individuals being stirred to do battle with the powers and principalities which promote the cult of Freemasonry, which has gripped our nation from its very beginning. Founded in England in the 14th century, Freemasonry was brought to our shores with white Anglo-Saxon culture. The cornerstone of the White House, U.S. Capitol and major federal buildings were laid in Masonic ritual. Because Masons have been intimately involved in the establishment of our U.S. government and institutions, it is very likely that Freemasonry is a root source of many economic and governmental confusions today.

To better understand the errors of Freemasonry, we asked Mr. John Metcalfe of Bowie, Maryland, to provide us with a personal testimony. Mr. Metcalfe, formerly with the National Geographic Society, was a Mason for 12 years. He renounced his Masonic involvements upon conversion to Christianity in 1971. He presently gives pastoral oversight to seven churches in the Baltimore area.

"They'll never ask you to join; you must ask them." The intrigue was high as I talked with a man about "the Lodge." "Who are these men, and what do they do?" I asked. "Mostly businessmen of the community, and their purpose is to

do good to everyone," was the reply.

My wife and I had just moved to a new community and were eager to be accepted. My wife's grandfather was a Mason, so she tried to gain membership in the Eastern Star, but was refused. Being a secret organization, she was never told why. For 12 years, I plunged my soul into spiritual jeopardy.

A friend instructed me that to enter the First Degree of Masonry I would need to answer the question, "In whom do you put your trust?" "In God?" I asked. "Well, that's up to you. Some say the Almighty, some say Allah, Buddha, anything you like—that's okay." Freemasonry, following after "primitive revelation," is universalist in nature and welcomes people of all creeds.

I began my spiritual journey through the "chairs," spending a year in each office. In eight years, I occupied the highest office of our local Masonic Lodge, that of Worshipful Master. Pledging myself to secrecy under an oath which carried a penalty of having "my throat cut across, my tongue torn out by its roots; and being buried in the rough sands at low-watermark," I spent many long hours at the Lodge Hall in secret meetings and rituals.

How, I wondered, could all this be reconciled to the Christian faith? Though the Bible was quoted, memorized and recited to new candidates, Jesus Christ and His atoning death and resurrection were never presented as the only way of salvation and redemption. Instead, we focused time after time on the death and resurrection of a former superintendent of the Ancient Craft, Hiram Abif. Biblical characters, like King Solomon and Hiram King of Tyre, were studied and presented for emulation so that we could "become as great as they were." I couldn't help but notice that secrecy, occult ritual, pride, and cooperative vain ambition marked

Washington, D.C. Masonic National Memorial.

(Continued on page 2)

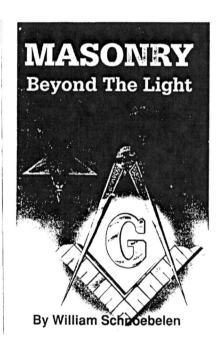

MASONRY
Beyond The Light

By William Schnoebelen

November 14, 1989

Mr Michael D Juzwick
Light Eternal Publications
101 Mt Lebanon Blvd
Pittsburgh PA 15228-0000

Dear Michael

Thank you for your tract on the effects of Pornography in the United States of America. I provides valuable information and touches the roots of Freemasonry at many spots.

Some masonic historians trace the roots of the ritual of Freemasonry back to Ashtoreth. Nimrod is one of the secret words in masonic ritual. The rituals of Freemasonry center around the generative nature of man with the square and compasses which appear at their altars representing the female and male generative organs respectively!

There is so much lust within the fraternity that the most common comment I heard from defecting masons is that they were oppressed by the sin of lust or the demons of lust. That is to be expected since the rituals center around sex though not clearly visible to the initiate. The degrees of Freemasonry are produced to deceive the Mason as Albert Pike, 33rd Degree Mason and writer of the higher degree rituals boldly declares. Pike was an avowed Luciferian who was a man of low personal character taking wagon loads out into the wilderness for drunken orgies in which he provided the women. Non the less, this reprobate is buried in the House of the Temple in Washington, DC in the Mason's highest place of honor and the United States government erected the only statue in Washington, DC of a Confederate, Albert Pike with his blasphemous book, MORALS & DOGMA under his arm. It is that book which describes the luciferian connection of the roots of the degrees he wrote and that are practiced in this country whose Congressmen are Masons in numbers totalling 70%! This fraternity is so strong that they were able to march into the Oval Office and declare Ronald Reagan a Mason on sight on February 11, 1988---an honor he thanked them for on February 22, the birthday of our first President who took his oath of office on a Masonic Bible.

I agree with the article that the United States will have to pay for the sins of pornography and abortion. Masons by their good works have a positive image but those who know their roots know also that they are at the roots of prostitution and abortion as well. They are satan's workers though, because of deception, they view themselves and are viewed by others as "good men". This organization with its secrecy also drives the wedge of secrecy between husband and wife and is responsible for many broken homes as a result. Their youth organizations lead our young away from God. One New York City group came just north of Albany and at their convention raped and sodomized on of their own! The Albany County DA and judge, both Masons, did not remove themselves from the case because they desired to use their power to fulfill their masonic obligation. The six indited on felonies saw their charges dismissed or reduced to misdemeanors and DeMolay continue to boast that none of their boys has ever been <u>convicted</u> of a felony. Such are the events of evil days but God will save His own. PTL!!

In Christian Love,

[signature]

REV HARMON TAYLOR
International Director

December 15, 1989

Mr Michael D Juzwick
Light Eternal Publications
101 Mt Lebanon Blvd
Pittsburgh PA 15228-0000

Dear Michael

We're glad you appreciated the truth about the root of the Shriner's Red Fez! That is a truth that Shriner's don't know and is part of the fraternal deception of their own. I praise God that and your son, Justin, were able to put Gospel tracts into the hands of many of these men. I with you in prayer that those words may take root and bear fruit in their lives and that they will abandon the Shrine organization and the idolatry that accompanies it.

You can certainly expect attack as you stand against the "whore" in New York Harbor. That monster is an abomination and Freemasons played an important part in its building and it its recent rededication. It will be a symbol of our destruction as well in the days that are coming very soon!

Enclosed is the tract that will be mailed to pastors across one of our states. Hopefully this will catch on and reach pastors across the country.

In Christian Love,

PASTOR HARMON TAYLOR
International Director

429

 **MINISTRIES** INC
Box 12 Newtonville NY 12128-0012

NEWSLETTER

Vol.II No.4   October/November/December 1989

SHRINER'S RED FEZ HISTORY BARBARIC AND ANTI-CHRISTIAN

When the average American thinks of the Shriners (a branch of Freemasonry or the Masons), the thoughts are of Children's Burns Centers and hospitals, and the Shrine circus, where handicapped children are often carried to the front row seats in the strong arms of weeping men who are wearing the Red Fez of a Shriner. Rarely do we see a parade without seeing Shriners driving up and down the parade route in their little cars and motorcycles, wearing the clothing of Arabian knights, bringing laughter to the children along the line of march.

They may also be seen on more serious occasions such as the laying of public building cornerstones or at the funeral service of a Lodge member. Here they are dressed in more somber attire, wearing their ornate sashes, medallioned chains of office and ceremonial aprons, performing with solemn dignity the rites handed down through centuries of their ritual secrecy. "Good me" they say, "becoming better."

YET, once you get past the good-old-boy fraternal act, the funny red hat of the Shriner, the fez, and the sheltered reputation of the local Blue Lodge of Masons, there is something beyond the colorful mask, an aura of mystery, power and intrigue, complete with undertones of false gods, blood oaths, conspiracy and back room politics.

The FEZ, the red hat of the Shriner, is an example of the double meaning of symbols that is rife behind the facade of all the branches of Freemasonry.

Worn and even carried to the grave with pompous dignity, the history of the Fez is barbaric and anti-Christian.

In the early 8ª century, Muslim hordes overran the Moroccan city of Fez, shouting, *"There is no god but Allah and Mohammed is his prophet."* There, they butchered almost 50,000 Christians. These men, women and children were slain because of their faith in Christ, all in the name of <u>Allah</u>, the same demon god to whom every Shriner must bow in worship (and proclaim him the god of his fathers) in the Shrine initiation ceremony.

The Shriners' blood oath and confession of Allah as god is found in the secret ritual book, **THE MYSTIC SHRINE, An Illustrated Ritual of the Ancient Arabic Order of Nobles of the Shrine,** (1975 Ed., pgs.20-22). Realize that Allah is not just *another* name for God. Allah is the name of *another god,* In usual fashion, the initiate swears that he will be inseparably obligated to this "most powerful and binding oath.", *in advance,* and that he may **NEVER** retract or depart from it.

During the butchering of the people of Fez, the streets literally ran red with the blood of the martyred Christians. The Muslim murderers dipped their caps in the blood of their victims as a testimony to Allah. These blood stained caps came to be called *FEZZES*, the Muslim badge of honor. The Shriners wear the red Fez today. The greatest tragedy is that the Fez is often worn by men who profess to be Christians themselves. It must cause God to weep! ####

TRUTHS THAT TRANSFORM

Request, at the following address, your copy of a two day radio program of Dr. D. James Kennedy by the same name which dealt with the issue of Freemasonry. You will want this tape featuring the late Dr. Walter Martin, Dr. Bob Morey, and Tom McKenney. Write: **Truths**

That Transform, PO Box 33, Fort Lauderdale, FL 33302-0033. It is perhaps the best single tape for introducing a Christian to the subject of Freemasonry.

Don't forget to enclose a gift ($5.00 suggested) to <u>their</u> ministry when you make your request. As with all ministries, theirs continues only with financial support. ####

FREEMASONRY & THE NEW AGE

Freemasonry and what is generally called the New Age Movement can no longer be separated. Doctrinally, and in terms of goals, there are many similarities. Many New Agers are also dedicated Masons of the occult, "enlightened" type. The official journal of the Scottish Rite (Southern Jurisdiction, "Mother Council of the World") is called "THE NEW AGE". Keith Harris, a pastor in Marion, Kentucky and researcher and writer in several areas including Freemasonry, recently received a letter from the Tara Center (New Age headquarters affiliated with Benjamine Creme). In the letter, the late Alice Bailey, the most influential New Age authority, is quoted as saying about the dawning of the New Age of their occult messiah "Lord Maitreya", "The three main channels through which the preparation for the new age is going on might be regarded as the Church, the Masonic Fraternity and the educational field." (Concerning the Church we can only assume she refers to the many non-Bible believing churches that pass themselves off as churches). She says, "In all these bodies there are to be found esoteric groups who are the custodians of the inner teaching and whose uniformity in aspiration and technique is one." (A.A. Bailey, <u>The Externalization of the Hierarchy,</u> pages 510-512). Interesting!

Alice Bailey admits that the majority of Masons are <u>not</u> in on this great conspiratorial move of Satan (they believe they are doing something good); it is only the esoteric (those with the truth, hidden knowledge and understanding in the higher degrees) the elite minority who realize how it all goes together. ####

MERRY CHRISTMAS

1,687 OUT!

We continue to rejoice and to thank God for his use of the Holy Spirit in prompting masons and their families to "see the light", the TRUE LIGHT - JESUS and to abandon the false light they received within the Lodge. Please pray with us this figure tops 2,200 in 1990!

Reviews & Recommendations

I am writing this in recommendation of Michael D. Juzwick's Symposium on Parenthood & Husbandry presentation. Michael's work is very well researched and has a strong Biblical base. It is stated in the symposium that families today are in a spiritual warfare. Parents need the " insight " of the Lord in order to raise children or "Trees of Righteousness" in this society. All around us we are seeing the breakdown of the family and family values. What is needed today is strong Biblical teaching and practical principles that can be implemented in child rearing. Michael gives us this! It is refreshing for me to see, as an elementary school Principle and father, an uncompromising view on parenting. For these reasons, and many more, I would recommend Michael D. Juzwick's Symposium on Parenthood and Husbandry.

Jeffrey A. Marshall - Principal
Hillcrest Christian School
Bethel Park, Pennsylvania

Michael D. Juzwick has a heart to help develop healthy homes and families. He believes in the premise that Godly parents beget Godly children. He calls for men and women to follow God's age-old standards of righteousness. I especially appreciate his call for older women to teach the younger women those Godly standards. The reminder to guard the ear and eye-gate is good advice to Christian women.

Karen Dillaman - Children's Church Administrator
Allegheny Center Christian & Missionary Alliance Church
Pittsburgh, Pennsylvania

While I have never observed Michael D. Juzwick's Symposium on Parenthood & Husbandry, I have, at his request, read his materials. While there were some minor premises that some would debate, I believe his major points and teachings to be Biblically based and doctrinally sound. The material would be edifying to any believer, and, if faithfully applied, would result in far-reaching, positive transformations in many families. This type of material needs to be known and applied by God's people, for the sake of the home, the church, and the nation.

Rockwell Dillaman - Senior Pastor
Allegheny Center Christian & Missionary Alliance Church
Vice President - Christian & Missionary Alliance Denomination

Recommended Parental Resources

The Symposium
On
Parenthood & Husbandry
— A Gathering Together to Drink the Water of God's Word
on Parental Oversight —

By:
Michael D. Juzwick

American marriages and families are failing for a lack of both knowledge and understanding of God's plan for them.

Keeping a proper balance between your marital duties to your life partner, and the various needs of your children, can be the cause of much distress, frustration, and disappointment. Psalm 127 warns us of attempting to do what only our Creator fully understands how to do. This three phase symposium guides you through the primary guidelines of marriage and nurture of children. Husbands and wives will learn together the forces that exist against their work of marriage and care of the children they both love. Michael D. Juzwick leads you through the vital principles of God's Word that addresses these most important subjects.

Marriage/Child Development
Light Eternal Pblns. ISBN: 1-887412-01-8
Suggested Retail Price: $17.95

Do you desire to obey Christ's commands to teach" every" creature ?
There are numerous falsehoods that are believed by Christian parents about involve -ment in local, state and federal politics. God has created the earth to not permit a spiritual vacuum in any area of authority. Including our nation's seats of government. Michael D. Juzwick has produced a short study of the blessed form of government we now have as Americans. He warns of the horrible consequences of ignoring God's commands to both pray for, and be committed to, preserving our constitutional laws, legislative, judicial and executive form of rulership we have with the priciples of His eternal Word. And moral principles of life on the earth. An easy read for educating your family.

Christ's Commands/Politics
ISBN:1-887412-03-4   Suggested Retail Price: $5.99

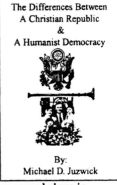

The Differences Between
A Christian Republic
&
A Humanist Democracy

By:
Michael D. Juzwick

THE ORIGINAL INTENT
OF
THE FIRST AMENDMENT
ACCORDING TO
THE FOUNDING FATHERS
One Nation

Under God

By:
Michael E. Citriniti
&
Michael D. Juzwick

Profaning and twisting this federal law has caused abuse in American families. Learn how this occurred and what parents can do to stop it!

Though daily, we are being bombarded by the liberal media's view, that despises the Christian world view, that most Americans hold. American parents have been brainwashed by antichrist opinions on this Christian law the Founding Fathers blessed this nation with. God wants His people to lift up their voice much louder than the secular media [see Isa.58:1]. If we do not, who will?
The Original Intent of the First Amendment will return our minds to those honorable purposes that made America great. Lest we see our children seduced by the God-hating secular forces arrayed against God's eternal purposes for them.

United States Constitutional Law
Light Eternal Publications ISBN: 1-887412-00-X
Suggested Retail Price: $13.25
College Discounts available

BOOK REVIEW

FOR THE TITLE:

THE ORIGINAL INTENT OF THE FIRST AMENDMENT - ACCORDING TO THE FOUNDING FATHERS

BY: Michael E. Citriniti & Michael D. Juzwick

The authors trace the philosophical wishes of the founders of the United States as they wrote the documents which govern the nation. Various historical documents are interpreted through the framework of the Bible in this study.

William Penn's Farewell Address to Pennsylvania, delivered in 1684 is included. In that speech Penn calls for the people to be committed to God. He desires temporal blessings for the people, but more significantly that they stay in line with God's plan spiritually.

The authors describe current events and how far the nation has strayed from its original Christian founding. They call for a return to the nation's spiritual roots.

—— Dr. William G. Covington, Jr.
Mass Communications Department
Edinboro University, Pennsylvania

Recommended Parenting Resources
– Publisher's Order Form on Back –

**The Symposium
On
Parenthood & Husbandry**
– A Gathering Together to Drink the Water of God's Word on Parental Oversight –

**By:
Michael D. Juzwick**

American marriages and families are suffering and under stress for a lack of both knowledge and understanding of God's plan for them.

Psalm 127 warns us of attempting to do what only our Creator fully understands how to do. This three phase symposium guides you through the primary concepts of both marriage and nurture of children. Husbands and wives can learn together the forces that exist against their work of marriage and care of the children they both love. Michael D. Juzwick leads you to discover, and apply, the vital principles of God's Word that addresses these most important matters for good success.

**Marriage/Child Development
Light Eternal Pblns. ISBN: 1-887412-01-8**
Suggested Retail price: $17.99

American Jurisprudence & Family Law is being assaulted by legal demands for equality among lesbian & gay social situations. Moral destruction is accelerating. The rising specter of the new American sodomy is now challenging the societal norms of what our national policy will be concerning what actually is marriage and family. Though the Lord God created the ordinance of marriage in the Garden of Eden, the corrupted wills of American social planners, are now working to re- define it. This is because of the great corruption and confusion the wounds of divorce, and other childhood abuses have created. This new release by Mat Staver fully addresses the great damage same-sex relationships are doing to innocent children. It also reveals the serious mental and physical health consequences it is bringing.

Marriage/Societal Development
Suggested Retail price: $10.00

Cataclysmic political challanges to the Judeo-Christian basis to our National establishments of Jurisprudence are occurring at every presidential election.

America was warned by our founders that *"..He who will not be Governed by God, would be ruled by tyrants.."* Witch Madalyn Murray-OHair, who single handedly banned Public School prayer & Bible reading, Norman Lear's -People for the American Way and ACLU lawyers have sought to reject this Judeo-Christian premise in our US Courts. Chief Justice Roy Moore clearly teaches the truth about God's rule in both Church and US Federal Governments. We are just beginning to experience Psalm 9:17 and Romans 1: 18 - 28.

Church-State /American Jurisprudence
Retail Price: DVD $15 or VHS $12

**THE ORIGINAL INTENT
OF
THE FIRST AMENDMENT
ACCORDING TO
THE FOUNDING FATHERS**

**By:
Michael E. Citriniti
&
Michael D. Juzwick**

The profaning and twisting of this federal law has caused abuse in America's families. Learn how this has occurred and what parents can do to stop it!

Though daily we are abused by America's secular and profane liberal media with lies about the First Amendment, most Americans hold the Christian world view. America's parents have been slowly brainwashed by the antiChrist and God-hating media. Liberal secularists, such as the ACLU and People for the American Way, seek to censor Christians in public places, while they gain great revenue from socially destructive pornographers. God wants His parents to lift up their voices much louder than these powerful media forces [see Isaiah 58:1]. If we do not. Who will? *The Original Intent of the First Amendment* will return our minds to those honorable purposes that made America great. Lest we watch our children seduced by these God - hating secular forces arrayed against His eternal purposes for them. Parents are God's first authority.

**United States Constitutional Law
Light Eternal Pblns. ISBN: 1-887412-00-X
Suggested Retail price: $13.25**

434

Light Eternal Publications

— Biblical Light For America's Christian Families —

PUBLISHER'S ORDER FORM

ISBN PREFIX # 1-887412   © **Light Eternal Publications - U.S.A.**

PRODUCT CODE	TITLE	PRICE [EA.]	NUMBER OF COPIES
1	The Original Intent of the First Amendment Citriniti/Juzwick — *The Profane Wresting of United States Federal Law* —	$13.25	
2	The Symposium on Parenthood & Husbandry Juzwick — *A three phase examination of Biblical & Cooperative Parental oversight* —	$17.99	
3	The United States Constitution, Bill of Rights & Declaration of Independence — *46 page Pocket Version of the Federal laws of America* —	$1.00 S/H .75	
4	The Differences Between a Christian Republic v. a Humanist Democracy — *A short review & analysis of United States Constitutional laws & government* —	$7.99	
5	Same Sex Marriage Mat Staver September 2004 — *A Legal & Societal analysis of the New Sodomy of America & its Negative effects on Children*—	$10.00	
6	Face the Truth Tour Presentation Video April 2002 [Adults only] -- *An Interview of Volunteers by Michael D. Juzwick on Pro-choice atrocities in America* –	$ 15.00	
7	Palm Beach WFGC - TV 61 - Video June 2002 – *Here & Now Program w/ Gwenn Adams interview of Michael D. Juzwick* —	$ 9.95	
8	The Symposium on Deliverance Juzwick — *A Fifteen part examination of God's war on Satan's kingdom for Mankind* —	$ 9.95	
9	I Do Exist DVD Dr. Warren Throckmorton – *A Documentary of 5 people who found God's Word & Grace to Overcome being Gay* –	$ 26.50	
10	Christian Modesty & the Public Undressing of America Compact Disc - CD – *God's Standards versus the rise of nudity & immodesty in America* –	$ 7.00	
11	The Law of the Land Chief Justice Moore DVD $15.00 or VHS $12.00 – *A Judicial & Biblical review of the Responsibilities of both Church & Government* –		
12	How Modern Churches are Harming Families John Thompson CD $10 Audiocassette $ 7 – *Segregational Groupism versus Discipleship development of Parental Leadership* –		

* Discounts available for Church, high school, college and university student textbook adoption & classroom use!

Vital & Defensive Marriage & Parenting Resources
– Titles Order Form on Back –

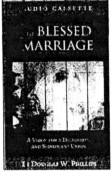

American marriages and families are suffering and under distress because of a lack of both knowledge and understanding of God's plan for them.

Marriage is God's Garden of Eden ordinance for one man and one woman under His Lordship. It is very evident that the very foundations for this blessing of our Maker are under assault by those who hate God and His purposes. Many marriages are failing due to a lack of knowledge and understanding about this gift of God to men and women. This audio message will introduce couples to some of the vital basics needed to succeed at this character development relationship children need to observe as young disciples in this world.

Marital Foundational Principles
Light Eternal Pblns. Title 3 Cassette/or CD
Suggested Contribution: $ 7. 85 + $1. 35 s/h

American Churches must center their discipleship upon God's call for ".. *all men to repent.."* **[Acts 17: 30]. Leadership of families must be developed in our day. Fathers & Husbands need prayer, honor, and respect if God's Spirit is to be free to use them. Satanic unisex equality curses this Bible principle.** This title explains Christ's command to make disciples. Training men, and male children, to assume Biblical responsibilities as spiritual leaders, and godly coverings over the family must be done by pastors. Elder women must do this with younger women & girls Titus 2: 3 - 5.

Church Leadership in the Home - Cassette/ or CD
Suggested contribution: $7.85 + s/h $ 1.35

The War Against Boys is a Must Read for all Parents that are unaware of the kinds of abuse our children are suffering because they are forced to be " *a captive audience* **" and be abused by militant feminists now taking over our schools.**

The lead professor over the Harvard School of Education - Carol Gilligan - has called for militant social engineering of our sons to effeminize them to meet her idea of what men should be. She has lead the charge to convert boys into her image using our Federal taxpayer dollars in the millions. Satan is creating confusion in both our boys and girls concerning God's Biblical creation of " ..male and female.. " by militant feminists now ruling in our colleges and universities.

Political Science /American Education - Book
Suggested contribution: $17.85 + $1. 85 s/h

Jesus called 12 men to be His disciples & Apostles. This would be considered a non - politically correct misogyny against women today in America. This unBiblical attitude is being fed into churches by the secular education, television & print medias. Learn how to create male friendly churches! We must not complain if we refuse to! As Pharaoh King of Egypt commanded *"..every male child to be thrown into the Nile river.."* [See Exodus 1: 16] so Satan is working overtime to rid our churches of effective male leaders over our families. This book provides key understanding for promoting a male encouraging environment in our churches.

Male Leadership/ Church Government
Light Eternal Pblns. Title 18 - Book
Suggested contribution: $15.00 + $1.85 s/h

BIBLIOGRAPHY AND SOURCES

AMERICAN HERITAGE SERIES: Volume LXX. #1, Dec.1968; pages 68-73.

CHICK, JACK T.: THE CURSE OF BAPHOMET - Chick Publications, Chino, CA.

GESENIUS': HEBREW - CHALDEE LEXICON TO THE OLD TESTAMENT - Baker Book House, Grand Rapids, Michigan. 1981.

HAMMOND, FRANK & IDA MAE: PIGS IN THE PARLOR- A Practical guide to Deliverance; Impact Books, Kirkwood, MO 1973. Or Children's Bread Ministry - P.O.Box 789, Plainview, TX 79073

HISLOP, ALEXANDER: TWO BABYLONS; Loizeaux Brothers, Neptune, NJ 1959

HOLY BIBLE, THE: THE OPEN BIBLE, KING JAMES 1611 VERSION, Thomas Nelson Publishers, Nashville, tn 1975

JUZWICK, MICHAEL D. : FATHERHOOD IN THE UNITED STATES OF AMERICA; Light Eternal Publ;ications; Pittsburgh, PA 152126 - 1985

LOS ANGELES TIMES; Thursday, January 23, 1986- front page - " Thousands of abortion foes rally in Capitol.

METCALFE, JOHN: INTERCESSORS FOR AMERICA NEWSLETTER; March 1986, Vol.13; Freemasonry: A personal testimony.

NATIONAL GEOGRAPHIC: December 1985 issue, volume 168 # 6, Pages 720, 730 & 758. A review of historical items at the Vatican.

SCHNOEBELEN, WILLIAM: MASONRY - BEYOND THE LIGHT; Chick Publications - Chino, CA 1991

WOODROW, RALPH: BABYLON - MYSTERY RELIGION [ANCIENT & MODERN] P.O. Box 124 Riverside, CA 92502, 1966.

WORLEY, WIN: DEMOLISHING THE HOSTS OF HELL - EVERY CHRISTIAN'S JOB; Pages 77 -79, Hedgewich Baptist Church - Lansing, IL 60438, 1978

ZONDERVAN BIBLE ENCYCLOPEDIA: Definitions and history of Baal worship - Pages 209-210

CPSIA information can be obtained at www.ICGtesting.com
Printed in the USA
BVOW07s0138090914

365958BV00001B/55/P